Howardena Pindell

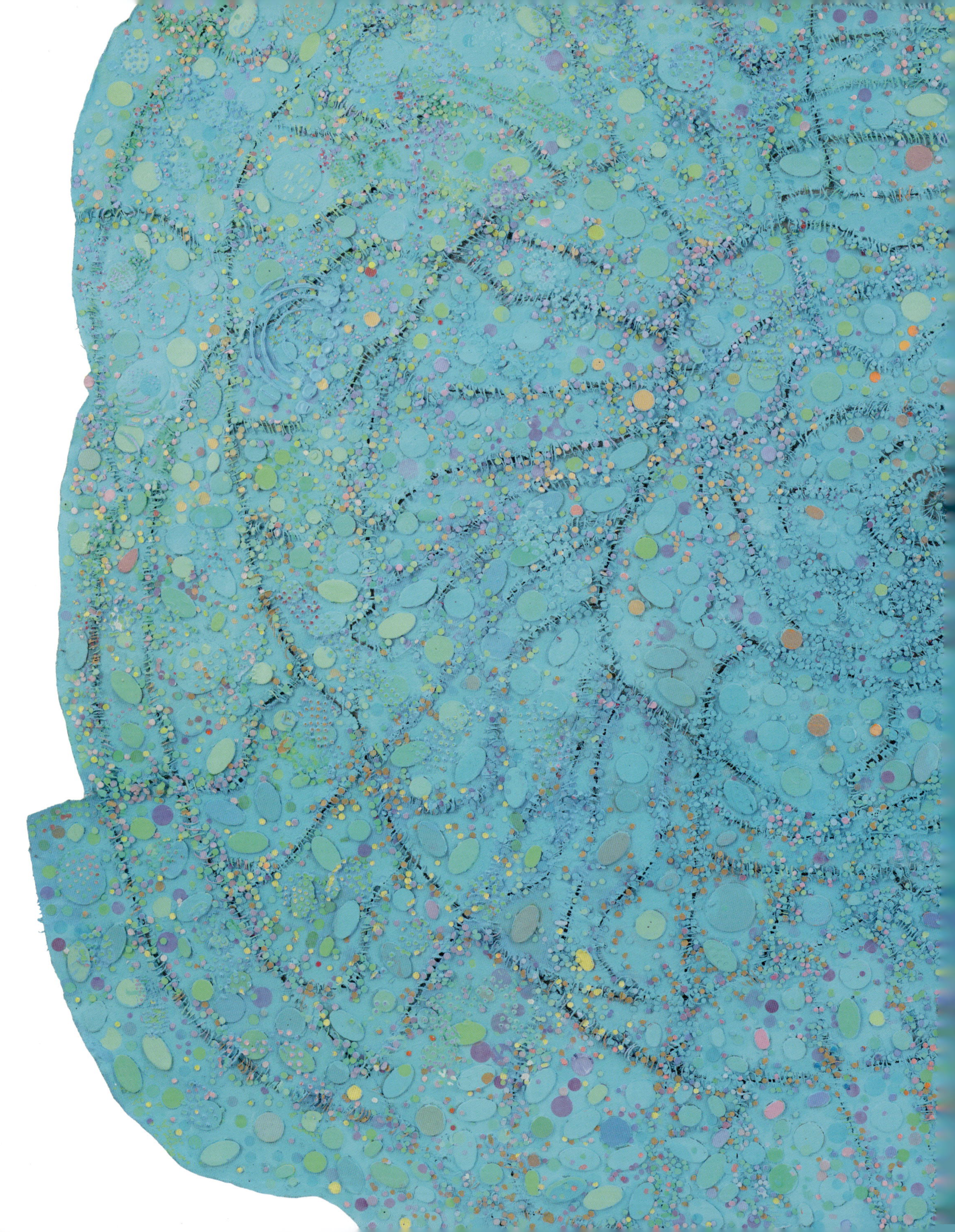

Howardena Pindell
Reclaiming Abstraction

SARAH LOUISE COWAN

YALE UNIVERSITY PRESS

NEW HAVEN AND LONDON

Published with assistance from the Nancy Batson Nisbet Rash Publication Fund.

Publication of this book has been aided by a grant from the Wyeth Foundation for American Art Publication Fund of CAA.

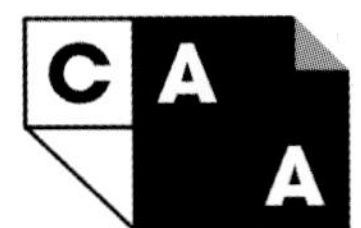

Published with assistance from the National Endowment for the Humanities. Any views, findings, conclusions, or recommendations expressed in this publication do not necessarily reflect those of the National Endowment for the Humanities.

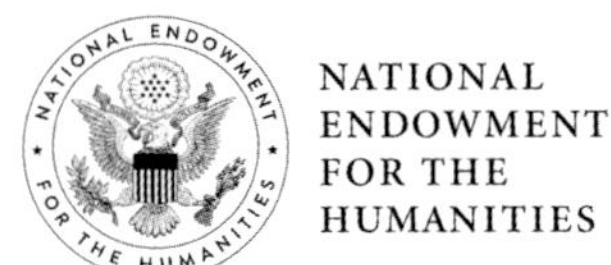

yalebooks.com/art

Excerpts of earlier versions of chapters 2 and 3 appeared as "Texturing Abstraction: Howardena Pindell's Cut and Sewn Paintings," in *Art Journal* 79, no. 4 (2020), published by the College Art Association.

Designed by Laura Lindgren
Cover designed by Laura Lindgren
Set in Ionic No. 5, IBM Plex Sans, and Lagom by Laura Lindgren
Printed in China by 1010 Printing International Limited

Library of Congress Control Number: 2021952610
ISBN 978-0-300-26429-6

A catalogue record for this book is available from the British Library.

This paper meets the requirements of ANSI/NISO Z39.48-1992 (Permanence of Paper).

10 9 8 7 6 5 4 3 2 1
Frontispiece: Howardena Pindell, *Night Flight* (detail of fig. 104)
Page vi: Howard Wells, Untitled photograph of Howardena Pindell (detail of fig. 64)

To Laura and Alex

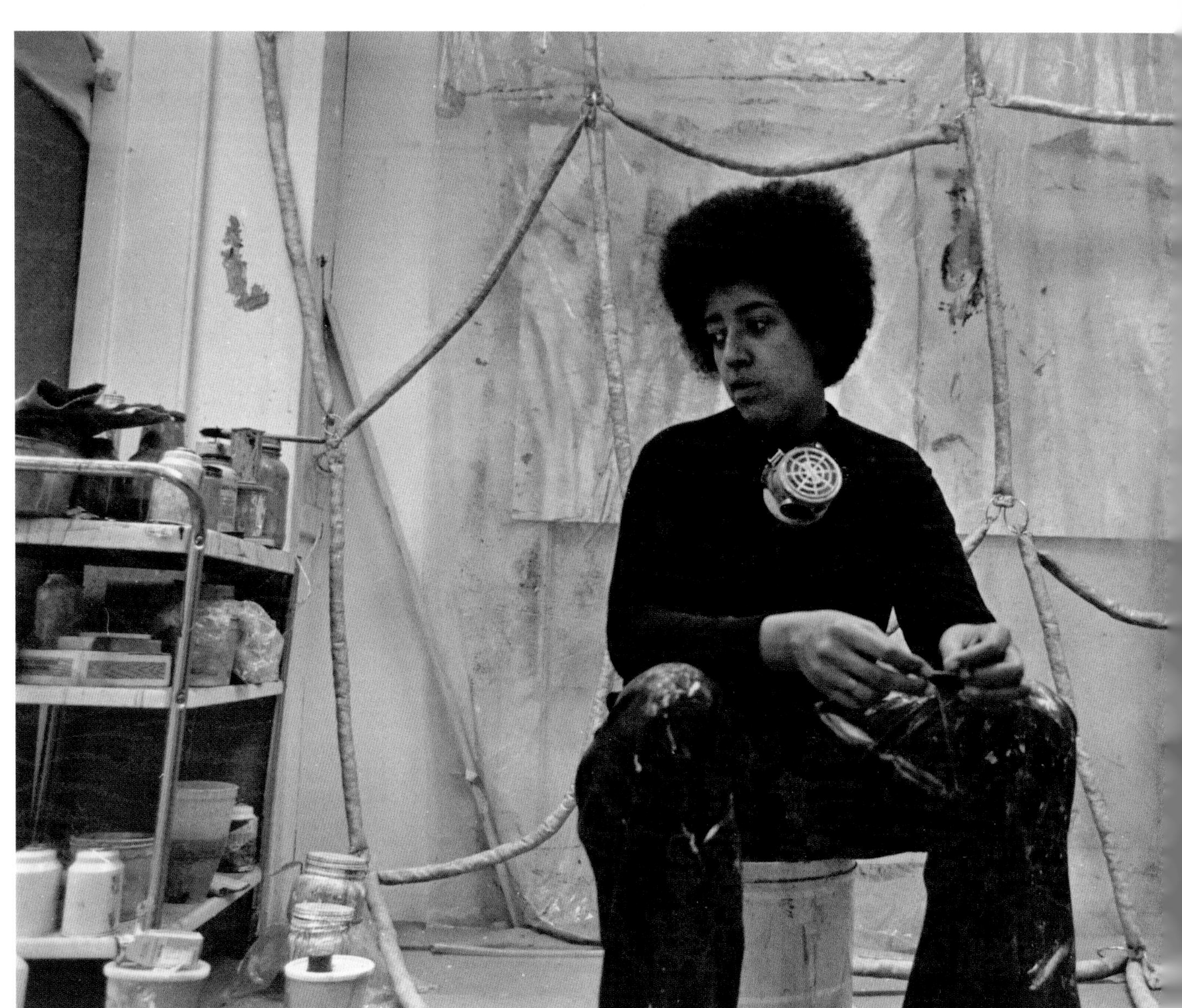

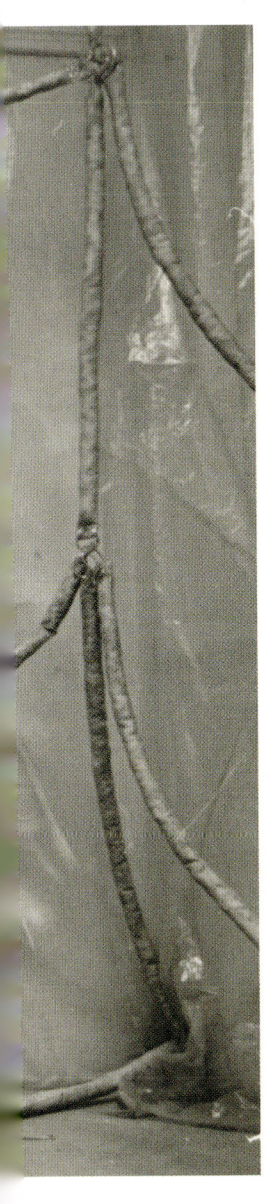

Contents

Acknowledgments

So many people helped this book come into being. My deepest appreciation goes to Howardena Pindell for her generosity across our conversations and correspondence. She shared her artworks and experiences with me from the earliest days of research. Her work as an artist, activist, and thinker has been a deep well of inspiration not only for this project, but in my life. I also thank the staff at Garth Greenan Gallery, especially Rachel Garbade and Alison Dillulio, for their cheerful, reliable support with archival materials and images.

My thanks go to all those at Yale University Press who engaged with my project, most especially Amy Canonico, Heidi Downey, Laura Hensley, Mary Mayer, and Raychel Rapazza, who shepherded me through the daunting challenge of a first book. Laura Lindgren did a wonderful job designing the book. Over the course of my research, I benefitted from the expertise of countless archivists, curators, librarians, registrars, and other professionals. I thank staff at Fales Special Collections at New York University, the Museum of Modern Art Archives, the Libraries and Archives of the Brooklyn Museum, the archives of the Whitney Museum of American Art, and Rutgers Special Collections. I am appreciative of staff at the National Gallery of Art Library, the Library of Congress, and the Archives of American Art, especially Erin Gilbert, Josh Franco, and Mary Savig. At Emory University, Randall Burkett and Pellom McDaniels III were exceedingly hospitable. I thank them and the rest of the staff there, as well as at the archives of Spelman College, and the David M. Rubenstein Rare Book and Manuscript Library at Duke University. My appreciation goes to curator Carol Thompson at the High Museum of Art in Atlanta for generously sharing her time. Patricia Hickson and Eileen Doyle at the Wadsworth Atheneum Museum of Art in Hartford, Connecticut, kindly pulled unwieldy materials for me. I am grateful to them, as well as to the staff at the Manuscripts and Archives at Yale University and the Yale University Art Gallery.

Throughout the development of this book, I have been fortunate to receive a number of fellowships and grants. This project has been supported by a National Endowment for the Humanities Summer Stipend, a DePauw University Fisher Course Reassignment, a Mellon/American Council of Learned Societies (ACLS) Dissertation Completion Fellowship, a Townsend Center for the Humanities Fellowship, and a Smithsonian American Art Museum (SAAM) Predoctoral

Fellowship. At SAAM, I must thank Melissa Ho and Carmen Ramos for discussing Pindell's legacy with me. This project was also supported by a Mellon Curatorial Internship Fellowship at the Brooklyn Museum. I am deeply grateful for the opportunity to learn from Carmen Hermo, Rujeko Hockley, Catherine Morris, Eugenie Tsai, and Stephanie Weissberg. I received travel grants from the Getty Research Institute and Rose Library Special Collections at Emory University.

Scholars known and unknown to me have supported my research through feedback, encouragement, and their intellectual model. First, I thank those who discussed Pindell's art and life with me, particularly Naomi Beckwith, Grace Deveney, and Valerie Cassel Oliver. They generously shared their insights and expanded the possibilities of Pindell research through their own work. My gratitude goes to Camille Billops and Jim Hatch, Linda Goode Bryant, Barry Rosen, and Lorna Simpson for spending time with me; I learned a great deal from them. Huey Copeland, Salah M. Hassan, and Steven Nelson provided intellectual inspiration and moral support. Others whose scholarship or encouragement bolstered this project in significant ways include Andrea Barnwell Brownlee, Kirsten Pai Buick, Eddie Chambers, Darby English, Lisa Farrington, Jacqueline Francis, Kellie Jones, Audre Lorde, Bibiana Obler, John Ott, Joshua Shannon, Freida High W. Tesfagiorgis, Michele Wallace, Judith Wilson, Tobias Wofford, and, especially, Lowery Stokes Sims, whose work has opened so many intellectual doors for me. My particular thanks go as well to Jordana Moore Saggese for her support and for incisively editing my writing about Pindell's cut and sewn paintings when it appeared, in a different form, in *Art Journal*.

This book emerged from my dissertation project, which I completed in the History of Art Department at the University of California, Berkeley. I am eternally grateful for the luminous intellects and kindness I encountered in Patricia Berger, Natalia Brizuela, Whitney Davis, Beate Fricke, Anneka Lenssen, Margaretta Lovell, Ivy Mills, Todd Olson, Sugata Ray, Andy Shanken, Lisa Trever, and Anne Walsh. My special thanks go to my committee members. The inimitable intellectual force of Darcy Grimaldo Grigsby has indelibly shaped my scholarship. I thank her for showing me how to dig deeper. One could not ask for a better guide through the strangeness of modernisms than Lauren Kroiz, whose patience is outshined only by her perceptiveness. Her astute advice was a balm in crucial stages of the project's life. Leigh Raiford generously inducted me into the field of Black studies through her assiduous, ethical scholarship and her ability to make community—I am forever thankful. Her smarts, vivacity, and commitment are an inspiration. Most of all, I am profoundly grateful to Julia Bryan-Wilson for the generosity with which she shares her incisive mind, her unwavering engagement as chair, and the humanity she brings to intellectual labor. Her courageous scholarship continues to motivate me to aspire to more in my own.

At DePauw, I am grateful to the many colleagues who supported the final stages of the book's writing, including Nahyan Fancy, Bridget Gourley, and fellow faculty writing group members. Particular thanks go to members of the Art and Art History Department, especially Meredith Brickell, Pauline Ota, and Natalia Vargas Márquez, for their encouragement. Brooke Cox, Bethany Fiechter, and Misti Scott graciously and skillfully helped me get the project over the finish line. I also am appreciative of the students I have taught there for inspiring me to keep asking questions. Special thanks must go to Alyssa Flory for her stellar assistance with copy editing and image permissions.

My deep gratitude goes to the fellow travelers who made intellectual life livable over the course of this project: Amanda Armstrong, Jamal Batts, Adam Benkato, Elizabeth Buhe, Mahasan Chaney, Ellen Feiss, Jez Flores, Aglaya Glebova, Essence Harden, Grace Harpster, Matt Kendall, Lex Lancaster, Munira Lokhandwala, Sigrid Luhr, Kappy Mintie, Ianna Hawkins Owen, Amy Rahn, Michaela Rife, Valentina Rozas-Krause, Ben Shestakofsky, and Jennifer Sichel. I am grateful for the radiant intellectual companionship of Olivia K. Young; this project is much richer for it. Sarah-Neel Smith patiently mentored me through the process of transforming the dissertation into a book. Her discerning feedback and innumerable pep talks kept me grounded and moving. Emma Silverman has been a constant interlocutor, an unflinching editor, and a dear, true friend for the life of this project. I thank her for keeping me afloat.

My family, chosen and otherwise, has supported me through this process. In the early years, the companionship of Rebecca Ewing, John Herbstritt, and Karly Stark carried me. Laurie Ellen Pellicano kept me fed and asking questions when I needed it the most. Christopher Fiorello is a firecracker of curiosity and an inspiration. When I need to phone a friend, I call Caitlin Howlett, whose wit and wisdom never fail. John and Kate Berry have become family, sharing celebrations, losses, and their comfy couch. The many branches of the Walter clan, including the Bacons and Garzolis, fill me up and keep me honest. Jonathan Love has been there since day one; what a gift. Libby is a rare gem of a sister. What would life be without the delightful Aurelius and Tallula? I am so grateful for my wonderful expanding family, especially Maria Roehrkasse, Meg Dorsey, Jack and Kara Dorsey, and Richard Roehrkasse and Ann-Caroline Davis. Elisabeth Smith has been a steadfast source of sunshine, wisdom, and strength for well over a decade. She lent her sharp eye to the manuscript at a pivotal moment. A person couldn't ask for a more life-affirming friendship than the ones I have with her and with Emma Silverman.

Alex Roehrkasse has been my partner throughout the life of this project and deserves boundless appreciation for his patient support. My world and this work are much richer for his emotional and domestic labors, his intellectual companionship, and his big, luminous heart. My mother, Laura, died long before I started asking the questions that motivate this book. But she taught me how to express love through labor. I jointly dedicate this book to her and Alex.

Introduction

Abstraction . . . doesn't have a concrete meaning, but can relate back to signification in the world.
—Howardena Pindell

Howardena Pindell (b. 1943) arrived in New York in 1967, skeptical of the city and her prospects for work. Fresh from the MFA program in painting at Yale University, the young artist associated the widely accepted cultural capital of the United States with the career ambitions of the white men in her graduating class. These peers followed closely in the footsteps of faculty mentors who arranged introductions for their favored students—seemingly small gestures that upheld a system of uneven resource distribution, which disadvantaged Pindell as a Black woman. Pindell wanted something entirely different for her artistic practice—to create work guided by her own "passion[ate]" artistic vision, without the need to appease a would-be patron's self-aggrandizements.[1]

In New York, Pindell launched a pathbreaking career as a curator, art world reformer, writer, and visual artist. Shortly after her arrival, she began working full-time at the Museum of Modern Art (MoMA), first as an assistant in the museum's International Exhibitions Department. Within a few years, she became the first Black American curator to work at MoMA, eventually rising to the rank of associate curator of the Department of Prints and Illustrated Books.[2] There, she became a savvy, if critical, art world insider. In the face of racism and sexism, she held a genuinely unique position, often the first or the only Black woman in roles of authority at predominantly white institutions. Pindell reimagined what it meant to labor as an artist as she insisted on her rightful place at the center of contemporary art.

During her first decades in New York, Pindell moved through art worlds embroiled in the rancorous debates of the period's social and political upheaval. The myth of a politically detached modernist art waned amid the exigencies of global crisis and domestic unrest. Demonstrations against the Vietnam War erupted on city streets and college campuses. In the art world, antiwar

Detail, fig. 25.

sentiments helped fuel the 1970 Art Strike that temporarily closed museums in Manhattan. Uprisings of the late 1960s in cities including Detroit and Newark attested to the failure of incremental legislative change to deliver widespread social and economic transformations. Support for Black nationalisms bloomed in the late 1960s and early 1970s, and many artists gathered under the banner of the Black Arts movement to espouse a revolutionary Black culture distinct from that of the white U.S. mainstream. Drawing on the strategies of the civil rights movement, the women's movement emerged at the end of the 1960s, and women agitated for a wide variety of legislative and societal reforms. The American Indian movement, Chicano movement, gay liberation movement, and others likewise contributed to a widespread rethinking of public life.

So-called advanced art in the United States underwent major transformations in these years, as artists drafted new relationships between their politics and artistic practices. These changes were especially profound in New York, home to a density of artists and high-profile art institutions. Artists including Benny Andrews, Jon Hendricks, Tom Lloyd, Faith Ringgold, and Jean Toche took direct political action, forming artist-activist groups such as the Art Workers' Coalition (AWC), the Ad Hoc Women's Committee of the AWC, and the Black Emergency Cultural Coalition that intervened in museum business. Members demonstrated against discriminatory practices and the military-industrial entanglements of the Metropolitan Museum of Art, the Museum of Modern Art, and the Whitney Museum of American Art. Alternative institutions abounded as artists sought to display and distribute their work outside mainstream circuits that failed to reflect the city's diversity.[3]

Dominant narratives of then-recent U.S. art cast abstraction as largely detached from the politics of the day. Artists who committed themselves to the social liberation movements of the 1960s and 1970s tended to view abstraction, particularly abstract art that lacked an overt extra-aesthetic purpose, as too far removed from the era's political urgencies. Leaders of the Black Arts movement, for instance, favored figurative work with an explicit political message. Feminist artists of this period largely considered abstract painting a secondary concern of the women's movement. From these perspectives, abstract idioms appeared increasingly complicit in the systemic exclusions that had consolidated advanced art around a small group of mostly white, male artists. Artist-activists' suspicious view of abstraction emerged in response to modernist critics' hegemonic reign over notions of artistic "quality."[4] This linchpin term implicitly linked artistic validity to race, gender, and sexuality.

Pindell challenged the terms of these critical conversations by rejecting the mutual exclusion of activism and abstraction. In her first fifteen years in the city, she worked primarily in abstract modes, producing collaged paintings and works on paper that drew on abstract expressionism, color field painting, and conceptual and postminimalist forms. The painting *Carnival at Ostende* (1977), viewed from a distance, presents a pastel field speckled with small dots of saturated color (fig. 1). A closer inspection of this unstretched, allover painting betrays a dense, protuberant texture (fig. 2). A tangible layer of thick paint covers the canvas. Small bits of matter sit atop and are embedded within this substrate. These materials include paper rounds created by a hole punch, the ubiquitous detritus of pre-digital white-collar offices. Intermingling with these bureaucratic remnants, glitter and sequins shimmer against the surface of the painting, lending it a light dusting of nightlife cosmetics and costumery.

Howardena Pindell: Reclaiming Abstraction considers how Pindell reclaimed abstraction as a set of aesthetic resources useful, rather than antagonistic, to a Black feminist project. In creating a context for her own artistic development, she took advantage of her proximity to a wealth of sociocultural institutions. Pindell participated in conversations about Pan-Africanism, the politics of administrative cultural labor, and feminist reclamations of handicraft, as she combined methods of making drawn from Ghanaian textiles, paradigmatically modernist idioms such as allover painting and the grid, and materials associated with the "feminine." Pindell culled her distinctive aesthetic from a wide range of conversations about what art could be.

In order to understand Pindell's orientation toward abstraction, I contend in this book with three historically entangled modernisms—an overlapping series of local and transnational, historical and ongoing conversations about art-making— rather than positing modernism as a globally agreed-upon artistic project. First, "modernisms" refers to a broad range of artistic practices that self-consciously address the conditions of art-making through attention to process, surface, materials, and discursive context. Modernist painting, for instance, might draw attention to the two-dimensional pictorial plane through means such as color blocking or pattern. According to a conventional art-historical narrative, this emphasis on the flat, literal surface of easel painting initially emerged in France in the late nineteenth century, as painters associated with the impressionist movement eschewed the imperative to model three-dimensional space that had dominated Western artistic paradigms since the Renaissance.

The term "modernist" also has operated as a designation used to marginalize and exclude Black people, Indigenous people and other people of color, women, working-class people, and LGBTQIA+ people from elite art institutions and art-historical narratives. This predominantly white construction of modernism, which I refer to as "institutional modernisms," encompasses rarefied cultural conversations that grant limited access to artists according to an elusive set of coded criteria. Lastly, "modernist" refers to attempts that artists have made

Fig. 1. Howardena Pindell, *Carnival at Ostende,* 1977. Acrylic paint, dye, paper, thread, glitter, sequins, and powder on canvas, 7 ft. 9½ in. × 9 ft. 9¼ in. (237.5 × 297.8 cm). Private collection, Palo Alto, CA.

since the late nineteenth century to build on a preceding generation of practitioners by working through specific conceptual, political, and formal problems. For instance, Afro-Chinese Cuban painter Wifredo Lam engaged with cubism while critiquing its colonialist underpinnings in the 1940s through an emphatically hybrid aesthetic drawn from Afro-Cuban cultural and religious elements.[5] Significantly for this study, for several decades throughout the twentieth century, nonrepresentational, or abstract, idioms functioned as the paradigmatic expression of institutional U.S. and European modernisms.

Pindell braided distinct modernisms together in her practice. Her approach to abstraction explored the conditions of art-making itself, critiqued the exclu-

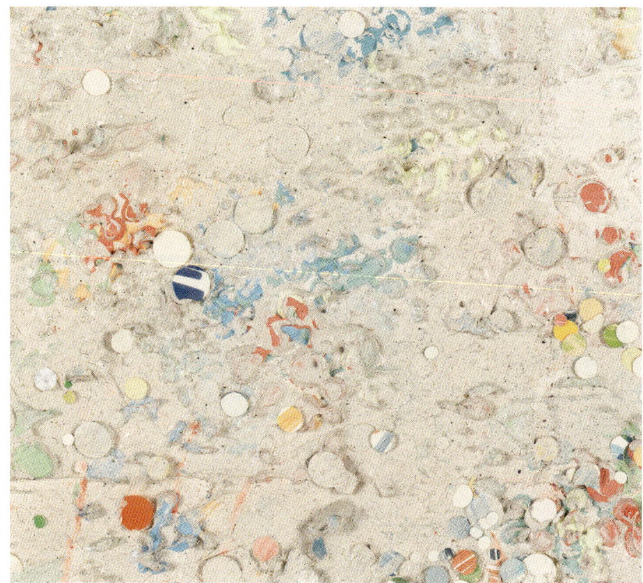

Fig. 2. Howardena Pindell, *Carnival at Ostende,* 1977 (detail; see fig. 1).

sions of rarefied artistic circles from within the institutional art world, and responded to the limitations of preceding U.S. artistic movements, particularly abstract expressionism and post-painterly abstraction. This study joins others in adopting an expansive rubric of modernisms that includes critical practices since 1960.[6] Deploying the term "modernism" in this context acknowledges that political and reflexive critique figured prominently in earlier modernist practices, such as Lam's, and centers the continuity of struggles for recognition faced by artists of color. In the late 1960s, Pindell carried on a modernist tradition in using the tools of modernism to extend and critique itself.

Contrary to the prevailing political-aesthetic logic of the 1960s and 1970s, abstraction proved an inimitable asset to artists in this period of social upheaval. Lynda Benglis, Betty Blayton, Melvin Edwards, Joe Overstreet, Joan Snyder, and Jack Whitten produced abstract art that stretched the bounds of prevailing modernist idioms. In light of social liberation movements, abstract art became a renewed site of material and aesthetic experimentation rife with political potential and metaphorical possibility. The burgeoning mediums of video, performance art, and installation aided these expansions, opening up painting and sculpture to new techniques.[7] Feminist artists in particular inaugurated innovations in the materials, mediums, and sites of advanced art, often incorporating ordinary, everyday gestures and objects into their works.

Nonetheless, Black artists, and Black women in particular, faced scrutiny over the "political rectitude" of their work. Pindell's decision to work abstractly defied expectations of the period that Black American artists represent themselves in their art in a literal way. Adrian Piper, one of the most well-known U.S. artists of her generation, expressed a common view when she called her abstract practice of the 1960s "the work I did in the Garden of Eden, before I found out I was a black woman."[8] Never one to mince words, Piper pointed directly at the naivete presumed to undergird a Black woman artist's decision to work abstractly. Her commentary references the sobering reality that this choice could result in artistic exile or dismissal.

Pindell, I argue, took up abstraction as a way to engage with yet defy racial and gender discourse, rather than flatly reject it. Her deployment of modernist idioms cannot be ascribed to naivete. A perceptive observer of art world discrimination, she understood that critical narratives and curatorial practices had colluded to exclude non-white artists from accounts of modernism. In her hands, the production of abstract art became a tool with which to disrupt limiting cultural assumptions and to process her experiences in an embodied way.

Modernism offered many artists an effective set of artistic strategies for exceeding the more dogmatic strains of 1960s and 1970s aesthetic-political discourses. In his 1967 essay "Black Is a Color," artist Raymond Saunders rejected a nascent Black Arts framework that burdened Black artists with the responsibility to use "their arts as political tools, instead of vehicles of free expression." Saunders countered that artistic latitude and freedom from political responsibility were requisites for meaningful cultural contributions with the potential to redress social inequities. In contrast to Saunders, whose text defaults to conceiving of the artist as "man," Pindell laid claim to her artistic vision as a Black woman. She could not readily secure her place in existing modernist narratives through reflexive leverage of either her racial or gender identities. The intersecting nature of racial and gender oppression compounded the elisions of each.[9]

To a greater degree than their peers, Black women artists have faced what art historians Arna Bontemps and Jacqueline Fonvielle-Bontemps have called a "special dilemma," namely, "the need to either protest racial or sexual discrimination against them or to somehow avoid it; to either rationalize the psychological impact of racism and sexism on them and their art or to transcend it."[10] This was never more true than in the late 1960s and 1970s, as prominent voices within the Black Arts movement and the feminist art movement aimed competing demands at artists. From her vantage point decidedly outside of these movements' narrow-sighted targets—Black men and white women, respectively—and of institutional modernism's guarded perimeter, Pindell chose differently. She engaged with modernisms in distinctly feminine-coded and African diasporic terms, defying the separation of abstraction and activism.

This book contends that the works Pindell made in the first two decades of her career exemplify what I designate as "Black feminist modernisms." This term signifies diverse creative practices that strategically utilize modernist idioms in order to unsettle racist and sexist logics. Black feminist thought—an open-ended, ongoing set of critical conversations and concrete actions sharing the goal of Black women's liberation—flourished in the United States as Pindell embarked on her career. A constantly negotiated terrain of activist, artistic, and scholarly work, Black feminisms encompass practices of policy reform and imagination, of protest and care that center the experiences of Black women. As participants in an ever-evolving discursive field, Black feminists have contested the aims, priorities, and tactics of their shared project to upend oppressions rooted in race and gender as well as class, sexuality, ability, and nationality. Black feminisms became increasingly institutionalized in the 1980s and 1990s; however, these diverse philosophies have existed in the United States as long as Black women have.[11]

Through Black feminist modernisms, artists critically engage with hegemonic cultural discourses and respond to the existence of intersectional oppressions within marginalized communities. In his book *Radical Aesthetics and Modern Black Nationalism,* GerShun Avilez considers how U.S. artists since the mid-1960s have drawn on the dominant ideology of Black nationalism to counter that philosophy's own constraints, particularly with regards to normative gender and sexuality. In other words, artists adapted nationalism to suit their own queer and feminist projects, finding artistic opportunities in its strictures. Avilez's study draws on queer theorist José Esteban Muñoz's germinal notion of "disidentification"—a strategy of "'working on and against' . . . that tries to transform a cultural logic from within, always laboring to enact permanent structural change."[12] Cultural actors might disidentify not only with a white, middle-class, masculinist, heterosexist culture, but also with conventional ideologies within, for instance, Black cultures, Indigenous cultures, or women's cultures.

Existing models of cultural critique, such as Avilez's and Muñoz's, highlight the intersectional nature of oppressions and artists' multivalent resistance to them. The concept of Black feminist modernisms extends these theories by further emphasizing the simultaneous existence of a range of "cultural logics" that artists engage and defy. As a Black feminist modernist, Pindell confronted a multiplicity of hegemonic discourses, including Black nationalisms, white feminisms, and institutional modernisms. Through each of these ideological nodes, she both accessed generative cultural conversations and encountered social constraints rooted in anti-Black racism and sexism. Most significantly, Black feminist modernisms as a concept recenters the practices of Black women artists.

Black feminist modernists of the 1970s contributed in myriad ways to the era's Black feminisms. These artists critiqued the hypocritical ways in which Black nationalist cultural criticism and white feminist institutions actively sidelined Black women's cultural achievements. In these pages I identify artists including Blayton, Ringgold, Beverly Buchanan, Janet Henry, Loïs Mailou Jones, Senga Nengudi, and Betye Saar as Black feminist modernists. They joined Black women artists such as Vivian E. Browne, Barbara Chase-Riboud, Maren Hassinger, Mary Lovelace O'Neal, Mavis Pusey, Alma Thomas, and Mildred Thompson in developing Black feminist modernisms in the 1960s and 1970s. These artists labored against the intersecting oppressions of race and gender

by reclaiming and remaking the traditions that excluded them. The particular aesthetic strategies of Black feminist modernisms vary by practice and, for many artists, have changed over the course of their careers. This study focuses on a single visual artist working in the years following the 1960s civil rights movement; in doing so, it proposes "Black feminist modernists" as a broader category with cultural and historical relevance. For instance, the careers of U.S.-born French burlesque star and civil rights activist Josephine Baker and Harlem Renaissance–era U.S. sculptor and educator Augusta Savage offered important precedents for this later generation of Black feminist modernists.[13]

THE HAPTIC

Pindell has made her most significant contributions to Black feminist modernisms through a haptic approach to abstraction she developed in the first two decades of her career. The term "haptic" refers to one's perception of the world through touch and the sense of one's bodily movement and position (proprioception). Haptic sensations entail physiological and psychological mechanisms through which humans relate to material dimensions. To a greater degree than touch alone, the haptic connotes embodied relationality. For instance, the feel of velvet under one's fingers might be described as tactile sensation, whereas the experience of walking across a room while draped in velvet cloth, sensing its weight, warmth, and resistance, would more accurately be called haptic perception.[14]

It was through her extended engagement with the haptic that Pindell ardently pursued African diasporic, feminist, and modernist aesthetics and critiqued the ideologies that undergirded them. She developed a handworked approach to abstraction through collage and handicraft as well as through an extended metaphor of mending and a textile logic—an aesthetic that conceives of the artwork's surface as a permeable, textured membrane.[15] With her expertise, Pindell innovated upon modernist models of surface, creating lavishly textured artworks that scramble positional descriptors such as "on" and "in."

Pindell developed these interrelated haptic strategies—collage, handicraft, mending, textile logic, and surface play—simultaneously, combining them in the same works. For instance, the raised collage elements of her works on mat board generate densely textured surfaces that attest to her haptic labors. Her intimately scaled collages, such as an untitled example from 1973 now in MoMA's

Fig. 4. Howardena Pindell, *Untitled #20* (*Dutch Wives Circled and Squared*), 1978. Acrylic paint, dye, paper, thread, glitter, sequins, and powder on canvas, 7 ft. 2 in. × 9 ft. 2 in. (218.4 × 279.4 cm). Museum of Contemporary Art Chicago. Gift of Albert A. Robin by exchange, 2014.15.

collection, place hand-numbered paper rounds in delicate, gravity-defying piles that overlay a grid made of thread (fig. 3). A coating of talcum powder covers every surface, unifying the variously industrial and craft-coded materials with a grainy texture. This layer evokes cosmetics, lending the works a feminine-coded finish and proposing an analogy between their surfaces and a powdered vis-age—a parallel redolent of French painter Jean Fautrier's abstract compositions. The collages' tactility and Pindell's arrangement of powdered thread in inter-secting sets of parallel horizontal and vertical lines contribute to a textile logic; the paradigmatic modernist grid melds with the warp and weft of textile. At the same time, the artist pushes the pictorial surface outward from the work, eschewing modernist flatness and pictorial recession.

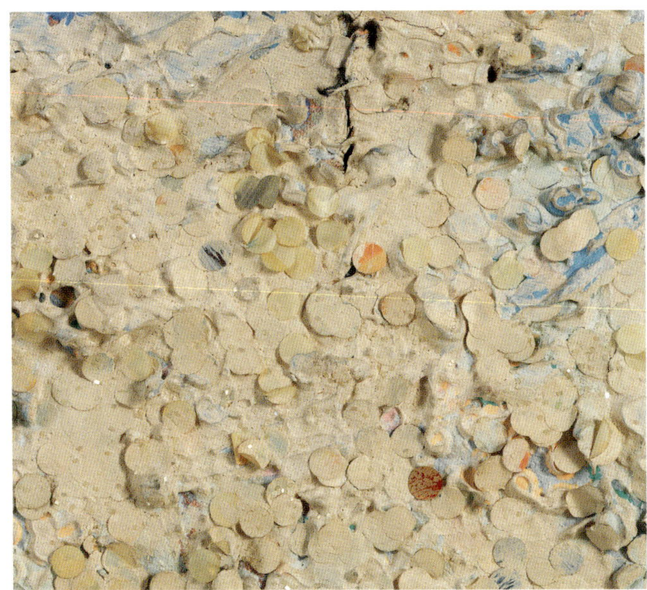

Fig. 5. Howardena Pindell, *Untitled #20* (*Dutch Wives Circled and Squared*), 1978 (detail; see fig. 4).

This haptic approach to abstraction reflects Pindell's broader concern for the phenomenological aspects of her works, particularly the relational dynamic between her art works, her labors, and her audiences. She pursued the haptic in part because she believed it could generate "empowering" psychological effects for herself as maker and for her works' viewers. While reflecting in the mid-1980s on the first decades of her career, she developed an idiosyncratic definition of "surface tension" to theorize this aspect of her practice. "Surface tension" describes her use of densely hand-worked surfaces to register her labors, generating a physical presence without recourse to figuration. In this way, Pindell used the haptic to assert her authorship abstractly, rejecting the representational imperatives of prescriptive cultural ideologies.[16] She also connected her theory of surface tension to scale, leveraging compositional size ratios to activate her audiences' bodily movements. Works including the untitled collage of 1973 repeat detailed forms (typically the round) in an allover pattern that tends to draw the viewer inward, outward, and back toward the artwork.

Pindell also explicitly—and presciently—positioned surface tension as distinctly African diasporic. In more recent years, scholars have drawn on affect theory, especially the insights of film theorist Laura U. Marks, to conceptualize the haptic as a minoritarian strategy. Queer theorist Eve Kosofsky Sedgwick, for instance, has argued that haptic experiences elicited by textured surfaces exceed the subject—object dichotomies that undergird Western materialist philosophies. Black feminist theorists Rizvana Bradley and Hortense Spillers critique this liberatory model of the haptic by contending that the salutary properties of touch must be understood alongside histories of touch as violence in the wake of the transatlantic trade in enslaved Africans.[17] The haptic's associations with healing and subjugation both hold relevance to Pindell's practice, which she developed not only from formative encounters with Ghanaian textiles, but also out of her frustrations with her disempowering position in a white-collar workplace.

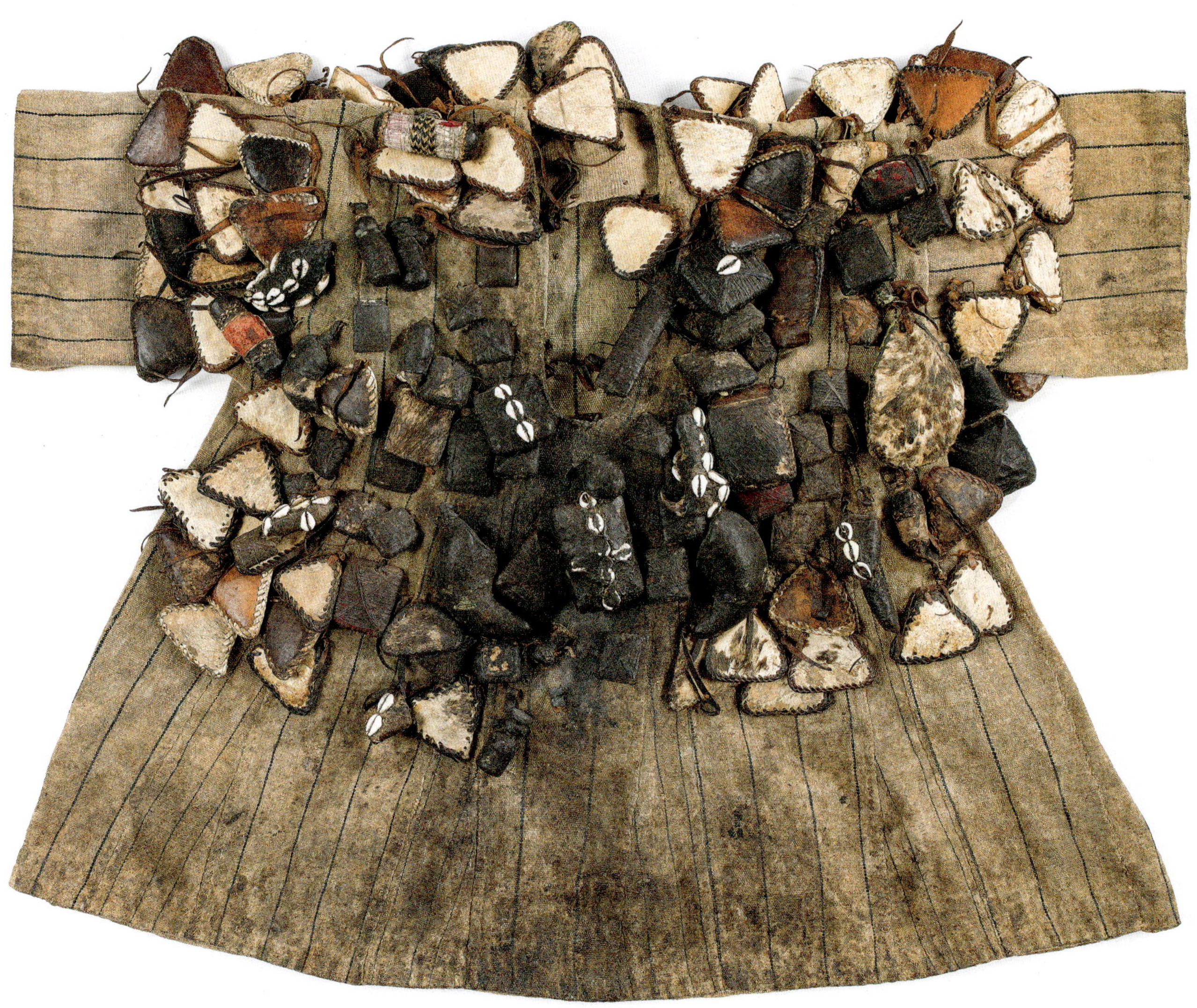

In her cut and sewn paintings of the 1970s, Pindell most directly investigates a haptic approach to abstraction. Inspired by Ghanaian textiles, she constructed these works through an elaborate series of steps that underscored her labor and expressed postminimalist concerns for process and bodily effects. *Untitled #20* (*Dutch Wives Circled and Squared*) (1978; figs. 4, 5) shares the loosely hanging, horizontal span of an Akan *batakari,* or war tunic, that Pindell encountered in an exhibition of African art at MoMA (fig. 6). She incorporated visible stitching and collage into her oeuvre after viewing this texturally dense Ghanaian textile in 1972. Triangular leather bundles bound with leather cord adorn the garment. These and other attached amulets contain words from the Koran intended to "safeguard" the wearer.[18] Pindell adapted the notion of protective accumulations to her own works, understanding them as a diasporic extension of African cultural practices. To create *Dutch Wives,* she pieced together scraps of canvas, treating them as textiles. The painting's collaged texture and visible, stitched seams rhyme with the garment's adornments and construction.

Through her expansion of modernist painting into West African textiles, Pindell produced what art historians Huey Copeland and Krista Thompson have dubbed "afrotropes"—"recurrent visual forms that have emerged within and become central to the formation of African diasporic culture and identity."[19] Ghanaian textiles such as kente cloth indubitably function as afrotropes in the U.S. context. Pindell joined many Black American artists in this period, such as Ed Clark, Houston Conwill, and Betye Saar, who approached "Africa" as a site of cultural Blackness accessible through characteristic aesthetic forms. These artists adapted a wide diversity of practices from the continent to the contexts of their own lives and artistic careers, operating at an intersection of cultural affirmation and cultural appropriation in response to social ruptures that originated with the Middle Passage.

Pindell joined a small cadre of these artists who innovated upon the era's artistic trends by engaging with afrotropes primarily through textural, rather than visual, characteristics. New York–based Black American painters, including Al Loving, Overstreet, Ringgold, and Whitten, radically altered their approach to the painterly surface in the 1960s and 1970s, experimenting with textures, dimensionality, materials, and scale. The concept of "surface tension" belongs to Pindell and cannot readily be ascribed to these diverse practices. However, each of these artists, like Pindell, defied the aesthetic hierarchies of Euro-American culture through the choices they made about surface.

For Black women artists in this era, haptic artistic strategies proved particularly significant as a way of engaging with both African diasporic and feminist aesthetics. They joined non-Black women artists in developing intensely tactile art-making methods. Through craft-inflected materials and processes such as sewing, feminist artists disputed the Western supremacy of the optical and connected their twentieth-century practices to histories of women's handiwork. Pindell, with her incorporation of visible hand-stitching, glitter, and pastel paints into her abstract paintings, embraced handicraft as a feminist recuperative strategy, working alongside others to redress the long-standing institutional trivialization of women's cultural contributions.

MENDING ABSTRACTION

Pindell's career offers an ideal springboard for a broader examination of how artists have renegotiated their practices in periods of heightened social interrogation, navigating the demands of their political commitments and aesthetic affinities. She is paradigmatic of Black artists who reclaimed abstraction in the late twentieth century, asserting an African diasporic artistic lineage that defied institutional modernism's proprietary claims. However, Pindell's experiences differed from those of most of her contemporaries in the sheer range of institutions through which she moved, which included both establishment and alternative galleries, museums, and publications. She leveraged insights gleaned from these various affiliations to develop enduring critiques of how art institutions and artistic reception actively produce systems of exclusion.

The only child of a middle-class family, Pindell's upbringing and training contributed to the complex interactions of class, race, and gender in her life. She grew up in Philadelphia, a city she has recalled as largely segregated. Pindell's mother and father each hailed from large families who struggled to make ends meet. The first generation of their respective families to attend college, they both obtained graduate degrees and worked as educators. They subsequently emphasized the importance of education for their daughter. The Pindells enrolled Howardena in a wide variety of enrichment programs from a young age, including extensive art classes. She attended an elite public high school in Philadelphia and received both a BA and BFA from Boston University in 1965, graduating a semester early. The following year, she entered the prestigious MFA program at Yale, focusing on painting. Pindell has reported that sexism was the norm and she was regularly mistaken for an international student during her time in New Haven. Upon completing her degree in 1967, she moved to New York, where she could live with a friend rent-free while looking for employment. An arduous, discouraging job search ended with an offer from MoMA that Pindell credited to a stroke of luck.[20] Despite her educational credentials, she made little money at the museum and struggled financially for years as she sought to support her artistic endeavors.

Pindell often found herself at the crosshairs of art world contention. At her day job at MoMA, colleagues treated her prejudicially, regularly dismissing or ignoring her. During her tenure, the museum solidified its claim as a preeminent modernist institution and became the primary target of the AWC. Although she attended some AWC meetings, Pindell's museum affiliation prevented her full participation in the activist group; in her telling, members including artist

Carl Andre labeled her a "spy." Her institutional post caused controversy within Black artists' circles in particular. Pindell has noted that some prominent artist-activists criticized her for not "opening more doors" for artists of color, though she felt powerless to do so.[21] Despite being sidelined within both the museum and the activist organization, she nonetheless agitated for art world reform alongside AWC affiliates throughout the 1970s.

During her first years in Manhattan, Pindell produced abstract geometric compositions and color field paintings, creating allover atmospheric compositions redolent of modernist works by Larry Poons and Ad Reinhardt, whom she has cited as influences. Pindell initiated her investigation of the tension between allover composition and granular, pointillistic detail with these paintings. Small rounds of contrasting colors flicker across these works, oscillating between pictorial recession and surface mark. Paint seeps directly into the unprimed canvas of these stained, spray-painted compositions (fig. 7). Over the course of the 1970s, Pindell brought texture and a textile logic to bear on her abstract practice as she labored to expand her aesthetic horizons beyond the predominately white male modernisms of Yale and MoMA.[22] In these years, she looked to Ghanaian textiles as a source of abstraction and as a route for accessing a Black cultural identity without recourse to figuration. With her collaged works on paper and paintings, she sought to incorporate what she called "covert" feminist messages into her work through the use of handicraft. Pindell's experimentations with abstraction culminated in her cut and sewn paintings of the late 1970s, works through which, I argue, she most ardently pursued a Black feminist modernism.

A series of cascading crises drastically reconfigured Pindell's life in 1979. That February, the publicly funded alternative gallery Artists Space opened a show entitled *The N—— Drawings*. (The anti-Black racist epithet was uncensored in its original context.[23]) The exhibition featured charcoal drawings and black-and-white photographs by a young white artist. Pindell helped to organize protestors that spring who argued that the exhibition's blithe use of a racist slur callously flaunted the systemic exclusion of Black artists from large swaths of the art world. The exhibition's supporters charged the protestors with censorship. In June, Pindell resigned from her position at MoMA, where she felt her colleagues scorned her, sharing the gallery's position that the protestors had overstepped. She began teaching in the Department of Art at Stony Brook University in August, a position she relished for the increased time it allowed her in her studio. Within two months, however, severe injuries she sustained in an automobile accident further destabilized her life; she suffered a head injury and temporary short- and long-term memory loss. Pindell adapted her artistic practice to this personal and professional upheaval, experimenting with figurative elements that hauntingly referenced her experiences. For instance, in *Autobiography: Earth (Eyes, Injuries)* (1987) a faintly visible silhouetted figure appears in the center of an unstretched, ovoid canvas (fig. 8). Collaged photostat images of eyes float in a painterly sea of deep blue hashmarks. According to Pindell, these disembodied eyes represent the passive onlookers who witnessed the car crash.[24] Following the Artists Space controversy and the accident—traumas that became deeply interconnected for Pindell—she gradually took on a more public activist role. By the mid-1980s, she was a prominent, outspoken critic of art world racism and sexism.

In recent years, scholars have tended to bifurcate narratives of Pindell's career into two distinct periods: the process-oriented work of the 1970s and the explicitly political art begun in 1980.[25] *Howardena Pindell* follows the arc of her artistic and professional development through the years of this purported break, and the events of 1979 figure prominently in its narrative of the artist's dynamic

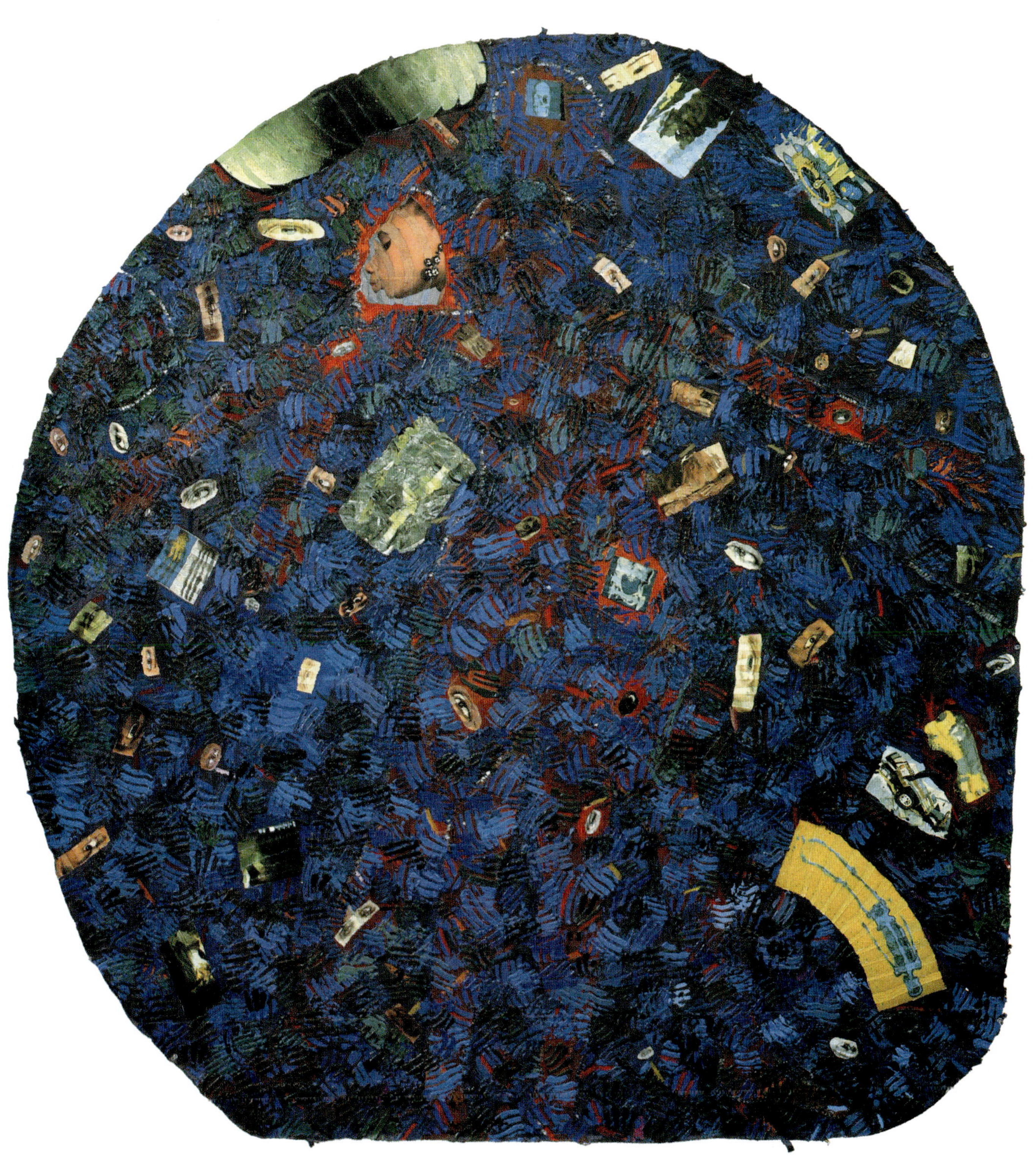

relationship to figuration and political expression. However, this account does not imagine the crises of that year, as many do, as a fissure between earlier concerns for formal effects and later efforts to redress art world bias.

Rather, I argue, interactions between modernism and activism, between abstraction and autobiography, defined Pindell's ambitious practice throughout the first decades of her career. Abstraction was never, for Pindell, a mode outside of or beyond her experiences as a Black woman. Instead, she favored this artistic idiom because it offered a framework for understanding the friction between individual experience and social identity. Pindell viewed abstraction as an inherently ambivalent mode of making that was poised, in her words, to "relate back to . . . the world" and to abstain from "concrete meaning."[26] She relied on these multivalent capacities throughout the first decades of her career.

Pindell turned to her most reliable artistic method, the haptic, in her continual efforts to reimagine what it meant to be a Black woman artist both before and following the events of 1979. The haptic recurs in her abstract and figurative art, and in her paintings, works on paper, and photographic and video practices. While her approach to the haptic changed significantly over these years, it remained a tool for interrogating the inextricability of abstraction and activism. This book identifies two structuring metaphors—mending and textile logic—that most exemplify the aesthetic, conceptual, and political reach of Pindell's haptic practice and of her contributions to contemporary art.

To mend is to repair something broken or damaged in order to extend its life. Mending is a process of piecing together, patching up, restoring, or healing. Pindell's practice engages with literal marks of mending, including the visible stitches of her cut and sewn paintings. Her mending also operates symbolically. She sought to "mend" abstraction, making it useful to her as an artist who experienced de facto exclusion from the category "modernist." Her abstract art stitches together the materials, the irreconcilable forms of labor, and the artistic conversations that shaped her life and career. In this way, her works made meaning of the seemingly incongruous spheres of modernist abstraction, bureaucratic labor, feminist reclamations, and West African textiles. Indeed, her artworks reveal these cultural formations to be inexorably linked. Pindell's art has the potential to help erode long-standing assumptions that place Black feminist cultural production and modernist abstraction in discrete silos, which are rarely imagined as coming into contact, much less shaping one another.

Of the works Pindell made between the late 1960s and the early 1980s, her cut and sewn paintings most overtly engage with the metaphor of mending. In *Carnival at Ostende*, for instance, short lengths of string skitter across the abstract surface, drawing attention to several visibly stitched seams (see fig. 2). The substantial layer of paint thickens the thread at these seams, which form a partial grid that divides the canvas into modular units. These details reveal that the painting consists of multiple pieces of canvas sewn together, rather than a single surface. The painting exemplifies how mending does not return an object to its original, whole state, but rather tends to it, expanding its usefulness. Pindell's works leave intact the traces of her efforts to bring together the spheres of her life. She developed mending techniques not only out of a belief that she could make meaningful art through abstraction and handiwork, but also from a need to reconcile aspects of her experience that failed to cohere under dominant ideologies.

Pindell's extended engagement with mending offers a reparative approach to the limitations of Black nationalist, feminist, and modernist discourses. Sedgwick has offered a theorization of reparative practices in contrast to the paranoid. Reparative motives, according to Sedgwick, "are about pleasure," about tending to needs and desires, often out of love. Pindell has conceived of her own artistic labors as both "pleasurable" and "meditative." She found refuge in them, despite the fact that they often involved tedious bureaucratic processes such as labeling and hole-punching. Thus, Pindell joins fellow Black feminist thinkers, notably poet Audre Lorde, in theorizing pleasure as a resource with particular resonances for Black American women, who in the public imaginary largely have been relegated to roles of suffering.[27] Black women's pleasure in art and in life offers a radical refusal of the interlocking hegemonic social controls of patriarchy and white supremacy.

Textility—a textile-based aesthetic—characterizes much of Pindell's most well-known abstractions. Her simultaneous involvement with abstract painting as an allover field, typically understood as optical, and as a tactile surface for "non-Western" handicraft operations, reveals textiles as the sublimated medium of the twentieth century.[28] Pindell exploited the metaphorical capacities of textiles as relational, vernacular materials imbricated in social, economic, and epistemological systems. Textiles are social membranes. They mediate the body's entry into the public sphere, interpolating us into a wide variety of social designations—class, gender, ethnicity, and life stage. The textiles that humans wear discipline our bodies through ritual, shaping our movements, gestures, and senses of self.

Amid the artistic expansions of the 1960s and 1970s, artists with diverse affiliations, including Sam Gilliam, Harmony Hammond, and Mary Heilmann, incorporated textility into their practices. Textile aesthetics played a particularly prominent role in feminist circles as part of efforts to reclaim handiwork as a culturally valuable artistic expression. Pindell encountered this artistic project in the predominantly white feminist artistic circles that provided her closest interlocutors in the first half of the 1970s.

Significantly, Pindell occupied an "outsider-within" position within these groups. In 1972, she cofounded the first women's cooperative gallery in the United States, A.I.R. Gallery, the only non-white artist to participate initially. She accessed this and other white feminist groups through her connections at MoMA, which included a formative friendship with white art critic Lucy Lippard. Many of Pindell's white feminist peers undertook earnest searches for a "woman's aesthetic." In contrast, she drew on her experiences as a Black woman to "signify upon"—or alter and redirect—notions of femininity, which in the Western world have been structured around whiteness. Pindell produced a waggish, overtly artificial, feminine-coded visual vocabulary, applying glitter, sequins, and "cheap" women's perfume to the surface of her abstract paintings.[29] Through her sidelong approach to feminist recuperations of materials and methods of making historically associated with women, she critiqued normative, racialized notions of femininity.

Pindell's artistic interventions into the discursive formation of womanhood must be understood in relationship to debates that construed whiteness as a prerequisite for non-pathological gender expression. In 1965, sociologist Daniel Patrick Moynihan (a liberal Democrat who later served as a U.S. senator from New York) published *The Negro Family: The Case for National Action,* a report written on his own initiative during his post as assistant secretary of labor. Eventually known as the Moynihan Report, it posited the "black matriarchy" as a driving cause of the economic woes of Black Americans.[30] The study, which synthesized the findings of several social scientific reports on poverty among Black Americans, controversially located the roots of racialized economic inequality in the "aberrant" formations of the Black family. Moynihan argued that families led by "dominant" Black single mothers perpetuated the systemic emasculation of Black men, who, in response, shirked familial duties. The solution, he concluded, was to foster feminine submissiveness among Black women.

The Moynihan Report reproduced long-standing stereotypes rooted in racist ideology. Black feminist theorists from abolitionist Sojourner Truth to artist Lorraine O'Grady have argued that, since at least the nineteenth century, Black women have been seen as "contentious and masculine," the "flipside" of womanhood that shores up ideal white femininity. For several decades after its initial publication, Moynihan's incendiary report served as a touchstone for Black feminist investigations of the racist and sexist underpinnings of normative accounts of the U.S. family and the racialization of gender. Critics charged the sociologist with laying blame for "the results of centuries of slavery, racism, and social and economic discrimination" at the feet of Black women.[31] The publication became a major flashpoint in the 1960s struggles for Black liberation. According to cultural critic bell hooks, the report had, among all the negative stereotypes assigned to Black womanhood, "the greatest impact on the consciousness of many black people."[32]

Black feminists in the early 1970s rejected the framework of the Moynihan Report as racist. Nonetheless, many conceived of Black womanhood as primarily operative in a family formation, particularly in the context of the Black Power movement. For instance, a special episode of the U.S. public affairs television program *Black Journal,* titled "The Black Woman" (1970), featured a panel of prominent Black American women.[33] In the episode, poet and community organizer Amina Baraka, along with most of the rest of the panel, construed Black women as wives and supporters whose labors should bolster the political work of Black men. This heterosexist framework excluded lesbians and unpartnered women from normative notions of Black femininity.

As a single, white-collar working woman, Pindell's biography did not conform to the predominant models of Blackness espoused within Black nationalist movements. The antipathies stirred by the Moynihan Report still hung in the air when she began contributing to the feminist art movement. Its "distortion" of Black women heightened the stakes of feminine presentation in the years Pindell began to incorporate pink and peach paints and women's perfume into her abstract artworks.[34] She used glitter, as well as sewing thread, to mend abstraction in the face of social narratives that denied the coherence of her experiences.

BLACK FEMINIST MODERNISMS

In a 1972 interview, when she was twenty-nine years old and five years into her career in New York, Pindell stated that she did not "know that many Black women painters." She felt isolated both as a Black person in a white art world and as a Black woman offered only partial membership in the Black Arts movement. Although making her art in seclusion, Pindell launched her career contemporaneously with a larger group of Black women artists who worked at the intersections of Black liberation efforts, feminisms, and modernisms. Their Black feminist modernisms formed as a series of practices with overlapping concerns, rather than a cohesive or monolithic group. In the post–civil rights era, Black feminist modernists brought emerging cultural expansions to bear on developments in "advanced" U.S. art, including color field painting, minimalism, assemblage, pop, and conceptual art. For instance, Blayton's stained, jewel-toned tondi innovated upon lyrical, color field modernisms (fig. 9). Their format evokes stained glass and the craft-inflected embroidery hoop. Beverly Buchanan's sculptural practice makes allusions to southern cultural histories through the idioms of postminimalism and land art (fig. 10). Her concrete block sculptures—some placed directly onto gallery floors, others into landscapes—resemble weather-worn ruins and minimalist forms put out to pasture. Black feminist modernists

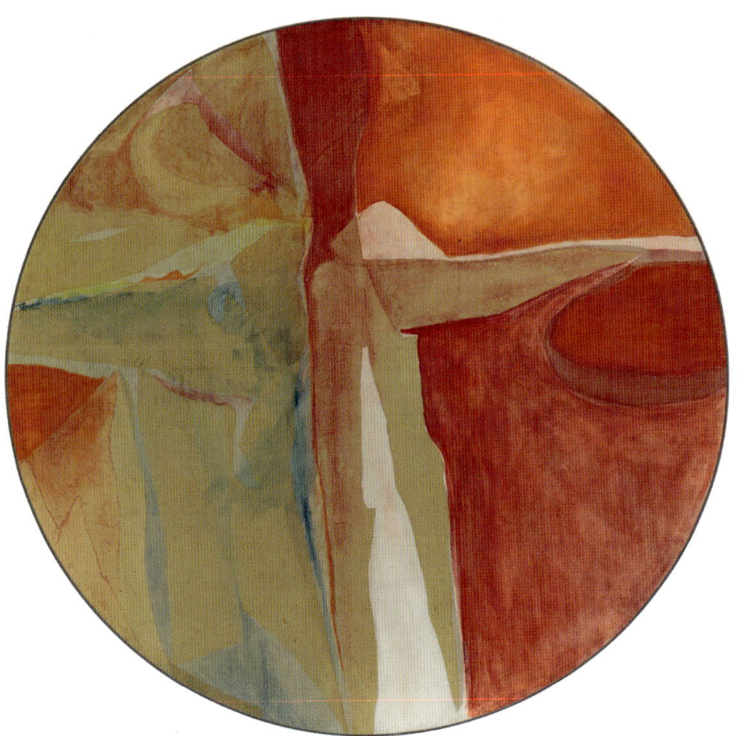

Fig. 9. Betty Blayton, *Reaching for Center,*
1979. Oil and collage on canvas, diameter:
58 in. (147.3 cm). Estate of Betty Blayton,
New York.

asserted their own belonging in the mainstream of U.S. art. They developed their
works in dialogue with a wider network of past and present Black women cultural producers who generated not only visual art but also poetry, prose, quilts,
and gardens.[35]

Over the course of the 1970s, Pindell came into contact with Black women
artists including Emma Amos, Blayton, Buchanan, Hassinger, Nengudi, Piper,
Ringgold, Saar, and Thomas. Pindell formed friendly relationships with some
of these women, for instance Buchanan and Blayton, whom she met at MoMA.
These artists each had their own complicated relationships to collectivity
informed by the realities of de facto segregation and tokenism. They moved
through some of the same art ecosystems, sharing gallerists and venues, occasionally agitating for art world reform together, understanding that they shared
a predicament, if not an artistic vision.

Black feminist modernists also worked alongside Black feminists who articulated their practices in opposition to modernisms. Artists such as Kay Brown,
Barbara Jones-Hogu, Dindga McCannon, and Ringgold made works with the
explicit intention of eschewing the aesthetic forms that predominated in
institutional art spaces such as MoMA. Jones-Hogu created the visually dynamic
screen-print poster *Unite* (1969/71), which depicts ten Black figures, fists raised
on sturdy arms above their heads, with a crisscrossing field of the titular word
(fig. 11). Purple, blue, red, and tan inks inject the imperative block letters with

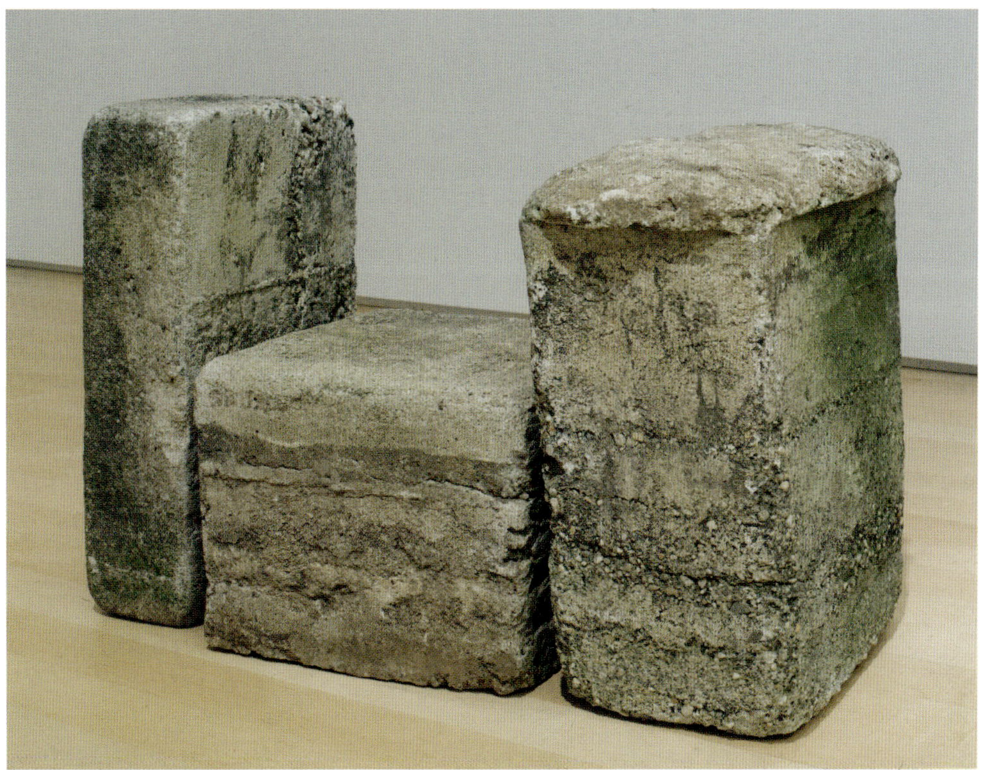

Fig 10. Beverly Buchanan, *Untitled* (*Frustula* series), c. 1978. Concrete, weight of all three components together: 625 lb. (283.5 kg). Brooklyn Museum. Gift of Arden Scott, 2017, 2017.9a–c.

movement. Sales from posters such as these supported the Chicago-based Black Arts movement collective the African Commune of Bad Relevant Artists (AfriCOBRA), of which Jones was a cofounder. In 1971, Brown and McCannon cofounded the Black women artists' collective Where We At: Black Women Artists in response to the Black Arts movement's marginalization of women artists.[36] The group embraced the movement's prioritization of art in service of social and political transformation. McCannon's *Revolutionary Sister* (1971) depicts a woman who literally exceeds the rectangular picture plane (fig. 12). Her crowned head, a reference to the Statue of Liberty, emerges from the top of a wood panel painted the colors of the Pan-African flag. Standing with arms akimbo, her hands just below a bullet belt that cinches a miniskirt, she appears poised for action. The women artists, such as members of Where We At, who maintained ties to the Black Arts movement espoused collective and community-centered practices, believing these would best serve the goal of political and cultural liberation. However, far from having a fixed orientation toward these Black feminisms, many artists engaged with a spectrum of approaches in their work, either simultaneously or over time.

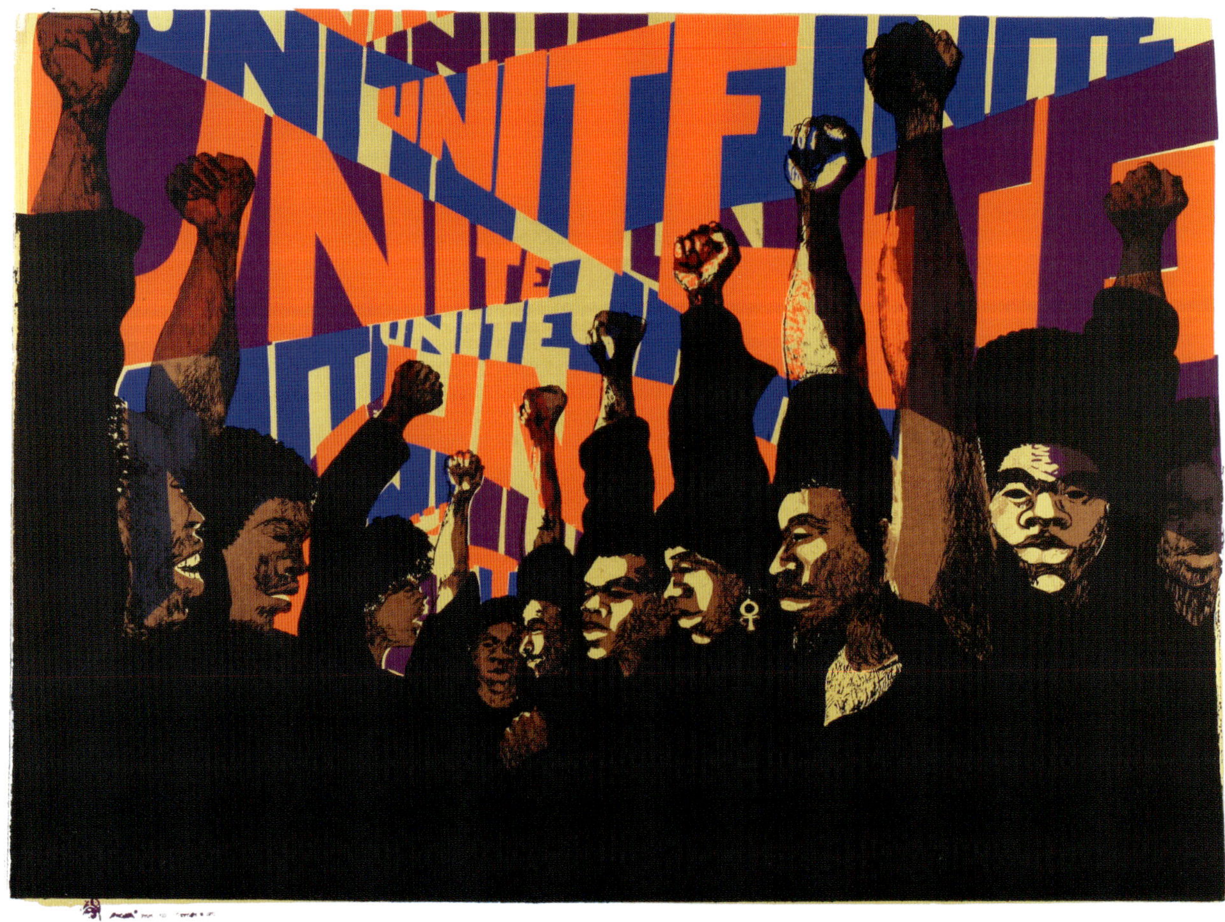

Fig. 11. Barbara Jones-Hogu, *Unite,* 1969/71. Color screen print on paper, image size: 22½ × 30 in. (57.2 × 76.2 cm). Collection of the Smithsonian National Museum of African American History and Culture, Washington, DC, 2008.13.

Particularly in the first decades of her career, Pindell faced structural barriers to forming community with other Black women artists. To support herself financially and maintain her artistic practice, she kept a grueling schedule, returning home from work around six in the evening and heading to her studio within an hour or two to paint until eleven or midnight. She spent her weekends painting as well, fulfilling her obligations to A.I.R. Gallery, writing, and otherwise managing her artistic career and personal affairs. Given these demands on her time, when Pindell met people, she generally did so through her predominantly white institutional affiliations. Nonetheless, over the course of the late 1970s and 1980s, she "became friendly with" Black women artists such Carole Byard, Janet Henry, Valerie Maynard, and Sana Musasama.[37]

Fig. 12. Dindga McCannon, *Revolutionary Sister,*
1971. Mixed media construction on wood,
62 × 27 in. (157.5 × 68.6 cm). Brooklyn Museum,
Gift of R. M. Atwater, Anna Wolfrom Dove, Alice
Fiebiger, Joseph Fiebiger, Belle Campbell Harriss,
and Emma L. Hyde, by exchange, Designated
Purchase Fund, Mary Smith Dorward Fund,
Dick S. Ramsay Fund, and Carll H. de Silver Fund,
2012.80.32.

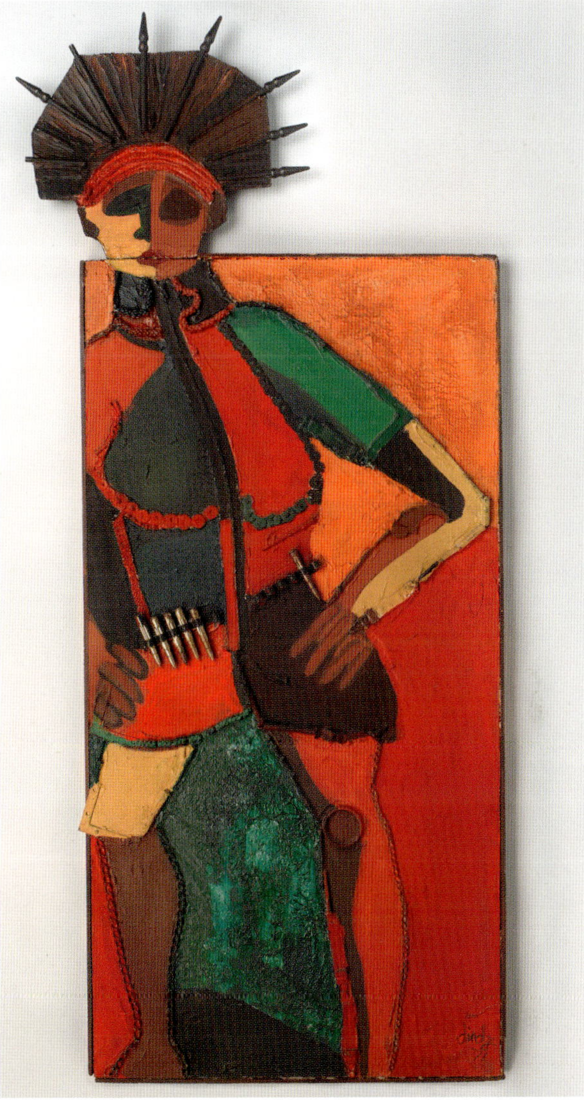

Pindell's family history and personality further contributed to her insularity. Her upwardly mobile parents raised her, she noted, to be "separate," providing enrichment and educational opportunities they hoped would shield her from the ubiquitous racial violence of their own childhoods. This method of rearing has shaped Pindell's reserved personality. As her friend and onetime gallerist Linda Goode Bryant has noted, Pindell is "very private . . . independent," and "not a collective kind of person."[38] Indeed, her labor-intensive, detail-focused method of painting reflects an introverted orientation to art-making that Pindell has held in tension with her public persona and outward-facing activism.

While recent scholarship has produced sensitive portrayals of the dynamic ways in which many Black artists have navigated their careers in close contact with one another, these analyses tend to sideline artists such as Pindell who have worked in greater isolation as a consequence of external barriers and individual preferences. A related issue lies in the perceived relationship between Black artists and a broader Black racial community. Art historian Kobena Mercer has critiqued the "burden of representation" placed on Black artists who face the impossible task of speaking as "representatives" of their race. Art historians Steven Nelson and Darby English have further theorized the impact of these uneven representational expectations on art-historical canons and artistic viewership, respectively.[39] These burdens weigh Black artists with an array of moral responsibilities that non-Black artists, to a greater degree, can eschew. Throughout her career, Pindell has weathered levels of scrutiny over her artistic choices and political affiliations that artists with different social positions rarely face.

During her first twenty years in New York, Pindell moved through eclectic milieus of cultural producers. She befriended white feminists in the early 1970s, including Lippard, artist Sylvia Sleigh and her partner, the art historian Lawrence Alloway, as well as artist Brenda Miller (who was also Pindell's neighbor at Westbeth Artists Housing). However, the racism and tokenism Pindell encountered in white feminist circles led to a profound sense of isolation. She left A.I.R. in 1975, feeling "yanked back and forth" between racial and classed exclusions from the gallery. Unlike most of her colleagues there, who were married, Pindell financially supported herself. Her distrust in predominantly white institutions mounted over the course of the 1970s. She increasingly suspected that her qualified entry into these organizations was intended to garner liberal goodwill rather than to achieve true inclusion.[40]

Beginning in the mid-1970s, Pindell frequently exhibited her work alongside other artists of color in alternative spaces such as Just Above Midtown gallery. She formed friendships with fellow Black artists such as Buchanan, Gilliam, David Hammons, Janet Henry, gallerist Goode Bryant, and art historian Judith Wilson. In this same period, she began contributing regularly to the *Feminist Art Journal* and the feminist arts and politics publication *Heresies*. Pindell participated in art world manifestations of the Third World Women's movement, working alongside artists including Ana Mendieta and Kay WalkingStick. She began conducting art world surveys, researching the demographics of artists represented in New York galleries and museums. The results, updated periodically, appeared in a series of articles printed in anthologies, exhibition catalogues, and art journals throughout the 1980s and 1990s. These texts include "Art (World) and Racism: Testimony, Documentation and Statistics," in which Pindell influentially contended that the art world constitutes a "closed nepotistic interlocking network" of galleries, museums, and dealers who exclude artists of color. The essay inspired the formation of PESTS—an anonymous offshoot of artists of color from the feminist collective Guerrilla Girls. Through this work, Pindell became a prominent voice in artists' efforts to redefine a women's movement outside of the whiteness that had monopolized mainstream feminisms in the United States since the early 1970s.[41]

ART-HISTORICAL INTERVENTIONS

Despite growing public interest in the abstract work of artists of color, the contributions of Black feminist modernists to contemporary culture have yet to be fully accounted for in academic scholarship. Throughout U.S. history, visual culture has served the social production of racial and gender ideologies that dehumanize Black women. Responding to this collusion, many Black feminist scholars have approached the visual, including visual art, with skepticism, dubious about its prospects for furthering liberation. As cultural theorist Michele Wallace and gender theorist Jennifer Nash have elucidated, within Black feminist scholarly discourse the visual has been understood largely through a lens of punishment—as an arena in which Black women are caricatured and stereotyped by others.[42] This perspective has contributed to a hierarchy of Black feminist inquiry that tends to marginalize Black women visual artists, especially those working in nonrepresentational modes.

The predominately white discipline of art history has maintained foundational hierarchies that have sidelined Black women artists. In the twentieth century, the institutional art world rarely looked to Black women artists as important contributors to modernism, despite their central role in U.S. social, cultural, political, and economic developments. Although a recent growth in scholarship on the abstract work of Black American artists has enriched the field of contemporary art history, the contributions of Black women continue to be minimized in these accounts. Black women are reinscribed as what Copeland has called "the sum of two differences rather than as individuals with their own ends and histories."[43]

In this book, I advance a Black feminist art-historical framework, responding specifically to art historian Freida High W. Tesfagiorgis's call for a "Black feminist art history discourse" that prioritizes Black women artists, whom scholars too often cast in a "defensive position." Similarly, art historian Judith Wilson has urged *"more* Black feminist visual theory" in order to further cultivate a discursive community around Black women's art. Tesfagiorgis, Wilson, Lowery Stokes Sims, Wallace, and other Black women art historians and critics working in the 1980s and 1990s sought to upend the disciplinary norms that required them to justify Black women artists' deviations from norms established to accommodate the experiences of white and male artists.[44] This study is indebted to these theorists, whose insights, though sometimes unacknowledged, undergird the discipline's more recent expansions.

Howardena Pindell argues that Black women visual artists have exploited visual and extravisual protocols to theorize and imagine forms of liberation, drawing on pain, pleasure, loss, and joy as they reckon with what it means to be human and what it might mean to be free. Drawing on interdisciplinary scholarship from Black feminist art history to queer theory, and from Black cultural studies to Americanist art history, this book insists on the co-constitutive relationship between race and gender and the visual. It participates in multiple strains of literature that simultaneously acknowledge the harmful historical and present-day realities of visual culture *and* highlight how Black women artists have refused to accept an irreparably detrimental visual field.

The first scholarly monograph focused exclusively on any aspect of Pindell's practice, *Howardena Pindell* follows from art-historical and interdisciplinary Black feminist methodologies for centering the works and lived experiences of Black women.[45] I draw on interviews Pindell has given over a fifty-year span, including those I conducted. This book seeks to "mend" the traditional form of the monograph. An art-historical genre, the monograph represents a lavishing of scholarly attention, only rarely granted to Black women artists, onto a single cultural producer. The existence or absence of such studies authorizes subsequent narratives and exclusions. Through its repetitive deployment, the monograph has granted mythic status to a few privileged individuals, typically white and male, who are anointed as bearers of artistic genius. By contrast, this monograph presents a model of decentering rather than consolidation. Pindell and her career are exceptional, but she has never stood alone as a Black woman making groundbreaking art. This project aims not only to provide a comprehensive, if necessarily partial, account of Pindell's practice, but more broadly to examine Black women's contributions to post–civil rights era debates around aesthetic hierarchies. The work of many of the aforementioned Black women visual artists, as well as the writing of Lorde, O'Grady, and Wallace, figures prominently in these pages. In giving concentrated attention to Pindell's career, this book aspires to stimulate future histories that fully acknowledge the ways in which Black women have led and defined culture in the United States.

As an art-historical intervention, *Howardena Pindell* reframes episodes in contemporary art around the experiences of makers often left on the margins of art history. This approach makes space for new questions, such as how abstract art in the United States changed as a result of the Black Arts movement and feminist art movement of the 1970s. It also reveals central, though neglected, tensions within contemporary art. For instance, the book examines the racialized and gendered messages about authorial agency encoded in the bureaucratic models of labor that so many artists in the 1970s embraced. Pindell engaged with these themes specifically in order to legitimate her practice as "advanced" at the same time that she challenged the social privilege unreflexively asserted through these tropes. Her experiences illuminate the contradictions that shaped U.S. art in the late twentieth century, a period that saw the rejection of some established hierarchies of medium and labor and the consolidation of others.

Each of the book's four chapters addresses a body of artistic work that enacts a distinct phenomenology of viewing through recourse to its own combination of conceptual and formal means. Alongside these analyses of Pindell's artistic development, I consider the contributions she made to contemporary art through her curatorial work, essays, and speeches. The study commences in 1967, with Pindell's arrival in New York. It concludes with a temporary turn to figuration in the early 1980s. This approach focuses the book on Pindell's refusal to represent herself in her art in a literal way, a stance that characterized her oeuvre in these initial decades of her career. By the late 1970s, she began questioning this position, and her artistic practice shifted gradually as a result. A further motivation for the book's scope lies in disciplinary needs. Pindell's abstract artworks have presented a particular challenge to art history; they do not readily model conventional narratives about Black women's meaningful artistic endeavors in these politically charged decades. Her figurative works of the 1980s and 1990s are more easily assimilated into art histories that view artists of color as working outside the mainstream of advanced art. By centering the first decades of Pindell's career, the book focuses the disciplinary question of how to reconcile artists' aesthetic and activist aspirations.

"Moving Modernisms," the first chapter, examines Pindell's initial forays into abstraction amid the ascendance of the Black Arts movement. Her spray-painted color field paintings enact a "choreography of viewing," activating their audiences' physical movements. These works drew on modernist theories promoted by Reinhardt and Josef Albers, and combined these formal concerns with her understanding of the circle and grid as social and cosmological signifiers. With her early modernist experimentations, Pindell thematized movement as a method for interrogating the complexly intertwined spatial, racial, and geographic dynamics of institutional modernisms. Ultimately, this early abstract art confronted the relationship between form and subjectivity espoused in modernist and Black cultural discourses.

Chapters 2 and 3 examine Pindell's emerging critiques of modernist abstraction through her haptic approach to works on paper and paintings. Chapter 2, "Paper Work," focuses on Pindell's collage practice, initiated around 1972, which engaged the technique's resonances within narratives of African diasporic, modernist, and feminist art. The collages deploy intimately scaled handiwork to underscore the artist's labors. Pindell's arduous mode of making participated in critical conversations about artistic labor emerging from conceptualist and feminist circles. She repurposed processes from her white-collar, bureaucratic day job to generate a pleasurable, potentially "healing" practice. In this way, the works assert a Black feminist theory of agential authority and knowledge production.

"Mending Abstraction," the third chapter, examines Pindell's growing investments in the haptic and its affective conceits in the late 1970s, as she posited her textural innovations as specifically African diasporic. With the cut and sewn paintings, Pindell turned to Ghanaian textiles as a source of abstraction, defying the persistent art world assumption that cultural Blackness should operate in the visual arts through a fixed set of primarily representational elements. The works embrace an avowedly feminine-coded aesthetic in order to reroute modernist expectations and theorize femininity as a racialized masquerade. In this way, they refuse the promise of modernist abstraction to register its maker's inner life. It is the cut and sewn paintings that culminate Pindell's efforts to "mend" abstraction. Through a series of structuring tensions, such as her postminimalist concern for the relationship between the handmade and the industrial, she most fully invested in a Black feminist approach to a nonrepresentational idiom.

The final chapter, "Screen, Skin," addresses Pindell's increasingly public activism and tentative use of figuration in the early 1980s. This shift occurred in the context of the artist's growing disillusionment with art world institutions and engagements with the Third World Women's movement. In the canonical 1980 video *Free, White and 21,* Pindell's most well-known work, she plays two characters who each deploy a series of gestures that thematize skin. These membranes, I argue, show Pindell using a mass medium to theorize representation as a series of imaginative, abstracting surfaces that interlace lived experience and mediated depiction. *Free, White and 21* frequently has been construed as emblematic of the end of Pindell's process-oriented, abstract practice. However, the video elaborates on the artist's long-standing concerns for textured surfaces, collage aesthetics, and textile logic. Pindell's figurative works continue her exploration, begun in abstraction, of the complex human experience of race and gender and the friction generated in the confrontation of embodiment and social identity. This continuity evinces how abstraction and figuration and modernisms and activism shade into each other. Pindell exploited a wide range of these aesthetic strategies as she adapted to changing personal and social circumstances.

In the book's conclusion, Pindell's increasingly figurative practice of the 1980s and 1990s takes center stage alongside her enduring artistic and activist legacy. Following the events of 1979, Pindell continued to pursue a haptic practice that engaged with abstraction; however, her concerns gradually shifted toward explicit questions about collective memory and the root of U.S. history in racial trauma. This reflective, content-driven artistic mode marked a departure from the emphatically nonrepresentational tactics she had used to redress modernist exclusions in previous decades. The conclusion also considers Pindell's most recent return to fully abstract works as she continues to raise contemporary art's most pressing questions over half a century since the beginning of her career. Her abiding attention to abstraction's activist potential has influenced a younger generation of artists working today. Contemporary Black artists such as Sadie Barnette and Samuel Levi Jones build on her insights by using new aesthetic forms to annotate the social scripts embedded in commonplace materials.

A joy and challenge of this project has been to track and participate in a recent uptick in Pindell's art world exposure, including a critically lauded career

retrospective, after decades of alternatingly waxing and waning public attention. Pindell has remarked on the reception of Black artists in the United States:
"Every ten years, the Euro-Americans come out and it's 'please tell us where
you've been all this time?' Suddenly we are of great interest and then the interest
dips and we hear nothing. . . . Every time the wave comes, we are there. We were
there all along. We've been doing our work. We've been plodding along."[46] As a
white woman, I take Pindell's insights as a call to sustained anti-racist action.
Her works urge a scholarly reconsideration at this juncture of renewed appeal,
an intersection that coincides with a "wave" of widespread institutional interest
and investment in inclusion. *Howardena Pindell* offers an extended, scholarly
consideration of Pindell's work, as well as the work of other Black feminist modernists, in the hope that this crest becomes a sea change.

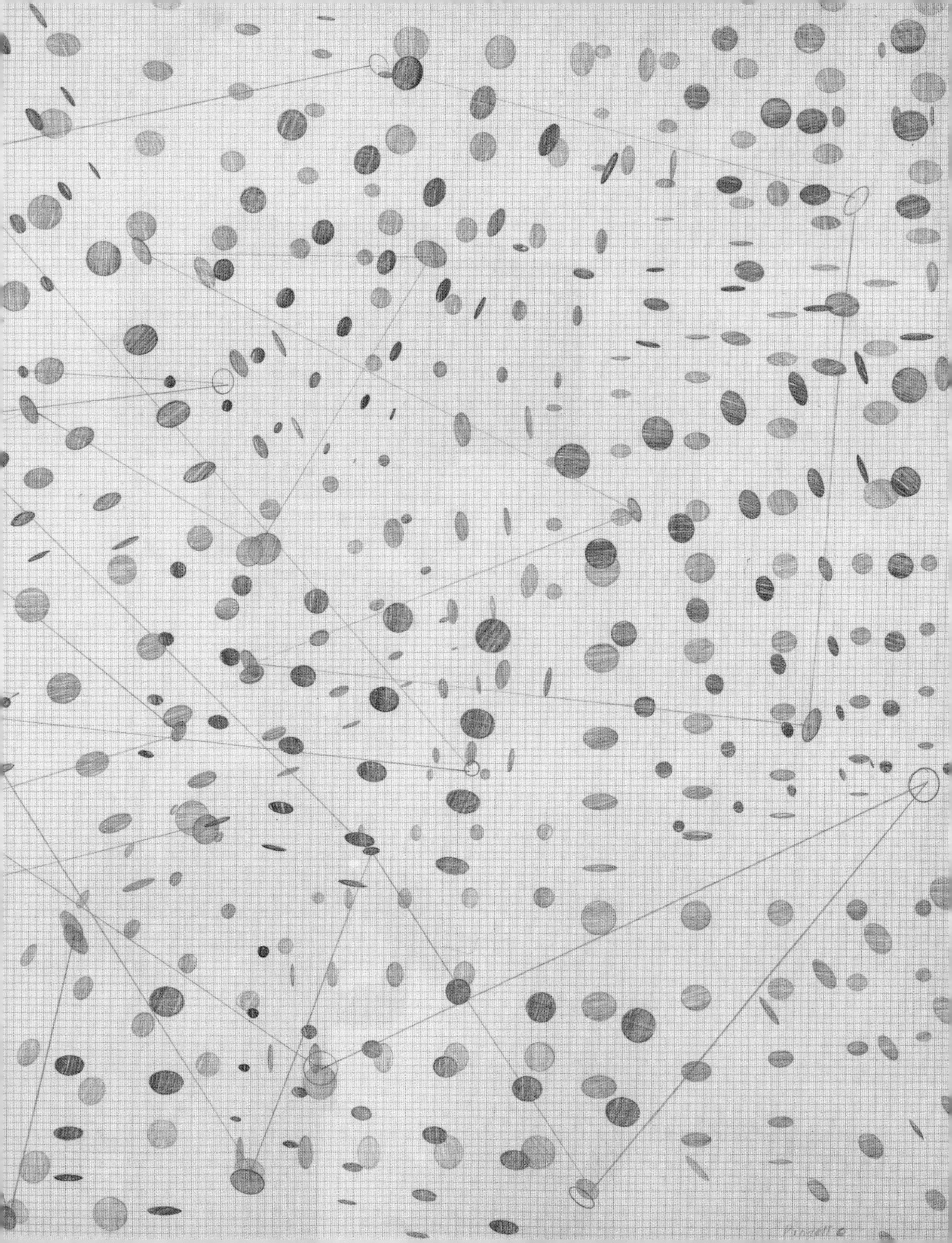

1 • Moving Modernisms

In 1969, artist Howardena Pindell carted several of her paintings uptown to the Studio Museum in Harlem. The recently opened institution, situated in a predominantly Black neighborhood, was established to provide quality exhibition space for living Black American artists. Pindell quickly regretted making the trip. Upon seeing her abstract canvases, the director of the museum, Ed Spriggs, roundly rejected her, telling her to "go downtown" and "show with the white boys."[1] As the retort lays bare, Pindell—like many artists in New York in the late 1960s—navigated artistic imperatives assigned on the basis of race and gender. These aesthetic expectations, mapped onto local New York geographies and onto artists' bodies, continue profoundly to shape art-historical narratives of the era.

This anecdote, which Pindell has shared in numerous interviews, instructs her audience in the fraught terrain she encountered as a Black woman artist working abstractly in this period. The paintings she took to the Studio Museum likely belonged to a series of brightly colored works in which geometric shapes overlay a hand-drawn grid (fig. 13).[2] Ellipses drawn in sunny shades of yellow, blue, and pink float atop an irregular grid. Lines dart from some of these shapes, injecting the composition with a sense of cybernetic motion. Produced in the years 1968 and 1969, the compositions were among the first of the artist's abstract works. With them, Pindell established some of the formal concerns that motivated her artistic production for the following two decades, including the tension between handmade and machinic forms and between pictorial surface and depth. Crucially, her practice in the late 1960s and early 1970s also established a framework through which she would challenge the exclusionary discourses around identity that structure histories of modernist art.

Pindell made these works in years when the stakes of abstraction shifted seismically. During their encounter at the Studio Museum, Spriggs voiced an increasingly prevalent view that abstract modernist idioms belonged exclusively to a white, male cultural tradition. In doing so, he echoed voluble contributors to the Black Arts movement, such as Amiri Baraka, Margaret Burroughs, and

Detail, fig. 15.

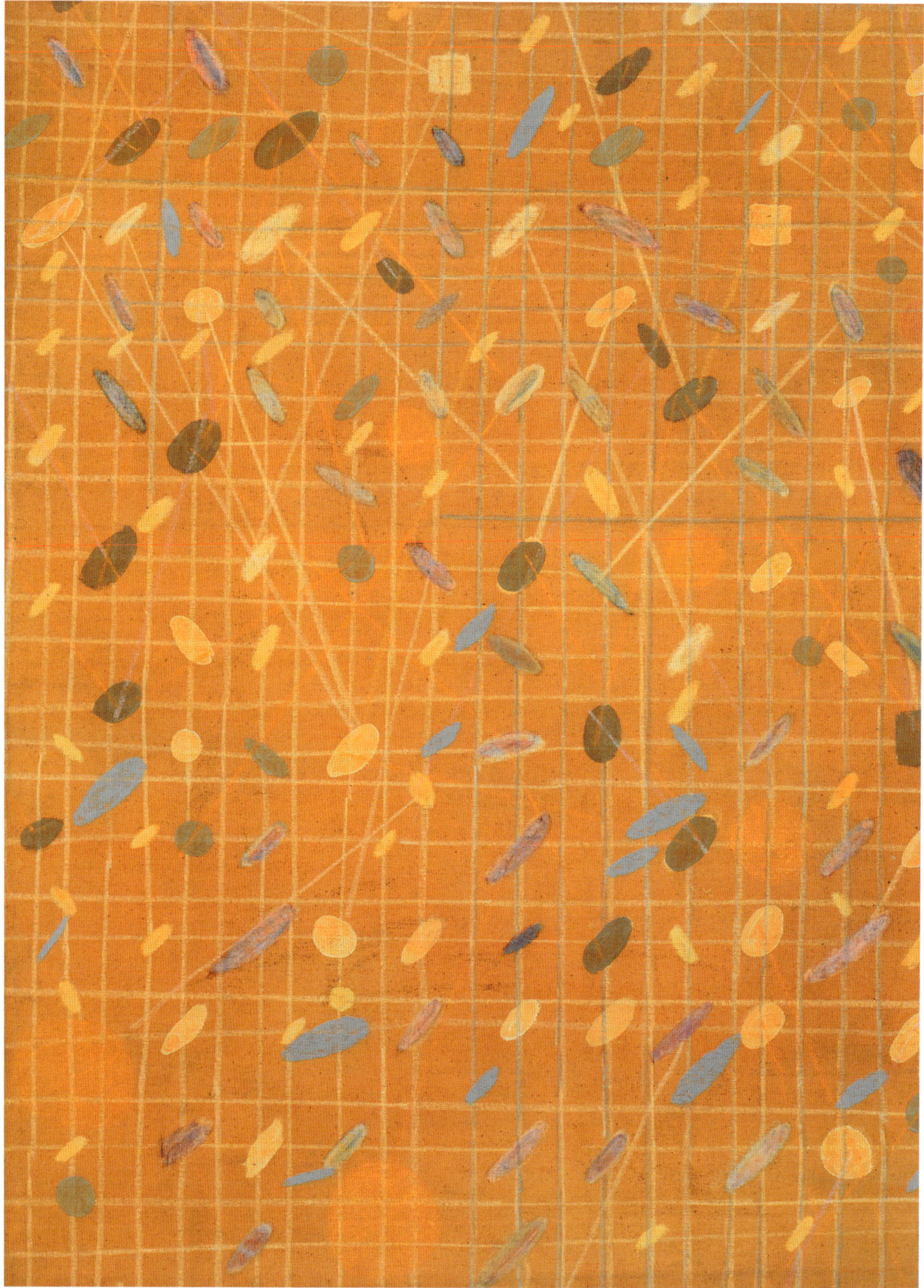

Larry Neal, who called for artistic efforts to support Black nationalist political projects in explicit, legible ways. The impetus fell on Black artists to articulate the redeeming social and political functions of their abstract works beyond merely being beautiful. This same dynamic appeared in other social liberation movements. In an era marked by civil unrest and the moral crisis of U.S. involvement in the Vietnam War, many cultural critics viewed the unfulfilled cultural project of modernism as irresponsibly disconnected from political urgencies, and therefore no longer viable.[3] Yet if Pindell refused the political imperatives placed on Black American artists to represent themselves in their art in a literal way, she also faced discrimination and exclusion from the "downtown" spaces that celebrated abstraction. Indeed, in New York in the 1960s and 1970s, modernist institutions remained largely inhospitable to artists of color, women artists, and openly queer artists as these groups agitated for greater representation.

This chapter focuses on Pindell's early abstract works—a body of several dozen paintings and drawings created between 1968 and 1973—to show how they contested the ways that dominant Black cultural and modernist discourses posited the relationship between artistic form and the artist's subjectivity. I argue that Pindell's practice defiantly refused formulations that prescriptively linked urban geography (downtown, uptown) with social position (white, Black) and location in the terrain of artistic practice (abstract, figurative). Instead, she consistently asserted her claim to New York modernisms as a Black woman by emphasizing movement through spatial investigations. In these artworks, Pindell deployed the circle as an individually meaningful symbol of motion that also situated her practice in relation to multiple cultural nodes. She utilized color to generate spatially ambiguous aesthetic fields that encourage the viewer's physical movement, activating a relational and embodied dynamic between the artwork and its audience. Lastly, Pindell appropriated the tools of cartography, such as the grid, as she wrestled with external efforts to place her in a literal art world geography and a discursive environment. In the face of attempts to fix her location, the artist generated artworks that thematize movement across a range of spatial scales. In the process, she both earnestly partook in modernist practice and rerouted its boundaries.

Despite knowing that the odds were against her in the predominantly white galleries and museums that showed abstract art "downtown," Pindell crossed geographic and conceptual borders to consciously situate her work in a lineage of modernist painting. In her recent book about the work of Black artists in Los

Angeles in the 1960s and 1970s, art historian Kellie Jones has contended that
"applying spatial theory to the art objects helps us consider . . . the importance
of place for those who don't have one or are always looking for one." While Jones
has focused her study on artists who migrated to Los Angeles from the Midwest
and South as part of the Great Migration, Pindell's reflections on her attempts to
navigate the art worlds of New York in the same period convey a similar sense
of dislocation and the need to "look for a place." Pindell and artists such as Al
Loving encountered what geographer Katherine McKittrick has called "cartographic rules," which naturalize inequitable geographies by fixing subjects in
conceptual and geographic locations.[4] These artists ardently, if critically, engaged
with modernisms in the racial-aesthetic border between uptown and downtown.
By incorporating movement into her modernist rubric, Pindell began exploring a
haptic relational aesthetic model through which she could defy those boundaries
and others that would limit her artistic ambitions.

Modernisms have been a set of ideas emergent in discourse—never fixed, singular, or free from contradiction. Pindell's initial engagements with modernisms
demonstrate a desire to be taken seriously as an artist and a belief that art had
value as a site marked by possibility rather than necessity. Her early abstract
work indicates that she saw tremendous opportunity in strains of modernism
espoused by major art institutions, despite the ubiquitous expectation that
a Black woman artist could not meaningfully engage with them. Throughout
this chapter, I use the term "institutional modernisms" to refer to rarefied U.S.
aesthetic regimes that prominent critics traced from abstract expressionism.
Institutional modernisms operated both as a set of formal tendencies deployed
by artists and a discursive constellation that upheld systems of privilege and
exclusion through recourse to increasingly outmoded ideas about art's universality and autonomy. As conceptual artist Charles Gaines has reflected, "Part
of the black experience of modernism was that historically it was an ideology
that helped discriminate against minority inclusion in the art world of the 1960s
and 1970s."[5] In these years, artist-activists such as Benny Andrews and Faith
Ringgold labored to unveil the foundational fiction of a hegemonic form of modernism: rather than a shared global aesthetic engagement, "modernism" was a
cultural gatekeeping project on a massive scale.

Pindell's engagements with institutional modernism defied its exclusionary
status quo. In particular, she challenged the institutional modernist expectation
that an artist ought to aspire to what art historian Darby English has called
an art "refracted by subjectivity itself"—that is, a subjectivity somehow beyond
its social construction.[6] By contrast, Pindell understood her inward world as
indelibly shaped by her experiences within racial, gender, and class positions.
She engaged with modernist painting as a site of interiority *and* understood

interior life as being formed and marked by social conditions. This is not to say that Pindell viewed her social positions as a Black woman as determinant of her artistic practice—indeed her choice to work abstractly in the context of the late 1960s suggests otherwise. Rather, she cannily deployed forms such as circles and grids. As I will show, these forms both held autobiographic significance and potential legibility as modernist gestures; through them, Pindell insisted that modernisms were relevant to her as a Black woman. This has been one of her most enduring contributions to modernist art.

Pindell held a unique position in the politicized landscape of the New York art worlds of the 1960s and 1970s. Within a few months of her arrival in New York, she gained employment as an administrative staff member of the Museum of Modern Art (MoMA). She would work at the institution for twelve years, becoming a curator of prints and illustrated books. In the early years of her career, MoMA provided access to a much wider range of artistic expression than she had encountered previously. In developing her own abstract practice, she drew inspiration from the many modernisms available to her in New York, making use of idioms from several of its seemingly conflicting versions, including abstract expressionism and conceptual art. These same years, artist-activist groups such as the Black Emergency Cultural Coalition (BECC), the Ad Hoc Women's Committee of the Art Workers' Coalition (AWC), and Where We At: Black Women Artists protested the rampant racial and gender discrimination of New York's art institutions.[7] Pindell's status as an "insider" (albeit one with qualified access to institutions entrenched in the era's racism and sexism) rendered her, in the eyes of many of her activist peers, an outsider to their radical movements. Nonetheless, ideas emanating from the Black Arts movement and feminist art movement profoundly shaped how Pindell and peers such as Sam Gilliam, Betye Saar, and Joan Snyder conceived of their modernist practices. These artists labored to bridge modernism and activism, viewing the boundaries between "Black art," "feminist art," and "modernism" as more relevant to critical debates than to their artistic practices.

This chapter offers the first extended scholarly account of Pindell's work as a modernist, focusing on the period most often overlooked in the growing literature on her oeuvre. Art history's reticence to address Pindell and her work as modernist is especially striking in light of her training and institutional affiliations. Yale was well-known as a training ground for late modernist painters when Pindell attended. Her education was steeped in modernist principles of medium specificity—she graduated with a degree in painting, and her courses focused on signal modernist pictorial elements such as color and composition.[8] When Pindell began working at MoMA, it was widely regarded as the favored home of U.S. and European modernisms in the United States.

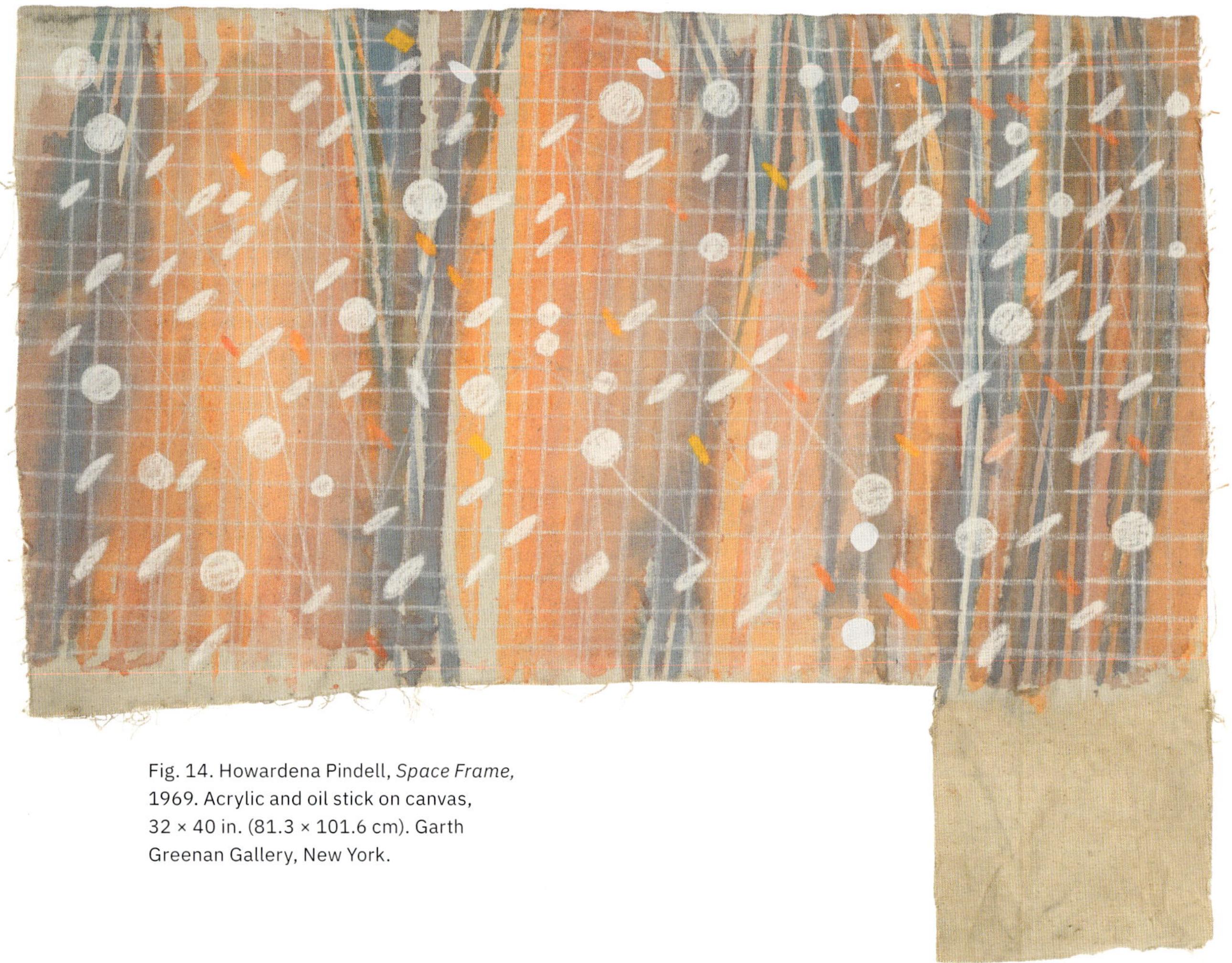

Fig. 14. Howardena Pindell, *Space Frame,*
1969. Acrylic and oil stick on canvas,
32 × 40 in. (81.3 × 101.6 cm). Garth
Greenan Gallery, New York.

This chapter's primary aim is to privilege the choices Pindell made with
respect to modernism. Rather than locating her early abstraction in a single
modernist narrative, though, it draws attention to how her work *moved* modernisms and moved within them, drawing on forms and techniques from a resplen-
dently animated New York cultural milieu in which experimental approaches
to art-making were common. Particular attention is given to Pindell's under-
studied engagements with formal concerns inherited from a U.S. tradition of
"post-painterly abstraction," or late modernist painting. The immense measure
of fortitude and conviction required to pursue one's art under these antagonistic
conditions motivates this attention to the formal vocabulary of the paintings.
Arguably never a comfortable home for her, modernism served Pindell as a set of
strategies and as an uninsured ticket to artistic recognition. With it, she insisted
that artists make choices that matter.

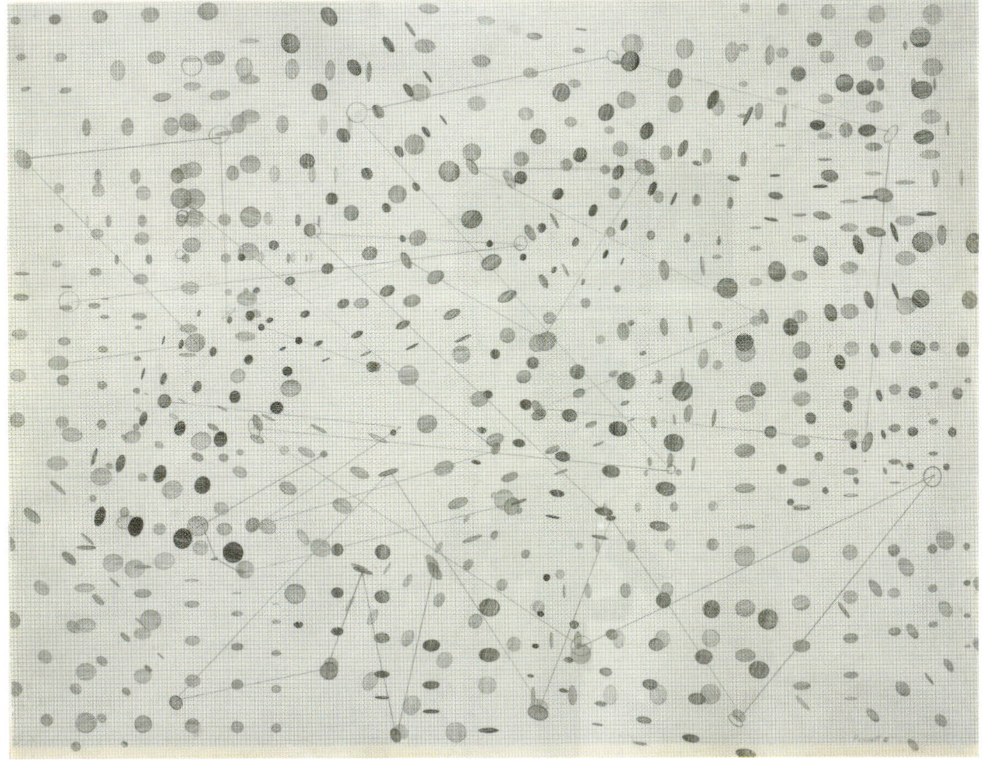

Fig. 15. Howardena Pindell, *Space Frame,* 1968. Graphite on graph paper, 17½ × 22 in. (44.5 × 55.9 cm). Museum of Art, Rhode Island School of Design, Providence, Georgianna Sayles Aldrich Fund, 2004.56.

CIRCLE

In 1972, shortly after launching her abstract practice, Pindell reflected that her development of a nonfigurative visual vocabulary emerged from turning inward, from a decision to paint "from within." She meant this literally. After moving to New York and starting her day job at MoMA, she had to paint at night, without the benefit of natural light. In the absence of adequate illumination, she "became tired of depending on things outside." She stopped arranging still-life objects to render them in paint. (During her years at Yale, she most frequently used a human skeleton for these purposes.)[9] Instead, she conjured forms from within her own imagination.

Two formal elements consistently appear in Pindell's abstract works from her earliest experimentations in 1968 through the 1970s: the circle and the grid. The salient associations of these simple forms shifted throughout this decade. Pindell's stated reasons for anchoring her practice in them changed over the years as well. What remained consistent, I argue, is that Pindell understood the forms she used as both originating in individual experience and participating in broader cultural discourses. Her case is paradigmatic of a generation of abstract

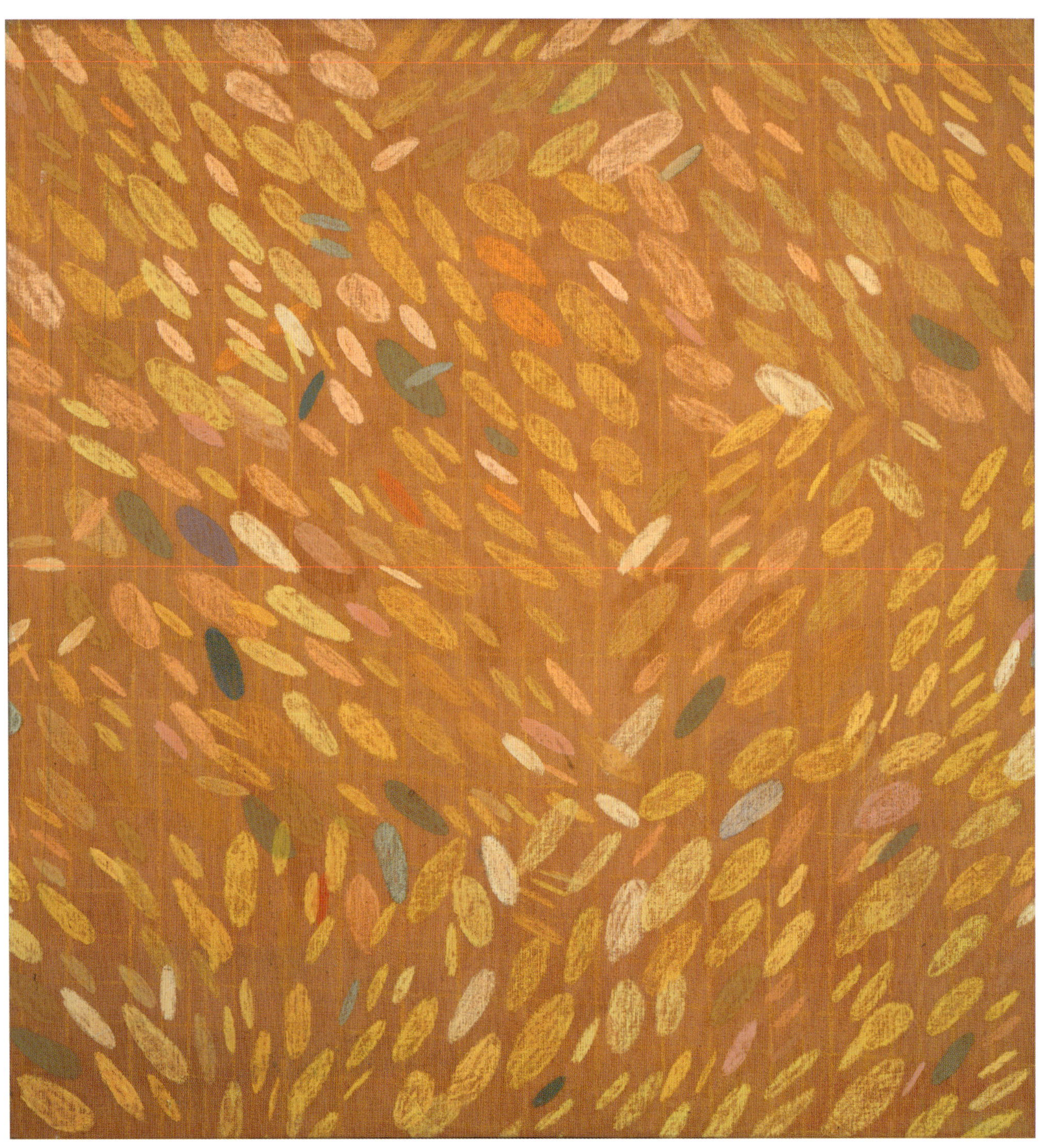

painters working in the 1960s and 1970s who insisted on the unique capacities of form, which they viewed as necessarily socially imbricated, to open possibilities foreclosed in the social world.

Some of the first abstract works that Pindell produced juxtapose a grid with a field of circles and ellipses to create a shallow sense of depth. She worked in this mode in both paintings and drawings in 1968 and 1969, alternatingly experimenting with loose marks in works such as the irregularly shaped unstretched canvas of *Space Frame* (1969) and more rigid forms in the identically named graphite on paper *Space Frame* (1968), now in the collection of the Rhode Island School of Design (figs. 14, 15). With these complementary approaches to geometric abstraction, Pindell drew on an emergent field of postminimalism and contemporary practices around conceptual art. She also conceived of her early abstractions in terms of an individual history shaped by the social realities of racial discrimination.

In the first years of her career, Pindell used autobiographically charged abstract forms to authorize her contributions to modernist abstraction. While "authority" often refers to a position of power over others, I use a different valence of the word in this chapter. I deploy the term "authority" to refer to Pindell's practice of making art with "confidence resulting from personal expertise," as in, she painted "with authority."[10] This authority or self-authorization is evinced by the artist's insistence on the significance of her artistic expressions despite a lack of critical support. It is inextricable from her status as an author. The notion of "self-authorization" may appear oxymoronic at first blush—authority generally implies external validation. However, the friction of this term expresses the contradictions of Pindell's unique position as a Black woman abstractionist with unparalleled access to institutional modernisms. Authority, however, does not cinch public recognition of one's authorship, or "authority" in its more common usage. So, while Pindell authorized her modernisms through appeals to her autobiography, art-historical discourse has largely denied her contributions to modernist art.

The circle—the single most enduring feature of Pindell's practice—provides a fitting starting point for an exploration of her modernist authority. Her accounts of her artistic interest in the circle vary, ranging from an argument for primary, even universal, form to an anecdote about racial segregation. Pindell introduced the round to her compositions in the early years of the women's liberation movement. In an interview conducted in the late 1970s, artist Sally Swenson asked

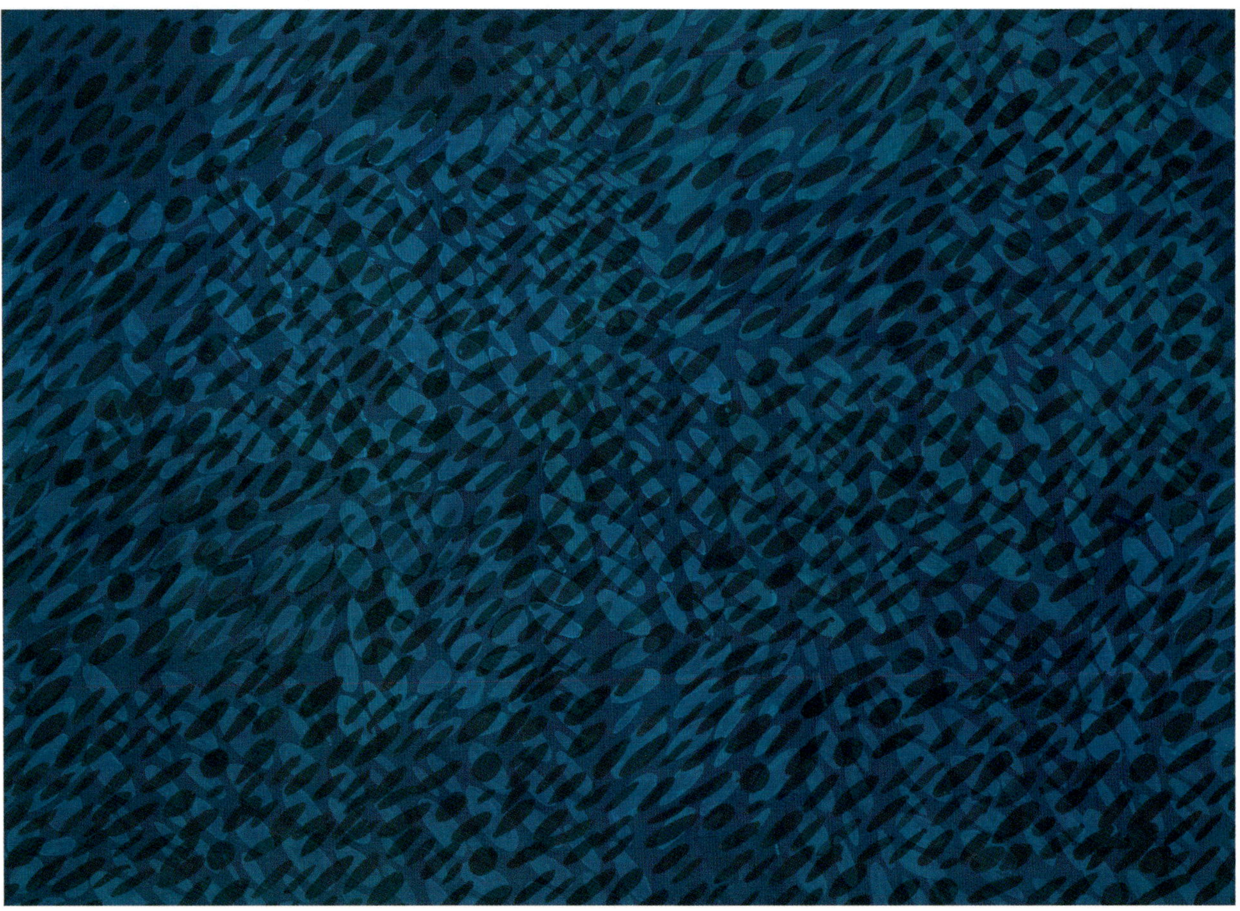

Fig. 17. Howardena Pindell, *Untitled,* 1969. Oil on canvas, 52 × 70 in. (132.1 × 177.8 cm). Private collection, Bellevue, WA.

Pindell if her use of the circle might be meaningful vis-à-vis feminist art critic Lucy Lippard's theory of the form as a "reminder of women's center in their art."[11] Pindell was familiar with this theory of "women's center," a term that implied the womb. She was at this point good friends with Lippard, who was well known in feminist artist circles, such as the all-women collective gallery A.I.R. that Pindell had cofounded.

Nonetheless, Pindell responded by telling Swenson that she "tr[ied] not to read too much," indicating her reluctance to merge her aesthetic language with a critic's sense of gendered form. Pindell continued, saying that her "attachment" to the shape came from her particular way of seeing "nature": "I thought of the circle in other terms. To me it's the simplest form. Our eyes are round; we don't have square eyes. Somehow it's primary for me. . . . The earth is round. . . . When gravity works, you get a mass that's circular . . . the sun is round and the stars are seen as points

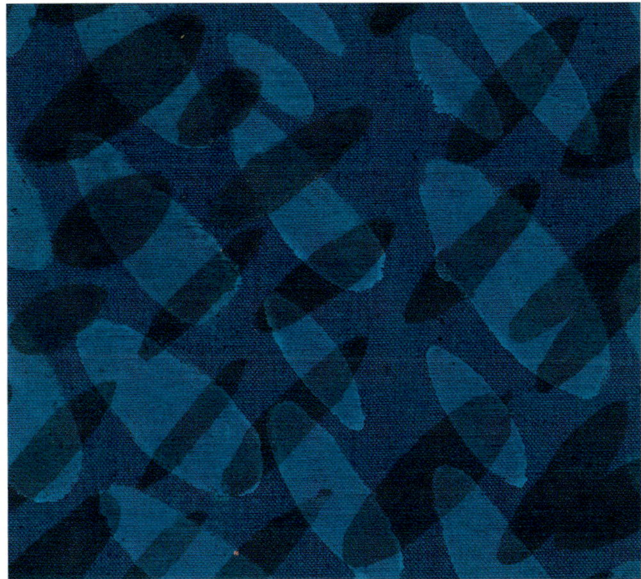

of light. I see everything as energy represented by little circles that move at a certain velocity."[12] For Pindell, the circle is primary—the basis of seeing (through round eyes), the shape that supports our bodies and lived environment (Earth), and the source of earthly light and energy (the sun).

Pindell suggested throughout the interview that she learned how to see in this way from looking at "nature." Here, she used the term "nature" in an expansive way, to refer to natural phenomena such as celestial bodies, birds, plants, and microbes, but eventually this concept spiraled out to "everything" that she could see. Rather than stemming from scholarly knowledge about the field of physics, Pindell was quick to point out, her theory of energetic perception arose from childhood encounters, experiences through which she began to learn how the world was organized. Her father took her on nature walks. She had a microscope through which she could examine microcosms, "like drinking water under high magnification."[13] Circles do not appear in Pindell's work because she is a woman, as Swenson's question suggests. Rather, she deploys the form because in the context of her art, the circle could formally convey her idiosyncratic way of internally visualizing the energetic forces and masses that comprise the universe. Her use of the shape emerged from an embodied epistemology.

Ellipses, or ovals, also appear frequently in the abstract paintings of the late 1960s, as Pindell experimented with a range of rounded shapes. In most instances, they accompany circles. The relationship between the two shapes suggests alternating states of stasis and movement, as if the ellipses depict circles on the move, distended by their propulsion. A pair of Pindell's early abstract works, *Untitled* (c. 1968) and *Untitled* (1969), contain no circles at all, but a dense field of ovals (figs. 16, 17). Pindell used *Untitled* for most of the abstract works she made in the first decades of her career, sometimes numbering her paintings and works on paper as well. This was one way she signaled her desire to be viewed as a modernist.

In each of these paintings, the ellipses are arranged in groups that share an orientation, lending the composition a sense of directional movement or energy.

Fig. 19. Howardena Pindell, *Untitled,* 1971. Acrylic on canvas, 71 × 95 in. (180.3 × 241.3 cm). Private collection, Bellevue, WA.

The 1969 example has a rich aquamarine ground overlain by two sets of transparent ovals, one in a dark wash, the other light (fig. 18). These shapes overlap, forming a web of subtle contrast that evokes the play of light through bodies of water. The painting's oceanic undulations stand out amid Pindell's highly saturated, gridded work of the late 1960s. It portends the deeper tones, the use of "veils" of color, and the recession of the grid in Pindell's spray-painted works of the following four years (fig. 19). Despite her compelling early use of the ellipse as a repeatable formal element, she carried the circle alone through her oeuvre of the 1970s.

When asked about her prolonged attachment to the round, Pindell has frequently spoken about an encounter during which she was "scared to death by one." Driving through northern Kentucky on their way to visit family in the early 1950s, when Pindell was around ten years old, she and her father stopped at a drive-through for root beer floats. When she finished her road trip treat, the young Pindell discovered a red circle on the bottom of her mug. Her father explained that the mark indicated that the mug was for use by "colored" customers, and that it reflected a broader culture of segregation that affected how Black Americans could travel, and where they could sleep or eat on the road.[14]

The experience of being literally, though surreptitiously, marked in this way—as an "other" whose bodily contact needed to be contained—was not new to Pindell. She grew up in Philadelphia, a then-segregated city where for Black residents, Pindell recalled, "you knew when you stayed in your neighborhood you were safe but . . . when you crossed that boundary you weren't safe. No one was there to protect you. Safety was in the community." By the early 1960s, the high school Pindell attended had begun to integrate, but vestiges of segregation remained in the city. In 1960, she joined students involved in the Philadelphia Youth Committee against Segregation to picket Woolworth's counters in predominantly Black neighborhoods. Inspired by the Greensboro sit-ins, the group protested Woolworth's racially discriminatory policies.[15]

Despite her lived familiarity with segregation, the road trip incident in particular stayed with Pindell for many years. Perhaps this accounts for why she has more often explained her use of the circle as originating with this experience, rather than one of the pedagogical vignettes of her childhood (such as looking through a microscope). The experience of being in a new place whose racial codes were not initially legible instilled her with an acute and traumatic sense of danger. As an adult, she purchased a mug of her own and painted a red circle on it, feeling that re-creating the traumatizing object might help "take the sting out" of the experience. Eventually, she would come to see the roadside encounter with racial segregation as a primary motive of what she has called her "obsession" with the circle.[16]

In both of these examples—circle as internal vision and as racialized stamp—the shape oriented Pindell spatially. As the fundamental unit of her self-generated cosmology, the round represented energy and the resonant repetition of familiar form across vast scales, from the microscopic to the cosmic. Pindell associated this circle with the animating physical and biological force of movement. By contrast, in its implementation as a biting instrument of white supremacy, the circle represented an external effort to contain Pindell, as a Black American, in a demeaning racial code. It signaled her passage into the Jim Crow South and tracked her intimate interaction with the physical world. The round can connect; it can also enclose.

Alongside her engagement with deeply meaningful individual associations, Pindell also deployed the circle to position herself in artistic and cultural conversations. The round has been ubiquitous in modernist painting. For instance, artist Betty Blayton, one of the few Black women Pindell met at MoMA, made

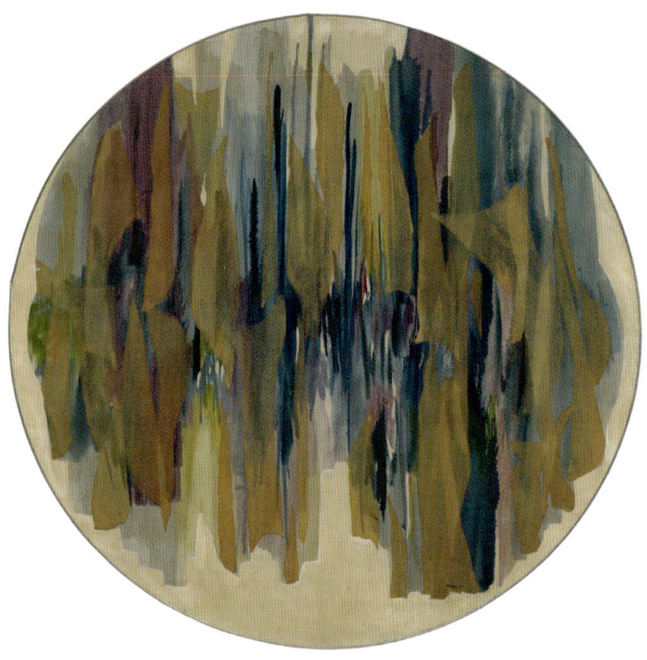

Fig. 20. Betty Blayton, *Consume #2,* 1969. Oil on canvas, diameter: 59 in. (149.9 cm). Virginia Museum of Fine Arts, Richmond. Arthur and Margaret Glasgow Endowment, 2018.352.

circular-shaped canvases stained in jewel tones in the 1960s and 1970s (fig. 20).[17] Jasper Johns and Kenneth Noland, each of whom Pindell has cited as an influence, made extensive use of the circle, specifically the bull's-eye, as a pop-inflected compositional device.

In the late 1960s and early 1970s, the circle also was redolent of the worldview espoused by proponents of the U.S. ecology movement, who emphasized the interconnectedness of natural and human-made phenomena. The circle became an important symbol of this "whole systems thinking," frequently expressed by images of planet Earth. Demands for photographs of the "whole Earth" emerged amid the space explorations of the 1960s. These calls reflected the belief that a photographic document of Earth from space would offer compelling visual evidence of humans' shared destiny, spurring its citizens to take sociopolitical action in the face of environmental degradation.[18] The politics of the ecology movement may not have been at the front of Pindell's mind when she introduced the circle to her abstract paintings. However, the title of two of her early abstract works, *Space Frame,* overtly references the 1960s Space Race that helped to spur "whole systems thinking," suggesting that these cultural conversations informed her notion of the circle as universal structure.[19] Her ability to find small circles of energy in everything from microscopic organisms to planetary masses resonates with ecologists' conceptualizations of Earth as a series of interdependent and structurally analogous systems.

The round held diverse meanings in the years Pindell began working with it—an emblem of the feminist movement, modernist painting, and the ecology movement. This range of valences contributed to the significance the shape held in the artist's biography. Her embrace of this symbolically potent form indicates that Pindell viewed the meanings adhering to individual experiences, social codes, and even cosmic structures as inextricable. She approached the circle as a tool for orienting herself, a compass for understanding her shifting locations in physical, social, and cultural universes.

In spring 1965, Pindell newly encountered what she called "an entire radical way of seeing." This experience alerted her to the existence of a fundamentally different use and definition of painting, which planted the seeds for her early abstract practice. The transformative meeting occurred at an exhibition entitled *Three American Painters: Kenneth Noland, Jules Olitski, Frank Stella* at the Fogg Art Museum at Harvard University. Michael Fried, then a junior fellow in the Department of History of Art and Architecture at Harvard, had organized the show as "a comprehensive statement of abstract art of the mid-sixties." The nineteen paintings on view at the Fogg were brightly colored, entirely nonrepresentational, large, and unlike any painting Pindell had seen.[20] This eye-opening encounter catalyzed her interest in modernist abstraction, encouraging her experimentations with spatial effects and color. When she began working abstractly several years later, she took up some of the signal concerns of the white, male late modernist painters whose work she viewed at the Fogg.

Pindell's deliberate and skillful use of color constituted one of her primary artistic investigations as an emerging modernist. Her approach to color, particularly in her stained, spray-painted canvases, exemplified a modernist concern for spatial ambiguity. Color field painting describes an informal movement that emerged in the United States in the 1950s and 1960s, inspired by European modernisms. Artists investigated color as a subject of painting, rather than the gestures and brushstrokes favored by abstract expressionists. Staining—the direct application of paint to an untreated canvas—was a common technique.[21]

Although Pindell was largely isolated from other Black artists in the first years of her career, in retrospect, she participated in a multiracial manifestation of the color field movement in the 1960s and 1970s. Black artists including Blayton, Gilliam, Peter Bradley, and Joe Overstreet extensively explored staining in their painting practices, often experimenting with unconventional formats such as round, unstretched, or draped canvases.[22] In fact, Pindell's spray-painted works bear a striking resemblance to the suspended canvases that Overstreet sprayed in deep hues, such as *Purple Flight* (1971). Overstreet's folded method of construction endows his sculptural paintings with a sense of fluttering motion that amplifies the dimensional oscillations of their pointillistic surfaces. The spatial tension paradigmatic of color field painting resonated with Black artists' social dislocation, or illegibility, as modernists who were rarely welcomed in institutions either "uptown" or "downtown," in contrast to the experience of the white, male artists whose work Pindell encountered at the Fogg. Pindell, I contend, exploited this disorienting capacity of color field to push against art world conversations—whether emerging from modernist quarters or the Black Arts movement—that would "locate" her. However, this discursive maneuver was not the primary function Pindell intended for her paintings; she made them first and foremost as objects of embodied aesthetic contemplation.

Three American Painters was Pindell's memorable point of entry to color field painting. On view in the exhibition were jewel-toned color washes by Olitski, striped shaped canvases by Stella, and Noland's pop-colored chevrons, such as the striped *Mach II* (1964; fig. 21). Each artist's contribution offered a dramatic departure from the version of painting Pindell was then studying in the fine arts program at Boston University, where she was pursuing an under-graduate degree. At Boston, which she later derided for its bland traditionalism, only the tasks of articulating muscles and rendering objects' volume mattered. According to Pindell, "Composition was a dirty word." She also observed, "The total painting was not important at all," and neither was color. *Three American Painters* presented precisely these aspects of painting—composition, concern for the full physical surface, and hue—as the privileged sites of interrogation of the most advanced art in the country. It asked its viewers to contend with pared-down geometric shapes, tonal juxtapositions, and the painting's ground in works absent any apparent markers of the artist's brush. While Pindell would continue to work figuratively for several years, the exhibition inspired her to apply to the MFA program in painting at Yale, where she knew she would get a different kind of education, one more in line with the artistic visions displayed at the Fogg.[23]

Fried, the show's curator, anticipated his exhibition would generate a new kind of viewing experience for the majority of its audience. The pedagogical focus of his catalogue essay helped readers through the difficult task of begin-ning to develop the "visual skills" necessary to understand the new painting. This tone is echoed in reviews of the exhibition. One reviewer cautioned visitors that they would need to "accustom" themselves to the new images, and advised them foremost to spend a substantial amount of time before the canvases.[24]

As art historian Courtney J. Martin has noted, *Three American Painters* was the final major exhibition of the 1960s to present a second generation of U.S. abstract painters as a "newly minted attraction." Dubbed "post-painterly abstraction" by art critic Clement Greenberg, the new modernist painting was characterized by an "investigative" approach to color, a consistently large scale, an absence of gestural brush marks, and the assertion of the painterly ground through shaped canvases or other means. These artists broke from certain

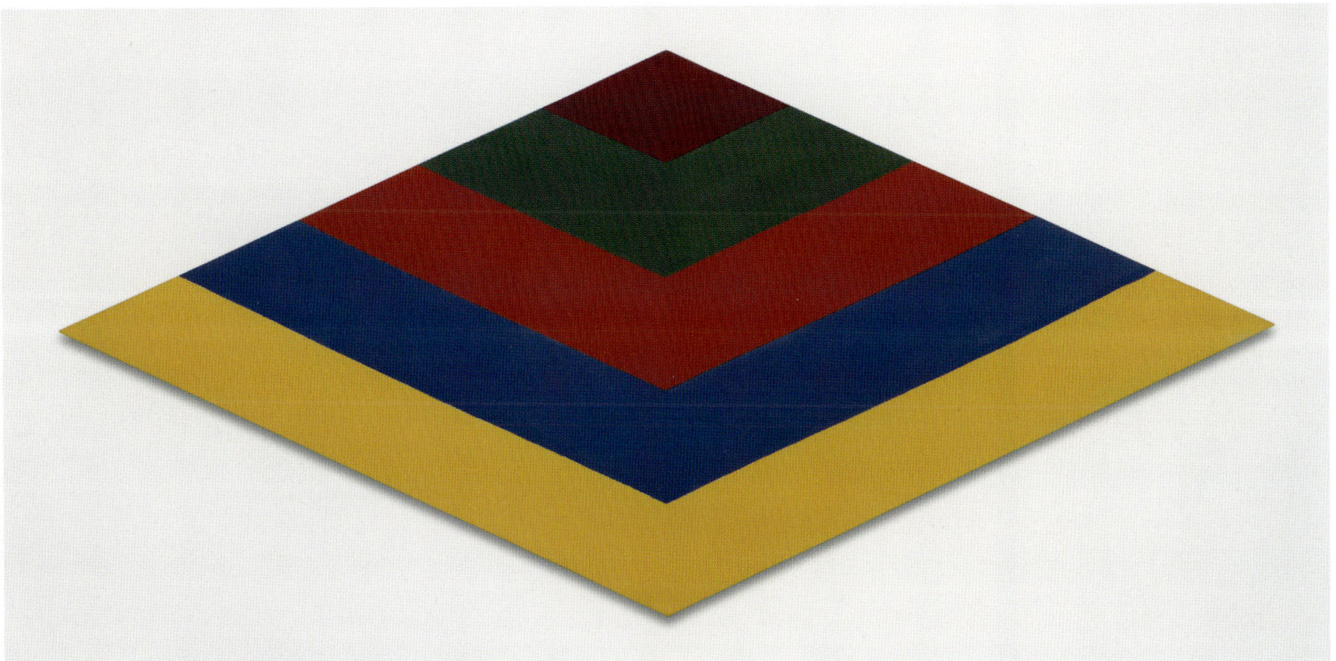

protocols of abstract expressionism, but the critical discourse around their work relied on the earlier movement's commitments to the uniqueness of inspired authorial vision and the primacy of painting as the site of advanced art.[25]

By the time *Three American Painters* debuted in 1965, modernist painting no longer could claim to be the singularly advanced artistic formation of the United States. Many of its artistic concerns had been adapted by simultaneously developing movements. Most notably, minimalism removed the artist's hand and asserted the material facts of the art object. Pindell would develop her abstract vocabulary from the entangled sources, including postminimalist, feminist, and conceptual forms, that characterized much of advanced art in New York in the late 1960s. However, from 1968 until 1973, the first years of her career as an abstractionist, her most salient references were the geometric and atmospheric compositions of late modernist painting.

Pindell first showed a group of her abstract works in November 1971, at the age of twenty-eight, four years into her curatorial career at MoMA. She presented four drawings and five spray-painted stretched canvases in a two-person show at Spelman College in Atlanta. The Black women's college was the first significant site of exhibition for Pindell's art, helping to launch her career. Displayed in the John D. Rockefeller, Jr., Fine Arts Building, the exhibition attracted little critical attention, although it allowed the artist to show a much larger number of her works than in the competitive gallery scene of New York.[26]

Curated by Hans Bhalla, acting chairman of Spelman's Art Department, the exhibition formed part of the Atlanta University Center (AUC) Coordinated Art Program, which brought the work of renowned Black artists to campus between 1967 and 1979. In the early 1970s, the program hosted exhibitions of work by

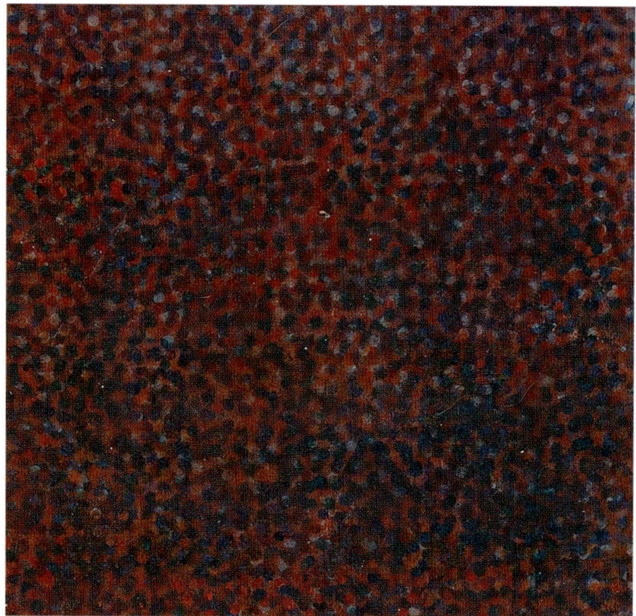

Fig. 22. Howardena Pindell, *Untitled,* 1971 (detail; see fig. 19).

Harlem Renaissance painter Charles Alston, Brooklyn-based sculptor John W. Rhoden, Jamaican painter Barrington Watson, and rising Black Arts star and BECC cofounder Benny Andrews. The program, spearheaded by Bhalla, also offered opportunities for emerging artists to exhibit their work.[27] Pindell, then little known outside of a small circle of colleagues, showed alongside New York artist Vincent Smith, who likewise was in the early stages of his career.

Through this robust roster, Bhalla made Spelman into an important site of inquiry into the possibilities for African diasporic aesthetics. Over the course of the program's lifespan, it hosted artists-in-residence Gilliam, Herman "Kofi" Bailey, and Floyd Coleman, enabling Spelman to acquire works by these artists for its art museum's collection. The program also sponsored lectures. In 1971, Regenia Perry, who was the first Black American woman to hold a PhD in art history (University of Pennsylvania, 1965), gave a talk entitled "Africa vs. Afro-American Art" as part of the AUC arts programming.[28] The array of ideas, mediums, and aesthetics presented at Spelman in these years—sculpture, painting, and drawing, social realism, abstraction, and folk-inspired art—suggests that Bhalla saw the program as an opportunity to expose the AUC's students, faculty, and staff to Black artists' wide-ranging approaches to their work amid a period of cultural contestation.

Given this expansive approach to art of the African diaspora, Spelman ostensibly offered Pindell an amenable site for the debut of her early abstractions. She presented allover compositions, both paintings and works on paper, comprised of layers of innumerable small circles. The sole review in a local newspaper favorably compared the pieces to the "very sophisticated work" of white abstract expressionist painter Mark Tobey.[29]

The large, stretched canvas of an untitled painting from 1971, one of Pindell's spray-painted works shown at Spelman, asks to be viewed from multiple distances (see fig. 19). On first approach, vermillion dots seem to float above a mass of deeper hues, including blue, burgundy, and violet (fig. 22). Small areas of steel

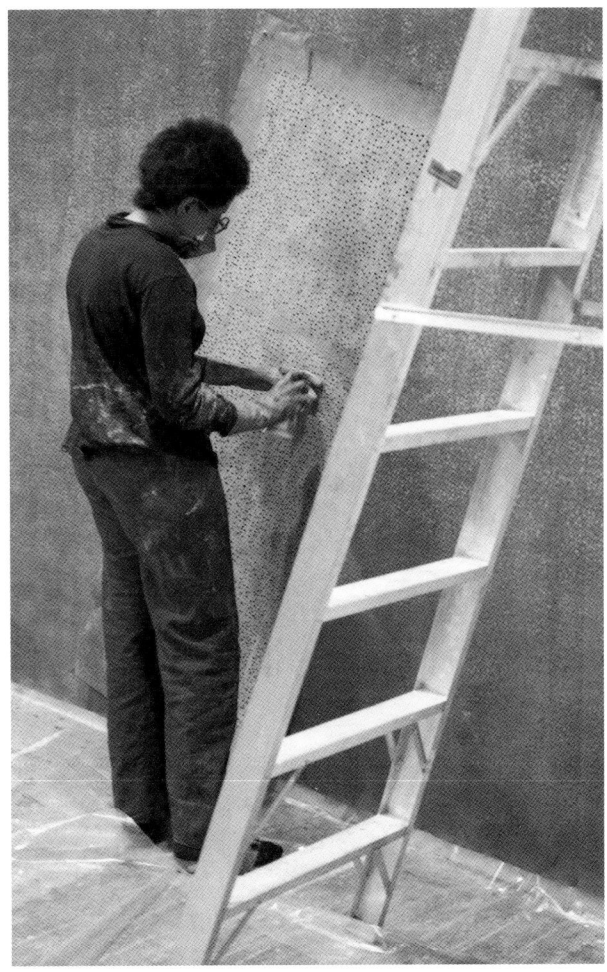

blue stand out as well, particularly on the right-hand side and in the center of the canvas. From afar the painting is atmospheric, its particles dissolved into an indivisible and allover tonal mass. Within a few feet of the work, the surface variation becomes more apparent and spots emerge from the field. Still, the cohesiveness of the composition holds, the enmeshed dots forming a visual cloth or web. Closer still to the painting, layers of colored dots appear. Blurred edges indicate that the circles were stained onto an unprimed canvas. Occasional glimpses of light tones might be views of the cloth but never resolve as such. The effect of the painting at this nearness is somewhat jarring. Where one might expect the rounds and their pictorial background to come into focus as distinct elements, there is instead an incessant repetition of indefinite shapes. The circles' leaky borders and semitransparency give the entire composition an air of diffusion, so that the individual forms cannot be firmly located.

Pindell made this work, like the others on view at Spelman, with a spray-paint gun. In a 1970 photograph taken at her studio in Westbeth Artists Housing in Manhattan, where she began living in the housing project's inaugural year, she works a spray-painted canvas (fig. 23). Pindell loaded acrylic paint into a canister and applied a misted stream of color to canvases and paper hanging in her studio. A hole-punched stencil mediated this process—she attached large, punctured cardstock sheets onto her wall, flat against the surface of her artworks. Pindell repeated this process dozens of times, shifting the stencil's position and changing paint hues until she had generated an atmospheric field of colors.[30] The spray gun became a popular implement for painting in New York in the late 1960s and early 1970s. Artists including Bradley, Olitski, Overstreet, Dan Christensen, Jane

Kaufman, and Lawrence Stafford used it to control their application of paint while also limiting their direct physical engagement with the surface of their works.

In the photograph, the protective respirator around Pindell's face, the spray gun she holds with gloved hands, and the stencil mediate her bodily contact with the painting. Nonetheless, she works very close to her canvas, applying pressure to the stencil with her left hand so that it lies completely flush against the painting's ground. Pindell also undertook a physically intensive process in the production of her stencils, as she incised them using a handheld single-hole punch. In her works, different from that of some of her peers, the apparent remove of markers of the handmade from the surface of the finished works belies the physical involvement the artist had in the production of the paintings.

Seen from afar, one might take areas of relative dark and light in Pindell's spray-painted canvases to indicate a painterly gesture; the artist must have applied the corresponding tones to those sections with deliberation. At close range, however, this sense of cause and effect dissipates. There are no signs of the artist's hand or of compositional order, only the repetitive proliferation of a simple shape in contrasting hues. The canvas leaves the viewer adrift in color. In the exhibition that arguably marked her debut as a working artist, Pindell foregrounded a color-driven aesthetic centered on spatial ambiguity. This contribution to Spelman's programming publicly signaled her development of a critical engagement with modernist form.

A CHOREOGRAPHY OF VIEWING

Three American Painters introduced Pindell to the way staining draws attention to the flat surface of painting. The slightly irregular edges and saturation of Noland's stained chevrons breathe subtle variation into his striking forms, while Olitski used staining to create immersive color fields pocked by occasional dabs or stripes. Pindell used the technique of staining, in addition to spray-painting, to achieve the spatially ambiguous, atmospheric colors that characterize her canvases. Thinly applied layers of paint seeped directly onto the surface of her unprimed canvas.

By the time Pindell began staining her canvases, she was also familiar with Helen Frankenthaler, who visited Yale during Pindell's time as a student. Frankenthaler innovated the use of stained, matte surfaces to avoid visible buildup of paint on canvas. In her texturally seamless works, color distinguishes stain from ground. Pindell's memories of Frankenthaler, however, suggest the famed artist lacked a generous and open-minded spirit toward young artists. According to Pindell, the esteemed painter "didn't even want to look at" her work on the basis of its figuration, an apparently painful event. In an interview in 1972, a year after the Spelman show, Pindell explicitly distanced her work from

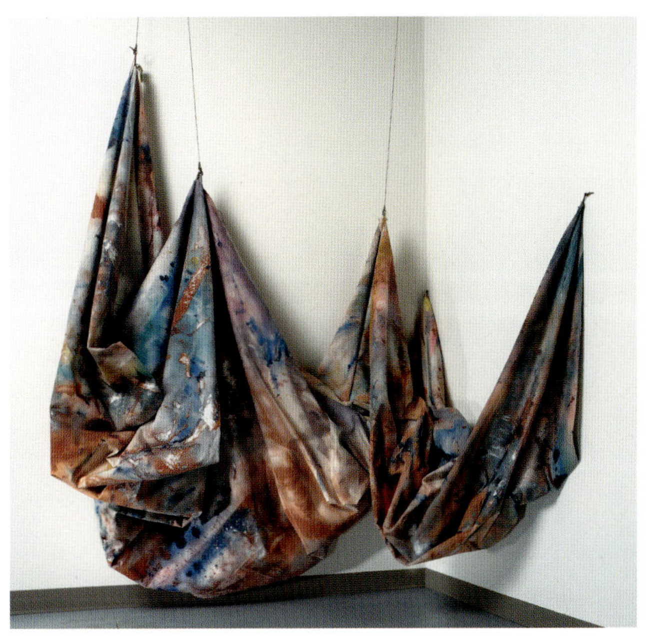

Fig. 24. Sam Gilliam, *Swing,* 1969. Acrylic and aluminum on canvas, 9 ft. 11⅝ in. × 23 ft. 6½ in. (303.8 × 720.1 cm). Smithsonian American Art Museum, Washington, DC. Gift of Mr. Edwin Janss, Jr. (1973.189).

Frankenthaler's. She reflected that some of her classmates at Yale had attempted to play a prank on the abstract expressionist by presenting work with "stains and blotches," and that Frankenthaler "loved it." Pindell irreverently asked, "How serious can you be if the jokes can be played?"[31] The encounter signals an early moment in Pindell's engagement with institutional modernisms, when she began to formulate skepticism about people in positions of power and the inherent aesthetic value of abstract form.

Fried framed the version of staining Pindell encountered at the Fogg as emblematic of how paintings could "address themselves to eyesight alone." His catalogue essay places Noland's and Olitski's staining practices in a lineage with Morris Louis's "optical" paintings. Opticality, the isolation of visual perception, was a primary concern in Fried's account of recent tendencies in advanced art of the mid-1960s, and formed the foundation of his assessment of modernism's highest achievements. Significantly, Fried posited opticality in opposition to tactility and to marks of the artist's hand. The stained edge, Fried wrote, "conveys the strong impression of not having been circumscribed by a cursive, draftsman-like gesture. It resists being read as *drawn*." Staining denies the viewer's tactile engagement, as well as the artist's, since it softens contours that would "[invite] one's touch."[32]

In some ways, Pindell's use of staining tracks with Fried's notion of modernist opticality, and the lineage of painters beginning with abstract expressionism that used the technique, as art critic Rosalind Krauss has argued, as "a way of avoiding the violence of a hardened contour."[33] The small circles of Pindell's canvases seep and bleed into one another and into the canvas ground. Paint seems to lose its material integrity, having no mass or texture of its own; it dissolves into color, leaving no obvious trace of the artist's hand. However, Fried's theory of staining overlooks the fact that, although the technique mutes the tactile properties of paint, the process generally leaves visible the texture of a painting's canvas surface, or ground. Thus, staining can operate as a method for revealing and exploring the textile basis of modernist painting.

Pindell leaves visible the textured warp and weft of her spray-painted canvases. She further emphasizes this textile logic in an untitled example of 1971 that features crease-like lines to create the illusion of folds. These creases draw attention to the canvas ground of the painting and evoke the stained, draped works that Gilliam made in the late 1960s (fig. 24). Pindell was familiar with Gilliam's work by 1971, when he had a *Projects* exhibition at MoMA; a few years later, they became friendly supporters of each other's careers.[34] In Gilliam's paintings, the sculptural folds of loosely hung canvas obscure the painted surface and activate a three-dimensional viewing space. By contrast, Pindell's creases raise questions about the painting's facture: Did the artist add these illusionistic marks with a brush or other instrument? Or did she rumple the canvas just after applying the paint? Whatever the cause may be, the effect complicates the optical thrust of the stained canvas by evoking the artist's tactile treatment of the work.

Other spray-painted canvases of the early 1970s likewise show Pindell diverging from a codified modernist model of staining with her introduction of "hardened" contours. A rectangular halo punctuates *Untitled* (1972), marking the off-center area where Pindell apparently placed a piece of paper before spraying paint around it (fig. 25). The straight lines of the shape interrupt the atmospheric field and disturb the tenuous illusion that color accumulated on the surface without intervention by the artist. By revealing the shape that the stencil blots out, the rectangle inverts the logic of the sprayed circles whose layering obscures the apparatus—the stencil—that formed them. The rectangle draws attention to the necessarily tactile process of its own creation, and thereby destabilizes what Fried called staining's purely "optical" basis. In a final example, one of the last spray-painted canvases Pindell would make, paper chads collaged flat onto the canvas give modest material mass to the spray-painted circles they repeat in size and shape. These chads portend Pindell's decades-long engagement with the material and with collage and texture.

Despite these spray-painted canvases' concerns for textile, texture, and contour, most of the paintings in this body of work register initially as meditations on color, surface, and pictorial depth. In the abstract paintings Pindell made between 1968 and 1973, she exploits hue to generate spatial tension. Under the tutelage of artist Sewell (Si) Sillman during her MFA training at Yale, she and her cohort learned the color theory developed by German émigré Josef Albers in the 1950s. (Sillman had studied under Albers at Black Mountain College as well as at Yale.) Albers's theory promoted a practice-based understanding of color. He asserted that color "is almost never seen as it really is," and that this makes

Fig. 25. Howardena Pindell, *Untitled,* 1972. Acrylic on canvas, 7 ft. 6 in. × 9 ft. 10¾ in. (228.6 × 301.6 cm). John and Susan Horseman Collection, St. Louis.

it "the most relative medium in art." By learning how to see and feel color in its relative forms, rather than acquiring knowledge about a theoretical system, students developed the skills needed, among other things, to exploit the varying "weights" of hues.[35]

In Pindell's spray-painted works, the principle of color weight, or what is typically called "value," accounts for the illusion that certain colors float above others. Regardless of the order of application of pigment, many of the lighter circles appear close to the surface of the work, on top of deeper colors that recede into pictorial space. The interaction between colors gives the impression of depth—a pictorial depth at tension with the surface emphasis of the unprimed canvas. This sense of recession relies on the contrast of colors. In an example from 1972, for instance, clouds of peach seem to float slightly in front of areas dominated by complementary blues (see fig. 7). The interlacing of blues and oranges in another example makes it more difficult for the eye to settle on a stable spatial organization (see fig. 36). These contrasting colors alternate coming to the surface, shifting as the viewer spends time in front of the canvas. In this way, Pindell expressed her interest in a signal concern of modernist abstraction as it had developed in the United States and Europe since the early twentieth century: experimentations with the tension between the flatness of the painted surface and the illusion of pictorial depth.[36]

Pindell's use of disparate hues also participated in late modernist inquiries into color, evoking Olitski's widely remarked ability to "prove that literally any colors can be combined successfully."[37] In one example of her spray-painted work, shades of taupe, black, brick red, lavender, and teal evoke an impressionist palette (see fig. 7). While the hues within an individual spray-painted composition are diffusely distributed across pastels, neutral tones, and saturated reds, the paintings' overall color impressions tend to be deep and cool, though in a few examples bright pinks or greens predominate. Three of the most widely exhibited paintings from this body of work favor maroon, a color that rarely appears elsewhere in Pindell's oeuvre and that recalls Mark Rothko's use of dense, deep reds to solemn effect.

The color experimentations of the spray-painted canvases take a variety of forms. In many cases, Pindell seems to relish the visual effects of close-value colors, which have similar levels of darkness or lightness. Regardless of hue, close-value colors often share similar color weights and appear to merge in space. The result is a variegated field of enmeshed dots. Three examples of Pindell's paintings from 1971 initially appear as nearly black monochromes, their palettes opening up to deep blues and violets with extended viewing. She has remarked that a fellow graduate student at Yale, Nancy Silvia Murata, inspired her to work with close-value color. According to Pindell, Murata "started working with Reinhardt's color thing where there's a lot of one color and then you see there is much more."[38]

Pindell referred to Ad Reinhardt's influential near-monochromatic works of the 1950s. She encountered his art as an undergraduate, when he visited Boston University's Art Department. The visit offered a unique opportunity to hear from a modernist in a program known for its conservatism. At first glance, Reinhardt's canvases appear as monolithic single-hued compositions. With time, they open, displaying subtle variations in hue, many compositionally organized along a three-by-three square grid, as in *Number 87* (1957). These paintings ask to be viewed over a span of time. Yve-Alain Bois has argued that Reinhardt's paintings of the late 1950s generate an increasingly long interval between the viewer's perceptions that "there is nothing to see, then almost nothing." The viewer

experiences this interval, Bois has contended, "as a 'narrativization' of his own
vision."[39] In other words, the hyper-close values of Reinhardt's colors generate
the conditions for a de facto male viewer to gain awareness of changes over time
in his own visual perceptions.

The values in Pindell's works are not as close or as dark as in Reinhardt's,
even in her darkest examples. But the spray-painted canvases also offer a shift
in the viewer's perception of color. From afar, a few deep shades of blue comprise
an untitled composition from 1971 (fig. 26). At close range, with individual circles
in view, this group multiplies and includes reds and greens (fig. 27). While time
is operative in this transformation, as in the one that takes place in front of a
painting by Reinhardt, the viewer's proximity to the surface of the work is also
significant.

Thus, Pindell's spray-painted compositions might be said to "spatialize" and
"embody" as well as "narrativize" vision. Although the works foreground optical
effects, they also prompt a "choreography of viewing" in the space of the gallery.
Their constituent dots draw the viewer physically inward, then the apparent
mismatch between the close-range color combinations and the overall hue of
the painting invite another look from afar. One might repeat this process, and
perhaps even identify the moment when, or the distance at which, perception
flips from individual dot to the synthesis of many dots. The paintings compose
themselves in the viewer's engagement with them, and they draw attention to
this process.

Pindell's choreography of viewing attests to her developing concern for the
phenomenology of art. Her paintings address themselves to embodied viewers,
rather than disembodied optical receptors. She shifts post-painterly abstraction
toward the multisensorial perception of lived experience and away from the
conceit of the purely visual. Pindell's introduction of full-bodied movement to
the viewing of post-painterly abstraction puts pressure on the tenets of medium
specificity by aligning painting with sculptural and performative viewing protocols. The works encourage observation from multiple points of view, and they
activate viewers' awareness of their location in the space of the gallery. With
them, Pindell offers a subtle challenge to the sensorial hierarchies of late modernist painting.

The political potential of a choreography of viewing extends far beyond the
normative terms of modernist art criticism. Art historian Sampada Aranke has
argued, in her discussion of works by Melvin Edwards, Kerry James Marshall,
and Jack Whitten, that through the activation of an embodied form of spectatorship, these Black artists have destabilized both the subject–object binary and the
ocular logics that undergird anti-Black racism in the West. In other words, their
artworks invite the viewer's physical movement in a gesture that challenges the

Fig. 26. Howardena Pindell, *Untitled,* 1971. Acrylic on canvas, 75½ × 75½ in. (191.8 × 191.8 cm). Garth Greenan Gallery, New York.

Fig. 27. Howardena Pindell, *Untitled,* 1971 (detail; see fig. 26).

ontological categories and hierarchical structures that have organized justifications for the enslavement, surveillance, and incarceration of Black people. For Aranke, this embodied, sensorial viewership has the potential to open audiences to an anti-essentialist relation to Blackness as an aesthetic. This artistic project had particular significance in the years Pindell launched her career as a modernist in the wake of the civil rights movement; Edwards and Whitten are her contemporaries. The semifigurative works that Aranke analyzes allude to anti-Black violence in far more explicit terms than do Pindell's spray-painted canvases. Nonetheless, Aranke's theoretical insights into the significance of an expanded relational field for Black artists who wish to defy the violent, conventional terms of the gaze shed light on Pindell's latent concern for these broader questions about the politics of looking and the stakes of offering up objects to view.[40]

In these initial years of her career, Pindell addressed viewers' bodies through movement that both positioned her work in institutional modernism and defied some of its limitations. The striking resemblance of Pindell's colorful dot paintings to a noteworthy dance backdrop underscores their choreographic operations. In 1958, Robert Rauschenberg began work on the décor for a new dance choreographed by Merce Cunningham called *Summerspace.* With the assistance of Jasper Johns, he created a cloth backdrop that flowed onto and covered the stage, spray-painting colorful circles directly onto this canvas as well as the leotards and tights the dancers wore (figs. 28, 29). Clusters of circles in shades of brown, yellow, green, pink, orange, and blue intermixed to give an illusion of blanketed depth to the backdrop, which Rauschenberg likened to a jungle. As an effect of the camouflage treatment, dancers' movements activated the backdrop, imbuing the field of dots through which they moved with a sense of motion.[41]

This figure–ground confusion caused Cunningham to remark on the success of the backdrop that even when he walked offstage, he felt like the dance continued.[42] While Pindell was not familiar with *Summerspace* prior to making her spray-painted paintings, they likewise set movement and surface, individual

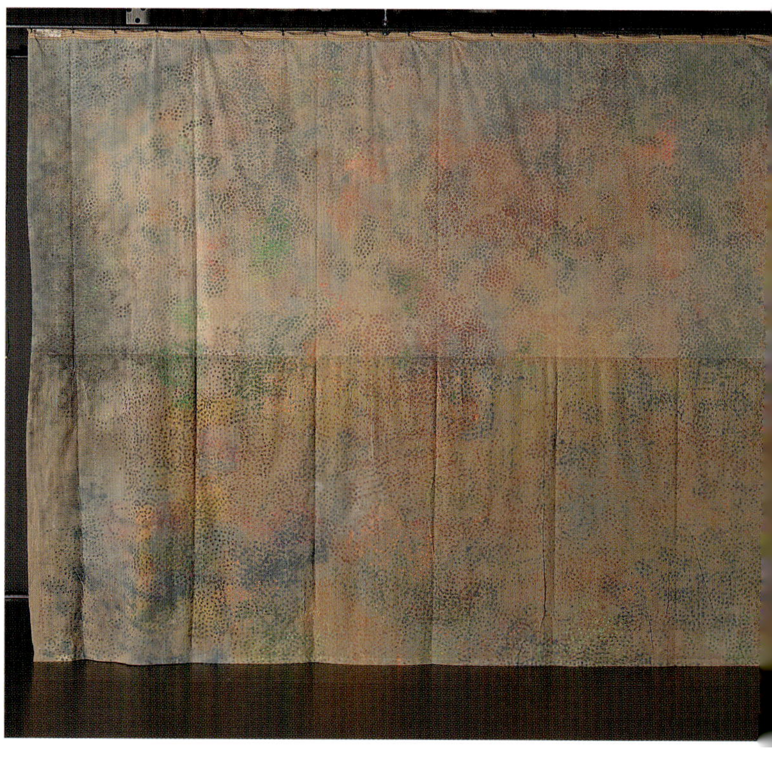

Fig. 28. Robert Rauschenberg, *Décor* for *Summerspace,* 1958. Enamel on canvas, 16 ft. 9½ in. × 43 ft. 10½ in. (511.8 × 1337.3 cm). Collection of Walker Art Center, Minneapolis. Walker Art Center, Merce Cunningham Dance Company Collection, Gift of Jay F. Ecklund, the Barnett and Annalee Newman Foundation, Agnes Gund, Russell Cowles and Josine Peters, the Hayes Fund of HRK Foundation, Dorothy Lichtenstein, MAHADH Fund of HRK Foundation, Goodale Family Foundation, Marion Stroud Swingle, David Teiger, Kathleen Fluegel, Barbara G. Pine, and the T. B. Walker Acquisition Fund, 2011.

Fig. 29. Robert Kovitch and Chris Komar in Merce Cunningham's *Summerspace,* 1977. Photograph: Jack Mitchell.

form and collective effect, in animated tension in ways that extend beyond their surface. Allover composition is central to these spatial effects. A diffuse, overlapping placement of circles rids the paintings and the backdrop of compositional focus and gives the illusion that the pattern might extend forever in all directions. The repetitive mark-making process, systematized by Pindell through the use of stencils, heightens the impression that equal attention and significance have been distributed to all areas of the canvas.

For Pindell, allover composition further signaled a desire to be situated in a modernist discourse around painting, and in a particular lineage emerging from abstract expressionism. Jackson Pollock popularized the compositional technique with his drip paintings in the late 1940s. As Fried has noted, allover composition allowed Pollock to weave elements together, to create a "homogeneous visual fabric which both invites the act of seeing on the part of the spectator and yet gives the eye nowhere to rest once and for all." Without a place to focus one's attention, the viewer of an allover painting is unable to identify figure–ground or inside–outside relations. For Fried, this left the viewer in "something like pure, disembodied energy," that is, in the realm of the purely "optical."[43]

With her compositions, Pindell wielded her coloristic acumen to generate fields of spatial ambiguity that operate visually as well as on the viewing body.

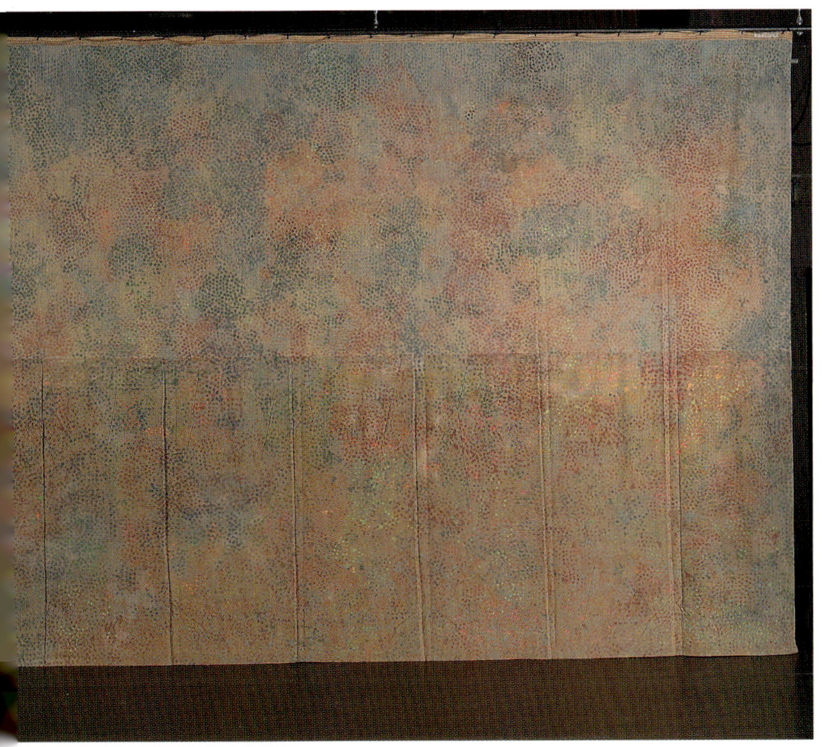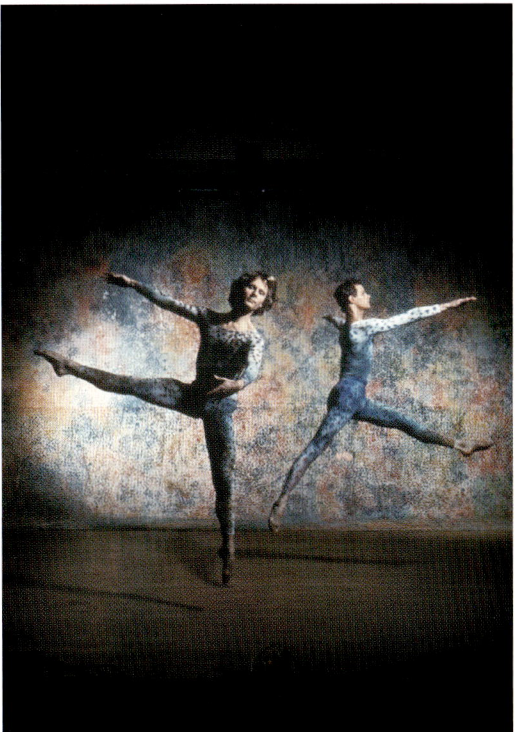

In contrast to Fried's theory, Pindell's paintings extend their interrogation of the figure–ground relationship to the structuring encounter between the viewer and the art object. The spray-painted canvases site the figure–ground question in the viewer's body, which moves toward and away from the canvas as the eye attempts to orient itself to the field of colors. Through this chorcography of viewing, as well as the assertion of her labor through her deployment of folds and contours, Pindell enlisted her audiences in a consciously embodied art encounter. Over the course of the following decade, she would continue to use the round and to rely on increasingly visible traces of her handiwork in abstractions that overtly thematize the bodily through the haptic.

The spray-painted canvases exhibit Pindell's nascent interrogation of the relational dynamics of art as an avenue for expanding a highly constraining discursive field. Given the pressing debates amid which Pindell developed her abstract practice, the spatial ambiguity of her spray-painted canvases offer a fitting formal analogy for the ambivalence she found and valued in abstraction and the placelessness she experienced as a Black woman abstractionist. Her commitment to spatial and discursive movement countered the expectation that her artworks locate themselves in relation to the sociopolitical project of Black nationalisms.

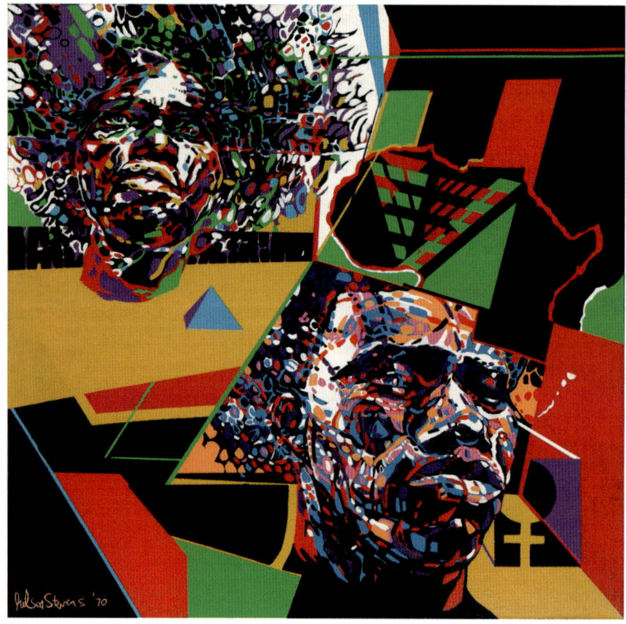

Fig. 30. Nelson Stevens, *Jihad Nation*, 1970. Acrylic on canvas, 42¼ × 42¼ in. (107.3 × 107.3 cm). Private collection.

CAPITAL "B" BLACK ART

Pindell became a modernist in a period of heightened political stakes around abstraction. While her concern for color was primarily formal in the late 1960s and early 1970s, a different, racialist sense of the term dominated the discussions of abstract art produced by Black artists in this era. The emergence of the Black Power movement saw a growing public platform for vocal proponents of a cohesive and ideologically driven Black art, which would serve to bolster the broader politics of Black nationalisms.[44] Under the auspices of Black art, representation, as both an aesthetic mode and political goal, was the signal aim of artistic production. Pindell and other Black artists confronted demands to represent themselves and their communities in their art using figurative means. This discourse left the abstract works of many Black artists adrift in a battlefield of critical negation.

In the late 1960s, spokespersons of the Black Arts movement called for art forms that would "[stand] for the spiritual helpmate of the Black Nation." The urgent need for "Revolutionary Cultural Consciousness" required Black artists to work collectively to supplant the images, values, and associations of a dominant white U.S. culture with a "capital-B" Black culture. Arbiters of Black culture such as poet and eminent Black Arts promoter Amiri Baraka and playwright Larry Neal deemed figurative, explicitly political work as the most expedient means to these ends.[45] They believed these idioms would be most legible to Black Americans with a wide variety of cultural experiences, and also most useful to the purposes of cultivating a Black culture apart from the white mainstream. African imagery—such as the outline of the continent against pan-African colors in Nelson Stevens's *Jihad Nation* (1970)—played an especially important role in these efforts at artistic and political consolidation (fig. 30). These cultural producers carried forward the work of those who had wielded artistic production as an aid to Black liberation struggles throughout the twentieth century.[46]

Calls for figurative Black art built on a widespread, historical coding of abstraction as racially white—a narrative that downplayed or disregarded "Africa" as a site and source of abstraction.[47] In the context of the Black Arts movement, Baraka argued that "'non-political' black artists do not actually exist in the black world at all. They are within the tradition of white art." Black artists working abstractly in this era encountered de facto categorization as "non-political," and those wishing to assert the political efficacy of their nonrepresentational work, such as Edwards and Tom Lloyd, bore the burden of explicating its social content. As art historian Lowery Stokes Sims has noted, this was the crux of the "dilemma" faced by Black artists of the 1960s and 1970s—"their ranks were divided between those who did 'black art' versus those who did 'mainstream' art (i.e., the styles championed by the art establishment)."[48] In reality, many artists worked at this intersection.

Baraka's and other critics' implicit assignment of abstract artists to a "tradition of white art" speaks, of course, to historical conditions. The abstract art on view in New York's museums and galleries indeed overrepresented white artists. In 1969, when Spriggs, the director of the Studio Museum, rejected Pindell's abstract work uptown, Black artists and women artists of all races rarely had been given space in museums or galleries downtown. That year, the Whitney Museum of American Art extended its first ever invitation for a solo exhibition to a Black artist, Al Loving.[49] Alma Thomas received the museum's first solo exhibition of a Black woman's work in 1972.

Gender discrimination was also rampant downtown. As the women's liberation movement began to gain traction in the early 1970s, *Time* magazine reported that in 1971, 96.4 percent of artists shown by "leading" New York galleries were men. Black women were excluded from museums and galleries on the basis of each of these individual forms of exclusion. They were underrepresented within the margin of exhibition space given over to Black artists, which went primarily to men, and the space for women, the bulk of which went to white artists.[50]

Further, in the 1960s and 1970s, midcentury modernist criticism continued to hold sway over New York art institutions, even as minimalist and conceptual art forms challenged their hegemony. These dominant narratives of U.S. art for decades forcefully posited a close relationship between abstraction and nonpolitical expression on the one hand, and between figuration and sociopolitical content on the other.[51] In this sense, modernist abstraction more frequently than not entered the public sphere as an apparently white and putatively nonpolitical cultural phenomenon. The most renowned modernist critics and institutions claimed it as such, either directly, in the case of its presumed apolitical mode, or through racially exclusionary practices.

Abstraction symbolized a political complacency in the wake of the civil rights movement that exacerbated the historically detrimental effects of abstracting processes. Literary scholar Phillip Brian Harper has theorized abstraction's role in the long history of Black people's subjection in the West. Harper has argued that abstraction is the central cognitive function of anti-Black dehumanization, enabling stereotype—a simplified image that comes to stand in for the individual. Abstraction underwrites "an exalted generic national personhood"—a white, generally male position that typically excludes Black Americans, Indigenous people, and other people of color. National histories of slavery and ongoing, everyday patterns of racist distortion rely on the subjection of Black Americans to relentless procedures of "representational abstraction."[52]

Harper has addressed a particular mode of abstraction—the inherently abstracting nature of white supremacy as an ideology that fabricates and violently enforces racialized fictions through everyday constructions and overt shows of force. This mode of abstraction generates racist images—and consequences—in abundance. Many participants in the Black Arts movement labored to supplant this harmful representational regime with figurative imagery that honored Black people. From an art-historical perspective, the cognitive abstraction that Harper has described, which often manifests in representational images such as caricatures, is distinct from nonrepresentational abstract art. Nonetheless, cultural discourses emerging from the Black Arts movement of the 1960s and 1970s cast abstract art as a product of a white supremacist culture with little use to Black liberation efforts. This period's debates stand as a momentary intensification of long-simmering tensions over the moral and political responsibilities of Black artists.

Darby English has noted that characterizations of abstraction as "irrelevant" to Black audiences limited the range of officially legitimated artistic means available to Black artists, thereby establishing an exclusionary basis for "Black art." Black artists working abstractly were admonished by spokespeople for the Black Arts movement as lacking political sophistication, or castigated as capitulating to their oppressors' cultural tastes. For instance, Tom Lloyd, a rare spokesperson who advocated for the political relevancy of his own abstract work, derided Loving and other Black abstractionists for showing their art downtown. Amid controversy over an exhibition at the Whitney, he referred to a group of Black artists working abstractly as "non-political 'cooperative' Negro artists whose bowing movements are readily spotted as talent."[53] The heady urgency of the Black Power movement, brought on by state-sponsored violence in the United States and Vietnam, led some Black Arts proponents to require art and artists to speak directly to a targeted range of concerns, including U.S. racism. Understated engagements with themes of Black experience or African culture, especially if

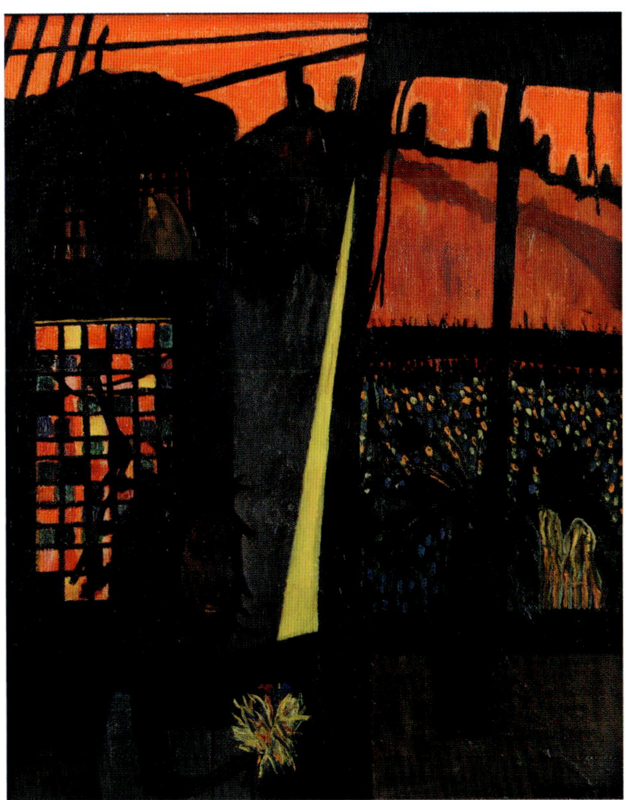

Fig. 31. Vincent Smith, *Easter Sunday,* 1965.
Oil on Masonite, 24 × 20¾ in. (61 × 52.7 cm).
Private collection.

rendered abstractly, typically registered for critics as "Black art" only
when artists prominently articulated
the political goals of their practices, as
Lloyd had.

A chapter from Pindell's early
career emblematizes the dilemma
faced by Black artists working
abstractly in these years and by the
critics who contextualized their work
in the era's debates. To accompany
Pindell's 1971 two-person exhibition
with Vincent Smith at Spelman,
curator and faculty member Bhalla wrote a brief text. In it, he established the
primary curatorial framework for the show—juxtaposition. Pindell's abstract
paintings and drawings "belong to the mainstream of the 20th century American art [*sic*]," while the figurative work of fellow New York–based artist Smith
"expresses the disenchantment of only Black people." Smith's works use red and
black to give warmth and gravitas to everyday subject matter, as indicated by
titles such as *Pot-Belly Stove* (1966), *Clothes Line* (1970), and *Store Front* (1970),
all included in the Spelman exhibition. Bhalla found value in both artists' work,
writing that each use their materials and techniques with "commendable discipline" and "fresh inventiveness." They deal "with their themes with authority
and subtle perceptiveness."[54] This framework suggests that Bhalla presented his
audience with strikingly differing practices as a way of concisely alluding to the
variety of aesthetic approaches being developed by contemporary Black artists.

By the end of the brief essay, however, the contrast between Pindell's and
Smith's works also serves to educate gallery visitors in the proper forms and
themes of the increasingly publicly visible "Black art." Smith's representations of
scenes from Black life, in Bhalla's estimation, "reveal something unique" about
"black experience and ethnic integrity." A painting of a young man kneeling at a
church altar, titled *Easter Sunday* (1965), sets a luminous orange-red background
against black architectural armatures to create a contemplative interior space lit

by stained glass (fig. 31). Bhalla opined that these works by Smith "for the most part, reveal anguish and disillusion of Black Americans in a white dominated society." Ultimately, he concluded that this art warrants the label "Black art" because it "rejects the traditionally Western oriented themes of styles [*sic*]" and instead "truly concentrates" on the artist's "own people."[55]

Pindell's spray-painted abstract paintings and drawings serve as a foil to Smith's "Black art," for her works "in no way relate to the themes of Black experiences or Black awareness." Instead, Bhalla identified varying sources for her art: Larry Poons's work, the colors of "Persian miniatures," and "the dream world of her subconscious." In the essay, this plurality of concerns indicated Pindell's primary investment in artistic freedom, a commitment ostensibly at odds with the imperatives of "Black art." Bhalla wrote: "Like many other Black artists, she wants to be completely *free* in choosing her visual statements rather than using one source."[56] He conspicuously skirted the question of the relevance of freedom as a political project in the wake of a major civil rights movement a century after U.S. slavery's end.

An article penned by Bhalla in the February 1972 issue of Spelman's quarterly newsletter, just three months after Pindell's show, indicates that he saw the diffuse aesthetics practiced by Black artists as an existential threat to the efficacy of Black art. In "The Dilemma of Afro-American Artists," Bhalla wrote that "Black art" was in peril of becoming merely "nominal," with "no practical convenience." With some Black artists embracing social protest and a "straightforward," "primitive" aesthetic, others exploring the representational and thematic imagery of African art, and others still rejecting these various concepts on the basis that "art is universal," Black art troublingly lacked coherence and, therefore, political efficacy.[57] This view accounts for Bhalla's efforts to preempt the viewer's identification of Pindell's abstraction with "Black art." The article further reveals that he worried that Black art had yet to develop an expression truly outside "the western idiom." Despite these reservations, and in contrast to more well-known tracts on Black art, Bhalla's pedagogical tone in the exhibition pamphlet for Pindell's show offers a diplomatic account of abstraction. He judiciously avoided overt disapproval or an explicit categorization of the aesthetic formation as racially white. Nonetheless, it seems that he too viewed the openness of abstraction as potentially detrimental to the politico-aesthetic aims of the Black Arts movement. Bhalla's discernments attest to the difficulty of the project that lay before proponents of the Black Arts movement—establishing and nurturing an aesthetic outside of white supremacist ideologies.

Despite the binds set up by art criticism, U.S. artists not only in the context of the Black Arts movement, but throughout the twentieth century, engaged with abstraction under explicitly political terms. Consider, for instance, sculptor

Isamu Noguchi's decades-long deployment of an emphatically modernist, politically charged artistic idiom. Neither the debates about the political efficacy of abstraction nor artists' defiant pursuit of political modernisms were new in the late 1960s, but both took on a renewed urgency under the banner of the period's efflorescent Black nationalisms. Although the most stringent defenders of the Black Arts movement advocated unequivocally for explicitly political art, artists such as Pindell engaged with the ideology of Black liberation that undergirded the movement through a much wider range of aesthetic strategies.[58]

ART WORLD ACTIVISM

Artists working in all manner of aesthetic modes agitated alongside one another for art world reform in the late 1960s, advocating for racial equality in New York's art institutions. It was thanks to the committed activism of these artists, as well as writers and critics, that museums began to devote gallery space to Black abstract artists such as Gilliam, Loving, and Thomas. Pindell actively participated in artist-activism in the early 1970s. This movement in turn shaped her life and career in both subtle and profound ways.

In 1969, the AWC formed, asking what artists, audiences, and public MoMA served. Pindell attended several AWC meetings at the encouragement of Lippard, but was eventually, in Pindell's words, "thrown out" as a result of her institutional affiliation. However, AWC files in the MoMA archives suggest that the group initially imagined that museum staff would liaise with the activists. Pindell's dismissal from the group under these circumstances suggests that it was not her institutional affiliation alone that prompted AWC suspicions, but perhaps its coincidence with her race and gender. In 1970, Faith Ringgold and Michele Wallace defected from the AWC to form Women Students and Artists for Black Art Liberation (WSABAL), a splinter group that protested the racism and sexism of the activist community.[59] Pindell did not join this group; for several years after her ouster from the AWC, she stopped pursuing membership in outside groups aimed at institutional reform. Perhaps her reluctance stemmed in part from her experience of being spurned by the AWC, the fact that she consistently encountered exhausting racist discrimination in her day job at the museum, or her demanding workload as a full-time curator and an artist. In these initial years of her career, her efforts to redress widespread art world discrimination centered on the little leverage she had at MoMA and on the development of her authorial voice as an artist.

In May 1970, MoMA's board of trustees requested a study of "the Museum's role in regard to artists of minority ethnic groups who have expressed serious grievances against major cultural institutions, including museums." The resulting group was known as the Byers Committee, named after its chairman, trustee

J. Frederic Byers III. Pindell joined these efforts to rectify racial discrimination at MoMA. According to her, the request to form the committee came in response to pressure from Black artists including Andrews and William T. Williams, who recently helped form the BECC.[60]

Pindell lobbied to become a member of the Byers Committee after an incident in which prominent museum benefactor and subcommittee chair Blanchette Rockefeller wrote a memo suggesting that there were no Black artists qualified to exhibit at MoMA. In a later interview, the artist recalled her determination to contribute her voice to the committee, proverbially "screaming and yelling" until she was granted membership.[61] Rockefeller's comment, it seems, pushed Pindell's frustrations with MoMA's institutionalized racism to a breaking point. (Ironically, MoMA later purchased Pindell's collage *Untitled #4* using funds from the Blanchette Hooker Rockefeller Fund.) To Pindell, a young professional, the Byers Committee may have seemed a rare opportunity to voice her concerns to those in power at the museum.

Supported by the expertise of Black cultural consultant Carroll Greene, Jr., the working group reviewed the museum's practices around racial inclusion. In a report submitted to the board in June 1971, it proposed changes to staffing and curatorial and outreach procedures. Pindell's contribution to the international exhibitions subcommittee focused on the museum's collection of prints and illustrated books, which she helped to oversee at the time. Her report, which includes a breakdown of artists' nationalities, foreshadows the statistical research that would play a prominent role in her more public art world activism of the 1980s.[62]

The international exhibitions subcommittee's seven-point recommendations to the museum placed great emphasis on the need to direct resources to the promotion of "African art and culture" within the museum's programming. Pindell would participate actively in and benefit from these efforts, traveling to six countries in East and West Africa in 1973 to identify sites for donated art libraries, and taking artistic inspiration from the museum's much-touted 1972 exhibition *African Textiles and Decorative Arts*. As a youth growing up in largely segregated Philadelphia, Pindell noted, she encountered a public cultural "embargo on knowledge related to Africa."[63] Her upwardly mobile middle-class parents took her to art museums, spaces designed to steward Euro-American cultural history. Her encounters with African art and culture as an adult would help to transform profoundly Pindell's artistic production later in the 1970s.

At the same time Pindell contributed to efforts to reform MoMA, her artistic career benefitted from the wins of fellow artist-activists. Perhaps most notably, examples of her spray-painted canvases appeared in two significant exhibitions at the Whitney in 1971 and 1972. Organized in response to the BECC's demands, the 1971 exhibition *Contemporary Black Artists in America* formed part of a

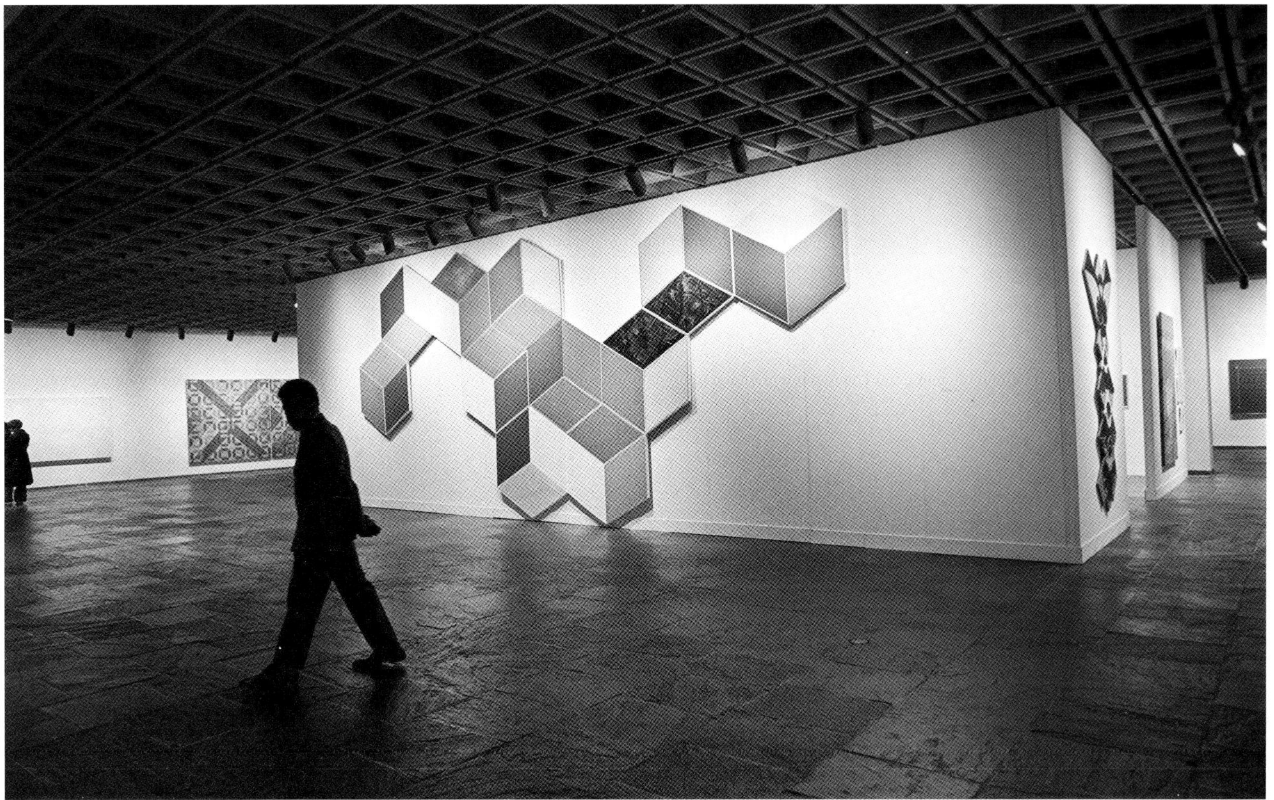

Fig. 32. Installation view of the exhibition *Contemporary Black Artists in America* at the Whitney Museum of American Art, New York, April 6–May 16, 1971. Left to right: Elyn Zimmerman, *#10* (1970); John Chandler, *Garvey's Quest* (1971); Al Loving, *WYN . . . Time Trip I* (1971); Walter Davis, *Black Bird Totem* (1970); Raymond Saunders, *Marie's Bill* (1970) and five drawings; James Lee, *Cleo II* (1970). Photograph: Tyrone Dukes/The New York Times/Redux.

twelve-show series (1969–74) intended to correct the glaring racial inequities entrenched in the museum's practices.[64] It formed part of a broader effort to incorporate Black art, Black curatorial input, and Black scholarship into the Whitney's programs. The exhibition, along with six solo shows of Black artists working primarily in abstraction, pointed to the museum's commitment to an expansive notion of what constituted "Black art."

Contemporary Black Artists in America, however, opened to controversy and received poor reviews. A full six months prior to the opening, Black artists slated to appear in the exhibition began protesting the museum's "abandonment of critical and intellectual responsibility." Nearly a third of the seventy-eight artists invited to participate eventually boycotted by withdrawing from the show. Rather than hire an outside curator with expertise in contemporary Black art, the Whitney delegated it to its own Robert Doty.[65] He dedicated a large portion

of the show to abstract works—over half of the eighty-four artworks on view. The
exhibition plan indicates that Doty placed abstract works in many of the show's
most significant sight lines. For instance, a large-scale, multipanel painting by
Loving dominated the exhibition's entry wall. Nearby works by John E. Chandler,
Walter Davis, and Lloyd repeated the honeycomb-like pattern of Loving's installation (fig. 32). While loose formal associations such as this one helped to organize passages of the exhibition, the show also generated stark juxtapositions
between abstraction and explicitly political figurative art. A work by Betye Saar,
Whitey's Way (1970), a small mirrored case containing two rows of white ceramic
alligators and a single black figurine—a reference to the racial predation of the
U.S. South—appeared alongside Pindell's spray-painted canvas and a hard-edge
abstraction by Mavis Pusey.

Many critics viewed the exhibition as incoherent, either as a result of the
museum's failure to take Black art seriously on its own terms, or as a consequence
of perceived deficiencies in contemporary Black art. Abstraction's pride of place
in the exhibition cast the figurative works on view in a subordinate position,
presenting them, as Susan E. Cahan noted, "through the lens of high modernism."
Doty's selections defied some artist-activists' expectation that the show would
reflect contemporary trends of the Black Arts movement by privileging figurative
forms expressly concerned with social and political realities. Exhibition reviews
in the mainstream press tended to detail the debates surrounding the exhibition
and suffered from critics' inexperience writing about—and prejudices about—work
by Black artists. A review by John Canaday in the *New York Times,* for instance,
belittled the work on view as "decorative attraction" and "imitators."[66]

Some of the most voluble and effectual protests of the exhibition came from
Black artists who worked primarily in abstraction. Seven artists who withdrew
from the exhibition admonished the museum for what they called "the worst
form of tokenism" in a letter published in *Artforum* in May 1971. These artists—
Edwards, Gilliam, Overstreet, Williams, John Dowell, Richard Hunt, and Daniel
Johnson—critiqued the exhibition as an "anti-curated . . . survey" with an ahistor-
ical approach to Black American art. They took particular umbrage at the exhibition's "primary focus on the racial identities of the artists" and only secondary
regard for their work.[67]

These abstract artists held complex and shifting ideas about the relationship
between form and racial identity, between aesthetics and Blackness. While their
artistic output seemingly placed them at odds with the protests organized by
the BECC, whose leaders disapproved of the emphasis on abstraction, there is no
evidence to suggest that these groups thought of their aims as antithetical. They
shared alarm at the show's deficiencies of intellectual rigor and care, and a commitment to actively combatting the art world conditions that produced the exhibition.

The Black artists working abstractly who boycotted *Contemporary Black Artists in America,* far from repudiating the pertinence of sociopolitical realities to their works, wanted to reserve the right to introduce such content on their own terms. As art historian Kellie Jones has argued, Black artists working abstractly frequently attempted to "make the social ferment of the time present in the work" through titles, materials, and themes. Gilliam has remarked that "figurative art doesn't represent blackness any more than a non-narrative media-oriented kind of painting, like what I do." He embraced the label "Black art" as a critique of the unwillingness of major galleries and museums to "show any work by any black artist." Gilliam and many members of his cohort, such as Whitten, Williams, and Frank Bowling, wanted to be acknowledged for the "artistic merit of their creations, rather than for the social content of their works."[68] Similarly, artists who heeded the calls of Black Arts movement leaders did so in a variety of ways. If Black nationalist cultural discourse sometimes prescribed imagery and content to artists, the lived reality was more complex as those artists chose how, when, and for whom to engage with Black cultures.

Pindell viewed abstraction as a site of ambivalence around social content, rather than a tool for its repudiation. As noted in the introduction, she has remarked that abstraction "doesn't have a concrete meaning, but can relate back to signification in the world."[69] Her comment locates the capaciousness of abstraction in the word "can," which signals the possibility and variation available to the artist and the viewer. Abstraction can produce meaning in relation to the social world, but it does not have to do so. Its power lies in its lack of fixity with respect to socially agreed-upon meanings.

Although Pindell was well aware of the controversy surrounding *Contemporary Black Artists in America,* she remained in the exhibition. It was her first opportunity to show her work in Manhattan, illustrious venue or not; she struggled to find anywhere to exhibit in these years. She stayed the course even when BECC cofounder Andrews petitioned her and other artists to withdraw from the exhibition, and further, to not show "in any of those racist institutions." Pindell understood that gender discrimination further stymied her career advancement. She later reflected, "My idea was that I have so few opportunities to show my work. All these men came to me telling me to withdraw work. They're the ones who are going to be shown anyway. I'll be the one that will be left out. So, I decided not to withdraw."[70] Her prediction has been proven astute. Although Black modernists were subjected to dismissal or censure by some of their peers, artists such as Edwards, Gilliam, Loving, and Williams also received enviable support from Black and white cultural institutions alike. Today, their works feature prominently in recently revised art-historical narratives that continue to overlook and marginalize women artists in accounts of Black American art and of abstraction.

It was also Pindell's insider knowledge of museums that motivated her to remain in *Contemporary Black Artists in America.* She knew that museums' goodwill toward artists of color might be fleeting and that, therefore, she could not count on future opportunities to garner such a large audience for her work as that offered at the Whitney. She also knew that MoMA, which she understood to be one of the "racist institutions" Andrews warned her against, recently acquired his painting *No More Games* (1970). Why should she step aside from the Whitney, she later asked, so that Andrews and others could speak on her behalf and leap at the opportunities they forbade her?[71]

Remarkably, Pindell found a measure of freedom in the unlikely site of gender inequity. She has noted that being perceived as falling outside of an artistic lineage (*any* publicly agreed-upon artistic lineage) in the early stages of her career allowed her to make the work she wanted: "As a woman, one is free to do your own work."[72] If there was no place for her in the art worlds she encountered in New York, she did not have to appease any of them. Of course, the converse remained true, as Pindell toiled for years to find a foothold in an art market largely disinterested in work by women of color.

The same year that *Contemporary Black Artists in America* opened, Pindell received an invitation to show in the Whitney's *1972 Annual Exhibition: Contemporary American Painting.* Her deep maroon painting in that exhibition contrasted with the bright, spring greens of the canvas that represented her in the slightly earlier show (see fig. 19). She painted both using her spray-paint stencil technique. In the final months before the annual exhibition's opening, the Ad Hoc Women Artists' Committee, a group that emerged from the AWC, wrote to Whitney director John I. H. Baur, urging him to assure equal representation for women artists in the high-profile show. The previous year, a group of committee members and coalition affiliates including Poppy Johnson, Brenda Miller, Lippard, and Ringgold had lobbied the museum to include fifty percent women in its Sculpture Annual and, of that group, fifty percent Black women. They staged sit-ins and demonstrations in the months leading up to the exhibition, placing unused menstrual tampons and uncooked eggs in the museum galleries and staircases. While the museum failed to meet their demands, the exhibition opened with twenty women out of one hundred total artists, up from the eight women out of 151 artists in the 1969 Painting Annual.[73]

For the 1972 annual, the Ad Hoc Committee sought to keep the pressure on the museum to represent women equitably. While Baur responded somewhat

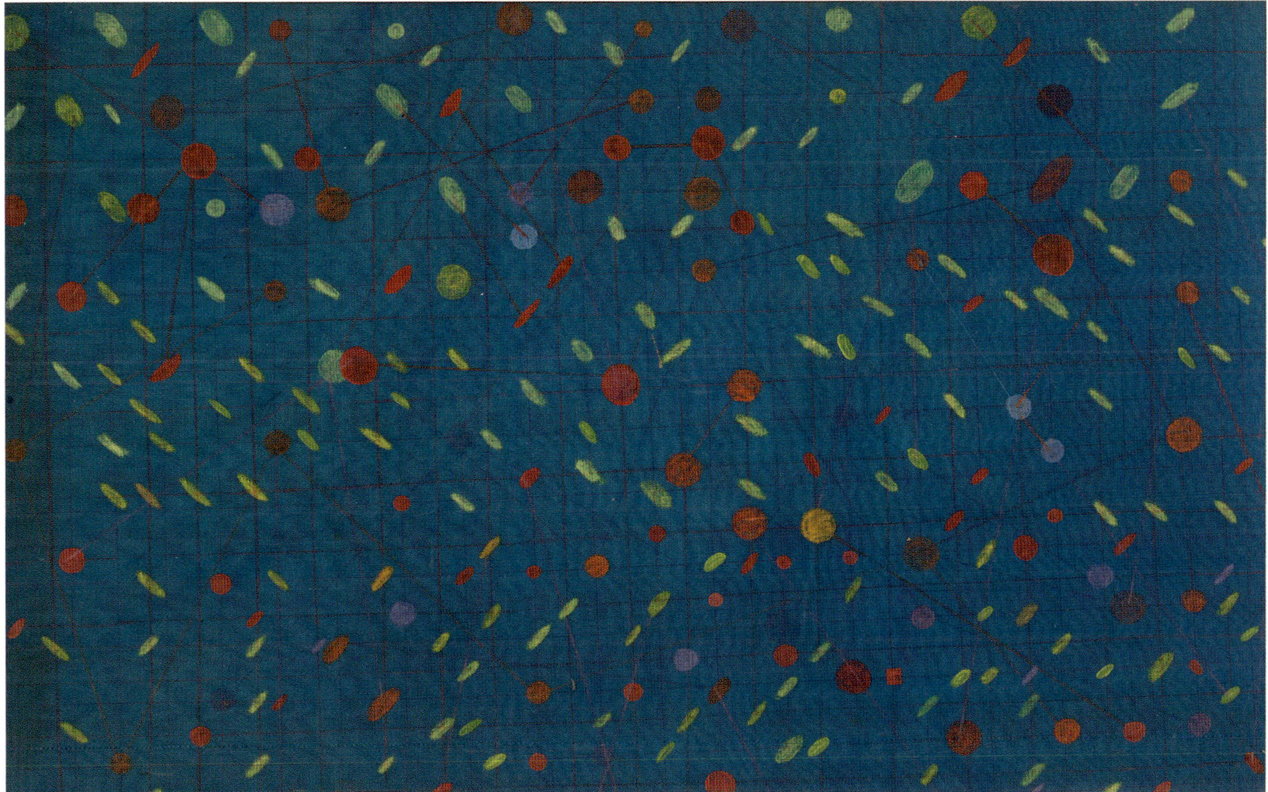

dismissively to the committee's demands, presenting the anemic argument that the museum had "no control over the percentage of slides by women submitted" to them, museum records indicate that curators made an effort to seek out women artists for inclusion in the exhibition. A memo from Marcia Tucker to fellow annual curators Doty and James Monte titled "Women Painters" lists several dozen women artists, Pindell among them, whose studios they planned to visit.[74] Pindell has credited her inclusion in the exhibition in part to the Ad Hoc Committee's efforts, though she declined to participate in the group when Lippard attempted to recruit her, feeling that her concerns as a Black artist would not be adequately addressed.[75]

Despite the hard-won gains in exhibition opportunities, working abstractly as a Black artist in the early 1970s entailed a particular set of risks. These included the risk of being illegible to some art audiences and unmarketable to art institutions looking to maximize the social cachet generated by their newly "diverse" offerings.[76] If leaders of the Black Arts movement were to be believed, modernist abstraction came from outside Black culture and was imposed by a colonizing, white Euro-American culture. Pindell clearly rejected this premise as she found even quite simple forms, such as the circle, powerfully imbued with social meaning. It was not expected in the late 1960s that a politically engaged Black woman artist looking "inward" would find forms that so seamlessly lent themselves to modernist abstraction. Pindell's case is instructive for considering how entangled personal vision and social structures can be and how insufficient broad social categories are for accounting for one's visual orientation toward the world. She used the grid, as well as the circle, to reimagine form as a resource for critically intervening in artistic narratives that adhered to her as a Black woman.

GRID

In many of her early abstract paintings, Pindell juxtaposes the "feminine" circle with a grid—a form in the 1960s associated with the civilizing, tradition-ally masculine-coded forces of modernity.[77] An untitled painting of 1968 sets a hand-drawn grid and warm-hued rounds against a steel blue background (fig. 33). In other works, Pindell used graph paper as the ground of drawing (see fig. 15). Swenson, in her interview mentioned above, followed her question about Pindell's use of the circle with one about the grid. "The grid," she asked, "is that modern civilization?" Many an abstractionist might blush, or bristle, at the suggestion of a one-to-one correlation between her forms and such concepts. Pindell responded in stride: "I'm not sure. Look at a map with longitude and latitude: these are points, and where they cross are points of energy."

The artist relates the grid to geographic space, but advances idiosyncratic definitions of common cartographic notations. For Pindell, grids are closely linked to the physical forces that form circles. "When gravity works, you get a mass that's circular, and somehow points along the mass are designated by lines drawn from A to B and they intersect," she told Swenson.[78] Here, the intersecting lines that comprise a grid, that constitute longitude and latitude, are overlaid on a "circle," or the sphere of Earth. These marks of energetic movement indicate motion and trajectories. Rather than accepting the neutral stasis of longitudinal and latitudinal lines, Pindell asserts that the taut, straight lines suggest propul-sion. They trace the forces of velocity, attraction, and drives.

This was hardly the prevailing artistic notion of the grid in the late 1960s. Over the course of the decade, the grid had become strongly associated with minimalist and conceptual art practices and a rationalizing or bureaucratic aes-thetic. Minimalist sculptor Carl Andre's floor pieces, for instance, mobilized the grid as a simple, modular structure, one encouraged by the protocols and forms of industrial materials. The decade also saw what one critic called "the great graph paper period," in which countless artists turned to the found material as a support for drawings, bringing both industrial and pedagogical allusions to their works. Graph paper posited the grid as a bureaucratic "container" for informa-tion.[79] Pindell herself would turn to this aspect of the grid in earnest in several collaged works on graph paper she made beginning in 1973.

The grid has had a long and varied career in modern art. Artists throughout the 1960s appealed to various aspects of its formal and conceptual resonances. Writing a typology of the grid in *Artforum* in 1972, John Elderfield outlined several common recent usages: the grid as "factual display" in the minimalist-inflected paintings of Agnes Martin; as a "framework" for Snyder's expressive brushstrokes; as "scaffolding" in the geometric abstractions of Poons; and as the "objectification" of Pollock's decentralized, allover compositions. Earlier that year, the Institute of Contemporary Art at the University of Pennsylvania had hosted an exhibition on the theme of grids. Lippard wrote an essay for the catalogue, noting that "the grid per se is of no importance" to the artists in the exhibition, and that nothing could be said to unite their artworks beyond the form itself. Despite, or perhaps because of, the glut of artistic practices that mobilized the grid and the many, disparate ends to which they did so, both Elderfield and Lippard emphasized the grid's status as a "neutral," "arbitrary framework."[80] Seemingly, it could be adapted to any use whatever. These observations helpfully pointed to the grid's ubiquity in modern art. However, these writers took this fact for granted, coming short of asking what underlying attributes of the grid had made it serviceable to such diverse practices.

To a greater degree than her predecessors, Rosalind Krauss struck on a unifying theory of the grid that sought to account for the form's particularities as a paradigmatically modern phenomenon. In a 1979 essay, at a remove of several years from the grid's minimalist-conceptualist heyday, Krauss contended that the structure announces "modern art's will to silence, its hostility to literature, to narrative, to discourse." It declares art to be autonomous and autotelic.[81] But beneath these features, which screen out the world in a gesture of refusal, Krauss found appeals to the spiritual. The grid reveals modern art's repressed spiritual function. Krauss considered, for instance, the gridded work of Kazimir Malevich, Martin, and Reinhardt. In them, the repetitive structure of the grid operates as a vehicle both for communicating the material facts of the surface and for accessing the metaphysical.

Among theories of the grid that circulated in the 1970s, Krauss's most profoundly shaped subsequent critical narratives of its role in modernisms. Like Pindell, she deployed a cartographic metaphor, writing that the grid "maps the surface of the painting itself. . . . The physical qualities of the surface, we could say, are mapped onto the aesthetic dimensions of the same surface." This formulation reveals several functions of the grid. First, through the "transfer" of physical qualities onto the aesthetic plane of the artwork, the grid displays its "naked and determined materialism," rendering visible the physical nature of that artwork. It makes what Elderfield called a "factual display" of the material ground of art by drawing attention to its surface, its measurability, its capacity

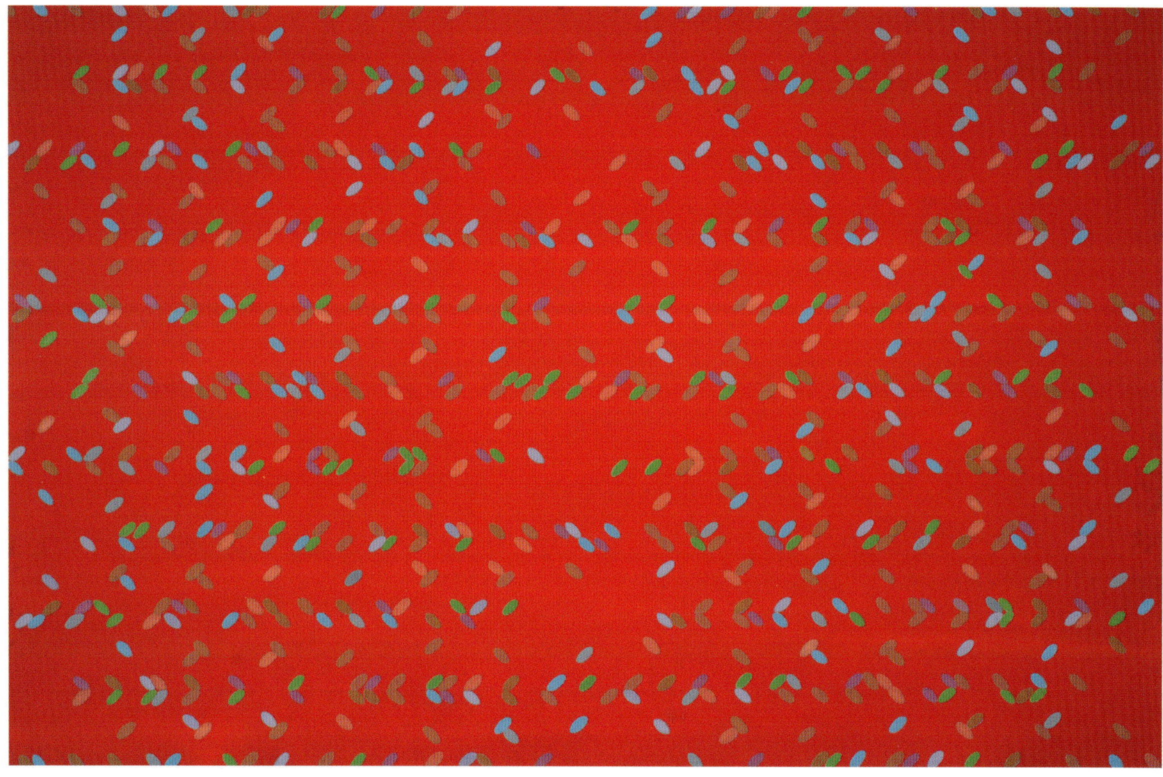

Fig. 34. Larry Poons, *Sangre de Christo,* 1964. Acrylic on linen, 90½ × 135 in. (229.9 × 342.9 cm). Audrey and David Mirvish, Toronto.

to be organized and divided like any other surface.[82] In doing so, it performs another of the grid's most significant functions: it makes the work of art legible as such, placing it in a matrix with other artworks. Among her most influential insights about the grid, Krauss asserted that it can locate the viewer in an intellectual, art-historical discourse by marking out the space of modern art.

Krauss's accounts of the grid take for granted the cultural context of a rarefied modernism. For her, the grid maps modernist terrain; she does not examine how or whether any given artist or artwork might be granted admission. Pindell, by contrast, recognized, as an artist whose entry into modernism was neither guaranteed nor encouraged, that the grid could be useful to her efforts. She approached the ubiquity of the grid with skepticism and opportunity in mind, as curator Naomi Beckwith has noted, seeing it not merely as "an aesthetic tool" but as "a vehicle for signaling the desire to be taken seriously as an artist."[83] As she became a savvy art world participant from her post at MoMA, Pindell realized that the grid, as an emblem of modernist art, might grant her work provisional entry into its hallowed ranks. If the grid maps "physical qualities" onto "aesthetic dimensions," as Krauss would assert, it could conversely be used as a device to render a physical surface into an artistic one. In other words, if the grid could symbolize the material fact of the work of art, its "transfer" function could also operate in the reverse, to indicate the presence of aesthetic intentionality on an otherwise merely physical surface.

With this insight, Pindell identified the discursive construction of the grid as an indicator of modernist intent. Her use of the form complicates Krauss's contention that the grid connotes artistic originality, declaring the artist's arrival at the scene of representation.[84] For Pindell, the fact that the grid had been codified as modernist form prior to her adoption of it was precisely the point. She deployed it, in part, in order to locate her practice in modernist conversations about surface. However, her understanding of the grid's utility did not preclude her earnest formal engagements with it, which endured through the 1970s.

In her early paintings, Pindell's use of the grid, especially its juxtaposition with circles and ellipses, closely resembles white American artist Larry Poons's canvases of the mid- to late 1960s (fig. 34). Pindell stated in a 1972 interview that she "liked" Poons's work, especially his use of patterned spots and lines to create a sense of unity. Poons, a once-frequently exhibited artist whose stature waned as modernist champions such as Fried lost ground in New York art circuits of the 1970s, subtly deployed the grid in paintings with optical effects. He utilized the form to help place geometric shapes across the surface of his canvas. Poons then painted over most of the grid in "acid" colors, almost entirely concealing the marks. His insistence that the grid played a merely supporting role in his works, offering his paintings "scaffolding," rather than structure, played a significant role in subsequent literature on the grid, especially Elderfield's typology.[85]

At first glance, Pindell's use of the grid in *Space Frame* (1969) evokes Poon's use of it as skeletal "scaffolding" (see fig. 14). A field of white and orange circles and ellipses appear to float above the grid, which is drawn atop pink acrylic paint striated with blue oil stick, mixing to create passages of sunset lavender (fig. 35). Thin, white diagonal lines connect some of the shapes. The grid, which is visible but drawn more faintly than the rounds and ellipses, helps to locate the shapes scattered across the canvas, nearly all of which are centered on at least one axis of a grid line. This grid's relatively rigid lines contrast with the round, loosely drawn shapes and the field of bleeding colors. Indeed, the formal rationale of the painting seems to lie in the juxtaposition of formal elements—circles with lines, vertical with horizontal, gestural with mechanical. Within this aesthetic system, the grid plays an important role. Its internal logic is one of predictable but visually interesting contrast between the stretch of verticality and span of horizontality.[86] In Pindell's paintings, the structure generates much of her works' compositional interest.

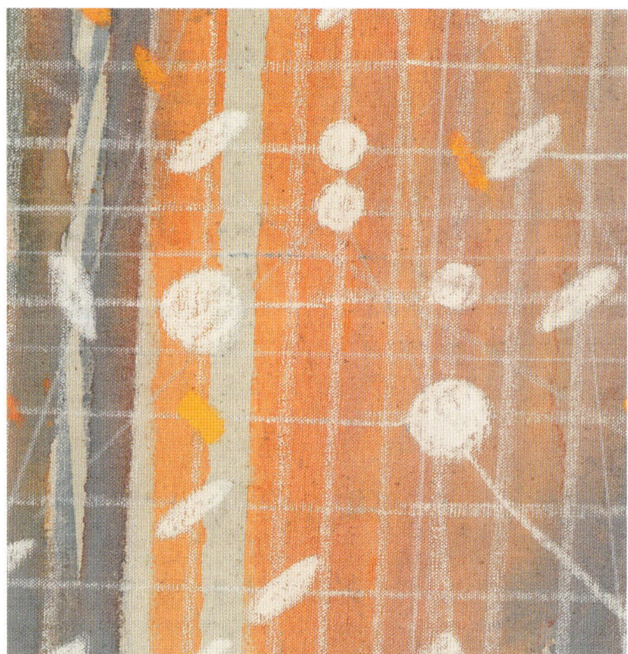

Fig. 35. Howardena Pindell, *Space Frame,*
1969 (detail; see fig. 14).

Space Frame of 1969 also participated in a postminimalist expansion
of the grid, evoking what Lippard
called its "temptingly despoilable"
perfection.[87] In this example, in
contrast to her other works of this
period, Pindell uses the grid to
introduce variation and irregular-
ity to her canvases. The lines of her
grid, though taut and straight, are
not perfectly parallel. Some of them grow gradually closer or further from one
another across the surface of the canvas, which may account for Pindell's decision to fracture the lines. In several passages, one line ends, and another begins
slightly higher or lower than the other, a small mismatch that suggests the artist
course corrected as she drew. These irregularities offer a glimpse into the artist's
process. The straight lines indicate that she used a ruler, while the imperfect
attempt at parallelism betrays that she did not pre-mark regular intervals for her
lines. Where the lines break, perhaps the artist observed the sloping and lifted
her ruler to commence drawing at a more secure position.

Space Frame alludes to the grid's rigid regularity and rationalizing associations without adhering to them. Instead, they are muted by apparently hand-
drawn elements as well as the painting's candy store colors. The work's title
references the ambitious nationalist project of 1960s space exploration, which
required mathematical precision as well as a great deal of ingenuity and imagination. (A "space frame" is a type of architectural structure with an interlocking,
geometric pattern.) On the surface of Pindell's work, rigor and confection are held
in productive tension. A highly skilled and trained artist, she consciously intervened in the rectilinear protocols of the grid by inserting overt markers of the
handmade. This gesture anticipates her imminent embrace of postminimalist
idioms, which place the industrial and handmade in dialogue.

Pindell's canny, extended commitment to the grid ran counter to the emerging perception of the form as analogous to a white male positionality. In 1971,
Black American poet Michael S. Harper published "The Nature of the Grid," a
treatise in verse that characterizes the grid as brutally destructive in its ratio-

nality. Harper, in an interview the following year, explicitly linked the violence of the grid to its "annihilation" of "nonwhites."[88] The literary scholar Phillip Brian Harper has situated the poet Harper's "suspicion" of the grid in the context of the form's centuries-long development in Western history as "effectively an avatar of the white-masculine form itself." In the United States, the apparent uniformity and rationality of the grid was mobilized to "conceptualize the ideal proto-republican citizen" as a white male landowner. A tool for measuring individuals against this ideal subject position, the grid also functioned as an administrative apparatus for partitioning land during early-republic settling. As the literary scholar Harper has noted, the grid's "nullity" and putative neutrality packaged land for easy consumption, belying the preexisting presence of Indigenous people and the politics of their forcible removal.[89]

Pindell may have been aware of these political and historical resonances of the grid in the late 1960s, but unlike Michael S. Harper, she did not reject the form on this basis. Rather, she exploited its potential utility in her efforts to establish herself as a modernist. Her astute appropriation of the grid "located" her work in a modernist context that did not, by convention, grant access to Black women. Pindell's awareness of these social barriers must have heightened her consciousness of the grid's potential as a signifier of aesthetic intentionality and a symbol of agential authority.

In addition to conceptualizing the grid as a tool for positioning her work in relation to modernisms, Pindell also embraced the cartographic valence of the structure as a symbol of both location and movement. The grid opened the symbolic possibility of remapping an artistic terrain parsed by racial and gender ideologies. Pindell's theory of the grid as a resource resonates with McKittrick's observation that cartographic rules are socially produced and alterable, that "there exists a terrain through which different geographic stories can be and are told." In response to dominant cultural discourse rendering Black subjects "ungeographic," Pindell developed her own theory of the grid as a source of energy. Her grid, a visualization of a universe in motion, countered the normative functions of longitudinal and latitudinal lines as methods of locating subjects in geographic space. McKittrick has observed that Black women have utilized the malleability of cartographic rules in order to struggle against "geographies of domination" that place them in positions of subjugation. Pindell's early modernist practice functions as a gesture of "saying place"—an enunciation that defied the ways in which others had located her.[90]

CONCLUSION

Pindell arrived in Harlem in 1969 with hope that the Studio Museum was "the place" for her in the Manhattan art world; instead, Spriggs directed her to the predominantly white downtown galleries and museums where she knew, as a Black woman, she would not be welcome. In addition to expressing the view that abstraction belonged to white men and in white institutions, Spriggs's rebuke of Pindell's modernist practice reflects a conviction deeply held in the New York artistic milieu of that era, that "my abstract painting is a proxy for my self-hood."[91] While Pindell and other Black artists pursued abstraction for its openness, critics nonetheless often evaluated their artistic propositions according to a distinctly racialized set of criteria.

Despite criticism, from 1968 to 1973, Pindell created several dozen striking abstract compositions that integrated the circle, delicately drawn grids, and fields of color applied with a spray-paint gun. Through this work, she rejected a fixed position, troubling the ways in which both Black cultural and modernist discourses have construed the relationship between form and subjectivity. Within Pindell's formal cosmology, circles and lines have the potential to operate symbolically as part of a violent system of social ordering and to speak to childhood pastimes. However, they also have the capacity to demarcate the effects of "primary" forces, which organize the universe on the levels of astrophysics and microbiology, shaping planets, microbes, and atoms. The broad swaths of conceptual terrain between these modes of signification constitutes an important site of inquiry in Pindell's art, a trajectory she used both to reject external attempts to locate her in established racial-aesthetic models and to reflect on her displacement from would-be art world resources. A perceived tension between the aesthetic choices Pindell made in these years and the politics of her later career has led to a scholarly blind spot around her engagement with modernisms. In fact, Pindell adopted institutionally sanctioned modernist idioms as part of a politically charged refusal to abide racially exclusionary aesthetic protocols.

Art-historical scholarship continues, at times, to suppress the ways in which Black American artists of this period worked across formal and sociohistorical concerns and rejected the idea that the two are mutually exclusive.[92] The first years of Pindell's career illuminate the ongoing need for scholars to give careful attention to how artists have defied the cultural conversations that framed their labors, generating practices that exceed the conceptual and aesthetic terms handed down through cultural institutions. Her strategic, informed, and at times sidelong approach to modernisms urges a reconsideration of how artists in this era imagined the dynamic relationship between their abstract artworks and their subjectivity.

Pindell had something to say about—and through—modernism. She expressed it repeatedly, through great effort, and at the risk of no one responding, or looking. At the beginning of the 1970s, she negotiated the tightrope of artistically addressing both abstract idioms and her sense of self as a Black woman. They were part of what she found when she looked "inward," and what she made as she moved through the world. In doing so, she created formulations of space and place that moved modernisms, defying the boundaries that had displaced her artistic vision.

The abstract paintings that Pindell made in her initial years in Manhattan also laid the groundwork for her aesthetic and material explorations of the next two decades. In particular, the circle and the grid continued to play significant roles in her career. Within a few years, both would become tactile. Rather than staining her rounds into a canvas, Pindell would lift them from her works, hole-punching paper scraps to create densely textured collages. The irregularities of her handmade grids would eventually materialize as the warp and weft of handwoven strips of textiles. For the remainder of the 1970s, Pindell's oeuvre explicitly rearticulated the putatively optical as the inherently tactile. She launched this intervention with collaged works on paper that reconfigure the tedium of administrative labor, generating a "pleasurable" feminist practice.

2 • Paper Work

Howardena Pindell completed a spray-painted canvas in 1973 that, at first glance, largely resembles the nearly two dozen she had made over the course of the previous three years. Deep maroons and violets serve as backdrop to thin layers of pastel blues, greens, and yellows in an untitled painting dated 1972–73 (fig. 36). The resulting high-contrast dappling makes the example one of the more visually dynamic of this body of work. This painting also contains Pindell's first use in the medium of a technique that would become paradigmatic of her oeuvre—collage. Paper chads affixed to the surface of the canvas repeat the rounds of color comprising what she called her paintings' "veils of dots."[1] Several dozen of the paper cutouts stipple the upper half of the canvas and extend downward on the right-hand side. Whereas earlier examples of the atmospheric stained paintings generate a sense of pictorial recession, the chads in this work draw greater attention to the literal fact of the painting's surface. Sitting atop the diaphanous field of color stain, they break the illusion that the painting's constituent materials had dissolved into purely visual phenomena.

This painting launched Pindell's decades-long abstract collage practice. Although the circle and the grid would continue to serve as the foundational structures of her oeuvre, with collage she stretched the ambitions of the artistic project she had initiated in 1968. A close look at Pindell's collage practice reveals the stakes of her "mending" operations—her tedious collage techniques, drawn from handicraft and administrative labor, offered a method for connecting with her body and asserting her authorship in defiance of the everyday erasures of her experiences as a Black woman artist and curator.

Over the course of the 1970s, I argue, collage became the single most significant element of Pindell's practice, the aspect she explored most deeply, and whose lessons she applied most diligently to her production. In 1973, she began gluing orderly chads flat onto graph paper, using collage as an instrument of categorical precision in over two dozen works that participated in conceptual art's bureaucratic themes. The same year, she began making collage works that engage with postminimalist concerns for repetition with variation, textured,

Detail, fig. 36.

handworked surfaces, and neutral colors. Powdered paper accretions pile on mat board and stumble over string in gravity-defying formations. Pindell used collage in similar ways in densely textured paintings throughout the 1970s and 1980s. Over the course of this period, she made dozens of increasingly colorful and chaotically composed works on paper that belie the meticulous processes she used to fabricate them. Pindell also would return eventually to figuration through collage: she used the technique in her photographic series *Video Drawings* (1973–76) to meld televisual broadcast imagery and an idiosyncratic notation system.

"Collage" denotes a wide variety of techniques. Its most common current day usage, and the one I invoke here, refers to both a method for adhering elements to a larger surface, which is often though not necessarily two-dimensional, and to the resulting collaged object. Though collage and assemblage share many features, including transformation, or recycling everyday materials and recontextualizing them as fine art, assemblage often takes a sculptural form and lacks a single ground, or surface. This distinction, though not absolute, locates these practices differently in relation to modernist discourses about painting and sculpture.

Variably claimed as a method of production, an aesthetic, and, occasionally, a medium, collage capaciously accommodates imagery and materials from disparate sources. Artists in the United States in the postwar era—notably Romare Bearden, Jasper Johns, Lee Krasner, and Betye Saar—turned to collage at pivotal moments in their careers. Like European cubists earlier in the century, they embraced it as a technique of collapsing distinctions between "high" and "low" culture. Insofar as collage scholars theorize it as a medium, a method of artistic production with its own internal logic, they cite juxtaposition—heightened visual, conceptual, and material contrast—as its defining rationale.[2]

With her introduction of collage to the surface of her canvases, Pindell cast aside her allegiance to the medium specificity that she had explored in her spray-painted works, but nonetheless remained deeply invested in the era's expanding modernist aesthetics. Collage opened her practice to a range of sources beyond the institutional modernisms she had explored, as she drew on the aesthetics of Ghanaian textiles and handiwork historically associated with women. However, Pindell continued through the 1970s to articulate this expanded artistic vocabulary with abstraction, couching these new sources in conceptual and post-minimalist idioms.

In contrast to artists such as Saar, who embraced a "junk art" aesthetic that explicitly incorporated found objects that remained identifiable in their new context, Pindell sublimated her collaged materials in allover abstract compositions. For instance, her untitled collage of 1974 presents a pale pink and beige field of delicately lifted rounds (fig. 37). Pindell tediously hand-numbered these individual chads in black ink, pinning them to her work surface with a needle or nail while she wrote. When she began working in this way, she initially numbered the chads sequentially, starting with single digit numerals, but eventually "gave up" and "just started numbering."[3] However, most works appear to contain a sequential set of numbers, with occasional repetitions; this example includes numbers over one thousand. She then applied the chads to the surface of the collage, randomly selecting them without concern for their digits. Subtle variations in the translucency of the pencil eraser–sized circles, the black gestural marks of the numbers, and a thin layer of powder atop the densely textured collage render the composition, which measures a humble eight inches across, a microcosm of understated abstract drama. To put a fine point on it, through squinted eyes, the collage resembles an ornate abstract expressionist painting in miniature. The paradoxically lush and restrained postminimalist aesthetic of the collage camouflages the specificity of its material means—the bureaucratic detritus produced by a hole punch.

Collage offers a productive angle onto histories of twentieth-century art because it has been central to institutional modernism and the resistance to it. As art historian Kellie Jones has argued, early in the twentieth century, Euro-American artists approached collage and assemblage as a set of practices without prior authorial claims. These artists, mostly white men, drew freely from the collage practices developed for centuries by non-Western makers, untrained artists, and women, mining these apparently authorless cultural formations for the "raw material" of their vaunted artistic careers. The cultural reckoning that accompanied the social liberation movements of the 1960s offered some resistance to this unchecked appropriation. By the 1970s, narratives espoused by proponents of Euro-American formalist modernisms, African American modernist art, and feminist art all traced their origins to collage. Postmodernism too, despite supposedly being a repudiation of modernism, shares the structuring metaphor of collage.[4] How is it that the technique has been so foundational to both modernism and to artistic formations that have issued challenges to it?

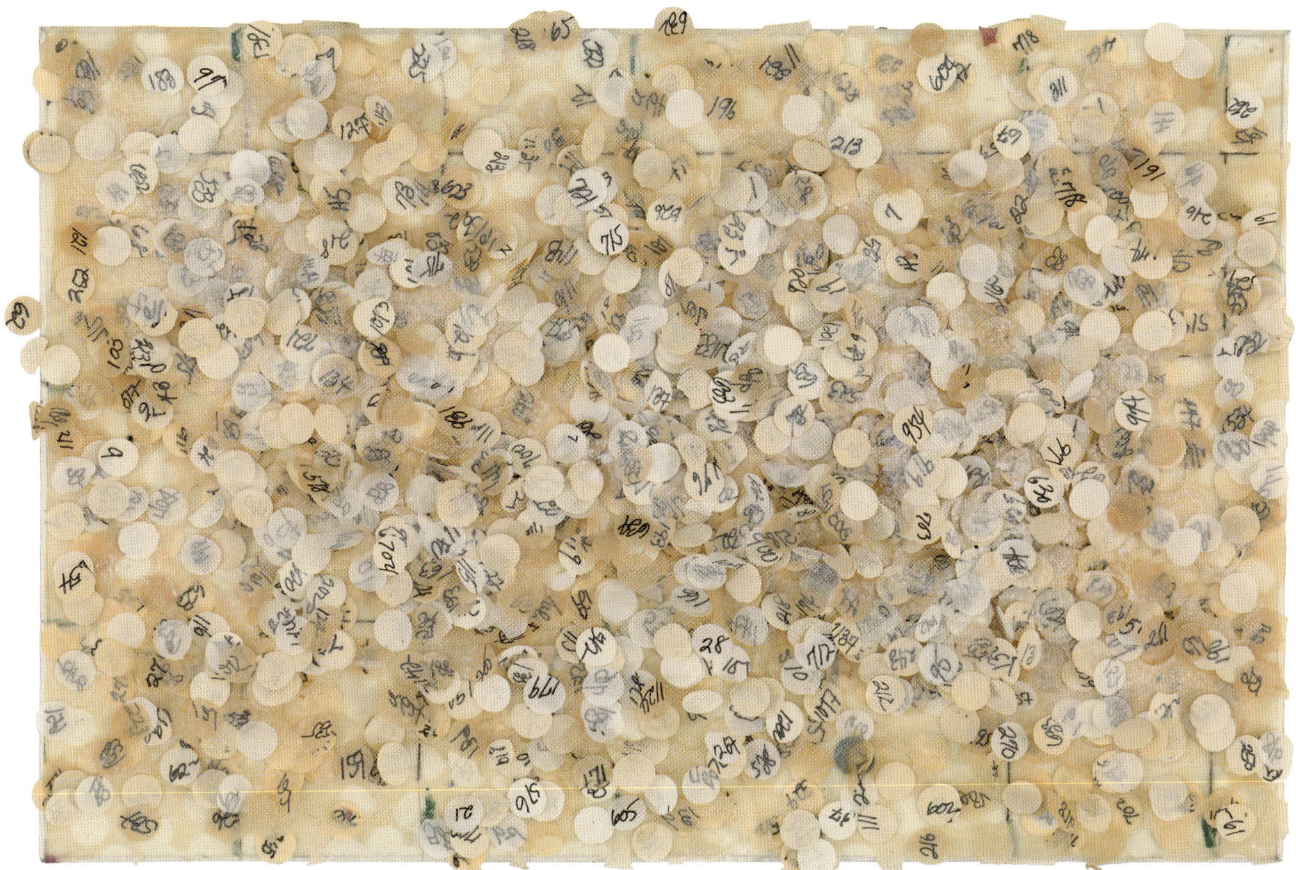

Many of these disparate accounts of collage hinge the technique's significance on its purported capacity to metaphorize aspects of modern life through
formal qualities such as fracture and disjuncture.[5] African diasporic and feminist narratives in particular note the resonances between collage's formal and
conceptual juxtapositions and the lived experiences of minoritarian subjects.
As feminist art critic Lucy Lippard has argued, "It is a collage experience to be
a woman artist or a sociopolitical artist in a capitalist culture." Other scholars,
such as literary critic Gwen Raaberg, have emphasized the ways in which artists in culturally marginalized groups have developed strategies for drawing on
collage's features—for instance, its pictorial malleability.[6] This approach tempers
what in the art-historical record occasionally veers into naturalized connections
between the technique and social marginality by underscoring the agency of artists of color and women. While narratives about collage as an artistic strategy for
redressing social marginalization tend to center on figuration, Pindell's abstract
practice points to the aesthetic variety of African diasporic and feminist engagements with the technique, challenging institutional modernism's exclusionary
claim to abstraction.

This chapter examines how Pindell approached collage in the 1970s as a site from which to build a practice that pulled from bureaucratic aesthetics and Black, feminist, and modernist cultural formations. With collage, I contend, she found an ideal strategy for engaging what art historian Mary Schmidt Campbell has called the "multiple inheritances" of Black American culture. This term recognizes how Black Americans have navigated the contradictions of a national cultural tradition that contains both the stultifying imperatives of the white mainstream and the possibilities and promises of Black liberation projects. Particularly in her collaged paintings, Pindell combined unexpected materials, such as cat hair and paper scraps. She hole-punched, attached string, and dusted powder onto the surfaces of her collaged works. In both the works on paper and paintings, she created protuberant surfaces inspired by sources including childhood games and conceptualist accounting. Like many Black American artists, she drew on cultural resources—Akan textiles of West Africa, feminist reclamations of women's handiwork, conceptual art's bureaucratic aesthetic—that, taken together, "[confounded] the taxonomies of conventional art," even in a period when the unconventional became routine.[7]

Pindell's approach to collage exemplifies the technique's ability to hold different things together. Through her collage practice, she both owned and disavowed modernism. For instance, she has credited an instructor in her graduate program at Yale, Knox Martin, with introducing her to collage as a potential method of producing large-scale abstract works in the mid-1960s.[8] In this context, collage presented a decidedly modernist strategy for engaging questions about surface. However, Pindell's first use of collage in painting coincided with a broader, decisive shift in her work typically understood in opposition to modernisms. She embraced collage in response to encounters with West African textiles and her entry into feminist artistic circles, especially the group at the women's collective A.I.R. Gallery.

Through these formative engagements, Pindell began to view collage as much more than a method of exploring surface as a modernist; she approached it as a vehicle for a discursive promiscuity that could blur the boundaries between her abstract practice and her activist concerns. Pindell used collage as a way to bring together aspects of her life that often felt fractured and disjointed—her experiences as a Black woman in the feminist movement and on the margins of the Black Power movement, and her status as an artist surrounded at the Museum of Modern Art (MoMA) by coworkers whose artistic careers had gone "dormant." In her hands, collage became a haptic, labor-intensive tool with which to address how specific formal problems intersected with constraints imposed by gendered and racial bias. Pindell explored, for instance, the assumptions about labor imposed by an aesthetics of administration in conceptualist practices of the early 1970s.[9] Through her collage practice, she critiqued how debates about feminist and bureaucratic labor in the 1970s elided the authorship of Black women in the same moment that the feminist movement became appropriated by white, college-educated women.

Both this chapter and the next consider the contributions Pindell made to U.S. postminimalist art and abstraction. Through the new materials and processes she introduced to her practice with collage, she launched a decades-long investigation into questions about Black women's labor and the possibilities of an African diasporic aesthetic. Strikingly, Pindell conceived of collage as a source of embodied pleasure. The technique, for her, held the possibility of "visceral" enjoyment.[10] This theory of collage as pleasurable stood in tension with the tedious labor needed to produce collage effects. Pindell developed this artistic-therapeutic practice as a way to cope with the difficulties of her workaday life. With the technique, she increasingly incorporated insights gleaned from her lived experiences as a Black, white-collar woman artist into her practice. Pindell innovated a Black feminist approach to collage; in her hands, the technique became a method of mending rather than a metaphor merely for fragmentation.

COLLAGE WORK

Collage has been recruited to perform all kinds of work for competing cultural camps. Modernist, African diasporic, and feminist artistic discourses enlisted collage throughout the twentieth century to articulate defining cultural ambitions. Once regarded as a frivolous, feminine pastime, collage technique momentarily ascended to a privileged position in accounts of the development of modernist Western art in the 1950s. For instance, in his 1959 essay "Collage," art critic Clement Greenberg discussed cubist artists Georges Braque and Pablo Picasso's purported "invention" of collage between 1907 and 1914. Greenberg claimed this innovation catalyzed the inevitable progression of modernist art toward its defining characteristic—a dynamic tension between flatness and pictorial recession.[11] His argument erased the widespread use of collage aesthetic and techniques by artists in non-Western cultures, women artists, and folk artists prior to the early twentieth century. Greenberg's commentary epitomizes midcentury modernist criticisms' proprietorial stance toward artistic innovation.

Artists in the early twentieth century turned to collage to thematize juxtaposition and difference. For instance, those working in cubist and dada circles in the 1910s and 1920s drew on its inherent capacity to inject everyday materials into the rarefied realm of so-called elite art. Some dada uses of collage and later surrealist experimentations generated psychological effects, using the technique's dissonances to address social crisis. Through juxtaposition and fragmentation, artists aimed to undermine conventional associations and shock the viewer "into a perception of a new reality—social, political, and psychological, as well as aesthetic." For instance, artist Max Ernst's dada collages morbidly address the moral absurdity of life in postwar Germany by producing hybrid creatures that combine humanoid and animal forms.[12]

Collage posed a danger to modernists invested in the maintenance of cultural and social hierarchies. In 1912, cubist painters Albert Gleizes and Jean Metzinger recognized that emergent forms of abstraction, which drew on collage aesthetics, problematically blurred the boundaries between design and art. Thus, they asserted, collage could muddle crucial distinctions between inspired artistic production and the rote machinations of merely skilled laborers. Gleizes's and Metzinger's historical theorizations of the "decorative" would inform Greenberg's abandonment of collage over the course of the 1960s, when he espoused modernist theories increasingly predicated on the separation of art from the outside world. Painting supplanted collage as the preeminent modernist medium, for unlike collage, its material means need not point to a broader sociohistorical milieu.[13] Collage's associations with craft and feminine pastimes prevailed by the 1960s. This shift in critical understanding occurred despite the widespread acknowledgment that collage's application to fine art contexts had been a necessary step in the development of Euro-American modernisms.

From her position at MoMA, Pindell encountered a range of modernist engagements with collage spanning the early twentieth century to her contemporary moment. She assisted with preparations for the 1968 exhibition *Dada, Surrealism, and Their Heritage,* curated by William Rubin, which prominently featured collage works. Several years into her curatorial career, in 1974, she looked to a later generation of modernists engaged with principles of collage in her own exhibition. Pindell organized *Printed, Cut, Folded, and Torn,* a show that presented textured works from the Department of Prints and Illustrated Book's collection. Her notably diverse selections included an untitled work by Alan Shields featuring interwoven strips of stitched paper, prints by Lucio Fontana with punched and pierced holes, folded paper works by Sam Gilliam, and collaged prints by Louise Nevelson.[14]

Pindell's own collage practice as she organized *Printed, Cut, Folded, and Torn* involved processes of puncture and layering. She punched and pasted materials onto graph paper and mat board. *Untitled #2* (1973), a work now in

1010 5718 3744 116 198 217 430 400 358 325 235 588 300 360 339 302 176 26 459 404 408 405 544 542 1416 438 1221 1433 1008 533 1613 209 451 1744 1677 1689 422 997 520
5775 5620 0802 117 243 317 240 632 153 170 124 451 272 226 380 235 1000 413 240 54 765 589 515 681 1415 854 815 457 1411 1488 626 734 1571 1883 1369 224 1044 835 109
1022 1200 5801 178 102 209 104 291 511 404 131 014 0885 51 1046 0880 326 302 111 401 466 519 584 475 703 1660 860 1752 657 666 746 527 1245 1028 180 933 591 1103 593
15106 15114 0835 657 0886 177 40 228 290 305 222 248 394 0572 108 303 200 390 236 584 527 163 455 588 789 601 574 576 1580 1189 1051 825 1243 1366 1404 915 1624 1153 875
15789 15274 15210 188 6048 448 205 759 325 215 397 0862 202 403 415 288 397 282 100 416 461 547 437 453 1170 1098 600 618 1652 1411 513 761 1016 673 1453 1093 1853 1971 784
5116 1852 1388 121 168 250 419 745 153 520 341 492 573 231 446 226 180 5288 155 419 411 421 640 412 1040 745 593 774 592 657 1528 1600 1442 1055 573 775 714 771 516
0847 1546 5100 1074 193 499 262 249 251 313 213 402 376 789 134 295 585 228 256 488 512 550 626 765 1611 1083 1170 1133 1736 728 841 620 612 1371 1410 823 673 1760 577
457 355 412 436 385 381 389 197 16 185 214 446 199 211 367 423 279 187 351 480 413 403 527 485 1083 1402 186 648 1114 624 758 1010 701 668 143 657 1567 1445 1162
191 82 190 259 363 158 204 210 195 105 283 1085 588 264 214 0008 444 178 247 411 515 573 475 561 1743 700 1113 512 839 700 101 1620 1616 703 1544 1670 1575 411 643
457 411 586 219 243 396 266 212 478 106 118 1000 891 189 588 234 185 588 270 500 525 570 404 588 1024 1586 737 1603 1477 826 709 1223 610 524 1688 1289 843 516 573
467 83 446 426 359 370 216 330 462 446 1008 313 581 348 165 23 761 581 445 660 431 53 918 806 1557 1461 1089 810 1577 805 587 1201 885 565 519 825 1244
0889 1886 110 387 1080 380 449 292 478 273 284 405 543 1820 1583 334 14 338 1638 660 410 469 420 426 651 1046 636 658 1622 1126 1362 614 1104 770 1131 710 1039 1489
409 15101 112 465 1520 468 1520 466 186 1612 289 200 281 439 322 442 1820 584 201 555 485 630 843 628 945 116 1151 809 482 973 585 911 1268 891 750 867 908 571 1266
303 464 760 162 331 430 472 297 278 1512 453 52 151 275 189 107 286 375 369 479 467 471 129 588 807 961 807 1684 1713 1208 625 1489 1161 1343 1067 608 820 719 116
1576 171 335 186 401 208 206 388 1922 173 1575 28 196 125 379 1521 163 208 536 544 322 530 485 589 614 564 713 1518 1325 798 1485 1489 1238 1249 1716 1570 1637 1523 709
175 257 200 268 352 1589 0874 258 137 443 263 020 1008 1582 317 316 227 5683 444 451 446 784 428 477 629 599 865 551 1635 901 287 151 882 760 1766 903 858 1445 1162
15845 15851 080 202 141 112 5297 444 157 382 221 350 135 586 457 544 480 474 555 568 488 493 500 541 1112 1558 944 1023 1169 930 907 1089 1348 1224 1635 1110 748 1702 1775
192 174 241 339 160 252 239 1513 1620 1679 454 359 1884 253 15103 574 490 490 421 523 51 491 123 724 902 605 942 1213 58 1300 1004 680 701 962 640 1137 853 528
1580 124 1084 441 395 368 704 225 332 277 404 311 166 1628 1682 583 445 473 473 683 40 459 365 899 1570 1164 677 1420 670 1688 161 603 104 1123 1488 1488 1109 987
123 141 329 112 74 65 124 413 1083 500 319 1770 342 899 38 508 418 527 442 464 508 781 511 153 566 1238 730 786 1474 1026 54 919 442 588 1822 1454 1748 1043
357 1544 1026 1881 36 287 341 56 298 447 304 642 50 141 183 432 440 440 553 44 520 58 441 661 544 413 759 78 1714 980 1333 1569 857 1473 1703 1029 582 164
181 344 174 219 399 1585 185 210 306 223 293 448 1571 1023 18 483 741 782 58 444 420 640 473 539 1644 846 853 682 1174 1303 608 569 776 0457 1069 732 776 977 158
1585 446 0804 101 152 48 254 224 244 299 388 1585 1507 204 372 554 1447 072 582 472 577 562 482 958 867 1646 1601 781 153 544 863 1735 465 1398 804 1668 166 1574 1889
314 447 458 268 336 169 1085 1845 119 120 347 146 143 336 0944 993 616 15 475 563 583 884 570 614 972 1510 1447 687 778 1292 1285 518 655 1332 118 916 924 2145
220 157 1580 1707 174 1885 217 28 346 1570 456 129 235 167 1624 448 571 343 804 449 569 1443 467 777 126 389 1112 888 1172 1604 600 1402 1366 997 1622 1730 1658 419
408 208 239 448 0886 294 309 404 105 1038 0837 40 230 157 1577 430 135 502 446 446 799 557 858 1183 1924 944 1090 606 1171 542 770 524 1715 1415 787 2063 2091 1880
1008 166 113 232 571 315 130 184 1088 765 1590 215 280 431 22 58 441 462 550 804 527 536 515 1185 1440 1108 1607 1647 806 1473 1312 824 796 1765 1878 2088 2040 2195
447 340 346 1585 341 44 378 856 140 510 1583 2140 29 1544 378 490 486 474 470 451 506 521 186 1117 1162 720 783 519 1448 1557 614 1755 1400 228 2134 2193 1885 220
1534 1656 1019 86 926 1679 796 1452 1563 768 671 585 1248 478 925 1771 664 682 973 558 595 458 446 830 991 663 1154 1744 668 609 1281 997 5051 363 8010 5577 3005 3108
1563 1464 627 1578 607 433 1439 1641 69 1066 1064 453 852 1847 1661 678 1199 1064 1715 913 604 963 928 595 707 1008 1229 1550 1443 1605 1591 1577 3100 3477 321 362 2142 37
773 139 1456 1417 1391 1208 1589 120 760 1234 1200 1046 761 1665 575 996 1500 648 954 1525 1384 195 762 801 943 121 1732 1687 530 1687 491 1158 1911 3469 1768 3019 3004 37
943 807 876 1536 1123 1005 270 1574 1582 703 1238 892 210 1288 760 288 934 910 1278 906 666 134 574 831 988 764 1544 1783 850 1548 646 3960 651 3164 3134 3046 3095 27

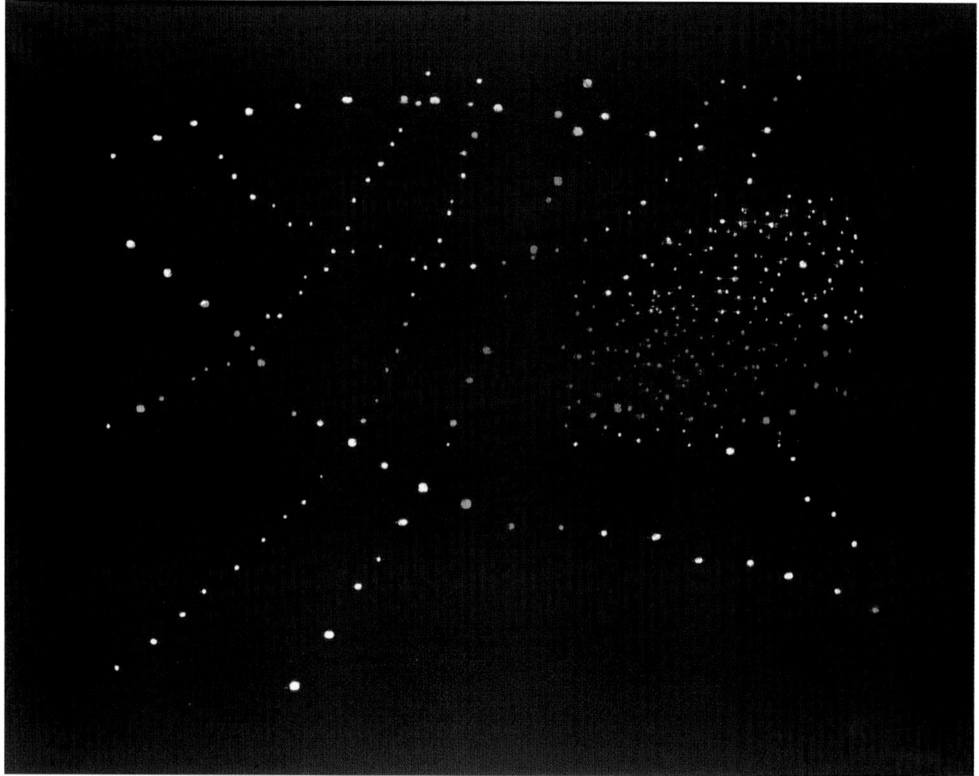

Fig. 39. Lucio Fontana, *Concetto spaziale* (Spatial concept), 1950. Oil on canvas, perforated, 32 × 39½ in. (81 × 100 cm). Musée d'Art Moderne et Contemporain, Saint-Etienne, France, AM1979–27. On deposit from the Centre Pompidou.

the collection of the Metropolitan Museum of Art, is typical of the graph paper collages (fig. 38). Pindell generated the paper rounds pasted onto her collages by hole-punching cardstock and other thick papers. She excised some of these chads from the stencils she used in her production of spray-painted color field paintings. Her manner of working with collage evokes the repetition of form in the spray-painted compositions, but with a difference. In those earlier works, two substances (color and canvas) merge to generate a unified surface. Here, Pindell layers a single substance (paper). Her collages challenge the distinction between the artwork's surface and its surface marks differently than her spray-painted works did. Paper constitutes both ground and the form atop it.

Many of the prints on view in *Printed, Cut, Folded, and Torn,* like Pindell's early collages, disrupt the two-dimensional picture plane through the use of excision. For instance, works on paper and paintings in Fontana's punctured series *Concetto spaziale* (Spatial concept) (1947–68) likewise deploy the repeated round to destabilize the singularity of the artwork's surface (fig. 39). Pindell avoided printmaking during her years as a curator of prints and illustrated books, in order to avoid what she called a "conflict of interest."[15] Nonetheless, the exhibition shows her exploring some of the formal and material concerns of her artistic practice through her curatorial work. She expanded the modernist category "print" by approaching the department's collection through the collage protocols of cutting, folding, and tearing.

It was not only a modernist, Euro-American model of collage that Pindell encountered at MoMA and drew from in her early engagements with the technique. Her exposure in the early 1970s to objects from a wide range of African cultural contexts also influenced her use of collage. The technique plays a prominent role in canonical accounts of African American art history as well, and many scholars have assigned it special status as a distinctly African diasporic medium. For instance, art historian Patricia Hills has argued that a generation of African American artists who came of age in the 1930s and 1940s, including Bearden and Jacob Lawrence, used collage to situate their practices in relation to European modernisms, their African ancestry, and localized cultural practices. They adapted cubist collage techniques developed by early twentieth-century European modernists, "knowing full well that those artists had themselves been influenced by African art."[16] These artists' embrace of the cross-cultural flows of Western culture reflected in part the model of philosopher and cultural critic Alain Locke. In these same decades, he advocated for regionalist art and the first self-consciously racial art movement in the United States.[17]

Bearden and Lawrence, according to Hills, each drew in their use of collage technique from "personal art histories." These included southern cultural practices such as quilting and the papering of domestic walls with newspapers and magazines. Bearden and Lawrence held positions of reverence in African American New York artistic circles of the 1960s and 1970s. A cohort of artists whose practices developed in these years, such as Benny Andrews and Faith Ringgold, expanded these artists' imagery and engaged more directly with subject matter such as African textiles. For Hills, what unites these generations is a commitment to paying "homage to a way of life that sees virtue in improvisation and in making do."[18]

Other art historians have focused on African American artists' use of collage as a strategy for addressing specific formal and conceptual problems. Kobena Mercer has argued that Bearden's embrace of collage in 1964 constituted a pivotal breakthrough that "answered a deep structural dilemma for African American artists" around issues of race, racism, and representation (fig. 40). That dilemma emanated from the prescriptive demands placed on non white artists to work in a "representative" way that would reflect the aspirations of African Americans as a group. In Bearden's hands, collage offered a possible way out of this "burden of representation" by pointing simultaneously to an anti-essential Black identity and the cross-cultural borrowings at the root of modernism. He achieves this in works that leave visibly torn seams between collaged source material drawn from popular magazines and art books. According to Mercer, these juxtapositions of African sculptures and documentary photography speak to the accumulative nature of representation, of identity itself as forged through cultural materials.[19]

Pindell's earliest experimentations with collage in the late 1960s evoke Bearden's famed figurative photostat works. She encountered Bearden's work by 1968, when she met the preeminent artist during preparations for the MoMA exhibition *In Honor of Dr. Martin Luther King, Jr.*[20] In this same period, she made two figurative collages that thematize the period's heightened racial strife. Fabricated from newsprint photographs, an untitled collage of 1967 presents a disjointed urban scene structured as a series of framing gazes, although visible seams, the inconsistent scale between pictorial elements, and a vertical horizon line on the bottom left of the picture plane undermine the composition's spatial

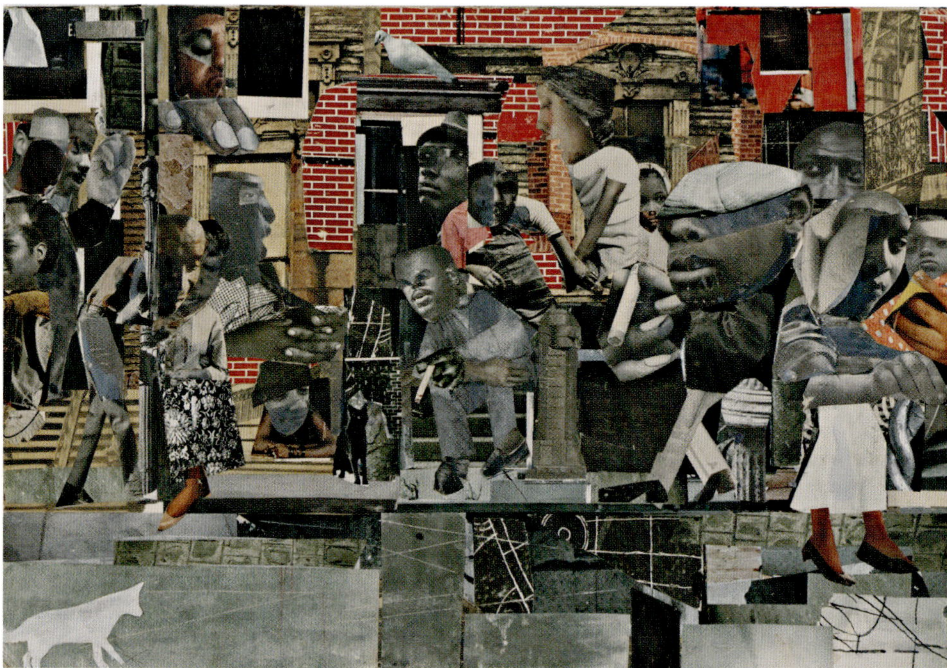

Fig. 40. Romare Bearden, *The Dove*, 1964. Cut-and-pasted printed paper, gouache, pencil, and colored pencil on board, 13⅜ × 18¾ in. (33.8 × 47.5 cm). Museum of Modern Art, New York. Blanchette Hooker Rockefeller Fund.

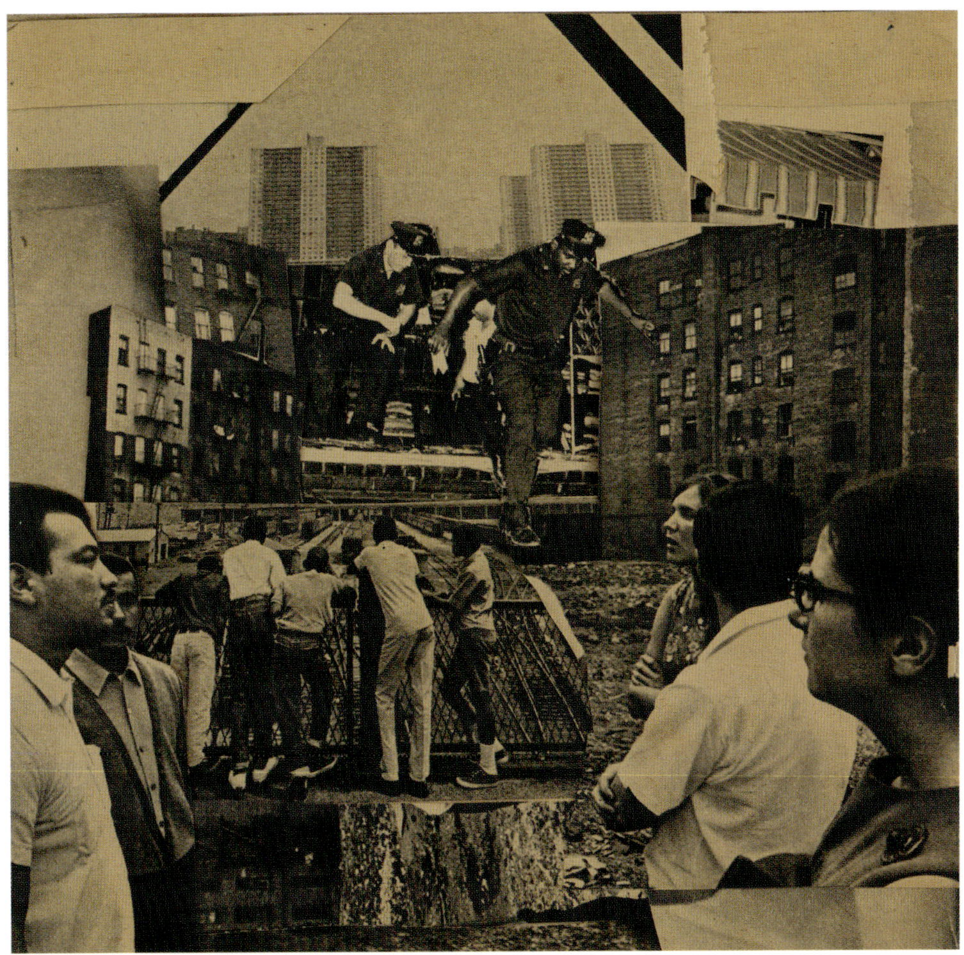

coherence (fig. 41). In the outermost register, two clusters of adults stand in an
empty lot surrounded by high-rise buildings. The adults, some identifiably white,
face one another, as if conferring. They flank five Black teenagers who stand
with their backs turned to the camera as they lean against a fence to gaze at a
set of railroad tracks, unaware of the scene unfolding directly above them. Here,
just above the center of the composition, two uniformed police officers, a Black
officer leading a white officer, hurriedly exit a structure. Together, these figures
form a circuit—the gazes of the adults and of the adolescents and the implied
movement of the officers—evocative of the racialized systems of surveillance and
policing that undergird U.S. anti-Black racism.

Specifically, this loop connects would-be stakeholders in the United States'
urban racial landscapes of the late 1960s. It calls up the era's rolling urban
unrest, much of which occurred at least partially in response to racist policing. The "long, hot summer of 1967" saw 159 riots in cities across the United
States, including uprisings in Black communities in Detroit and Newark. These

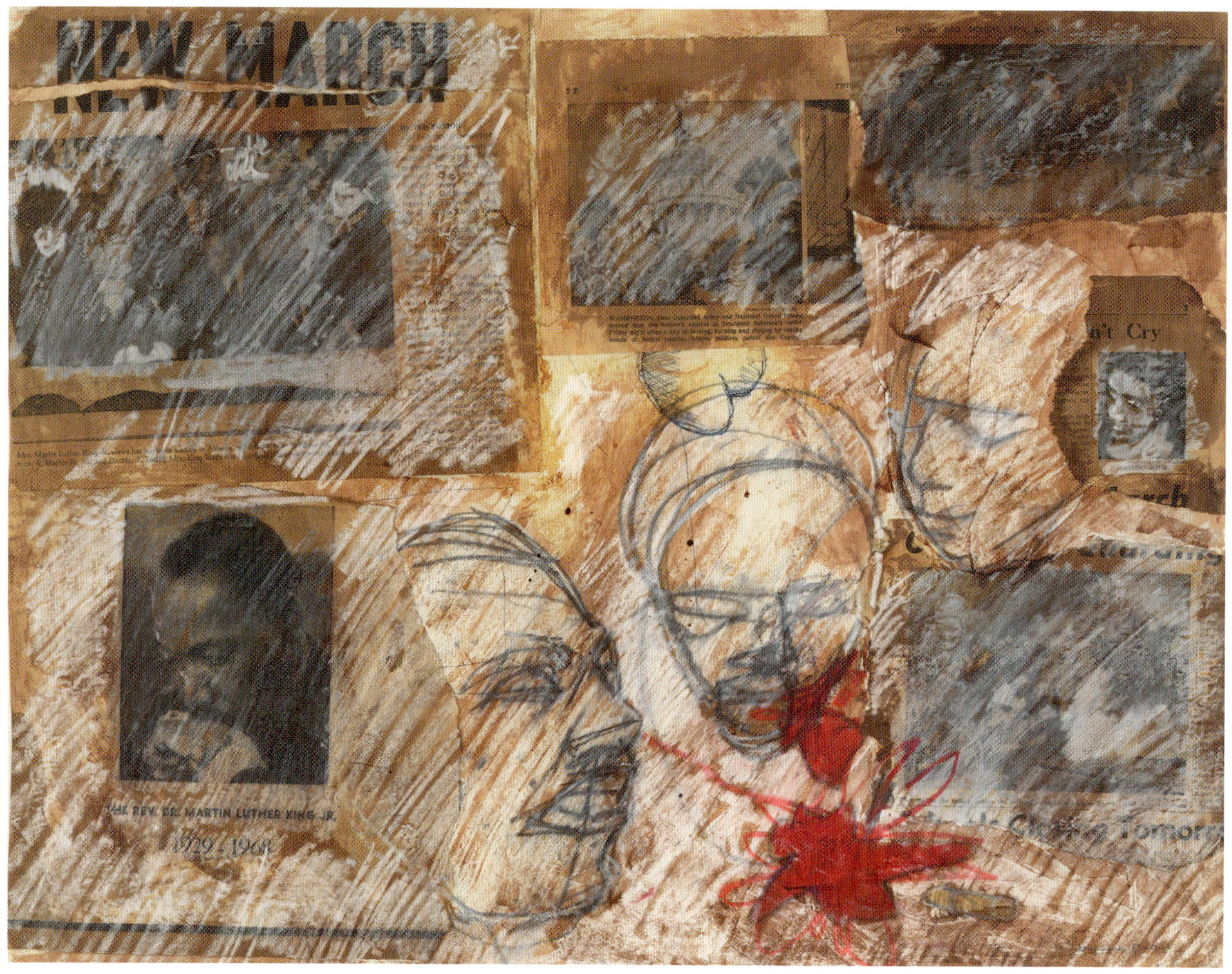

events reduced several city blocks to burned-out rubble and resulted in scores of deaths and injuries when police and National Guard officers responded to protestors with force.[21] Pindell's collage abstracts from specific historical events, but her visually dense composition nonetheless presents an urban landscape as a metonym for national racial politics in this moment. The disorienting visual junctures between compositional elements speak to factious intimacies. Prying gazes of unknown adults and the police claustrophobically frame the adolescents' train-watching. Further, these elements are each fabricated from newspapers; the city emerges from a collection of circulated representations of its inhabitants. The scene offers an ominous take on Bearden's collaged cityscapes, further underscoring how popular representations create public identities.

In another collage, *Memorial—Homage to Martin Luther King* (1968), Pindell pays tribute to the recently assassinated civil rights leader Dr. Martin Luther King, Jr. (fig. 42). A burst of red ink near a blunt sketch of the reverend's visage evokes a bullet wound as well as the sudden, puncturing violence of his death in the national psyche. In this work too, Pindell literally handles the news of the day in her creation of collage, and generates new imagery from the period's unfolding visual archive. Bearden likewise viewed collage as a tactic for entwining social content and aesthetic concerns, though the two artists' approaches to the technique vary in significant ways. In his works, Bearden disarticulates the human form by collaging individual figures from differing sources at varying scales. The boundaries between his human subjects and their environment frenetically blur in expressions of elapsed time. By contrast, Pindell's collages scramble the built environment and represent groups of figures from single-source materials.

Significantly, Pindell promptly ended her experimentations with figurative collaged elements, pursuing the technique instead through abstract idioms. In this way her project differed from artistic programs, such as Bearden's, that used collaged pictorial representation to address African diasporic identity and experience directly. Existing accounts of collage technique as an African diasporic cultural practice tend to center figuration. Pindell's case helpfully illuminates the much broader range of choices African diasporic artists have made when working with collage. Her nonrepresentational collage practice is paradigmatic of those that have issued a challenge to Euro-American modernisms' purported monopoly on abstraction.

An exhibition titled *African Textiles and Decorative Arts* catalyzed Pindell's early use of collage. The show opened at MoMA in fall 1972. Guest curated by Roy Sieber, an Africanist based at Indiana University, the exhibition presented two hundred and fifty examples of textiles, jewelry, and other objects of bodily adornment from sub-Saharan Africa. For the four-month run of the New York showing, Pindell visited the exhibition several times a week, taking advantage of the opportunity to view its galleries when they were closed to the public. There, she saw a panoply of objects, the vast majority of which were designed to be worn, held, or applied to the body—"complex woven . . . cotton and silk from Ghana and Nigeria . . . strip weave from Upper Volta" and "cosmetic accoutrements," such as "combs, hair-pins, wigs, and tweezers."[22] The show introduced her to a wide range of African cultural objects for the first time and motivated her to travel to West Africa the following year.[23]

This exposure to African art and culture profoundly affected Pindell's art-making practice, with particular consequence for her use of collage.

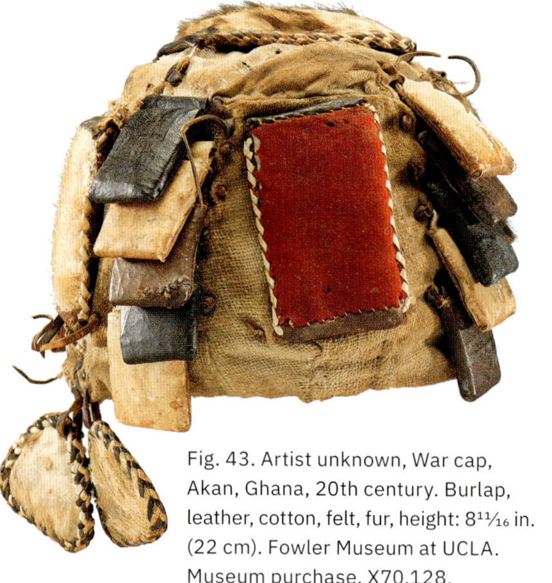

Fig. 43. Artist unknown, War cap,
Akan, Ghana, 20th century. Burlap,
leather, cotton, felt, fur, height: 8¹¹⁄₁₆ in.
(22 cm). Fowler Museum at UCLA.
Museum purchase, X70.128.

According to Pindell, her encounter in *African Textiles and Decorative Arts* with a charm- and amulet-encrusted Akan batakari, or war tunic, spurred her to experiment with dense accumulative textures (see fig. 6).[24] The tunic was displayed with its matching cap (fig. 43). Small works on mat board made shortly after the exhibition represent her first efforts at lifting collage elements off a two-dimensional surface (fig. 44). Clusters of hole-punched paper chads held together by spray adhesive and talcum powder pile on top of sewing thread that forms a grid. Several of these hole-punch scraps protrude from the board as they balance improbably on their paper-thin edges. The accretive results of Pindell's tedious fabrication process evoke, though on a smaller scale, the adherence of packets, horns, and shells to the batakari. These three-dimensional elements push the collage from the picture plane, defying the flat modernist surface in their accumulative logic.

Pindell's introduction of an intensely tactile approach to the surface of her art profoundly affected her artistic production over the course of the following decade, when she would increasingly favor loosened, hand-wrought forms. Her engagement with the textured batakari as an aesthetic model reflects a broader tendency emerging from the Black Arts movement and feminist art movement to embrace cultural inheritances that had been systemically devalued by modernist discourse. Many Black American artists turned to culturally specific ideas about "Africa" as they sought to resuscitate cultural claims suppressed in predominantly white art worlds. Textured accumulations in particular figured prominently in U.S. notions of African aesthetics. Pindell herself penned an article that cites accumulation as a distinctive trait of African art.[25]

In contrast to the figurative work many of her contemporaries produced in the pan-Africanist vein of the Black Arts movement, Pindell's lifted collages draw on West African textiles as a source of abstraction. Though such implicit engagements with Black cultural heritage remained marginalized in Black Arts discourse, they played a significant role in art in this period. For instance, Loïs Mailou Jones's prolonged study of Haitian Vodou practices propelled her use of collage to mimic the additive character of the creolized Afro-Caribbean religion's

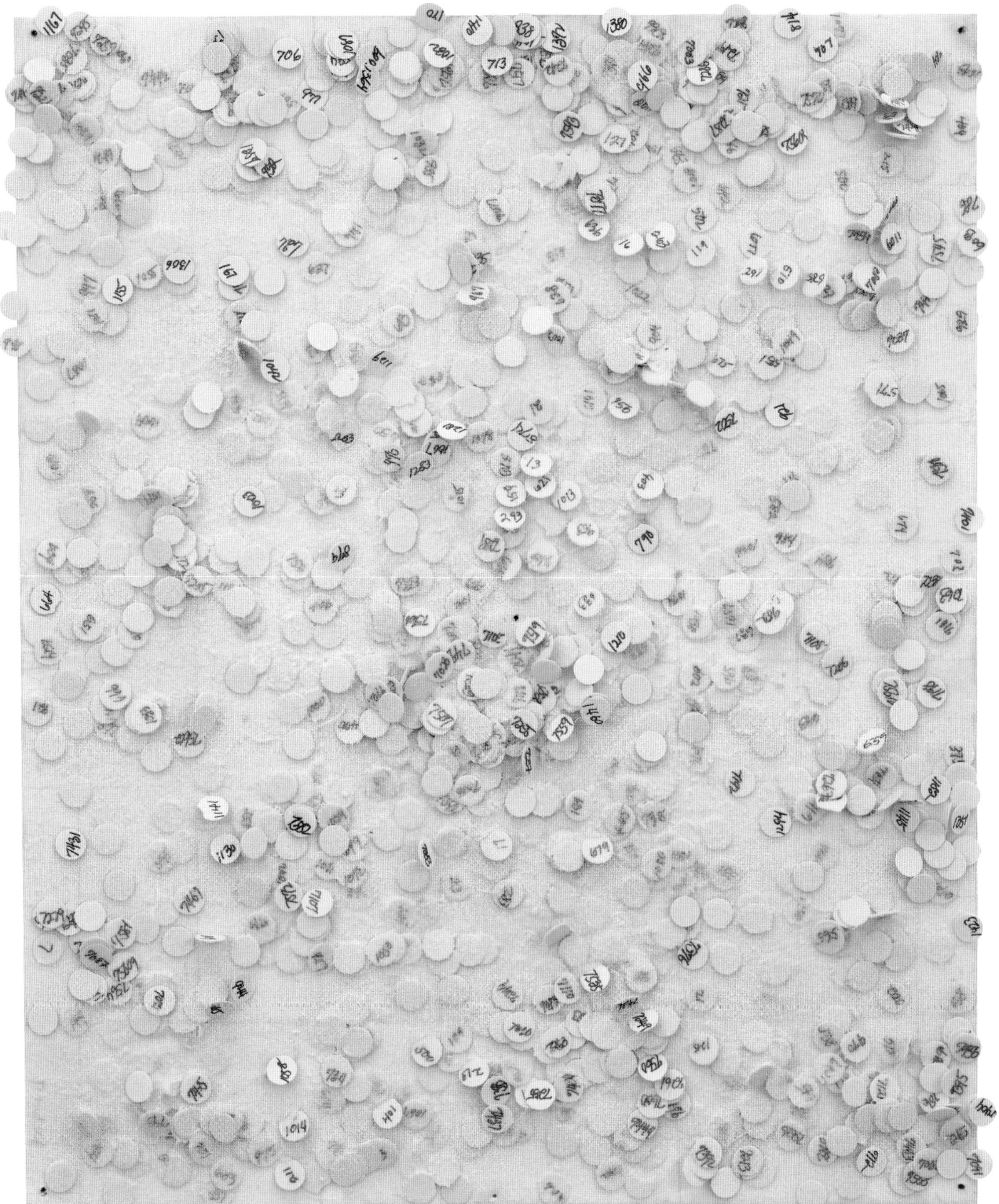

rituals. As Rebecca VanDiver has argued, Jones's Haitian collages of the 1960s evince the artist's "complex diasporic literacy" and reflect the "hybridization" of diasporic experience. Like Pindell, Jones developed an abstract, collaged idiom to investigate an affinity for an African diasporic cultural practice.[26]

Most accounts of African diasporic collage share a defining thesis—the technique's capacity for juxtaposition and fissures make it an important metaphorical resource for artists investigating the syncretic character, the "disjuncture" and "relocation," of diasporic identity.[27] African and European resources, as well as fine art and everyday visual culture, meet on the collaged surface, generating new contexts for artistic meaning in their contact. In the 1970s, feminist artists too embraced collage's ability to collect vernacular objects and images and recontextualize them as artistic material.

"WOMEN'S WORK"

Collage figured centrally in feminist critiques of art world gender politics in the 1970s. A multiracial cohort of feminist artists, including Saar, Emma Amos, Dindga McCannon, Miriam Schapiro, and Vera Simons, embraced collage as well as the related practice of assemblage, mining their associations with domesticity and resourcefulness. For some feminists, collage offered a way to celebrate women's ability throughout history to make aesthetic interventions with few material resources. Domestic handicrafts such as collage remained accessible to women throughout history because, in contrast to fine art mediums such as painting or sculpture, they require relatively little access to training or specialized materials.[28] Indeed, this accessibility to women and working-class people accounts in part for its devaluation in modernist hierarchies of art. For Pindell, too, collage offered a venue for artistic production when material realities required her to be resourceful. She, however, continued in her collaged works to participate in and critique discourses about advanced art, rather than repudiating modernist ambitions, as some feminist artists pointedly chose to do.

Pindell's most immediate artistic circles in the early 1970s included predominantly white feminist artist groups. Though painfully fraught, this white feminist "inheritance" was also artistically fruitful for Pindell. She endured the racial apathy of colleagues who chose to ignore the relevance of racism to feminist efforts. Her involvement with these groups resulted both from shared artistic concerns and from the segregated realities of her work life—the overwhelmingly white offices of MoMA served as her primary point of contact with New York art worlds in the first years of her career.

In 1972, Pindell cofounded A.I.R. Gallery, the first women's artistic collective in the country. Here, she became emboldened to embrace feminine-coded aesthetics—a consequential decision for her collage practice. Artists including Dotty

Attie, Mary Grigoriadis, Susan Williams, and Barbara Zucker had approached her, as well as thirteen other women, about establishing the cooperative. At the time, women artists were almost entirely shut out of major galleries in Manhattan. For Pindell, the group served initially as an alternative to the intimidating downtown "bar scene," a term that refers to the male-dominated artist socializing that took place in "art bars" such as the Five Spot, Dillon's, and Max's Kansas City. The camaraderie forged in these locales provided the artists who patronized them with professionally advantageous connections. Although some women artists, such as Carolee Schneemann, joined their ranks, getting "hit on" was the norm. Given these circumstances and the various domestic responsibilities that tended to burden women artists, they often undertook their practices in isolation. Lacking institutional support, many women artists, including Pindell, made and showed their work in whatever corners of their homes or borrowed spaces they could muster.[29]

Pindell helped to name the women's gallery, proposing Eyre, a reference to the self-reliant protagonist of Charlotte Brontë's famed bildungsroman. The group adapted the name to their local context, borrowing the homonym A.I.R. ("Artist in Residence") from fire codes used to designate the occupation of nonresidential buildings by artists. A.I.R.'s conveners learned of Pindell's art from critic and curator Lippard, who had included her work in the Women's Slide Registry, a collection accessible to galleries and museums with the express purpose of promoting greater inclusion of women artists in New York shows.[30]

Pindell's relationship with Lippard proved consequential in other ways as well. In fact, the artist has attributed her induction into feminist art circles to the critic. The two met at MoMA in 1967, where they worked together in a now-defunct Department of Circulating Exhibitions. In her first years at the institution, Pindell assisted Lippard, among other employees, with curatorial administration. For a period, the two worked together "almost daily," even though Lippard was not a full-time employee.[31]

According to Pindell, Lippard distinguished herself from other colleagues when early in their working relationship she "asked [her] opinion" about Max Ernst's collage studies. (Lippard worked on the aforementioned 1968 exhibition *Dada, Surrealism, and Their Heritage.*) This professional overture broke with an implicit institutional policy to exclude subordinates from any aspect of curatorial decision-making. Shortly thereafter, the critic asked to visit the young artist's studio, a request that left Pindell "in awe." Her proximity to curators, critics, and other art world power brokers rarely translated into access to their time. The majority of these professionals, in Pindell's estimation, prejudicially failed to view her as "an equal" worthy of their attention. The studio visit impressed Lippard. As a result, she included Pindell in the Women's Slide Registry and selected three of her works for inclusion in an early influential feminist exhibition, *26 Contemporary Women Artists,* held at Larry Aldrich's gallery in Ridgefield, Connecticut, in 1971.[32]

Pindell debuted her collage works at her first show at A.I.R. in January 1973, a joint exhibition with Harmony Hammond. A.I.R. served as a platform for Pindell's most pressing artistic experimentations, offering opportunities to exhibit her abstract works in Manhattan at a formative period in her career. Her contributions to the show included works on mat board as well as examples on graph paper.[33] This approach to collage, which incorporated the grid and the handmade, meshed with the predominant postminimalist aesthetic typically on display at the gallery. Broadly speaking, postminimalisms of this period tended to thematize loosened geometric forms, repetition and seriality, and tensions between handmade and industrial processes and materials. They also often favored "neutral" colors such as beige. As Hammond has noted, "Most of the work exhibited at A.I.R. was abstract, material-based and/or conceptual. The emphasis was on materials and their natural color."[34] The density of postminimalist idioms at A.I.R. reflected in part Lippard's affinity for them. She gathered many of the slides that populated the registry from which the gallery's founders drew their selections. (A.I.R. also promoted a wide range of styles, including figurative work by Judith Bernstein and Nancy Spero.)

Art critic Robert Pincus-Witten has noted that postminimalism's "relationship to the women's movement cannot be overly stressed."[35] Artists simultaneously expressed their engagement with feminist and postminimalist discourse by emphasizing process, soft materials, and the expansion of mediums. At A.I.R., Patsy Norvell's diaphanous sculptures, Rachel bas-Cohain's warped grids, and Rosemary Mayer's gauzy structures operated at the intersection of these artistic vocabularies. The gallery's unofficial visual program was instructive for Pindell, helping to shape the aesthetics of her collages when her color field paintings became impractical due to spatial and financial constraints.[36]

Collage was particularly well suited to feminist efforts of the 1970s to endow artistic projects with personally meaningful materials. Some artists, such as Hammond and Norvell, used a collage sensibility to import objects directly from their local, largely female communities and reframe them in the gallery.[37] Participation in women's consciousness-raising groups (abbreviated as "CR") motivated many artists' introduction of overtly feminine-coded content into their practices. Meeting in circles, women spoke about topics such as family obligation, work, and sex. By surfacing realms of experience previously left unspoken, CR helped to generate feminist frameworks of personal and social inquiry. Artists used these openings in their work.

Pindell participated in CR by 1972, when she reported sharing a group with Lippard. Like many of her peers, Pindell credited the supportive discussions

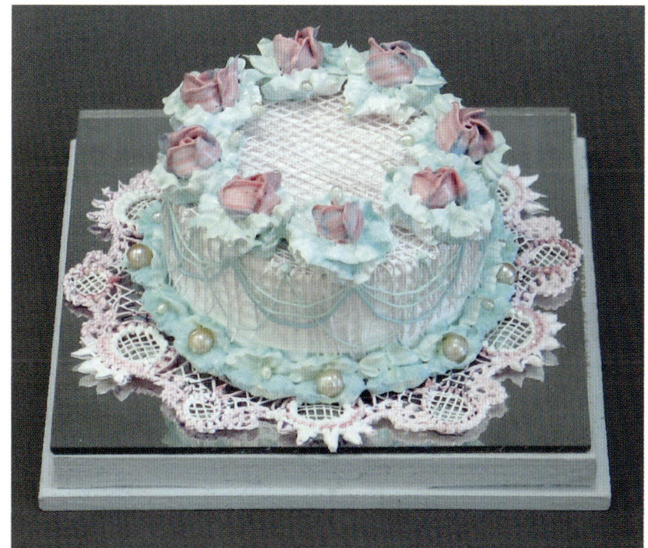

Fig. 45. Pat Lasch, *Untitled,* 1974. Acrylic, wood, mirror, and Plexiglas, 3½ × 6 × 6 × in. (8.9 × 15.2 × 15.2 cm). Meredith Ward Fine Art, New York.

that unfolded within the group as a source of artistic validation and encouragement.[38] In the years immediately following her entry into feminist groups, she incorporated materials from her everyday life into her practice—the paper scraps produced by a hole punch, sewing thread, and mat boards, which she recuperated from a dumpster at MoMA.

When feminist artists turned to autobiographically charged objects as artistic materials, they drew on much longer histories of women's engagement with collage. Women in the United States had created scrapbooks by collaging treasured memorabilia and found materials since the nineteenth century, and had employed collage aesthetics in the creation of objects such as valentines, birthday cards, and quilts for much longer. Collage connected the labors of twentieth-century artists to makers whose creations, as a consequence of sexist hierarchies, largely had been relegated to the footnotes of cultural history. In the 1970s, the technique offered a method for resuscitating "women's work," including textile-based practices and other "decorative" arts, as a site of culturally valuable creative production.

The typically intimate scale of collage, both as a method of making and as an artistic object, helped to secure its associations with feminine-coded labor. As literary theorist Naomi Schor has argued, the detail has been gendered as feminine in normative Western aesthetics, the inverse to masculine concerns for monumentality. Historically, the small scale of feminine-coded cultural practices such as collage and embroidery served socioeconomic purposes. Through delicate detail work, socially privileged women could cultivate feminine ideals such as refinement. By laboring in contained areas, sometimes their own laps, women also could quickly put aside creative endeavors in order to perform other household duties.[39] Collage could be performed with scraps of time and materials, and contained within the strictures of conventional gender roles.

In the early 1970s, when feminist artists began incorporating traditional women's work into their art, commentators noted a coincident "size race" among male artists making increasingly unwieldy sculptures and land art. Some feminist artists used collage and detail work to signal their rejection of this implicitly colonialist impulse. Artist Pat Lasch, for instance, lavishly adorned her cake-like sculptures with small baubles and beads (fig. 45). Pindell's painstakingly constructed lifted collages on mat board also plainly embraced the textured detail, even in the face of censure. One critic derided her work by asking, "Oh goodness, how many Lord's Prayers can you get on the head of a pin?" The query likens Pindell's detail work to a spectacularized display of technical skill. At the 1915 Panama–Pacific International Exposition in San Francisco, Swedish American engraver Godfrey Lundberg gained fame for exhibiting his handiwork: a gold pin with the Lord's Prayer engraved on its head. This comparison suggests that, for the critic, too much detail could undermine the status of an artwork, potentially relegating it to the realm of oddity. The admonishment reflects the modernist tenet that detail could render an artwork overly technical or "excessive"—a term that evokes stereotypes of women, especially women of color, as immoderately emotional and unrestrained.[40]

Many feminist artists critiqued hypocritical modernist narratives that championed the technique but rejected its associations with feminized practices. Saar, for instance, influentially collaged personal mementos and flea market finds in compositions that intertwined overt references to keepsake practices and the avant-garde artistic discourse of West Coast junk art. Feminist artists working with collage both accessed a historical lineage of women's art and advanced a visually recognizable critique of institutional modernisms. Some prominent white feminists viewed collage as a form of modernist disavowal. Lippard, for instance, who influentially theorized feminism as an artistic and political mode that operated outside of modernism, placed a "collage aesthetic" at the center of feminist practice.[41]

While Pindell shared with her white feminist colleagues a concern for collage's gendered associations, her engagement with the medium differed in significant ways. For her, the technique had the potential to connect her practice not only to women's history, but also to African diasporic cultural transmissions. Collage presented an opportunity to engage multiple artistic inheritances, drawing on and contributing to African diasporic, feminist, and modernist understandings of the technique. In working at this intersection, Pindell's practice echoes Black feminist lesbian poet Audre Lorde's theorizations of her own "collaged self-construction." Through the collaged genre of "biomythography," Lorde asserted her own avowedly heterogeneous identity, which she conceived as an inherent feature of Black womanhood. For Lorde, collage metaphorizes the process by which one accumulates histories, including collective memories, and assembles them into a sense of personhood. Lippard too theorized collage as a strategy for suturing the fragments of a socially fractured identity. She wrote that in feminists' hands, "Collage is born of interruption and the healing instinct to use political consciousness as a glue with which to get the pieces into some sort of new order."[42]

Pindell's collage practice asserts the technique as a discursive method of mending—a way to bring together aspects of her life in the face of social fragmentation. With collage, she could place this, plus that, on the same surface, articulating her collage experience as a Black feminist modernist. Her use of the technique to draw together African diasporic, feminist, and modernist conversations illuminates the flows between these practices, particularly the foundational, if suppressed, roles that work by Black and women artists have played in the formation of institutional modernisms. Pindell also conceptualized her art-making process in terms of mending operations. In published essays and interviews, she has theorized the tedious labor required to create her collages as reparative. Through her distinctly bureaucratic and feminist engagements with collage work, Pindell developed a method of tending to the splintering pressures of her career.

OFFICE WORK

In her earliest body of abstract collages, made in 1973, Pindell assigned handwritten numbers to dozens of chads and pasted them onto graph paper (figs. 46, 47).[43] These works make a tidy display of their own tedious fabrication. Pindell painstakingly hole-punched her chads, often from manila folders. This process could be expedited by layering the papers, but only with a corresponding increase in the exertion needed to squeeze the tool's metal handle. She then tidily handwrote digits in ink onto each of these rounds, using a needle to still the paper. Finally, she pasted each of the chads onto the surface of the graph paper, meticulously positioning each within a square formed by the graph paper's intersecting light-blue lines. The neatly inked digits seem to enumerate the repetitive gestures of this miniaturized cataloguing process.

These works, whose production was concentrated in 1973 but would continue until 1975, engage with conceptual idioms of order, "low" materials, and bureaucratic systematization. The industrially printed pages of graph paper continue Pindell's exploration of the grid from her collages of the late 1960s, but newly approach the modernist structure through a bureaucratic aesthetic that she culled from her everyday life. To a degree, the collages are formulaic, each produced through a methodical process with discrete steps resulting in works of slight variation. Despite their dry aesthetic, they offer abundant visual interest. The paper rounds sit on the graph paper in subtly different ways. Barely visible dabs of adhesive outline some of the chads, and the handwritten numbers enigmatically suggest a numerical pattern without resolving into one. These studies of seriality dramatize subtle variation.

15809 0987 15773 15129 16018 16494 6065 15939 14288 6300 1629 1670 15647 16049 15864 16418 1690 1690 1692 16240 16223 16204 16001 16179 15647 15809 5895 16082 1641 15926 16708 16044 16259 15934 16049 16056 15491 6056 15880 16299 15724 15874 15848 16236 1594 2816 3266 3061 8363 3064 3017 5286 15294 15856 5283 840 7357 8396 15849 984 15044 16200 2890 5203 5314 16644 8218 16664

0984 15904 15782 15526 16712 15286 1620 1498 4052 15623 15604 15315 15770 16215 16802 15785 16179 1699 16172 15660 16265 15816 4070 15504 16093 15608 15536 1608 15866 15903 16221 1609 0996 15701 15872 15491 15874 15726 16122 15871 15874 15726 16122 16210 15704 15276 2065 3044 3087 1586 15106 3397 3242 3262 15828 3018 15800 6263 15844 5232 3082 5316 15873 8291 15144 8316 15667 2001 3209 15294 3362 15805

15851 3025 15109 1589 1613 1608 15508 16218 1687 15897 15716 16311 15942 16213 1522 15676 15784 1686 16199 1689 15324 14304 1009 15782 15981 1567 15914 15590 15660 16130 15941 19760 16019 1686 15622 6405 15871 15466 15682 15920 2014 15113 16183 3275 3243 8286 15746 3247 15809 1585 3441 15189 15220 15525 15792 3262 2358 2366 15896 2001 0890 15277 5861 3267 15220 63031 15213 15175

18856 15217 6859 0803 16275 16298 15317 1601 15522 15702 16200 14187 15809 1624 1851 16283 5765 15867 6479 15160 16259 11406 15532 2448 2732 2668 2584 2511 2614 8 2723 2716 2667 2803 6 2477 2646 2746 2532 2613 15210 3301 3374 3218 2006 3208 5863 15780 15877 2897 16448 15466 1584 3410 2338 3001 5044 2254 15771 15194 15167 5240 15826 16213 3289 3259 3483 15224

15213 1584 16245 15732 16287 1514 6787 16800 15510 14076 16476 1588 1665 16029 1641 15811 16604 15180 1624 16490 16251 15476 16081 2467 11 4534 2258 2838 6617 2741 2522 200 2448 2454 2203 2465 2443 2456 2444 2465 2453 2400 2444 2603 3397 1585 1992 2364 3355 15771 15680 15799 2648 2009 916 15811 15228 364 15103 15079 15869 15776 16225 2680 15809 16050 2880 2806 3066 15282 3269 3462

15990 15738 1621 1809 1624 1643 16222 1689 1584 16023 15921 15859 15677 15887 15767 1623 16271 1608 15714 15628 15669 15655 1816 2717 2467 2463 2550 2903 4465 2648 2741 2105 2686 2685 2868 2556 2730 203 300 2730 203 300 1590 1584 3319 3877 15825 2000 15277 15899 15238 2392 9393 5396 15903 15809 3412 1511 3447 15877 15206 4016 3816 15862 15560 16021 15859 15584 15223 15785 2336

15897 15880 1589 0986 15906 1609 0936 15625 0880 16712 15272 1584 15520 15521 6448 16215 16226 16468 1609 11054 15913 15167 16259 2445 2490 2754 2590 12 2877 2577 2811 2478 2520 2465 2487 2476 2778 2597 15216 2476 2758 7593 15216 2444 4044 15888 6326 15701 5474 8286 3096 3044 2261 15907 3698 15221 7802 15770 8740 15877 5276 15713 3177 8023 12284 17246 15108 2285 1958 5851 2330 4707

15146 5288 15874 15783 16222 15305 15507 1609 16258 16491 5658 16161 16647 1604 6163 15988 8974 16107 6811 1608 1604 1655 15783 2009 21132 2517 2005 2447 56 2446 2756 2840 8215 2468 2450 2477 2205 2624 2250 2477 2205 2624 2250 11464 15777 8260 15772 8288 15177 15185 15230 15844 1614 5896 15185 8025 2244 3289 15880 15701 15246 2377 8307 15990 15222 2368 1029 6875 2441 3012 15283 15805

15117 15074 15524 0840 15827 16200 16164 1485 15854 1600 1204 16483 16411 1605 15738 16277 16259 16217 16205 1600 15841 8992 15012 2778 2800 2724 2425 2605 2751 2853 2572 2776 2602 2744 2473 2749 2714 2755 2707 2451 2728 2754 15989 2421 3026 15801 15120 3405 16732 15219 3804 2352 15888 14887 15411 16201 15280 15237 15588 15246 3209 16281 13721 15887 1818 15769 6415 3201 15821 3862 3370 3208

16234 15893 15918 16910 1608 1628 15621 16014 15930 15874 15477 15901 16007 16230 16091 1608 15912 16851 1609 15666 16307 11004 16216 2631 2576 2702 2407 2638 2847 11 1405 2451 2499 2611 2554 2613 2443 2524 2816 10 2462 4557 2468 2584 2514 2509 15442 15208 2277 3002 15996 355 2252 3043 3042 15118 6839 3371 3263 1959 3004 3361 368 6853 15844 16245 2287 15775 8388 3578 1601 3308 2889 3292

6866 0884 15824 15822 1626 3005 15831 15880 15915 15921 16050 15804 15999 1583 16739 15728 15877 15851 15979 1613 14917 15721 1604 2761 15 2 2700 2644 2677 2418 2455 2640 2462 3 2717 2499 2510 2725 9 460 2566 256 595 2739 2722 1980 326 1888 15817 1187 15845 1614 8046 15219 15825 15272 15885 3358 3378 5011 3082 8009 15765 15859 15244 6341 5446 3373 6247 3860 15901 15288 8287

0865 15842 10751 15897 1608 1604 1593 16203 15757 1628 15886 4271 15875 16114 15987 15613 15910 15666 16278 1602 15880 15460 16001 2746 2253 2617 7 9640 2383 2745 2465 2446 2631 2595 2590 2451 3679 2754 2573 15451 2401 2661 2477 4074 3077 15226 3874 15242 3603 2728 2424 3237 1628 1586 3818 1589 15244 15274 1516 15226 3223 1580 17791 3280 3044 5271 15774 15765 15269 15247 15711 2020

15778 15202 15805 15753 15884 1603 15898 15800 4056 1606 15760 15845 15276 14116 16062 15768 15902 16001 15965 6700 15189 1588 16083 2566 2775 2602 1994 2490 5460 2724 531 2715 4460 2623 2784 4582 4587 5468 2501 4434 4900 2587 2410 15560 3385 3291 2865 1594 0460 2222 15771 4580 6064 3043 3680 15294 15641 387 15233 1594 1918 2220 1932 306 5215 15048 15121 2865 15247 2261 3284

15754 16231 6830 15710 1049 15809 16021 520 6221 6256 1011 1431 15851 15685 16692 15645 15776 6110 16231 16628 18022 16186 1603 2472 2722 2597 2669 2521 2553 1643 1493 2290 261 2411 2603 2630 256 595 2739 2710 2049 441 205 15783 1586 3284 15823 2218 3280 1523 15112 5275 6853 3404 1511 1904 3372 3002 2857 1960 1594 15247 15844 5877 1624 3205 5241 2521 354 6245 17717

15857 16221 1589 15821 1689 5415 1607 1609 15829 1606 6007 5460 15998 15871 5721 1640 1604 1642 1609 16051 15815 15603 15720 2622 2752 2768 8743 2560 2456 2789 2790 2722 2574 18 2592 2453 2701 2602 2487 0447 2861 2579 2649 4611 15155 3359 0369 1561 15226 1601 3305 0360 2358 6806 2276 2080 1514 1508 2224 3446 1581 15827 15774 4890 2014 15167 15646 1561 16023 1586 15280 1591

15778 15751 1584 16191 1688 15904 15761 1304 16175 1525 0828 1500 1606 15845 16008 15125 1628 16309 1625 1601 1620 1620 15910 2457 264 2 400 2722 203 2404 2723 17 2730 269 2564 4597 2424 4900 2587 2400 15808 3064 15065 15268 1581 15861 2272 15229 15249 1824 5873 325 820 8361 2590 15914 3401 1522 5769 15643 16716 2261 6260 3371 1880 16997 2305 3229

1886 16020 15508 1622 15685 15615 15877 16048 5912 16897 15674 4360 1605 1604 15800 6441 1655 15721 1605 1620 16497 15913 15565 2724 2356 2712 2917 2644 4044 2650 2583 2516 2580 2434 2585 2778 2710 2491 1441 2583 2516 2580 2434 2585 2775 2710 2491 1441 2584 2577 1622 15916 15016 15343 16716 2208 6260 3371 1880 10997 2305 3229

1628 15916 15669 4624 15651 1687 16194 1624 15997 15867 16271 6005 5646 1624 1583 15161 1568 15530 1622 16115 15859 15910 1628 2554 2703 2716 2497 2649 2450 2559 1608 2430 2644 2706 2446 2447 2561 2579 2447 2578 2447 2561 2578 3205 5241 2521 354 6245 17717

15994 15521 460 16277 1608 5985 1624 7841 1608 15883 15668 1489 16160 1609 1620 15914 15977 15145 16118 1588 1604 5940 15659 2734 2591 2721 2644 2446 2571 2778 2649 4 2757 1586 2053 9877 2667 2476 2564 2411

[illegible] [illegible] [illegible] [illegible] [illegible] [illegible] [illegible] [illegible] [illegible] [illegible] [illegible] [illegible] [illegible] [illegible] [illegible] [illegible] [illegible]

15744 15804 15463 15603 0158 16192 15883 15656 1623 15602 1693 16003 1560 1693 1585 15622 15646 16927 16094 1616 15737 1691 5703 1592 2592 2736 2558 0462 2712 2711 2465 2717 2728 14 2789

15602 15755 6078 15787 15873 16291 15992 1592 6442 16077 15646 1652 15520 16012 16020 15862 1586 15892 16023 16712 15788 1601 15744 15972 2729 2718 2644 2471 2785 2697 2281 1468 2744 5 2592 2648

15728 6295 15713 15691 6867 5880 1620 1600 15641 15709 16037 8644 1628 15693 16211 15778 1602 1620 16968 15123 15628 1601 16298 16418 2164 2742 2358 1587 2640 2576 2578 7724 2624 2441 2748

15918 16094 15863 16497 15945 1624 1681 1601 1568 15624 1669 16916 15321 1622 0894 1852 16277 1628 1460 05817 16085 15528 2647 2559 2740 2457 2533 2705 9725 2557 2464 2443 2415 2447

16203 1647 1560 15771 5763 1567 16205 16258 1467 15940 16767 15918 16118 15943 1689 1609 1607 1479 15641 15483 16028 1444 15977 1567 0871 1460 2337 2463 1799 2496 2723 1523 2413 2475 2780 1702

16802 16601 15697 5663 1604 15771 16196 052 1644 16020 1691 5620 1460 0736 1629 15912 15486 6298 1577 1624 15554 16730 1602 1607 2724 22 2555 0978 256 2577 2469 2578 2597 2 2482 2486

15646 15761 1609 1628 1627 1591 5875 6833 0795 1607 1623 15623 1567 1581 1593 1589 6285 1645 16235 5944 15794 15694 1609 1606 2452 2565 2495 4561 239 1400 2716 2404 2646 2779 2489 2784

2000 15571 15724 5862 16283 1621 15606 1586 6298 16021 1675 1603 1473 6733 1618 15516 6779 15652 1694 6270 1594 1382 1591 15770 6601 2636 2442 2522 2497 0919 2719 2584 2448 2749 2462 12

16310 1603 15824 1650 1688 16291 1574 1634 1587 15802 1584 5632 6200 8212 16028 15941 1689 11711 15924 6448 0888 5482 16926 15655 2781 2993 216 2713 6555 1561 1 2740 2489 2722 2629 2746

16708 16267 16608 16244 15871 6648 15629 2393 15890 1649 16030 15873 1627 15897 15975 16801 16026 16031 1626 1609 15955 6057 15584 16207 2752 2592 2687 2617 2483 2985 2593 2659 2469 2640 2449 2448

16293 8214 16295 16035 15945 15738 1582 16305 6341 15602 6016 1496 15812 5662 1566 6230 1624 1621 2570 2563 1918 28658 2674 2574 2485 2735 2710 2488 2600 2470 2712 2716 4556 2485 2315 2746

16004 16892 6035 16801 1587 16245 19790 15678 2005 2003 2007 2009 2062 1483 1814 1608 1637 2364 2579 25206 1582 2560 2575 15837 2311 2468 2444 2649 2530 2429 2446 2491 2440 2780 2550 2741

0956 6095 1621 15892 5757 2524 15890 1608 1944 1911 1836 1985 2004 1483 2117 2007 2007 7852 25920 25900 28966 2809 26340 26780 2184 2488 2730 2552 2742 2439 2755 2449 2557 2716 2744 8642

15602 15914 6276 16791 1593 4252 15601 6772 1926 1901 1906 9850 2004 2042 2086 2611 6044 28872 28953 2560 4887 2602 2574 25673 2331 2576 2551 2672 2020 2591 1690 3735 3183 3079 3628 3144

1907 1861 1991 2012 2623 1888 1992 1911 1985 2086 1858 1888 2006 2002 1855 1411 1921 2571 5846 2577 2572 2672 2576 2573 1575 5710 2575 2784 2 2915 5862 2574 2733 2836 3629 3638 31633

1892 2009 1980 2106 22807 2004 1534 1991 2006 1993 1902 1951 1994 1966 1860 2074 1985 2089 2007 5556 20700 2501 1596 2560 0850 2570 2565 2585 0782 3780 3101 3670 5625 5059

1899 2005 1768 1992 6030 1890 2043 6002 1862 4111 1889 2007 6988 1980 2024 2024 2064 2581 2384 2583 2925 2440 2552 2575 2526 2509 2572 2581 2580 2554 5013 3103 5289 31638 310

1998 2007 2064 1770 1809 9725 2019 1997 2004 2000 1999 1985 1969 2004 2441 2004 2501 2464 2571 2561 2762 2575 25596 2558 2578 2059 2554 2654 2457 2869 5632 4675 3673 3915 3105

2006 1997 1992 1807 1981 2008 1980 1994 2009 2008 1944 1999 20005 1959 2013 1940 1952 2571 2445 2978 1582 2560 2568 2573 2875 2353 2569 25556 2531 25623 2579 2505 2024 2576 3618 3608

1995 1989 2005 2000 1802 2009 1999 1491 1951 1996 1664 1851 2004 1960 1992 2560 2551 2595 1044 2578 2564 2858 2567 2602 2578 2583 2522 2937 2581 2554 0826 3618 3660

16029 1978 1957 2012 2023 1695 2002 1914 2028 1954 2019 2004 1927 1930 2010 2014 1985 2584 2589 1581 2571 2583 2593 2809 2084 2596 2387 2557 2855 2786 2501 2014 2001 2050 3764 3101 34

19847 1995 1584 2004 2007 1990 2021 1866 20 6020 1982 2012 2013 1992 1920 1984 1995 2504 1587 2656 2578 2846 2565 2576 2586 2564 2573 2576 2894 2555 2521 3000 2594 3782 2040

20120 1870 1985 2000 1494 1820 1946 9504 2004 1994 1986 20104 2046 1993 1874 2015 1986 2567 2852 2569 2570 2852 1574 2579 2580 2586 2575 2359 2606 2582 1612 2580 2523 36807 3558

1950 5088 1887 1957 1787 1982 1996 2044 2010 1642 1928 1186 1417 1984 1982 1983 2575 2556 2558 652 2576 2806 2591 2570 2575 2556 2573 2581 2606 6236 2574 15626 2804 3560 31162

1953 1814 2063 1953 1998 1883 1992 1946 1995 2046 1958 1609 1621 2011 2008 1908 1995 2566 2445 2526 2694 1886 2576 2578 2577 2590 2601 2551 2560 2564 2615 1544 1526 1860 3688 3157

1996 1926 2064 2026 1991 2084 2009 8889 2040 2002 1949 1997 1935 2044 1938 2008 2828 2809 6200 1701 1566 2516 2009 2594 2909 2580 2577 2558 2601 2584 2509 1578 3558 5568

1487 2045 2007 1845 1178 1943 1900 2009 2025 1856 1930 2003 1980 1907 216 2565 2567 2558 2370 2538 2810 2654 2572 2606 2551 2585 2584 2588 2891 2884 4509 1564 1604 2560 2580 3559

1998 1917 1983 1986 1928 1689 1718 1924 1961 1980 1936 1996 2061 1837 2018 2018 2576 2577 2601 2579 2559 2572 2578 2557 2353 2580 2552 2560 2564 2544 2561 3780

1980 1940 1805 1984 2013 2064 1989 1995 2010 2000 1930 1944 1998 203 2007 1849 2009 2021 2345 2589 2556 2584 2554 2589 2788 2925 2576 2877 2577 2070 2011 2064 2018 2011

2011 1094 1986 2124 1877 1490 1966 1904 1991 1992 2003 1689 1911 1995 2024 1852 2016 2064 2389 2576 2544 2569 2586 2582 2585 2610 2582 2526 2010 2609 2005

1856 2009 20125 2085 1983 1998 1622 2009 1980 2004 2089 1957 1920 1995 2093 1997 2016 2046 2083 2017 1844 2016 2062 2015 2310 2680 2020 4478 2064 2080 2070 2007

2009 2097 2007 1876 2002 1897 1988 1974 1985 2077 2008 2028 1908 1905 1915 2012 2026 2013 2058 2015 2006 2064 1952 2076 1328 2016 2017 2018 2015 2577 2017 1885 1619

1 19 1987 15153 1604 1411 1633 1879 1939 1736 1685 1686 1669 1987 1455 5569 1940 1818 19308 1576 1952 1803 1951 1568 1456 1941 1980 1900 1849 1667 1971 1562 1575 1923 1930 1910 1599

1930 1660 1942 5877 1820 1932 1878 1301 1987 1499 1447 1425 1676 1248 1565 1622 1848 1980 1301 1568 5077 1861 1624 1862 1983 1945 1889 1980 1921 1304 1938 1944 5920 2566 1980 1450

1949 1411 1571 1924 1982 1950 1945 1564 1564 1986 5648 1528 1561 1816 1852 1851 1607 1983 1952 1851 1445 1929 1950 1941 1587 1363 1939 1562 1466 1957 1852 2068 1945 1887 1303 1957

1938 1948 1448 1930 1553 1560 1644 1741 1560 1436 1941 1901 1047 1940 1344 1859 1565 1909 1570 1927 1436 1801 5654 1529 768 1980 1958 1515 1938 5664 1991 1832 1566 1605 1946 1949

1542 1596 1934 1265 1735 1538 1439 1930 1935 1542 1934 1446 1911 1945 930 1944 1852 5622 1516 1560 1508 1935 1601 1588 1983 1677 1568 1929 1954 1381 1910 1654 1560 1858 1894 1987

1580 6235 1987 1687 1981 826 1940 1952 1950 656 1906 1144 1826 930 1952 1953 1985 1561 1993 1981 5632 5623 1602 1882 1456 1935 1446 1897 15640 9448 9302 1463 1840 1894 1867 15659

1956 1990 1314 5607 900 1681 1787 7092 1782 1822 2099 1850 2121 2740 2242 1623 1816 2445 1027 2299 2249 1832 2155 1702 1578 6201 1360 14442 1958 1810 1981 1664 1886 1987 1938 1846

5629 1905 1934 1464 17 1066 2311 2315 2819 1621 1993 1608 9135 1819 1690 2007 1817 1644 2631 1061 1827 2001 2099 1958 2143 9701 1963 1892 1361 1808 1986 1564 1560 1924 2405 580

1591 7668 1984 217 1728 2068 1469 1914 1663 2497 1783 1941 180 2387 1290 352 1761 2193 2342 1995 2237 2044 1679 2132 1655 2135 1940 1907 1515 1936 1946 9307 4455 1982 2040 1950

1685 1852 1680 2296 1964 2022 164 2067 1812 1700 2013 2249 2228 2348 2229 1803 2009 2486 2304 2159 1648 1719 2321 2037 1799 2136 1826 2283 15689 1651 9109 2009 15221 4069 4509 1526

1809 1682 1954 1708 1661 2091 2052 1939 1665 1900 2048 5000 2608 2230 1947 2276 2434 1609 1760 1961 1409 3205 2301 2127 2099 2064 2064 1810 200 3438 2227 1615 15212 15104 84 15222

1749 1631 2040 1621 1698 2080 1695 1799 1923 1957 7029 2081 1653 1865 1606 2181 630 2114 2061 2208 1954 2161 1628 1851 2262 2241 2163 1702 1803 1611 1953 2010 60 189 121 15189

168 2007 1641 1730 1856 1648 2308 2009 1632 1994 1658 2074 1900 2082 1885 267 1986 1807 2290 2214 2354 216 2061 2006 1804 2265 1615 2112 2102 1752 2010 1976 444 2057 40 2262

[illegible] [illegible] [illegible] [illegible] [illegible] [illegible] [illegible] [illegible] [illegible] [illegible] [illegible] [illegible] [illegible] [illegible] [illegible] [illegible] [illegible]

[illegible] [illegible] [illegible] [illegible] [illegible] [illegible] [illegible] [illegible] [illegible] [illegible] [illegible] [illegible] [illegible] [illegible] [illegible] [illegible] [illegible]

Fig. 46. Howardena Pindell, *Untitled #3,* 1973. Ink on paper collage, 22⁵⁄₁₆ × 17½ in. (56.5 × 44.5 cm). Collection of James Keith Brown and Eric Diefenbach, New York.

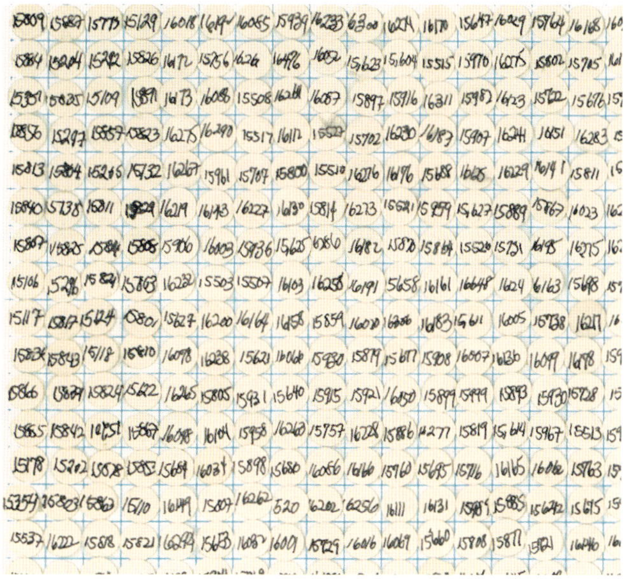

Fig. 47. Howardena Pindell, *Untitled #3,* 1973 (detail; see fig. 46).

Perhaps surprisingly, Pindell thought of these rigorous collages as both playful and pleasurable. She has remarked that she made them "just for the sheer pleasure of writing a number and seeing the clusters of dots as color and seeing the variations of grays and darks." Pindell found what she calls "visceral" enjoyment in the tedium of office work.[44] The collages hold labor and pleasure in tension. As a Black woman and a bureaucrat, Pindell understood the stakes and politics of administrative labor differently than her white colleagues. In her collages, she engaged with everyday materials in an embodied, labor-intensive way in order to redress the prevalent notions of artistic authorship that failed to account for her.

Pindell used numbering and bureaucratic material such as the hole punch, graph paper, and manila folders—some of which she appropriated from MoMA—to place her works in leading discussions of conceptual art and reference her post as a white-collar worker.[45] The procedures of hole-punching, labeling, and sorting chads resemble the bureaucratic assignments, including extensive paperwork, she performed at the museum. Pindell worked as an assistant curator from 1971 to 1977, when she received a promotion to associate curator of the Department of Prints and Illustrated Books. Though prior to this promotion she curated twelve of her own exhibitions, regularly published, and traveled abroad under MoMA's auspices, she continued to perform administrative tasks for her department and spent the majority of her working hours in the museum offices.[46]

The paper chads that proliferate on Pindell's collages and paintings of the 1970s allude to this administrative labor. A commonplace office instrument in the pre–desk-computer era of the 1970s, the hole punch functioned to prepare documents for filing. With the squeeze or press of a hand, a worker could produce a series of uniform perforations in a stack of papers, which could then be secured with a ring, or in a file or binder. The handheld hole punch that Pindell used, in contrast to three-hole punches, also carried associations with handicraft, particularly children's art projects. Nonetheless, the hole punch offers an apt metonym for the physically repetitive, mundane tasks Pindell fulfilled in her remunerative role at the museum. Although employed at an eminent art institution in positions that nominally gave her some creative latitude, she chose a metaphor for her work—hole-punching—that exemplifies the drudgery of secretarial labor. Nonetheless, it is precisely through the durational and physical aspects of this handiwork that Pindell asserted her authorship.

As art historian Julia Bryan-Wilson has argued, in the late 1960s and early 1970s, artists in the United States attempted to redefine artistic labor; these efforts coincided with the deindustrialization of U.S. cities and artists' growing distrust of rarefied art institutions. For example, conceptual artists frequently conceived of bureaucratic labor as a set of impersonal procedures that would allow them to remove a degree of their subjective voice from the work of art. In 1967, artist Sol LeWitt voiced a nascent view of artist as bureaucrat, writing in the pages of *Aspen* magazine: "The aim of the artist would . . . [be] to give [the viewer] information. . . . He would follow his predetermined premise to its conclusion avoiding subjectivity. Chance, taste, or unconsciously remembered forms would play no part in the outcome." What LeWitt called the "serial artist" does not produce enchanting objects, but functions instead as a clerk who catalogues results.[47]

LeWitt's view of the "cataloguing clerk" evokes social theorist Max Weber's consequential theory of modern bureaucracy. Weber argued that bureaucracy develops more "perfectly, the more it is 'dehumanized,'" a condition that requires the elimination of emotional and personal inputs from individuals.[48] The precision and continuity of the modern bureaucracy, valued traits in a capitalist society, are ensured by officers who act according to codified roles. According to Weber, management of the modern office is based upon its files, or written documents, rather than the subjective capacities of its functionaries.

Like Weber, LeWitt posits the artist as a worker whose tastes and preferences are subordinated to the task of administering information. Both authors write of the bureaucratic labor performed by a clerical worker, rather than a high-flying executive. Ironically, the work LeWitt himself typically performed in relationship to his own artistic production was more managerial than secretarial; he often submitted specifications to manufacturers or institutions to distribute to laborers who fulfilled his "order."[49] His appropriation of bureaucratic procedures evokes the way avant-garde artists throughout the twentieth century had approached collage—as a method of production free from authorial claims and therefore ripe for the taking.

Conceptual artists in this period masculinized white-collar office aesthetics. Note how LeWitt used the term "clerk" rather than the more common and implicitly feminine gendered "secretary" to describe the administrative labor of the serial artist. Women, however, were the secretaries executing the clerical tasks that distributed and recorded information in U.S. offices in this period—punching holes, typing, and filing. When women of color managed to gain employment in offices in this period, most often they worked as secretaries. Indeed, Pindell has recalled an occasion in which a visitor to the museum—trustee and esteemed social psychologist Mamie Clark, herself a Black woman—assumed that Pindell, as the only other Black woman in a meeting, was a secretary.[50] LeWitt's authorial repudiation traded on the idea that women's office work was rote and mechanical. Custodial staff too, whom he neglected, performed the vital work of cleaning and maintaining bureaucratic workplaces. Read critically, LeWitt's conceptual renunciation of artistic agency upheld long-standing sexist and classist hierarchies of labor that denied the subjectivity of women and working-class people.

Labor was a signal issue of feminist struggles over the public recognition of women in the late 1960s and early 1970s. White, middle-class, and college-educated feminists protested their consignment to unremunerated domestic work and the limited employment options most white women could find in the formal employment economy, such as poorly paid secretarial work. Many of these women fought for access to the broader capitalist job market, demanding equal pay for equal work. In 1971, writer Toni Morrison critiqued the hypocritical oversights that allowed upper-middle-class white women to pursue a white, male model of success while relegating domestic labor to low-paid Black women. She wrote, "It is a source of amusement even now to black women to listen to feminist talk of liberation while somebody's nice black grandmother shoulders the daily responsibility of child rearing and floor mopping and the liberated one comes home to examine the housekeeping, correct it, and be entertained by the children." The "liberation" of white women, Morrison argued, came at the expense of Black women, who took on low paying domestic work that enabled white women to work in better-paying positions outside the home. She concluded, "If Women's Lib needs those grandmothers to thrive, it has a serious flaw."[51] White middle-class feminists prioritized their own liberation; making political commitments to women of color and working-class women would have required them to challenge the racial and socioeconomic status quo in ways that could have undermined their own narrowly defined self-interests. Ironically, at the same moment that white, middle-class women repudiated unpaid "women's work," white feminist artists embraced labor-intensive handiwork processes.

Unlike many of the artists who turned to an aesthetic of administration in the late 1960s and early 1970s, Pindell was herself a practicing bureaucrat. Her intimate knowledge of administrative labor generated a different artistic approach to bureaucratic idioms. Pindell's case helps to illuminate some of the limiting assumptions that art world commentators brought to changing ideas about artistic labor. For instance, Lippard wrote of conceptual practices of the late 1960s that "art is not just play, it is the counterpoint to work." Her gesture toward the socially liberatory promise of conceptualisms hinges, in this example, on the antithetical relationship between art and work. This dyad fails to account for someone such as Pindell, whose day job at an art institution both funded her artistic practice and helped to shape her aesthetic. Art historian Benjamin Buchloh has countered Lippard's view, arguing, "What Conceptual Art achieved . . . was to [temporarily] subject the last residues of artistic aspiration toward transcendence (by means of traditional studio skills and privileged modes of experience) to the rigorous and relentless order of the vernacular of administration." His argument follows from LeWitt's model. Conceptual artists subordinated "artistic aspiration" to the rational confines of bureaucracy through means such as dematerialization, de-aestheticization, and the prioritization of linguistic structures.[52] Pindell, to the contrary, engaged with the aesthetics of bureaucracy in part as a means of accessing a transcendent pleasure. How does her insertion of administrative labor into her reparative collage practice push against these models that oppose (Lippard) and collapse (Buchloh) two aspects of her daily life?

With her use of bureaucratic materials and processes, Pindell challenged the notion that bureaucratic labor, of the type performed by a functionary, necessarily entails a renunciation of agency. Her collages point to the dehumanizing effects of bureaucracy. However, she intently endowed these materials with the possibility of visceral enjoyment, putting pressure on a model of the bureaucratic-artistic laborer as lacking, to borrow LeWitt's formulation, "subjectivity." In contrast to Buchloh's model of conceptual art, which understands the movement's "success" in the subjection of art to an administrative vernacular, Pindell submits the administrative tools of the hole punch and file folder to a process, or set of "rules," of her own artistic devising. Her extraction of these symbolic materials from the rationalizing context of the bureaucratic office points to the fluidity of her lived experiences shuttling between the roles of artist and bureaucrat. For Pindell, the bureaucratic could be wielded to bring an aspect of daily life into her collages, rather than to renounce the pertinence of her subjective experience to her artistic creations.

Pindell's gesture of authorial assertion counters what she has called "the basic dishonesty of the society at large which simply says [as a Black artist] you're not supposed to be there." Perhaps, as a Black woman, Pindell felt she could not afford to forsake her claims to agential authority, as some conceptual artists did. For in rarefied fields of cultural production, Black women, in the words of cultural theorist Michele Wallace, "are systematically denied the most visible forms of discursive and intellectual subjectivity." In Pindell's work, the durational and physical aspects of collage handiwork could function as anti-erasure gestures through which to assert, rather than renounce, authorship. As artist Lorraine O'Grady noted in her germinal essay, "Olympia's Maid," there is a cruel irony in the fact that "the idea of subjectivity itself . . . [became] 'problematized'" in the very decades when Black women began to publicly articulate their life experiences as part of a process of theorizing Black female subjectivity. Indeed, conceptual denunciations of individual authorship emerged in a period marked by the growing public visibility of artists of color and women artists.[53]

With her collages, Pindell investigated the relationship between Black women's labor and commonly held assumptions about authorship. In the same years she made graph paper collages, she also innovated a body of works on mat board that opened her practice to new textures and materials. Gravity-defying accumulations of collage elements brought further questions about artistic labor to the surface of her works. For instance, *Untitled #20* (1974) diverges from the tidy restraint of its graph paper counterparts (fig. 48). Hand-inked chads pile atop the surface of the work. A grid comprised of sewing thread divvies this rectangular surface into squares of about one inch. These paper rounds not only defy the confines of the grid, crossing its fibrous borders, but also the flat surface of the support itself. They pile atop one another, lifting from the board. Their three-dimensionality marks a vastly different angle onto collage than the graph paper works, although they share basic forms and materials. Visually, they are far more ebullient. If the graph paper chads seem to stand at attention in their assigned modules, these paper rounds bustle and careen.

In contrast to their graph paper counterparts, the mat-board works raise immediate questions about their own facture. It is not evident how the artist managed to affix the lifted paper rounds to the mat board, or to achieve the flawless monochrome, though clearly a meticulous process undergirds these effects. The inscrutable aspects of the works' production generate a good measure of visual interest. In fact, Pindell tediously adhered collage elements, including hand-numbered chads, to the boards using tweezers and pins. She fixed these paper scraps in place with a photo-mount spray adhesive. Each collage took about two months of evenings and weekends to complete. This finicky, detailed work so strained Pindell's eyes, even as a person in her early thirties, that an eye doctor recommended visual exercises to keep her sharp vision intact.[54]

Pindell embraced collage as a demanding form of both bureaucratic and feminist labor. Her arduous engagements with the technique came at a personal cost, but were supported by her belief that her transformative recombination of materials offered her something in return. With collage, she found an expedient—and affordable—means of intervening in debates about artistic labor that directly affected her.

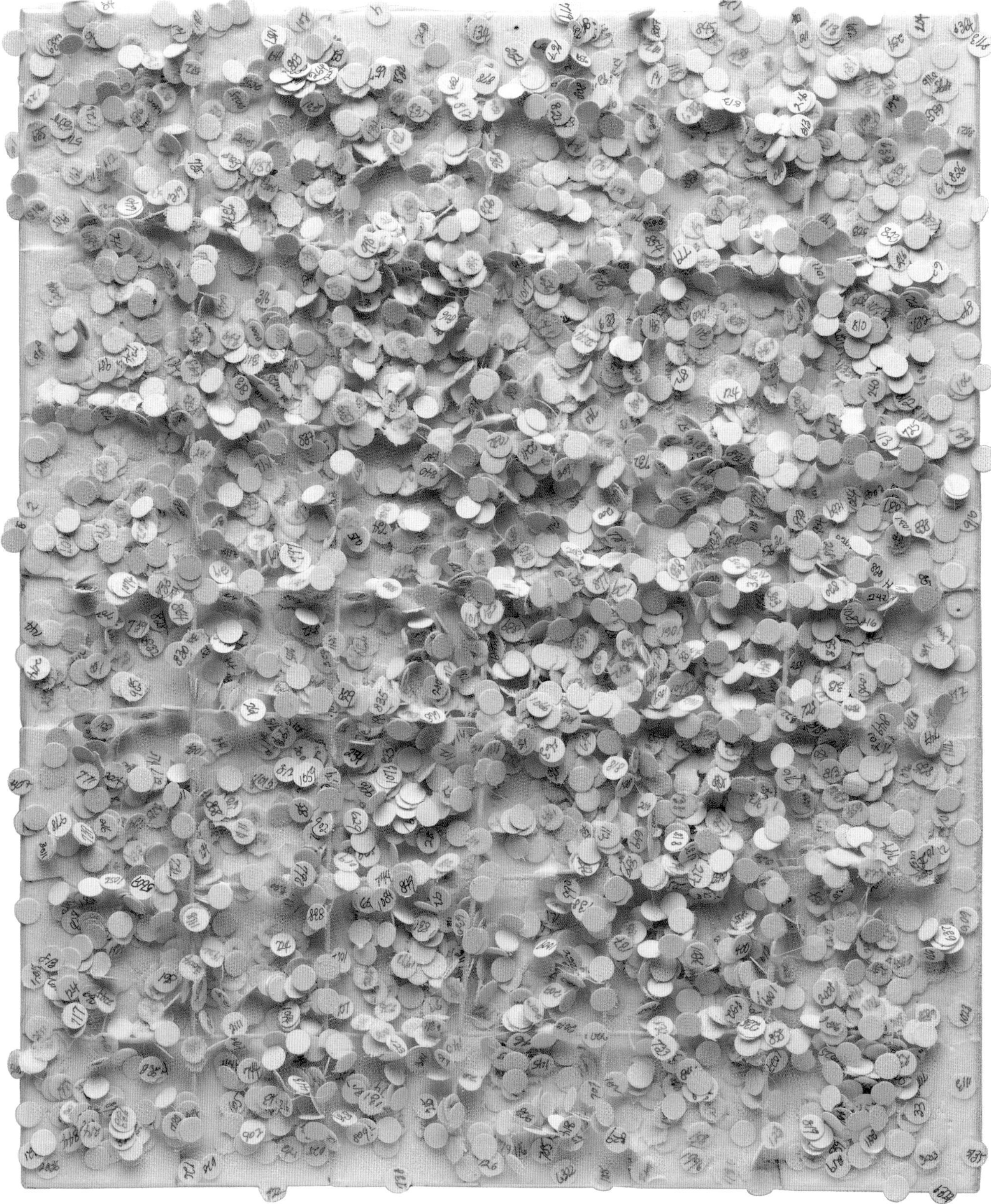

Fig. 48. Howardena Pindell, *Untitled #20,* 1974. Collage with hole-punched paper dots, pen and black ink, monofilament, and talcum powder on oak tag paper sheet, 12 × 9⅝ in. (30.5 × 24.5 cm). National Gallery of Art, Washington, DC. Dorothy and Herbert Vogel Collection 2007.6.303.

MAKING IT WORK

Like many Black American and women artists who came before her, Pindell turned to collage in part out of necessity. Collage provided her an economical means to make art in a period of financial strain and amid spatial limitations. According to the artist, she was "in a limbo period" during preparation for her debut exhibition at A.I.R., facing uncertainty in her living and work situation. She began working intensively with the technique when she could no longer afford the large canvas rolls needed for the atmospheric sprayed paintings she had produced for several years. Further, Pindell decided to produce small-scale works for the exhibition, rather than the larger paintings she had been making, because she could store them more easily when they were returned to her at the conclusion of the show.[55] She had run out of space for large works in her studio at Westbeth Artists Housing. This calculation suggests that despite some successes early in her career—selling a painting to the Whitney, for instance, or securing a two-person exhibition at Spelman College—Pindell remained skeptical of her market prospects. Collage, thus, offered a pragmatic solution to the material constraints she faced as an upstart.

In the early years of her career, Pindell has remarked, her "life was concentrated around getting supplies." The search for artistic materials took on a new intensity when she started working with collage, as she mined her everyday surroundings. For instance, the mat boards that serve as ground for many of her collages came from dumpsters in the basement of MoMA.[56] During this period, Pindell lived in a SoHo loft where, due to zoning restrictions, she could not access the building's refuse. She took her trash to the museum, where she discovered that the framing department disposed of the cutouts produced as a by-product of the matting process. These archival, one hundred percent rag, beveled boards were a boon to the financially strapped artist, and she collected them in garbage bags.

There is a poetic irony to Pindell's transformation of these discarded materials. She exchanged her own refuse for the museum's, turning the excesses of her employer into the raw materials for a career she sustained on the side of her poorly paid day job. The "negatives" of the mats that adorned the artworks on view in the rarefied institution where she worked became the support for her

collages. Thus, Pindell repurposed modernist art for her own use, both through
her artistic innovations and on this literal dimension. Her intervention here
evokes and inverts the ways in which Euro-American modernisms had co-opted
collage practices. As an employee, Pindell had access to the museum's infra-
structural underbelly, but as a Black woman artist, her chances of entry into the
institution were dubious. Nonetheless, one of these mat-board artworks, *Untitled
(#7),* now belongs in MoMA's permanent collection (see fig. 3).

Access to the museum dumpsters was a lifeline for Pindell—without some-
where to deposit her garbage, her affordable living situation would have been
untenable. However, this arrangement also marked the gulf between her and her
colleagues. That Pindell needed to lug her trash on the subway, up the A Line, to
the modernist temple at Fifty-Third Street and Fifth Avenue suggests the strain
in her life. As a young, Black, unmarried woman artist, Pindell lacked many of
the financial resources and privileges that her coworkers enjoyed, including a
sense of distance between her professional life and domestic needs. Garbage
stinks, and sometimes it drips. It is not difficult to imagine that Pindell would
have deposited her trash surreptitiously, trying to avoid other curatorial staff.
Her trips to the basement would have placed her in contact with the museum's
custodial staff and other blue-collar workers employed or contracted by the institution, many more of whom would have been people of color. Perhaps this, too,
served as a lifeline, as a respite from the stark whiteness upstairs.

Aside from the mat boards, Pindell sourced most of the other materials used
to make her collages from scraps or items she already had on hand, including the
paper chads. She punched some of these from manila folders she took home from
museum offices. Many more chads were generated in the production of stencils
used to make her spray-painted works. This decision to recycle materials from
one body of work to the next attests to her predisposition for resourcefulness
and also a continuity in her material concerns. To form grids on the mat-board
collages, Pindell pulled thread from her home sewing kit, the same spools she
used to sew her own clothes when she could not afford store-bought versions.
(Eventually, she would purchase sturdier threads produced for applications such
as sail fabrication and crochet.)[57]

Alongside this scrappiness, Pindell was fastidious about her materials. Her
time at MoMA alerted her to the pitfalls of non-archival materials. A contact-
induced allergy to lead attuned her to the dangers of toxic art supplies. (This sen-
sitivity motivated her to switch from oil to acrylic paint in the late 1960s.) Pindell
researched and tested her materials. For instance, she sourced the photo-mount
spray used to fix many of her collage materials from the industrial manufacturer
3M after meeting in her studio with a chemist from the company who showed
her adhesive samples. Pindell selected an adhesive to set her collages that would

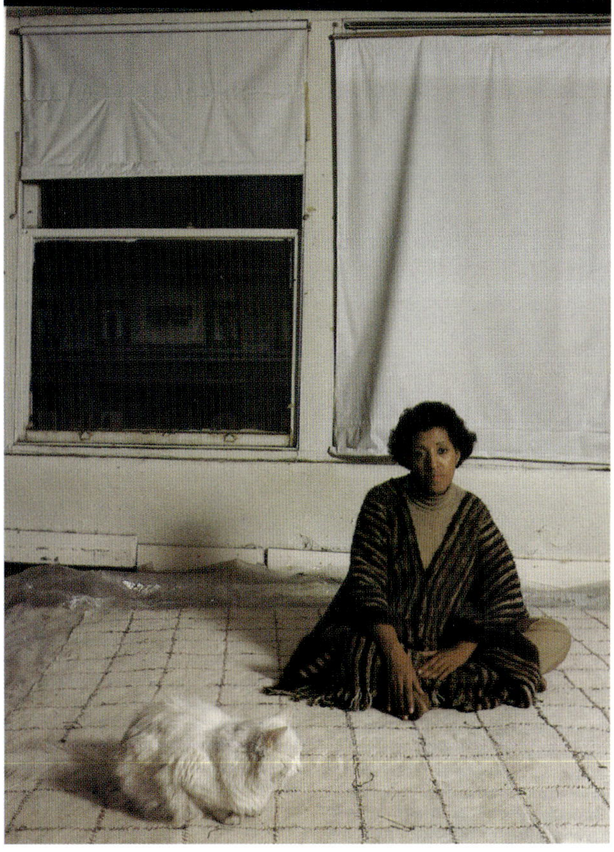

Fig. 49. Lilo Raymond, Untitled photograph of Howardena Pindell, c. 1977. Published in Richard Lorber, "Women Artists on Women in Art," *Portfolio* (February/March 1980).

not become brittle or yellow over time, having learned about photo-mount spray in a photography course at Yale.[58] Its role in her collage process resembles photographic procedures—the adhesive "fixed" the aleatory effects of gravity on the chads, as film seems to capture a moment and chemicals freeze photographic development.

Other aspects of the collages demonstrate a more freewheeling approach to materials. Strands of cat hair appear suspended in the talcum powder glaze of many of the matboard works. The hairs wafted into the collages in Pindell's studio home, where her pets roamed freely. She had several cats throughout the 1970s, though no more than two at a time. As a photograph dating to this decade illustrates, the pets were no stranger to her artworks (fig. 49). A collage in the collection of the National Gallery of Art features scores of hairs, some of them in small clumps (see fig. 48). Pindell thought of the hair as part of her finished artworks, though she never included it on her materials lists or intentionally applied it to the surface of her works.[59] Given that critics rarely granted artists of color and women the same agency as white men artists, this decision entailed the risk of castigation as sloppy or amateur.

The inclusion of cat hairs in Pindell's work exemplifies her broader interest in the tension between control and chance in her collages. Despite her scrupulousness, she nonetheless allowed the "mess" of cat hair into her work. The pet hair compounds the domestic associations of the collages' talcum powder and sewing thread. Pindell's willingness to adapt to the presence of cat hair on her artworks' surfaces attests to the continuity of the various spheres of her life at the time. The private space of her home, where she cared for pets, was the same place where she constructed large, abstract paintings for public view. Carolee Schneemann also incorporated cat content into her works in this period. Her collaged paintings and video works speak to her intimate fondness for her pets and to the cultural meanings attributed to felines. According to Schneemann, the cats that appear in her work over the course of five decades symbolically refer to the alleged elusiveness of feminine sexuality. Cats function simultaneously as an intimate marker of Schneemann's movements through life, and as muses who offer lessons on "improvisation," "risk," and "tenderness."[60] By contrast, these themes remain implicit, even hidden, in Pindell's work, which refers metonymically to cats through inclusion of their hair. Both Pindell's and Schneemann's use of cat hair disrupts the traditional divide between home and work, domestic privacy and public arena, to which so many feminist artists of the 1970s applied pressure.[61]

While found materials proliferate in histories of modernist art, the pivot in Pindell's production from fine arts supplies to reused detritus speaks as well to the specific material conditions of 1970s New York. She began culling artistic materials from MoMA's dumpsters, her cache of used art supplies, and other personal troves such as her sewing kit out of financial necessity. The agitations of the civil rights and feminist movements resulted in incremental legislative changes that promised to equalize pay across race and gender, but actual improvements to the wage gaps were sluggish. In fact, in 1973, the year Pindell's financial situation put a stop to her spray-painted canvases, the gender wage gap grew to the largest it had been since the U.S. Census Bureau began tracking earnings across gender in 1960. On average, a Black woman working full-time, year-round earned forty-eight cents for every dollar made by her white male counterpart. White women fared slightly better, making fifty-seven cents for every dollar earned by white men in a comparable position. Pindell has noted that museums such as MoMA hired women in the late 1960s (unlike the dozens of university art departments to which she applied after the completion of her MFA), but they did not pay them well.[62]

Pindell joined other Black artists in the early 1970s developing practices that used found materials and remnants to fabricate their artworks. Art historian Kobena Mercer has argued that contemporaries Saar, Robert Colescott, and David Hammons worked with found objects in order to speak "a double-voiced mode of address." By asserting vernacular cultural materials in the rarified sphere of artistic contemplation, these artists recuperated their materials' normatively designated "low" social value and inducted them into the "semantics" of the avant-garde—a space devised for the endurance of a particular white, masculine power structure.[63] Pindell likewise positioned everyday materials as both personally and culturally meaningful signifiers, thus interrupting institutionalized hierarchies.

In New York, many artists culled their artistic materials from the abundant urban refuse that littered the city's streets in the 1970s. Filmmaker and gallerist

Linda Goode Bryant has identified a specifically Black American conceptualist approach to these found materials in a group of Black artists, whom she calls "Contexturalists." Contexturalists, according to Goode Bryant, layer "context meaning" in their works through the use of "remains"—ambiguous materials that, in contrast to readymades or discards, never had a socially assigned function. Examples include Wendy Ehlers, whose *Three Inches Equals One Week of Laundry* (1974) features laundry dryer lint in the rationalizing confines of a Plexiglas grid. In David Hammons's *Bag Series* (1975–79), rib bones, glitter, and greasy brown paper bags evoke a "material culture" of the artist's Harlem neighborhood.[64] Goode Bryant included works by Ehlers, Hammons, and Pindell in an exhibition entitled *Contexturalists* at her Just Above Midtown gallery in 1978. Pindell's hole-punch scraps, the seemingly useless and valueless remnants of administrative processes, are remains that help to situate the viewer in the particular context of the bureaucratic office.

The materials Pindell wielded to create her collages interweave allusions to her white-collar job and everyday life, conceptual art practices, and craft and domestic labor. In this way, her collages bring together disparate social conversations in the white cube of the modern art gallery.[65] This feminist gesture conveys the interrelationships that, though unrecognized by normative discourses around gender, race, and labor, characterized Pindell's complex life and careers. The tension generated by the surprising juxtaposition of materials such as hole-punch remains and cat hair furthermore points to the fact that viewers can assign gender, race, class, and other social statuses to even the smallest pieces of visible matter.

HANDIWORK

Pindell labored for many hours to achieve her delicate collage work. This labor intensiveness is apparent, and, for many, an entry point into deeper consideration of her practice. However, little scholarship asks how Pindell theorized these effortful processes.[66] The artist has called her artistic labor part of her attempts to "heal" herself from the "traumatic" isolation of her working life at MoMA. In a candid, unpublished manuscript from 1994, Pindell wrote of the working process she developed in the 1970s: "I utilized a repetitive process of hole-punching in the construction of works made of accumulated circles to heal myself of the stress of fending for myself in a job category often inhabited by dormant, frustrated artists who had permanently stopped producing art to work in a museum. This accumulation process therefore reflected my emotional state. . . . Produced in isolation, these were symbolic works evoking my painful experiences working in isolation straddling two worlds, the museum and that of an artist's life."[67] Pindell counterintuitively connects the repetitive, many would say tedious, bureaucratic labor of hole-punching to a self-healing practice, giving insight into her motivations for

undertaking such painstaking work. The isolation of the labor and the process of
accumulation it garnered healed the artist not by opposing, but by, in her words,
"evoking" and becoming "symbolic" of painful experiences of isolation.

This sophisticated theory of therapeutic collage labor and accumulation
bears on the practice Pindell would pursue well into the 1980s. The "healing"
she envisioned in hole-punching evinces the liberatory possibilities she imagined
for her practice. In the passage quoted above, Pindell situated her recuperative
strategies in relationship to specific sources of pain. She located her stress in
the particular trauma of feeling isolated as an artist—at MoMA, she noted, she
was surrounded by "dormant, frustrated artists" who no longer made art. Not
only would she return home to her studio each evening and on the weekends to
work in solitude, she stood alone among her artist-coworkers in doing so. The
terms Pindell used to describe her colleagues—"dormant, frustrated"—imply a
disaffected state of inertia. Many of us who have spent time in a shared work-
space can attest to the deleterious effects of coworkers' resentments on workplace morale. A disgruntled colleague can turn workaday drudgery into a welter
of blame and dread. It is easy to imagine that in her early years in New York,
Pindell, as a young, recent Yale graduate succeeding in her efforts to produce
art, could have become a particular target of envy and a reminder to her colleagues of their own lack of artistic fulfillment. That she was a Black woman
achieving her artistic goals may have compounded the unjust ire she drew from
her coworkers.

When the occasional opportunity to connect with other working artists arose,
Pindell often encountered the burden of expectation. According to her accounts,
fellow artists of color and women artists asked her to wield her position to open
the museum's doors to their work.[68] She found herself powerless to instigate
widespread institutional change, stymied by bureaucratic slog and the prejudices
she faced as a Black woman in a white-collar workplace. The trouble she encountered in "straddling two worlds" lay not only in her professional double identity
as artist and curator, but also in the Sisyphean tasks assigned to her as a Black
woman with institutional stature amid struggles for social equity.

Elsewhere in describing her experiences of seclusion at MoMA, Pindell
emphasized her "token" status as often the only Black woman working on curatorial staff. She felt discouraged from being a full participant in the dynamic
social-professional life of curatorial work. On several occasions, Pindell found
herself the only member of curatorial staff not invited to important museum
social functions that doubled as professional networking opportunities. She
has recalled an unsupportive atmosphere in which colleagues and supervisors
overlooked her contributions and discouraged her from progressing professionally. (The sole exception, she has noted, was her friend Lippard.) Throughout the

1970s, in Pindell's words, she felt that she had "no protection" from the head of the Department of Prints and Illustrated Books, who "was very threatened" by her and "would never promote" her.[69] In 1979, tensions reached a fever pitch over the controversy surrounding the racist title of an exhibition held at the alternative art gallery Artists Space. The resulting heated debates led to Pindell's resignation from the museum.

Pindell has remarked that the institutional art world of the 1970s regularly denied the mere existence of Black women artists. Exclusionary museum exhibitions and a paucity of reviews in major newspapers and magazines effectively obscured Black women artists from the public eye. Pindell's account evokes what artist Adrian Piper has called the "triple negation of colored women artists," who are erased from the "Euroethnic" art world on the basis of race, gender, and vocation. Often this exclusion entails the complete denial of one's status as an artist, if not one's ability to make "meaningful art"—a code for work legible to white critics. This negation was not unique to the visual arts. Black feminist literary critic Barbara Christian has noted that when she approached publishers in 1978, over a decade after the height of the civil rights movement, with proposals for her book *Black Women Novelists,* most presses "could hardly believe black women were artists."[70]

How did the repetitive process of hole-punching alleviate the traumatic stress of being a Black woman artist and curator and even offer Pindell visceral enjoyment? The administrative labor of hole-punching, which evokes what David Joselit has called the "disciplinary beat of repetition," may seem an unlikely strategy for combatting isolation.[71] However, this tedious labor formed the foundation of Pindell's theory of an "empowering," specifically African diasporic, approach to art-making.

In 1982, Pindell began using the term "surface tension" in an idiosyncratic way to name the textural effects of collaged works on paper and paintings. For Pindell, "surface tension" describes the "empowering" presence of dense, handworked textures. She illustrates the effect through a negative example: surface tension contrasts with the "manufactured" finish of works such as Richard Serra's Cor-Ten steel sculptures, whose vast surfaces, though textured by the metal's protective weathered layer, lack marks of the artist's hand. Pindell believes that through their repudiation of human-scaled labor, such works propose a "dominant" orientation toward the viewer. The artist has removed himself, in some significant way, from the surface of his sculpture. According to these criteria, much of minimalism belongs to this category of the "disempowering." Pindell also has assigned the handworked, monumentally scaled paintings of Anselm Kiefer this dubious distinction. The imposing scale of his works renders the viewer "submissive." Surface tension, by contrast, entails a combination of texture and scale (whether overall or in detail) that makes the artist present for the viewer.[72]

Touch and texture are intimately related in Pindell's collages. Their surfaces, with their rich density of information, seem intent on enticing touch. They suggest that the viewer's digits could understand something their eyes cannot glean about the stability or constitution of these materials. As queer theorist Eve Kosofsky Sedgwick has written, to touch is "also to understand other people or natural forces as having effectually [touched the same surface] before oneself, if only in the making of the textured object."[73] Textural perception occurs through both visual and tactile means and necessarily entails, Sedgwick has declaimed, a cognitive procedure that includes curiosity about how the surface came to be thusly textured. This generates a conceptual exchange between viewer, maker, and object and emphasizes the relational dynamics of art-viewership. The textural density of Pindell's collages infuse the works with her past labors, lending her human presence to the abstract compositions (fig. 50). Each chad on a collage indexes a squeeze of Pindell's hand against a hole punch and a subsequent meticulous application. The direct, textural recording of these past moments of creation communicates to viewers that we are not alone with this object. Someone was here before us; someone left the traces that we now investigate.

Pindell's theory of surface tension draws on her understanding of the textural effects of African art. She has posited textural variety and a sense of "surface tension" as common characteristics of a Black American artistic tradition that stems from a diverse set of African cultural inheritances. According to Pindell, artists of the African diaspora share a "spiritual" concern for art and an appreciation for the spiritual power of beauty—all characteristics she found in African cultures. Through her engagement with U.S. literature that framed West African textiles as affectively charged objects, she viewed examples including the bata-kari as empowering and apotropaic, or protective against malicious forces.[74] Over the course of the 1970s, Pindell adapted the conceit of the apotropaic functions of African art objects, especially textiles, to her own work. She explicitly embraced the position that handworked textures could endow objects with the potential to "empower" viewers.

The apotropaic also implies a power against the viewer, an ability to protect art and maker from the outside. This aspect of the apotropaic resonates with Pindell's frustrating attempts to navigate a racist and sexist art ecosystem and to find a sympathetic viewing public for her practice. Pindell has reported that the extensive handiwork of her collage practice offers an empowering function for her, as well as for viewers. Tactilely intensive work helped her, in her words, to "connect with [her] body" when the "constant disapproval" she encountered as an artist and curator caused experiences of "dissociation." In psychoanalytic

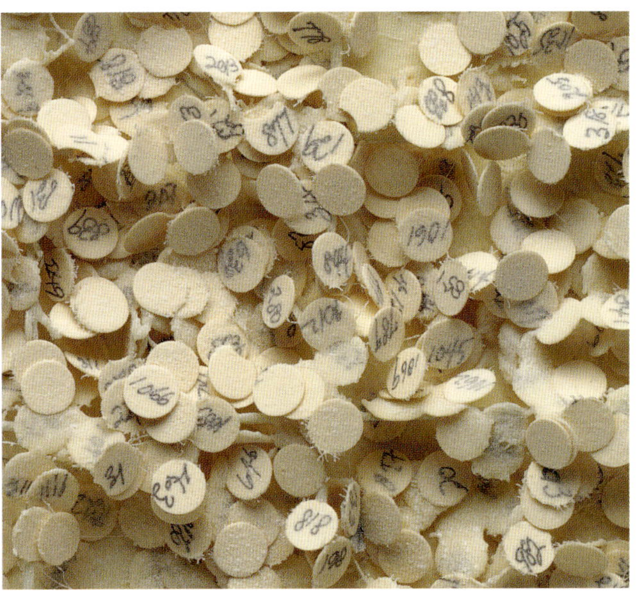

Fig. 50. Howardena Pindell, *Untitled #20,* 1974 (detail; see fig. 48).

discourse, "dissociation" describes a pathological condition, often resulting from traumatic stress, of "split[ting] apart" or fracturing normally unified psychic experiences.[75]

Artistic labor became a refuge for Pindell. Through repetitive tasks, she connected to her body and to what she experienced as "empowering" cultural expressions such as Akan textiles. She has described hole-punching as "a kind of a comfort . . . almost a kind of meditation or prayer. . . . [A] slowing down, shutting down . . . and then stepping into another space that was very peaceful." Her strategy of turning to her body for self-healing resonates with the work of Lorde. Pindell's contemporary, Lorde saw the self-definition of her own heterogeneous identity as a necessity of Black womanhood. She wrote and spoke extensively about the use of the embodied self to "reintegrate" the parts fragmented by oppression.[76]

In 1978, as Pindell intensified her use of collage in abstract cut and sewn paintings, Lorde delivered a talk at the Fourth Berkshire Conference on the History of Women at Mount Holyoke College entitled "Uses of the Erotic: The Erotic as Power." In it, she inverted popular understandings of "the erotic" by theorizing it as a source of power that "lies in a deeply female and spiritual plane," and that is "firmly rooted in the power of our unexpressed or unrecognized feeling." Encompassing but also operating beyond the sexual, the erotic provides the basis for female authority by removing "the necessity for certification of one's ideas by the dominant group." Lorde rooted the erotic in her own experiential position as a Black lesbian, but at the same time expansively framed the "resource" as something that could be shared among women in general, should they be willing to accept the responsibilities that attend it. For once accessed, the erotic requires us to feel "acutely and fully," to live lives of "excellence."[77]

"Uses of the Erotic," like other texts in Lorde's oeuvre, identifies the embodied self as a source of authority. Throughout the speech, Lorde located the erotic in acts of physical, mental, and emotional exertion. The erotic is potentially present in the painting of a fence, the writing of a poem, and in physical and spiritual "woman-love," which Lorde poetically described as "moving into sunlight against

the body of a woman I love." In the essay's sole narrative passage, Lorde offered
a metaphor for the erotic that illuminates the concept's intertwining with
the physical, material world. The evocatively descriptive passage requires full
quotation:

> During World War II, we bought sealed plastic packets of white, uncolored
> margarine, with a tiny, intense pellet of yellow coloring perched like a
> topaz just inside the clear skin of the bag. We would leave the margarine
> out for a while to soften, and then we would pinch the little pellet to break
> it inside the bag, releasing the rich yellowness into the soft pale mass of
> margarine. Then taking it carefully between our fingers, we would knead it
> gently back and forth, over and over, until the color had spread throughout
> the whole pound bag of margarine, thoroughly coloring it.

Lorde found the erotic in the ritual manipulation of an everyday household
product. She lavished attention on the touch of hands, which "pinch" and whose
fingers "knead," "back and forth, over and over."[78] Through corporeal, intentional
feeling one can bring color to a "pale" world. The artificial and domestic associations of margarine—a foodstuff that is not always considered one—underscores
the vernacular, "low" potential of the erotic. A butter replacement made from
refined vegetable oils, margarine has been variously villainized, outlawed, and
embraced by the U.S. public. Lorde's passage both emphasizes and overturns its
artificiality by focusing intently on the yellow coloring packet and through simile
rendering it a gemstone. The simile illuminates the fact that jewels, like margarine, are highly processed goods derived from materials in the earth. It challenges the idea that "high" culture entails feats of human ingenuity and "low"
culture constitutes cheap substitutes for something more authentic. One's material resources, in other words, do not determine their proximity or access to the
erotic. Rather, even the constraints of wartime rations, the context for Lorde's
margarine vignette, might serve as the seedbed of an emotionally transformative
erotic encounter.

In contrast to Lorde's luxuriantly sensual description of margarine, Pindell's
theory of surface tension chastely absents the bodily potential for orgasm and
sexual pleasure. This difference aside, Pindell, like Lorde, found in her body a
resource for bringing herself back together. Through her fabrication of collages,
she turned painstaking tasks, work that seemingly reinforced her social isolation, into a process of "healing." This meant using her hands in "comforting" and
"meditative" ways.

Pindell has remarked that through this handiwork process she made "something beautiful, almost to put beauty where [she] found ugliness." Her haptic

approach to art-making confounded the widespread denial of Black women's authorship, evoking what interdisciplinary scholar Gina Dent has called "black pleasure, black joy." Dent has theorized Black joy as an outward-facing knowledge that "signals" Black people's "more democratic hopes and dreams for the future."[79] Working with her hands, Pindell found a source of pleasure through which she could reconfigure, if imaginatively, the realities of her workday life. She used collage as a form of introspective mending, a way to tend to the distress caused by the conditions of her labors.

Numbers also offered Pindell a method for exploring the tension between labor and pleasure in her work. In her early collaged works on paper, numbering formed an important part of a cataloguing aesthetic that opened onto broader questions about the role of rationality in art, the ability of base material to hold meaning, and the capacity of ubiquitous aesthetic markers to secure artistic validity. Pindell began engaging the conceptual trope of numbering after an interaction with a gallerist. During a studio visit in the early 1970s, Cincinnati-based critic and gallerist Carl Solway asked her how many spray-painted dots appeared in one of her large, stretched canvases. Diligently frugal, the artist had saved the chads generated when she made hole-punched stencils to create the stained works discussed in Chapter 1 (fig. 51). These by-products sat in garbage bags in her studio. As a riposte to Solway's inquiry, she began hand-numbering the rounds with a Rapidograph, a kind of technical pen used by engineers and artists, and collaging them to graph paper.[80]

Numeric digits proliferated in conceptual art shown in New York in the 1960s and early 1970s. For instance, dozens of artworks in MoMA's 1970 exhibition *Information,* which gathered an international cadre of young artists working in conceptual modes, featured numerals. These digits performed functions such as ordering, counting, and measuring. Mel Bochner's *Measurement Series: By Formula (Circle)* (1970) consisted of a black wall with a circle and its dimensions neatly written in white chalk. Siah Armajani's *A Number between Zero and One* (1969), a centerpiece of the exhibition, comprised a printout "of all the digits between zero and one."[81] At over nine feet tall and five hundred pounds in weight, the work purported to exhaustively catalogue these numerals using an advanced administrative machine. Thus, it offered wry commentary on the productive capacities of technological innovation.

While the purposes of such numerical exercises remained opaque, even confounding, to some visitors to *Information,* the rationalizing function of the numbers themselves stayed reassuringly in place—digits follow a pattern, or they quantify a real spatial relationship. Curator Kynaston McShine explained that the artworks on view demoted aesthetics to an emerging function: "The style . . . is . . . simply a method of distributing information that interests the artist." While

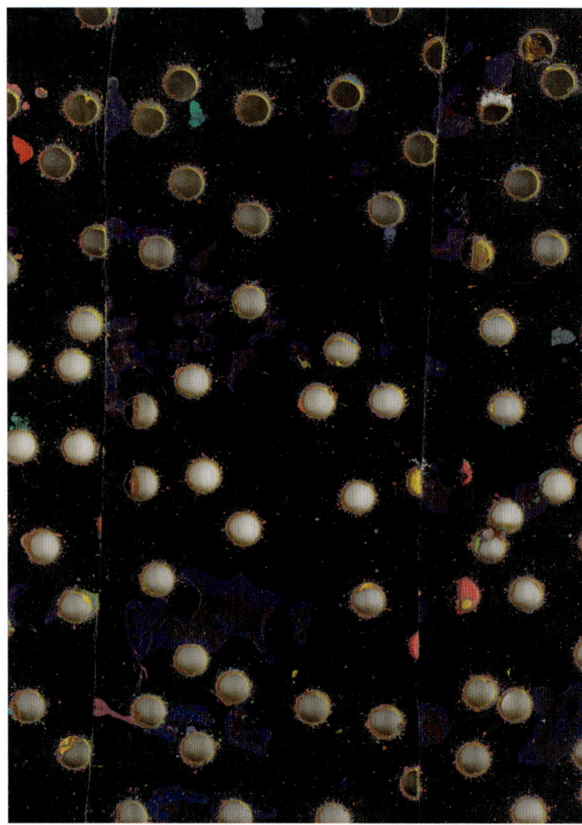

Fig. 51. Howardena Pindell, Detail of untitled hole-punch stencil, 1970. Acrylic on paper, 35 × 81 in. (88.9 × 205.7 cm). Garth Greenan Gallery, New York.

many of the exhibited artists may have intended to deploy digits purely as an effective means to communicate information, their works necessarily carried aesthetic effects as well; the museum context ensured it. *Information* introduced a bureaucratic artistic aesthetic to a large audience and inaugurated the mainstream institutionalization of conceptual art. Pindell not only had convenient access to the show at MoMA as an employee, she also had personal relationships with several of the artists in the exhibition, including Lippard and Carl Andre.[82]

Many artists in this era who incorporated numerals into their work, including those on view in *Information,* rejected hitherto prevailing aesthetic hierarchies by generating visual boredom through use of repetition, a narrow color palette, the demotion of the hand, and lowly materials. Pindell's collages share these characteristics of this conceptualist anti-aesthetic, but also counter them. Humble handwritten digits are given heft through their proliferation on the hundreds of chads that speckle each of the collaged graph paper works. This accumulation of the modest hole-punched paper scraps participated in conceptualist concerns for "dematerialization," an era term that in its broadest meaning refers to the subordination of material preciousness as an artistic investment.[83] A logic of accretion likewise operates in Armajani's *A Number between Zero and One.* Similarly to Pindell's collages, it underlines the physicality of low-value materials through an enumerated, accumulative mass.

In discussing her use of numbers, Pindell has positioned her collages in contrast to conceptual projects that entail "mathematical problem-solving" and "philosophical theories." Instead, she intended the gesture, she has said, as a "dig at the conceptual stuff" other artists were making. German artist Hanne Darboven's *Century Book 00–99* (1969), which appeared in *Information,* offers a paradigmatic example of how conceptual artists approached numbers in this

period. With this work, Darboven initiated a years-long investigation of calendrical systems using mathematical logic in handwritten text on paper. The series
built on her engagement with numbers as an artificial, readymade language in
works such as *Konstruktion/Perforation New York* (Construction/perforation
New York) (1966–67), in which mathematical procedures determine the artist's
mark-making choices (fig. 52). For Darboven, numbers offered a convenient logical system for a potentially endless procedure that she likened to writing.[84]

The fastidious numbering of Pindell's collage work evokes the rational systems pervasive in emerging artistic practices. However, rather than being
beholden to what she called an "elaborate psychological rationale," Pindell
parodied the emptiness she perceived in those procedures. Art historian Judith
Wilson has noted that Pindell "thumb[ed] her nose at her colleagues' obsession
with 'meaning' by placing her meticulously inked chads randomly."[85] Pindell, in
other words, embraced the aleatory as a method of overcoming the constraints of
rational meaning. Other artists, of course, also deployed conceptualist methods
ironically, self-consciously, or for aesthetic effect. Nonetheless, the binary Pindell
has constructed between her practice and others' productively illuminates more
distinctive features of her take on conceptual idioms, particularly the primacy of
her insistence on the "healing" capacities of repetitive physical gestures.

Crucially, Pindell dealt "with numbers on a visual, visceral level." She has
been adamant that she approached numerals as a form of drawing, rather than
signs in a rational informational system.
By designating her numbering as drawing, rather than writing, Pindell has
emphasized her tactile engagement with
the indexical forms. This approach to
numbers as handworked form is evinced
in an untitled painting from circa 1967
(fig. 53). A field of undulating gray and
black "2s," interrupted by a single "3,"
deconstructs the sign, through repetition, into a tightly curved shape
attached to a flat one. In the collages,
Pindell's "visceral," haptic engagement

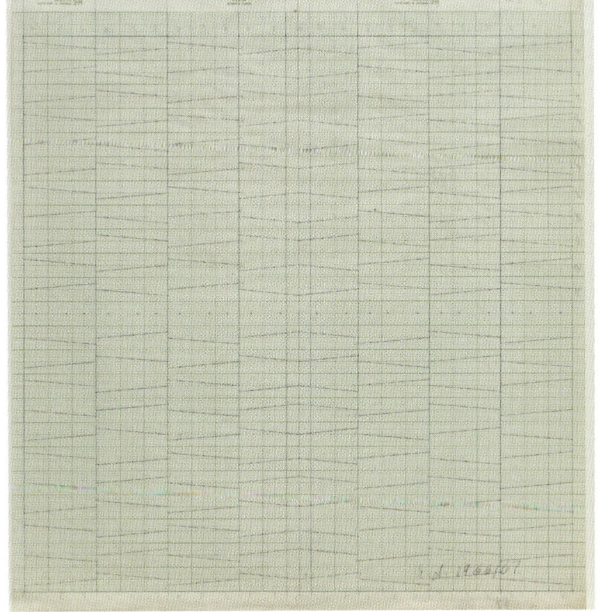

Fig. 52. Hanne Darboven, *Konstruktion/Perforation
New York* (Construction/perforation New York),
1966–67. Pencil and ballpoint pen on graph paper,
perforated, 26¼ × 24 in. (66.7 × 61 cm). Sprüth
Magers, Los Angeles.

with numbers is underscored by an intensely physical production process. Each one of the chads pasted onto Pindell's works passed through her hands several times. She hand-punched the paper rounds, wrote a number on each one, and then individually pasted them to a graph paper sheet or mat board. The title of an article penned by Pindell in 2004, "Numbering: Counting on My Fingers and Toes," further illuminates her enduring conceptualization of digits as both numerical and physical phenomena.[86] With their dense and abundant traces of her labor, the collaged graph paper works attest to the artist's physical copresence with her materials. If her numbers catalogue anything, it is the time and care she invested in their production, the delicate handiwork required to achieve their effects.

In addition to using numerals to situate her work within and to critique conceptual idioms, Pindell also has understood her numbering practice as carrying autobiographical significance. Her father, an accountant and statistician, kept ledgers of numbers. He used these in professional capacities—for instance, in his work tutoring high school students in high-level mathematics, as well as for domestic purposes such as recording readings of the family automobile's odometer.[87] In these contexts, numbers performed their normative functions. They partook in a process of quantification that rationalized an aspect of the world— tracking changes in student performance or measuring gas mileage. As an artist, Pindell created her own tidy rows and columns of digits. Her numerals convey, quite differently, an individualized sense of order secured by fond, and emotionally charged, memories of a scrupulous parent. From this intergenerational transmission of the visual form of rows of digits, she made her own meaning, using numerals as a convenient unit of draftsmanship.

With the collaged works on paper, Pindell continued the approach to abstraction she had developed with her deployment of the circle and grid in paintings of the late 1960s and early 1970s: she forged an embodied aesthetic arena in which to test individual meanings and play with the apparent universality of modernist forms. The artist's strategic deployment of digits placed her work in dialogue with other modernist models, notably Jasper Johns's proto-pop work. In December 1970, MoMA opened a survey of lithographs by Johns. The exhibition included over a dozen examples of his numeral prints. Hosted by the Department of Prints and Illustrated Books, in which Pindell worked, the show did not fall directly under her purview. Nonetheless, her prolonged artistic engagement with Johns's oeuvre over the course of the following two decades suggests it made a

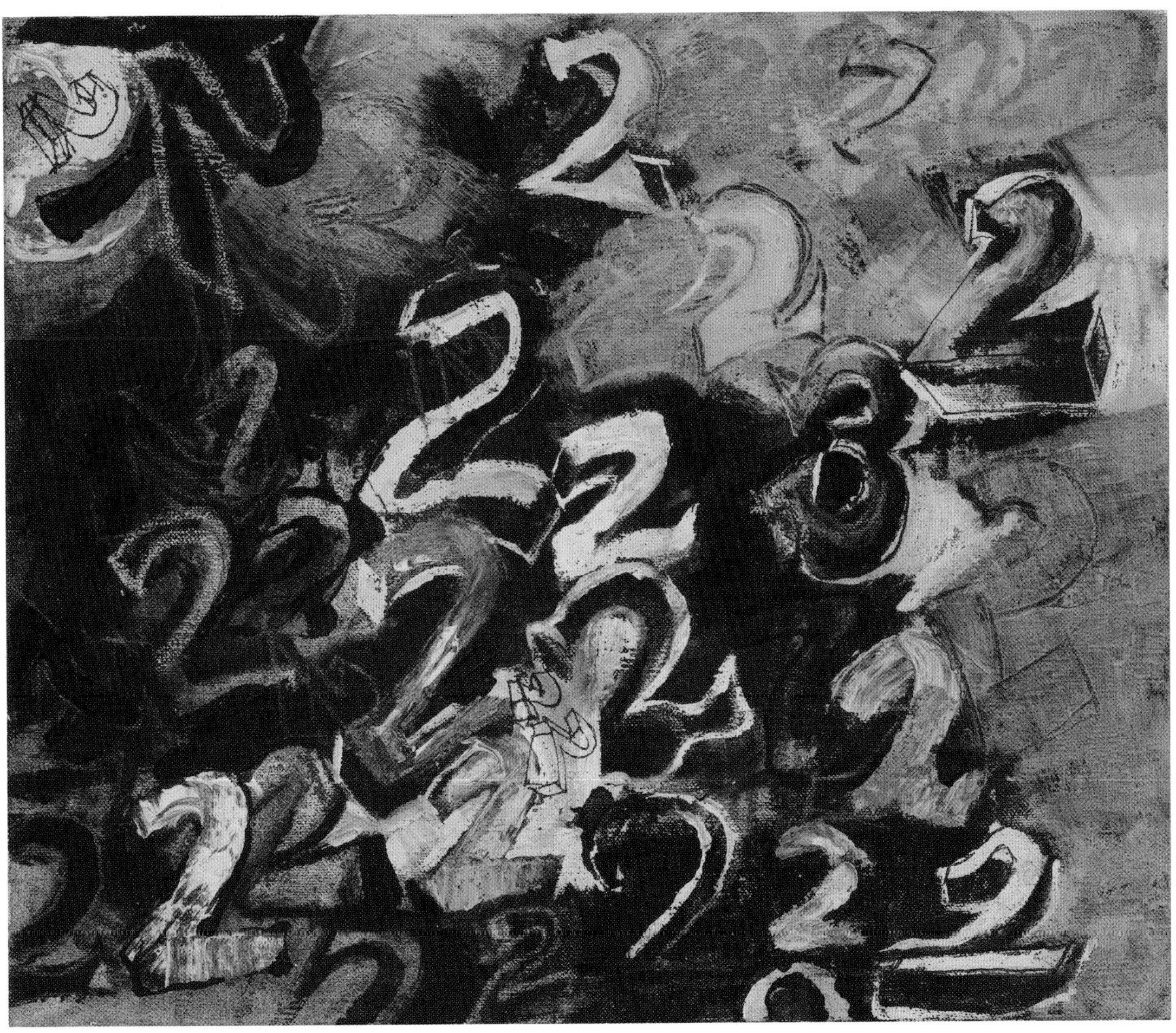

strong impression. Pindell would title a painting after a Johns print that entered her department's collection in 1978—she adapted the title of *Dutch Wives* for her *Dutch Wives (Circled and Squared)*, and several of her most ambitious paintings of the 1980s employ bold hatch marks redolent of Johns's signature canvases of the 1970s. The press release for the Johns survey emphasized the lithographs' success in "forc[ing]" the viewer into "a new awareness" of common visual material.[88] Her position at MoMA situated Pindell ideally to reckon with a proto-pop legacy of rendering banal signifiers as aesthetic units.

Through her engagement with collage, Pindell brought together automation and authorship, rather than simply countering conceptualist repudiations of artistic agency. The labor of fabricating her collages—hole-punching, numbering, pasting—created a processual scaffold that she followed in the production of dozens of works. She relied on this process inflected by the bureaucratic to give her collages what she has called a "sense of abandonment or non-decision."[89] LeWitt has noted that bureaucracy seeks to eliminate chance. Pindell, by contrast, has held chance and control in tension in the collages. Paradoxically, it was through her renunciation of decision-making that she imbued bureaucratic materials with authorial agency. Pindell asserted her subjective choice through handiwork procedures that transformed conceptual idioms from "meaningless" to "healing."

CONCLUSION

Feminist theories of collage have ascribed radical possibilities to the technique. For instance, Lippard has argued that the collage aesthetic "is a kind of dialectic exposing by juxtaposition the disguises of certain words and images and forms and thus also expressing the cultural and social myths on which they are based." Collage makes reality perceptible by denaturalizing its structuring components. Lippard continued that the connections between unlike parts forged through collage "is also a metaphor for the breaking-down of race, class, and gender barriers, because it moves out from its center in every direction." Thus, the collage aesthetic is "a metaphor for cultural democracy."[90] For Lippard, collage permits a rearticulation of the social order by creating new relationships between the objects it gathers.

Pindell's view of her collage practice as "random" and free of the burden of rational meaning counters the lofty sociopolitical aspirations Lippard ascribed to the technique. As a Black woman, she was less optimistic about the possibilities for this kind of widespread social transformation through aesthetics. Rather than positing collage as a metaphor for identity writ large, Pindell understood it first and foremost as "visceral, visual" work. Through collage, she ardently investigated a "meditative" artistic labor, which would become a central theme of her oeuvre. In this sense, Pindell's use of collage tracks more closely with Lorde's theorization of the technique as a Black feminist strategy for maintaining a sense of self amid the fracturing violence of intersecting racial and gender oppressions.[91]

Collage extended the materials, forms, and effects of Pindell's work. It brought the outside world and the artist's interior life to the surface of her art in increasingly overt ways. The technique introduced texture and references to everyday biographical cultural practices, such as sewing, to her previously staid modernist aesthetic, opening her artistic production to further biographical and politically germane resonances. With it, she innovated upon African diasporic, feminist, conceptual, and modernist conventions. The meditative labor of collage served as an outlet for a form of authorship that had been denied to her by mainstream art criticism. Pindell's abstract collages reconfigured the terms of artistic and bureaucratic work, both centering pleasure and beauty, on the one hand, and tedium and the therapeutic replication of trauma, on the other. With her haptic engagement with collage surface, Pindell imbued the bureaucratic form of the grid with the sensuousness of the weave.

In the early to mid-1970s, Pindell deepened her exploration of her artistic production as a form of mending—a process of using one's labors to create something new from worn remnants. The persistence of collage in her oeuvre attests to the artist's enduring belief that this kind of reparative work could be pleasurable and that it depended on haptic engagements with the material world. Throughout the decade, Pindell continued to pursue collage as a site of "healing" labor. Her Black feminist modernism reached its culmination in densely collaged paintings of the late 1970s that stake out the structuring tensions of so-called advanced art and the project of liberation. Through her deployment of the technique in the elaborate fabrication of these cut and sewn paintings, Pindell fully realized a Black feminist theory of abstraction that positioned the work of her own hands at the center of modernist art.

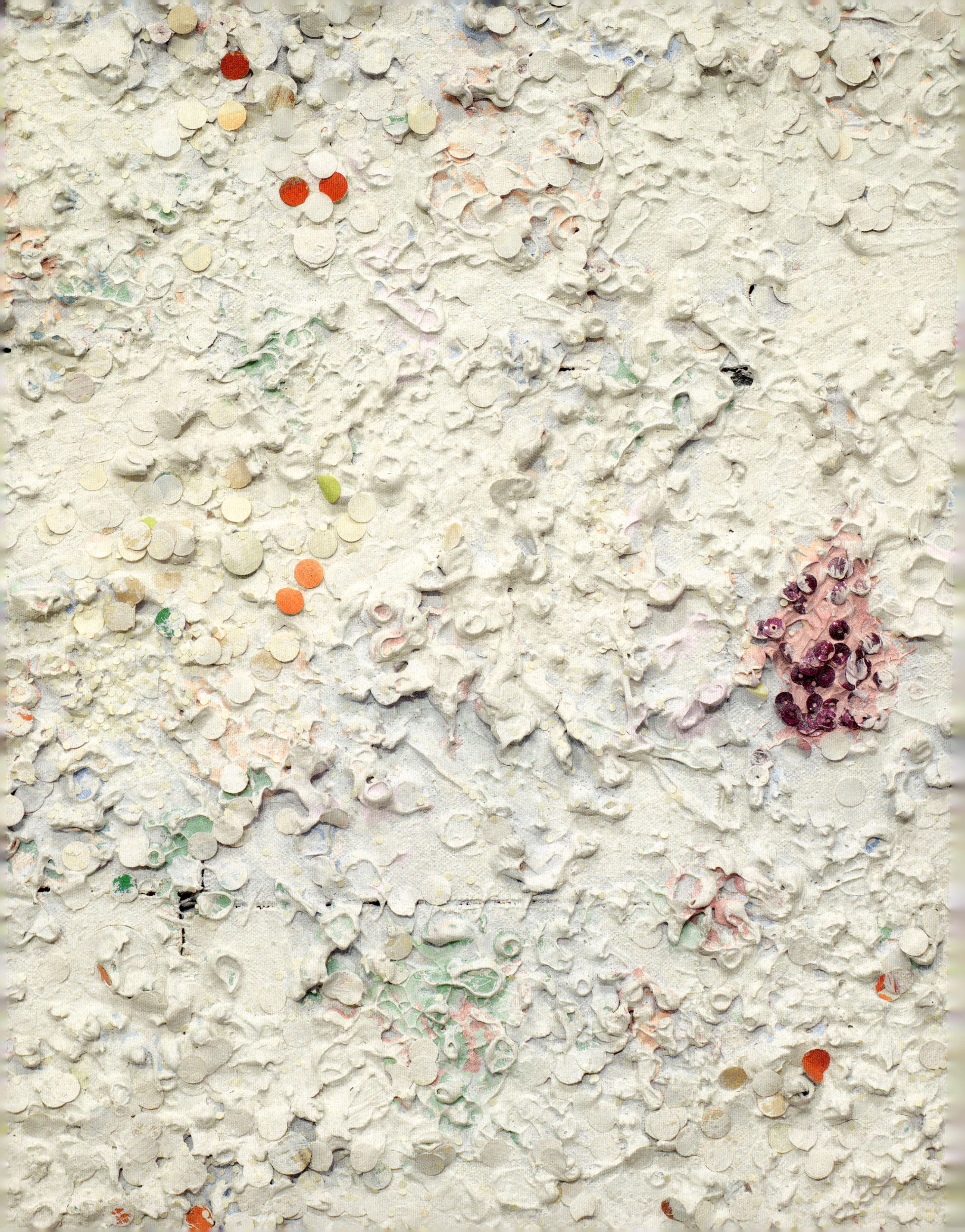

3 • Mending Abstraction

In 1976, Howardena Pindell began making paintings by cutting strips of canvas, sewing them together into a large rectangular grid, and covering them with collaged and painted materials to form an abstract field.[1] Pastel hues dominate these allover compositions, though specks of more saturated color mottle their surfaces. From afar, an untitled example from 1978 repeats the principal formal theme of Pindell's spray-painted works—layers of small circles. However, a closer look at the unstretched canvas, invited by the colorful irregularities, reveals a seam-ridden surface (figs. 54, 55). Small pieces of paper—chads produced by a hole punch—camouflage without entirely concealing the ruptures between swaths of textile. These countless paper rounds, ossified in gesso and acrylic paint, extend from the surface, carrying the collage concerns of Pindell's works on paper to the rarefied form of allover, abstract painting.

Between 1977 and 1981, Pindell completed six abstract cut and sewn paintings. On average, each of the paintings took two months to make and measures around seven by eight-and-a-half feet. Some of the works hang horizontally, in the traditional format of landscape paintings, while others are vertically oriented, like portraiture. With the cut and sewn paintings, I argue, Pindell extended her horizons beyond New Haven and New York as she developed a textility—or textile logic—in her abstract paintings. Largely inspired by her exposure to textiles from Ghana earlier in the 1970s, she pursued an increasingly urgent concern for aspects of painting beyond the strictly visual. Pindell introduced raised, textured surfaces to her paintings for the first time with these works and experimented with scent; she spritzed several of the cut and sewn paintings with "all kinds of cheap perfume," which gave the works an olfactory dimension when they were shown in the 1970s.[2]

Through this sensorial extension, I argue, Pindell developed a Black feminist abstract practice that both engaged with and challenged institutional modernist painting. Her cut and sewn canvases enlist their audiences in a realignment with the external world through "haptic activation"—an attunement to the embodied nature of perception, including vision, touch, and smell.[3] Pindell accessed the

Fig. 54. Howardena Pindell, *Untitled,* 1978 (detail; see fig. 55).

haptic through an extended exploration of textile logic. Both a mode of making and an aesthetic, textility connected her modernist ambitions with Black women's cultural practices associated with memory transmission and the expression of cultural authority. Thus, she stitched together her investments in post–Black Power feminisms and allover modernist abstraction. With the cut and sewn paintings, Pindell extended the haptic concerns of the collages on paper she had made earlier in the decade. She both literally and resonantly textured these compositions, mustering layered aesthetic interactions, entwining artistic media, and provoking multisensorial viewing experiences.

Pindell's haptic orientation toward abstraction put pressure on commonly held assumptions about the relational exchange of art-viewership. Queer theorist Eve Kosofsky Sedgwick has argued that haptic experiences, which conventionally refer to the combined perceptions of touch and the corresponding psychological registration of bodily position and movement (proprioception), can undermine the subject–object binary that structures conventional Western philosophies. She has written that touch "makes nonsense out of any dualistic understanding of agency and passivity." In other words, to touch is always to be touched.[4] Sedgwick's theorization participates in a recent body of scholarship that draws on affect theory to conceptualize the haptic as a specifically minoritarian strategy. Black feminist scholars, notably Rizvana Bradley and Hortense Spillers, have articulated less sanguine views on the liberatory potential of touch. Both Bradley and Spillers have contended that any emancipatory properties ascribed to touch must be contextualized in histories of touch as violence, particularly with respect to the transatlantic trade in enslaved Africans and histories of chattel slavery. This emerging theoretical discourse, particularly Spillers's notion of the "twinned" capabilities of touch as a site of both intimate "mutuality" and subjugation, resonates with Pindell's deployment of haptic strategies in her practice.[5]

Pindell's haptic work engages with the paradox of touch. On the one hand, she authored her own intensely physical involvement with her canvases for the express purpose of engendering pleasurable, "healing" encounters. On the other hand, she innovated this method of art-making out of a sense of loss. Pindell has understood her production of the cut and sewn paintings to be a response to her disconnection from her ancestral African cultures in the face of a hegemonic white U.S. culture. The canvases, I argue, represent Pindell's development of a distinctly African diasporic theory of painting, which she articulated in several prominent publications and lectures.[6] The works also emerged from her investigation of the alienating effects of her daily labors. She derived many elements of her fabrication process from the tediously repetitive administrative labor she performed at her day job. Through her haptic practice, Pindell both evoked and tended to sites of harm.

Without recourse to figuration, Pindell thematizes embodiment in her cut and sewn paintings. The canvases are visual artworks, and they maintain the modernist prohibition on touch. Nonetheless, they insist on vision as an embodied experience always enmeshed with other bodily senses, challenging the optical bias of institutional modernisms. Through their activation of a sensorial spectrum, the paintings bring a surrogate bodily presence—one that is decidedly feminine-coded—to the gallery. Their scented, bejeweled surfaces present this "femininity" as a masquerade. With this sidelong approach to feminine presentation, I argue, Pindell intervened in feminist reclamations of the era that centered whiteness. Instead, her abstract paintings conjure, without literalizing, an African diasporic feminine presence.[7]

Through her engagement with haptic textiles, Pindell opened her most formally ambitious works to a quotidian sensibility. Textiles are vehicles of everyday textures and odors; clothing, linens, and furnishings enrobe mundane encounters. Pindell positioned her practice in proximity to the lived textures of Ghanaian clothing, feminine adornment, and feminist handicraft. Her conceptualization of painting as textiles has endured. She recently described the medium as "a fabric of sensations, emotions, and feelings."[8]

Pindell also continued to contextualize her work in the realm of so-called advanced art, particularly modernist idioms associated with conceptualism and abstract expressionism. For example, the paintings utilize the paradigmatically modernist form of the grid to structure their allover abstract compositions. Most of the cut and sewn paintings are untitled and numbered according to their order of production, following modernist protocol. A pair—*Carnival at Ostende* (1977) and *Untitled #20 (Dutch Wives Circled and Squared)* (1978)—allude to works in the prints and drawings collections of the Museum of Modern Art (MoMA), which Pindell helped to oversee until 1979 (see figs. 1, 4).[9] Even as she expanded her affiliations far beyond elite East Coast institutions, she continued to engage with the aesthetic debates they fostered, expanding and critiquing their terms. The cut and sewn paintings are rigorous confections, couching sensorial exuberance in modernist visual protocols.

Throughout the 1970s, Pindell maintained a modernist practice while eschewing aspects of these traditions that failed to accommodate her ambitions. Her cut and sewn paintings deploy the conventions of abstract, allover painting in order to rearrange its dominant associations with a white, male subject position. In 1971, artist and critic Frank Bowling argued that sculptor Melvin Edwards exemplified Black artists who used abstraction to "signify" formal modernist languages and "re-route" them to address Black experience.[10] Pindell likewise enacted signifying interventions into modernisms. Her primary strategy for doing so, I argue, was a method of "mending." This concept refers to her use of a haptic, textile-based approach to art-making as a tool for critiquing institutional modernism's constraints. It underscores the role of lowly handiwork, particularly stitching, in these critical engagements. Mending also gestures to the reparative dimensions of Pindell's haptic practice. To mend is to extend the life and usefulness of otherwise worn-out textiles. Pindell mended abstraction, joining modernist idioms with African diasporic and feminist handiwork in order to make it useful to her.

The mending operations in the cut and sewn paintings represent the culmination of Pindell's Black feminist modernist project; they are the methods through which she most adamantly defied the racial and gender logics of modernisms. These works also allow for a renewed understanding of the possibilities and constraints held by abstract art of the 1970s more broadly. The cut and sewn paintings surface the tensions embedded in disciplinary silos, which continue to define—and unjustly circumscribe—the contributions of Black artists to contemporary art. Indeed, part of the paintings' punch aims at the capricious, socially determined nature of artistic reception. With her haptic approach to allover abstraction, Pindell expanded received notions about art in order to better accommodate her own lived experiences.

AFRICAN TEXTILES

On July 24, 1973, Pindell addressed a postcard from Nairobi, Kenya, to her friends art critic Lucy Lippard and artist Charles Simonds: "I will return forever changed. We are so ignorant of Africa. Kenya is full of contradictions." Written on the artist's second day in Africa, the text captures her earliest impressions of the continent—an experience that challenged her expectations and promised to alter her "forever." It also demonstrates Pindell's particular position as a Black American artist who approached "Africa" as a source of inspiration with a degree of longing and, perhaps, romance. U.S. artists and critics in this era frequently, if inadvertently, conflated the vastly diverse cultural and societal practices found in Africa.[11] For Pindell, who worked and had trained in predominantly white institutions, "Africa" may have offered a potent point of access to a cultural Blackness that was absent from her workaday environs. Over the course of the following two and a half decades, she would publish four articles on African art and culture and speak on numerous occasions about the relationship between her work and African diasporic art. Her extended engagement with African art, textiles in particular, led to extensive changes in the way she approached her canvases.[12] This shift in her practice foregrounded the pertinence of West African textiles to the aesthetics of modernist abstract art. These specific involvements with African art intervened in the figurative protocols espoused by proponents of the Black Arts movement in these years.

Pindell and Lowery Stokes Sims, then an educator at the Metropolitan Museum of Art, spent two months traveling throughout Africa in the summer of 1973 as colleagues and friends.[13] They visited Nigeria, Kenya, Ghana, Ivory Coast, and Senegal and made unscheduled stops in Uganda and Mali. The two young art professionals traveled under the auspices of MoMA's overseas books program. Their primary objective, according to MoMA records and reports, was to identify appropriate recipients for the donation of books to several art libraries. An additional, and we might imagine for the two aspiring curators, driving motive was to visit artists' workshops and studios. In Oshogbo, Nigeria, they saw printmaking workshops where drop-in locals could carve wood blocks and where artists combined personal experience and Nigerian mythology in their works. They witnessed the effects of colonial suppression in Ivory Coast and Senegal, where Pindell reported she heard "stories of French art instructors telling African students to draw street scenes of Paris." In Kenya, a nonprofit gallery provided studio space for artists to practice their painting, dance, music, photography, and printmaking. During their travels, Pindell and Sims saw artists make pottery, batik, and kente cloth. Pindell concluded from her trip that, although artists were often poorly resourced, there was "abundant talent" in Africa.[14]

While formative in the breadth of artistic material it introduced to her, the visit to Africa was not Pindell's first encounter with African art. MoMA hosted the exhibition *African Textiles and Decorative Arts* in fall 1972. Guest curated by Roy Sieber, the exhibition presented two hundred and fifty examples of textiles, jewelry, and other objects from sub-Saharan Africa. Pindell visited the exhibition several times a week for the four-month run of its New York showing, taking advantage of the opportunity to view its galleries when they were closed to the public. Critics and visitors alike embraced *African Textiles and Decorative Arts*. An oft-repeated point of praise was the exhibition's dispelling of the myth of "primitive" Africa. Sieber diverged from the well-worn trope of African culture as frozen in time, underscoring the contemporaneity of the materials on display. He wrote on the first page of the catalogue, "Nearly all of the objects have been produced within the last century; many are recent, and some are new. Almost all represent technical processes that are still in use and reflect contemporary African taste."[15] The exhibition also highlighted materials designed for the body—the titular "textiles" included clothing, and the majority of "decorative arts" on display were intended for bodily adornment. This thematization of embodiment may have further vivified diverse African cultures through references to everyday and ceremonial enactments.

Reviews show that the survey was favorably received, in no small part for its welcomed focus on materials previously little known to museum visitors. African sculpture, particularly masks, had become familiar to modern art enthusiasts through their appropriation by European and Black American artists earlier in the twentieth century. The show was also timely for its appeal to a larger number of Black visitors than the typical MoMA exhibition, which catered to white audiences. Since the late 1960s, artist-activist groups in New York had agitated for the city's art museums to attend to glaring inequities, particularly around issues of public engagement and racial and gender inclusion. An early episode in this period of heightened artistic activism occurred, for instance, when the organizers of MoMA's 1968 fundraising exhibition *In Honor of Dr. Martin Luther King, Jr.* failed to involve a single Black artist or juror. Artists' protests resulted in the expansion of both rosters, though work by most of the Black artists appeared in a separate gallery.[16]

The following year, MoMA became the primary target of the newly formed Art Workers' Coalition (AWC), which sought to democratize the art museum with free entry and greater public accountability. A roster of AWC demands in 1970 included an "exhibit showing the impact that the artists of African [*sic*] and South America have had upon the twentieth century western cultural revolution in painting, sculpture, music and dance." Whether or not *African Textiles and Decorative Arts* directly fulfilled this demand, one reviewer argued that it presented "evidence of the self-reliant creative powers of [Black Americans' African] ancestors."[17] The exhibition appealed to growing public interest in Pan-Africanism, which had been spurred in part by Black Arts movement leaders' efforts to promote Black cultural heritage.

Although Pindell did not subscribe to the tenets of the Black Arts movement, *African Textiles and Decorative Arts* piqued her appetite for African art and motivated her to travel to Africa. This exposure to African art and culture profoundly affected her art-making practice, with particular consequence for the development of the cut and sewn paintings. Most markedly, she never again stretched her canvases, instead allowing her paintings to "hang free" like the "flowing garments from South Africa, Senegal, and Nigeria" on display in the museum.[18] This decision to unstretch her canvases marked a departure from a fundamental facet of modernist abstraction as developed by painters including Piet Mondrian, Jackson Pollock, and Frank Stella. It also aligned Pindell's painting practice with the work of Black, abstract artists such as Sam Gilliam and Joe Overstreet, who had unstretched their canvases to generate sculptural effects in the late 1960s and early 1970s (see fig. 24).

While Gilliam draped and billowed his canvases like expressive, oversized curtains, and Overstreet tautly tethered his stained textiles in a manner evocative of sails, Pindell nailed her rectangular, unstretched canvases directly to the wall. This more staid display echoed her initial encounter with the African source material. Installation photographs from the MoMA exhibition show that some of the textiles and garments hung from the ceiling, suspended vertically in the middle of the gallery (fig. 56). Others, including kente cloth, were hung like paintings, flat against the wall. In the African contexts referenced in the exhibition, such textiles would generally be worn—wrapped and folded around the body and therefore never fully still. The director of MoMA's Department of Architecture and Design, Arthur Drexler, arranged the objects for the New York presentation, focusing on rendering the textiles immediately visually accessible. In other words, he maintained the protocols of a modern art museum in the display of functional and ritual objects. As art historian Doran Ross has noted of a subset of the textiles on view, "With their electric colors, vibrant geometry, and impressive scale, the weavings worked well (in the early 1970s) as dynamic examples of modern, if not contemporary, art."[19] In other words, the color, abstract design, and display of the textiles located them in proximity to modernist, abstract painting. Pindell's first encounter with this culturally diverse array of African textiles, then, foregrounded their pertinence to a form of contemporary art with which she was already intimately familiar.

The study of African textiles also inspired Pindell to incorporate a new way of handling materials into her production of the cut and sewn paintings—weaving. Several of the canvases, including *Untitled #19* and *Carnival at Ostende,* partially comprise interwoven strips of canvas, though thick paint and collage largely obscure this facet of their fabrication (fig. 57, see fig. 1). Pindell constructed the cut and sewn paintings through an elaborate series of steps that underscored her labor and situated them in postminimalist concerns for process and bodily effects. Notably, the paintings are not "painted" in the sense of applying brush to canvas, but fashioned through a process of accumulation. Pindell began by painting sheets of card stock and oak tag in rainbow hues, then excised small dots of color from these paintings with a hole punch, effectively destroying a two-dimensional work in order to create a three-dimensional one. With these dots set aside for later use, she fabricated her canvases. While methods varied across the cut and sewn works, each first required an arrangement of canvas pieces to compose the ground. Pindell started to work with scraps of canvas, left over from other artworks, when she could no longer afford to buy new rolls of canvas on her modest income at MoMA.[20]

One cut and sewn painting comprises approximately eight-inch squares arranged to form a grid, which is both the paradigmatic modernist form and the underlying structure of weaving (fig. 58). Some other examples combine this approach with a "woven" pattern; in sections of the canvas, Pindell folded six-to-eight-inch-wide strips over and under one another, "like a basket."[21] Another work, *Feast Day of Iemanja II, December 31, 1980* (1980), is made of long, two-inch-wide strips (fig. 59).

In each case, with the canvas arrayed, the artist then hand-sewed the pieces of fabric to form a seam-ridden and slightly irregular field. The degree to which the composite character of the canvas remains visible in the finished works varies across examples. In *Feast Day of Iemanja II,* lattice-like stitches bridge strips of canvas, revealing slivers of gallery wall, whereas in *Untitled #19,* stitched fissures are perceptible only in select passages, as paint and collage elements cloak many of the seams (fig. 60).

To achieve these densely textured surfaces, Pindell applied thick layers of acrylic paint to her canvas, then pressed a hole-punched stencil onto the wet

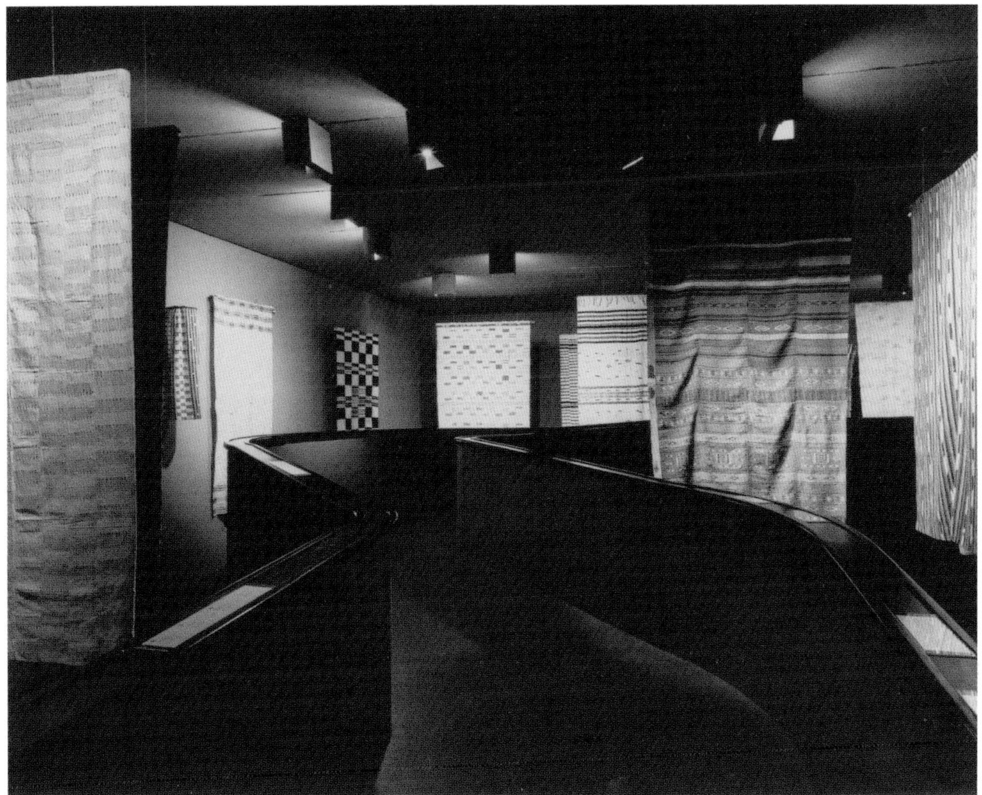

Fig. 56. Installation view of the exhibition *African Textiles and Decorative Arts* at the Museum of Modern Art, New York, October 11, 1972–January 31, 1973. Photograph: George Cserna.

surface, pushing the paint through the screen. The raised paint increased the surface area on which she could collage the previously painted chads. Pindell individually lodged thousands of these paper rounds into globs of paint, layering them atop one another, on their sides, and in the seams of the canvas with tweezers and photo-mount spray. More layers of paint, which often collected cat hair from the pets that roamed the artist's studio-home, a careful application of glitter and sequins, and a final dousing of "all kinds of cheap perfume" completed the paintings.[22] The smell of these perfumes, which has disappeared over time, would have activated a sense typically thought tangential to the perception of abstract painting. A strongly artificial odor would have permeated the areas around the paintings, perhaps attracting some viewers and repelling others.

The cut and sewn canvases critically took up the expansions and experimentations with painting that marked the medium's production by artists in 1970s New York.[23] Pindell developed the works from less heavily collaged canvases such as an untitled work of 1974–75, whose unstretched surface consists largely of monochromatic paint that is punctuated by brightly hued chads. Although the

Fig. 58. Howardena Pindell, *Untitled,* 1977. Acrylic paint, dye, paper, thread, glitter, sequins, and powder on canvas, 74 × 88 in. (188 × 223.5 cm). Collection of Mr. and Mrs. Lee Broughton, Cambridge, MA.

Fig. 59. Howardena Pindell, *Feast Day of Iemanja II, December 31, 1980,* 1980. Acrylic, dye, paper, powder, thread, glitter, and sequins on canvas, 7 ft. 2 in. × 8 ft. 7 in. (218.4 × 261.6 cm). Studio Museum in Harlem. Gift of Diane and Steven Jacobson, New York, 1986.2.

later works function as paintings in Pindell's oeuvre, they also thoroughly engage with the protocols of collage, comprising various materials adhered to a backing.

At the same time that the cut and sewn canvases were rooted in the medium of painting, Pindell used them to explore a textile logic. More than any other body of work, they play with the artistic surface as a tactile, textured, and olfactory membrane with accrued social meaning. For instance, the basic structure used to assemble the interwoven components found in some of the works resembles that of kente cloth, the most internationally recognizable of African textiles, which Pindell and Sims saw being woven on narrow looms in Kumasi, Ghana. In fact, Pindell has opined that her cut and sewn works have more in common with

kente or Ewe textiles from Ghana
than with the quilts to which critics
sometimes compare them.[24]

The term "kente" can be applied
to a wide variety of textiles, patterns,
and techniques. In the West African
context Pindell cites, it generally
refers to a strip-woven textile used
as festive dress and royal regalia by
the Asante people of Ghana and the
Ewe people of Ghana and Togo. This
arduously fabricated cloth consists
of three-to-four-inch-wide strips
of cotton or silk sewn together in
an alternating over-under pattern
to create textiles of various sizes.
Kente's meanings span both gener-

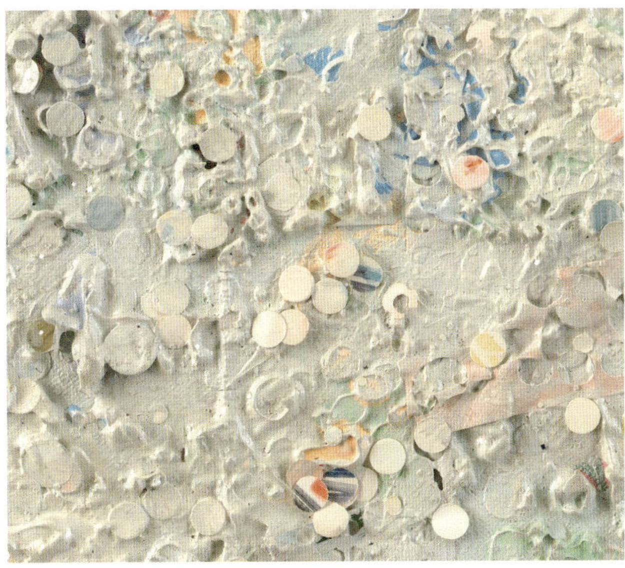

Fig. 60. Howardena Pindell, *Untitled #19*, 1977 (detail; see fig. 57).

ations and continents. As cultural critic Doreen St. Félix has noted, "In Ghana,
kente is prized as a link between ancestry and the present, a totem of tradition.
In America, kente is a magnet for a broad and diffuse desire for 'Africanness,'
the yearning to participate in the black diaspora. It is an organization of thread
expected to resolve the primal problem of our black Americans' continental
orphanage." Pindell encountered kente on both the African and North American
continents, as a Black American seeking an ancestral connection in the wake of
the Middle Passage, and as an artist expanding her abstract vocabulary.[25]

In contrast to kente, the woven strips of canvas in Pindell's paintings are
not apparent in most cases. Thick layers of paint and stitches camouflage the
canvas's interlacings. Intermittent slivers of green paint in the crevices of
Untitled #19 hint at the underlayer of canvas. As a technique for binding materials, weaving has its own relationship to concealment, since it creates hidden
layers. Visible passages of textile conceal those beneath them, only to be hidden
in turn. This alternating relationship between visible and concealed surface
undulates in two enmeshed directions. Given the additional labor and materials
required to achieve the woven passages of her paintings, why did Pindell obscure
them to such an extent? By interlacing portions of her canvas, she heightened her textile-based approach to the medium of painting. In obfuscating the
layers with collaged paint, she privileged these other artistic forms. The tension
between textile and painting here points to the fact that the ground of most
modernist painting is, of course, a textile. By conveying this tension through
means of diminished visibility, the works might be understood as thematizing

how textiles' foundational role has been sublimated, or hidden, in accounts of modernist painting that foreground medium specificity.[26]

Given Pindell's relish for West African textiles, it is notable that throughout the 1970s her paintings conveyed her interest exclusively through material means, particularly through their textures. In fact, she joined several others in this period, such as critics Sharon Patton and Arnold Rubin, in viewing dense texture as a distinctly African aesthetic. Pindell wrote that "the accumulation and aggregation of elements is a distinctive characteristic of African aesthetics." She drew a direct line between these textures and her own treatment of the surface of her works in the cut and sewn paintings.[27] This textural tactic for engaging African culture contrasted with ideologies of Black art that were being generated at the time and that favored figuration. In 1973, when she first unstretched her canvases as a result of her encounters with African art, Pindell entered a lively discourse about the relationship between art made by Black artists in the United States and African cultural heritage.

Dozens of Black American artists, several of them Pindell's colleagues and friends, traveled to Africa in the 1960s and 1970s. They gleaned inspiration from cross-cultural contact with nations newly independent from colonial rule as the United States lurched through its own civil rights struggles. Sculptor Martin Puryear lived in Sierra Leone from 1964 to 1966 and studied local approaches to woodworking. Artist Vivian E. Browne, an acquaintance of Pindell's, went to Nigeria in the summer of 1971 "as an artist looking for new experiences," "realistic about the fact that American culture" was the only one she had ever known. In 1977, dozens of U.S. artists including Faith Ringgold, Betye Saar, and William T. Williams traveled to Lagos and Kaduna, Nigeria, for the Second World Black and African Festival of Arts and Culture (FESTAC), dedicated to the "revival, resurgence, propagation and protection of black and African cultural values and civilization."[28]

For a Black American artist explicitly to evoke Africa in her work at the beginning of the decade was to invite the politics of Black Power to the reading of her art. While artists turned to African art as a potential source of artistic inspiration with a wide array of intentions, many of them, in contrast to Pindell, produced works that overtly referenced African cultures. Betye Saar, for instance, incorporated forms from African masks into hanging sculptural works such as *Gelede* (1971) after she and David Hammons first encountered a substantial collection of African art at the Field Museum in Chicago.[29] Artists who explicitly aligned themselves with the Black Arts movement, such as Nelson Stevens and members of the Chicago-based collective AfriCOBRA, frequently incorporated outlines of the African continent into their work (see fig. 30).

While Pindell's artworks do not overtly evince a Pan-Africanist consciousness, her travel companion, Sims, has situated their trip to Africa squarely in this discourse of the Black Arts movement. She wrote: "It was a startling revelation for us both, and we both arrived back in the United States having been jolted to a new plane of awareness about the actual relationship we could have with the Motherland that had haunted our consciousness as African-American women. We have often reminisced about that trip."[30] In contrast to prevailing discussions of the role of African heritage in a diasporic consciousness, Sims emphasized that she and Pindell gained greater awareness of their potential relationship with Africa as "African-American women." The gendered distinction further underlines the feminine denotation of "Motherland." Her comments suggest that she and Pindell charted a woman-centric, museum-sponsored ancestral homecoming of their own, opening a professional Black women's space for relating to "the Motherland" by leveraging the resources available to them at their respective institutions. This Black feminist political consciousness, which centered the women's experiences in professional roles rather than in family formations, countered what some saw as the Black Power movement's stiflingly patriarchal social structure.[31]

Pindell turned to the texture of textiles, a covert site of cultural engagement that exceeds the visual, in order to forge a different kind of interaction with African culture than that pursued by many of her peers. The inspiration she took from her encounters with Ghanaian art was no less profound. Her unstretched cut and sewn paintings echo the "free-flowing" textiles on view in *African Textiles and Decorative Arts* in their gentle draping quality. Nailed directly to a gallery wall, the canvases form a series of subtle concentric ripples, rather than tautly spanning stretchers or hanging perfectly flush with the wall. This additional layer of texture imbues the works with a sense of motion and emphasizes their membranous materiality. Pindell also explicitly drew on the accumulative textures of textiles on view in the exhibition, such as a batakari, or tunic, and an Akan cap (see figs. 6, 43). These objects, which the artist has cited specifically as an inspiration, appeared in a display case alongside other examples of heavily adorned garments (fig. 61).[32] Pindell's cut and sewn paintings share the textiles' dynamic treatment of surface through their collage of three-dimensional elements onto a hand-stitched textile.

Speaking retrospectively, Pindell has said that her attraction to Ghanaian textiles translated into an exploration of what remained a "subconscious" connection to Africa that she possessed as a Black American with ancestral ties to the continent. Further, she understood her textural form of engagement itself as evidence of her "ancestral memories" of concealment as an African cultural idiom. Scholar and poet Kevin Young has theorized an African American "tradition of hiding . . . a second sight to redress freedom in a culture designed to destroy any remnant of Africa or inherent humanity of an African being." Since the dawn of transatlantic slavery, Black people living in the New World have

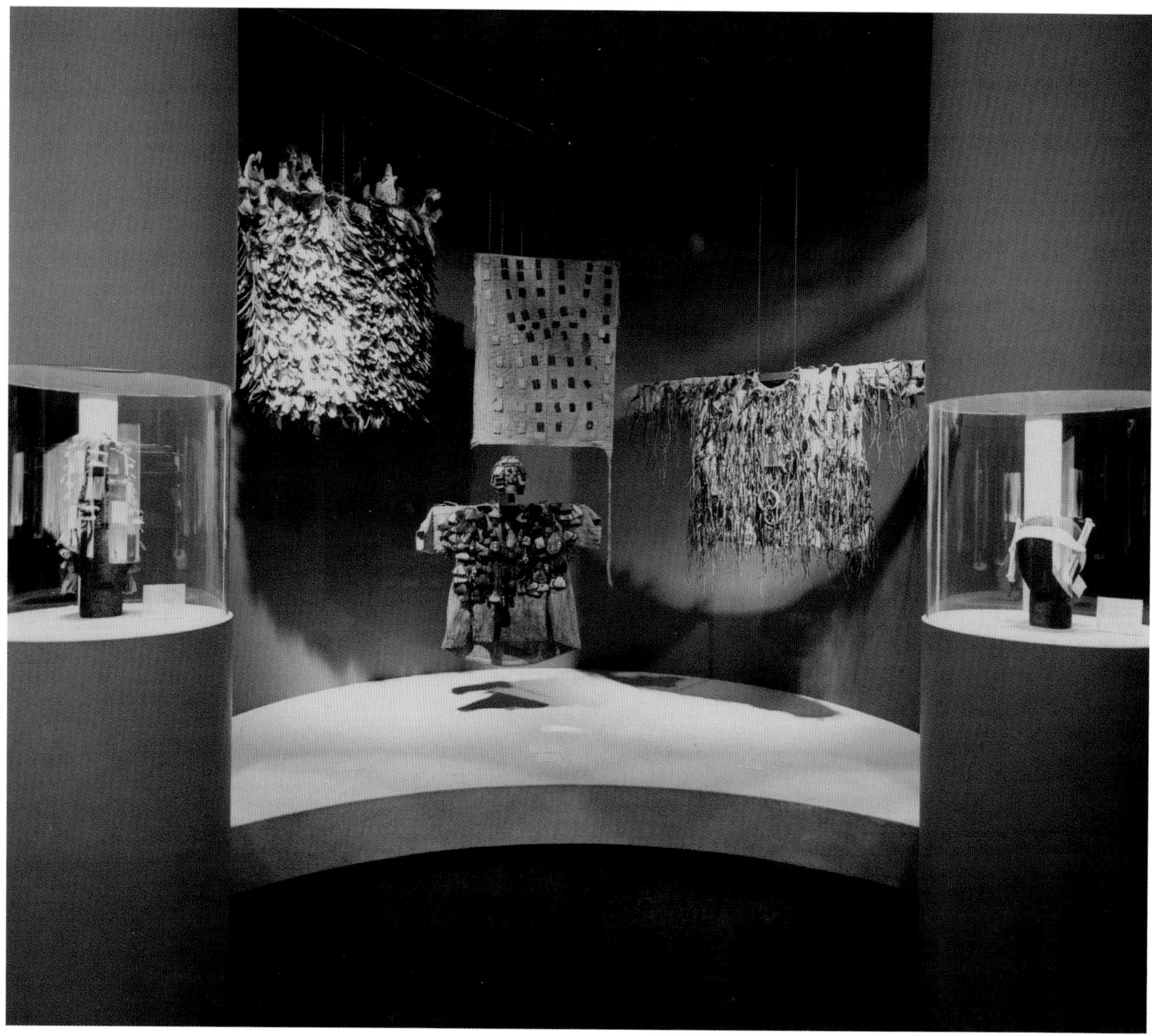

Fig. 61. Installation view of the exhibition *African Textiles and Decorative Arts* at the Museum of Modern Art, New York, October 11, 1972–January 31, 1973. Photograph: George Cserna.

"hidden, squirreled away, storied" cosmologies that white people wishing to maintain the racial status quo have deemed dangerous, illicit, and uncivilized. The suppression of African cultural inheritances within mainstream U.S. society helps to explain why Pindell, despite her early exposure to art museums, felt bereft of this cultural resource.[33] Textiles became the medium, and texture the content of Pindell's investigation of West African art as both a continuation of an African diasporic "tradition of hiding" and as a renunciation of the particular aesthetic-political regime of the Black Arts movement.

By the mid-1980s, Pindell's "subconscious" affinity for African art had resolved into a theory of Black diasporic artistic sensibility and overt allusions to African diasporic culture. For instance, in 1980, she broke with her practice of titling her works according to the protocols of modernist painting with *Feast Day of Iemanja II, December 31, 1980* (see fig. 59). Named after a Brazilian holiday celebrating the Candomblé goddess of the sea and of love, the work was the last wholly abstract cut and sewn painting she would make for several decades. Pindell encountered ceremonies in honor of the goddess during her travels to Brazil in 1977. The painting offers an early example of her turn toward more overt references to her travels.

African art represented one set of aesthetic interests among many for Pindell and her peers in the 1970s, some of whom also approached African art as a source of abstraction. April Kingsley's 1980 exhibition *Afro-American Abstraction* at MoMA PS1 brought together Black artists, including Ed Clark, Houston Conwill, and Pindell, who evoked African art in their abstract works through titles, materials, or their own narrations.[34] Each of these three artists was inspired to do so by trips to Africa in the 1970s. By presenting a wide array of abstract practices that drew on diverse sources from Africa, the exhibition challenged the notion that abstraction was only or even primarily a Euro-American inheritance. African diasporic artists have long worked in meaningfully complex ways both to engage with African artistic themes and to interrogate their own cultural notions of "Africa."

Many U.S. artists, including Pindell, have pieced together—or collaged—a relationship to African art and culture from a range of experiences. In discussions of her encounters with African art, Pindell has interwoven firsthand encounters in East and West Africa and curated viewings in New York museums. At MoMA she "was continually introduced to a confluence of Western and non-European visual art." Recall that her first extended encounter with African art occurred in an exhibition there, where garments hung like paintings. Black American artists in the 1970s took African art and culture as a set of traditions—not their own, but potentially relevant to their work and experience—that could expand artistic thinking in any number of ways that were not predetermined. Materials, shapes, colors, textures, and forms, themes, patterns, and senses of rhythm and order became the basis for cross-cultural art that was not necessarily about a literal Black identity but in which Black artists could seek a multi-voiced "mode of address."[35] For Pindell, for several years, the cut and sewn paintings served as a fecund site for germinating intertwined ideas about West African, postminimal, feminist, and modernist forms.

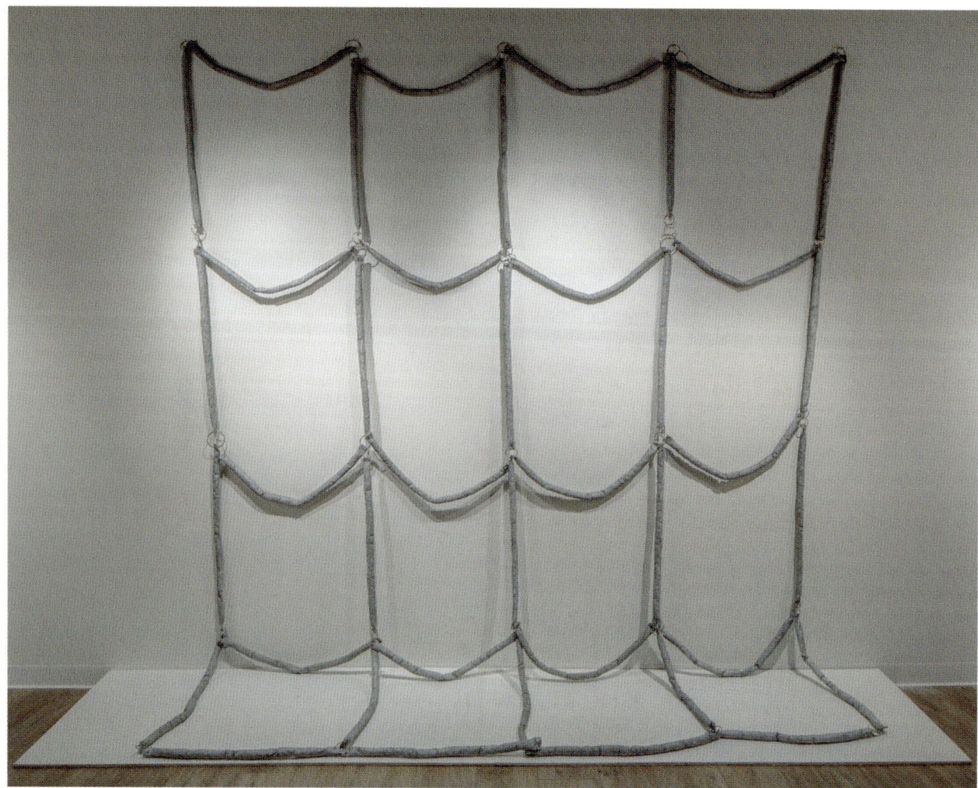

Fig. 62. Howardena Pindell, *Untitled,* 1968–70. Canvas, enamel, grommets, and foam, 12 × 12 ft. (365.8 × 365.8 cm). Mott-Warsh Collection, Flint, MI.

STRING GAMES

Pindell launched her artistic exploration of textiles through the gradual incorporation of thread into her oeuvre, experimenting first in sculpture, then working on mat board before moving to canvas. With thread, she introduced a material associated with handicraft into her practice. In her collaged works on mat board, she used it to develop a conceptual, textile-based visual language. With her use of thread in the cut and sewn paintings, she positioned her practice in relation to a Black American women's cultural inheritance. The shift brought on by thread began at the end of the 1960s, when Pindell began sewing the first of two soft grids—some of the only sculptures in her oeuvre (fig. 62). These early works participated in postminimalist idioms that would become an enduring theme in her work. Overlooked in many scholarly accounts, the soft grids offer insight into Pindell's early thinking about the fruitful tensions between industrial materials and craft processes, geometric regularity and variation, and the rational and irrational. She would pursue these themes further in the cut and sewn paintings.[36]

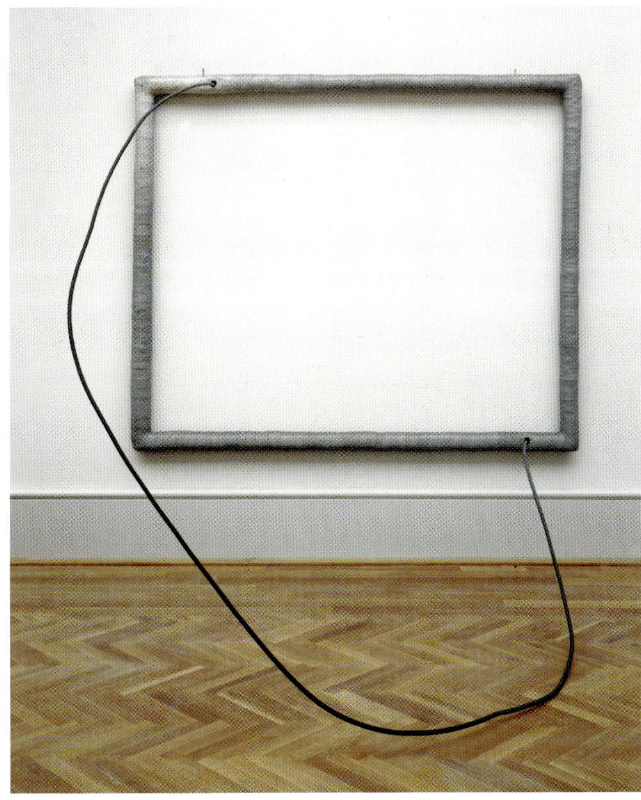

Fig. 63. Eva Hesse, *Hang Up,* 1966. Acrylic on cloth over wood; acrylic on cord over steel tube, 72 × 84 × 78 in. (182.9 × 213.4 × 198.1 cm). Art Institute of Chicago. Through prior gifts of Arthur Keating and Mr. and Mrs. Edward Morris, 1988.130.

Pindell finished the two soft sculptures while living at Westbeth Artists Housing in the early 1970s, where she initially had enough space to produce three-dimensional objects. To make the works, she cut scraps of canvas into thin rectangles and sewed them with a machine to form tubes. Pindell stuffed the tubes with polyurethane foam, and then tucked and sewed both ends of each tube. She sprayed the canvas surfaces with metallic silver paint and punched one to three grommets into the ends of each tube.[37] Metal rings connect the tubes, which are slightly lumpy. The entire sculpture hangs from the wall so that the bottom row of squares drapes onto the ground. These drooping grids make tongue-in-cheek allusion to bodily de-composure. The overall effect of the works suggests a jungle gym set of the first half of the twentieth century, though the sagging sculptures plainly could not support the weight of a human body. Pindell's sculptures thematize the rational giving way to irrationality. The sculpture's hardware follows its own rules rather than adhering to a logic of engineering efficiency. At any given joint, the number of grommets and rings varies. In some cases, three rings attach four tubes that each have one grommet; in others, one ring connects three tubes, and grommets are left empty.

The soft sculptures engage with a model of postminimalism exemplified by Eva Hesse's *Hang Up* (1966; fig. 63). Both works playfully deploy industrial materials to sensuous effect. Robert Morris likewise used the industrial in surprisingly somatic ways that countered the formal closures of minimalism. In *Untitled* (*Pink Felt*) (1970), segments of the titular material form an undulating pile on the gallery floor. Morris's emphasis on process disarticulates expected forms such as orderly stacks and grids and draws attention to the physicality of artistic labor. Postminimalist propositions by Pindell, Hesse, and Morris share a structuring tension between the body and the machine that speaks to their ongoing entanglements under late capitalism against the heralding of technological innovations that would putatively reduce the role of labor in daily life.

Hesse and Pindell achieve this effect in part by humorously contorting painterly form. As art historian Katy Siegel has observed, Pindell's grid sculptures "not only parod[y] the flatness of the modernist picture plane but [let] the 'painting' sag off the wall onto the floor, suggesting the play between painting and sculpture so key to artistic debates at this time." This artistic discourse placed painting in an inferior position relative to sculpture and incessantly harkened its "death."[38] In this context, many painters staked out ever more expansive definitions of the medium in the early 1970s and did so in part by scrambling elements of sculpture, performance art, and video art with the conventions of painting. Lynda Benglis's latex paintings (1969), poured directly onto the floor and allowed to harden, relocated painterly colors and gestural flows to the site of minimalist sculpture. In an inversion of Benglis's strategy, Pindell's soft grids place sculpture where painting ought to go—on the vertical wall—though they playfully droop into the horizontal realm of minimalist and postminimalist sculpture. By mobilizing the modular form of the grid to bridge the two mediums, Pindell suggests that recent sculptural practices had not so much exploded the logic of painting as reoriented it.

Shortly after its production, the second of Pindell's grid sculptures appeared in Lippard's consequential exhibition *26 Contemporary Women Artists*. The exhibition, held at Aldrich Contemporary Art Museum in Ridgefield, Connecticut, in 1971, featured the work of twenty-six women artists who had not yet received solo exhibitions in New York. Hailed by the Aldrich as "the first major exhibition of women's art since the Women's Movement," it "constitute[d] an attempt to remedy traditional neglect, to show how much good art by women has simply never been seen." Artists in the exhibition included Mary Heilmann, Adrian Piper, and Jacqueline Winsor. Works engaged with a spectrum of figurative, abstract, conceptual, and sculptural idioms, and intentionally so; Lippard wished to convey the expansiveness of "women's art" in what she called "a form of personal retribution to women artists [she]'d slighted, unintentionally, in the past." Pindell was represented by the 1970–71 grid sculpture as well as two irregularly shaped, abstract paintings. The sculpture returned to New York, where the artist stored it in her studio (fig. 64). Indeed, she made the work from light, soft materials in part because these qualities made for easier transport.[39]

Pindell's soft grids stayed in storage for years, as she archived this foray into sculpture.[40] However, she quickly developed a more lasting experimentation with textile logic. Pindell introduced sewing thread to collages on mat board in 1973, as in *Untitled #20* (see fig. 48). Thread, which she used to form a grid on the sur-

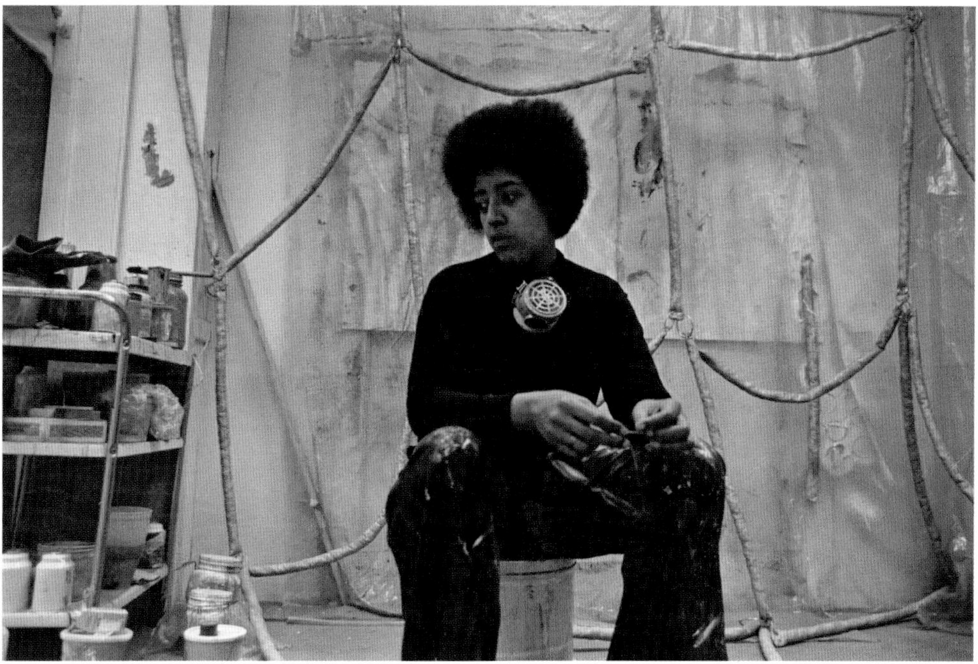

Fig. 64. Howard Wells, Untitled photograph of Howardena Pindell in her studio on West Street in front of *Untitled* (1968–70), c. 1972.

face of these collages, brought new kinds and degrees of texture to her work. The mat board collages extend the sculptures' chance operations and monochromatic palette. Pindell has stated that she "sprinkled" the chads onto the boards before affixing them, suggesting a random application, though she clearly intervened in gravity's effects by mounting some of the paper scraps directly on their edges. With the exception of the black inked numerals, the collages made in 1973 are all beige monochromes. *Untitled (Talcum Powder)* stands out for its darker beige tone, a muted ocher, as well as its deviance from Pindell's numerical titling system (fig. 65). It is likely an early experiment with the titular substance. A snow-like dusting of talcum powder covers the entire surface of the collages, including the vertical surfaces of lifted chads. This finish lends them a "frosted" texture and their even, monochrome palette. Pindell began applying the powder because she did not like the fibrous "patina" that spray adhesive left on the collages. The substance introduced another layer of corporeal associations to her practice through talcum powder's intended bodily application. Its texture also closely resembles cosmetics, reinforcing the implicit parallel between the fabrication of the collaged surfaces and rituals of feminine adornment.[41]

In 1974, just one year into her production of the mat-board collages, Pindell began replacing their beige monochrome with a vibrant palette. *Untitled #69* (1974) is mottled with deep blues, oranges, and reds (fig. 66). Pindell's decision to

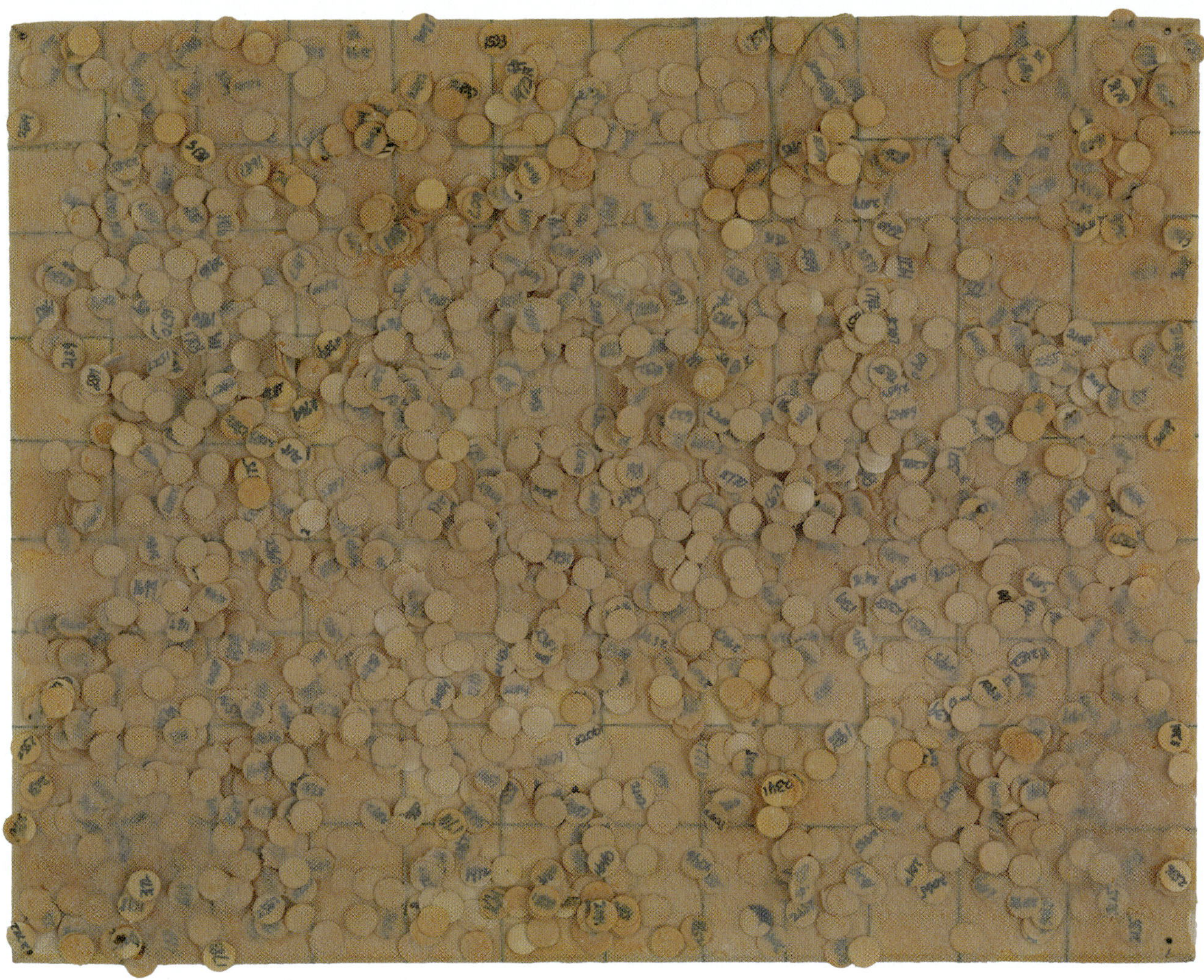

introduce a colorful palette to her collages starting in 1974 marks a departure from the muted tones of postminimalist and conceptualist idioms. (However, Pindell would continue to produce predominantly pastel paintings until the end of the 1970s.) Her recent encounters with colorful Ghanaian kente and other West African textiles likely helped to inspire this chromatic shift. As Africanist Robert Farris Thompson noted in 1983, "African cloth has for centuries, as it is today, been distinguishable by deliberate clashing of 'high-affect colors,' . . . in willful, percussively contrastive, bold arrangements."[42] The palette of Pindell's colorful collages evokes the saturated tones of textiles she saw at MoMA, though her dappled compositions more closely resemble the buzzing visual pattern of her spray-painted canvases than the "percussive" geometry of the Ghanaian cloths.

Pindell has credited her use of saturated colors to her coincident experimentations with televisual imagery in the photographic series *Video Drawings* (1973–76). Her turn toward the televisual around this time stemmed from earlier investigations. She thought of her spray-painted canvases of the early 1970s, through which she adamantly pursued the lessons of Josef Albers's color theory, as "a blown-up TV screen with all those little dots" (see fig. 36).[43] In Pindell's metaphor, the stained points of color that seem to dematerialize into the canvas are analogous to the ephemeral grains of electromagnetic current that comprise the televisual image. *Untitled #69,* in its layering of saturated hues through overlapping circles, resembles the atmospheric studies of surface and depth Pindell pursued in those spray-painted canvases (fig. 66). But whereas the circles of those earlier works sunk into the ground, as the textile absorbed the stained acrylic paint, the chads of the multicolored works on paper extend from the surface, almost seeming to push away from it.

Chads abound in the color collaged works—slender slivers of the mat-board surface peer from the clustered mass of paper only at the works' edges. The collage elements lift as much as an inch from the board, creating a much denser and more three-dimensional texture than any of the artist's previous works. No hand-inked numbers appear on these collages, which in their stead offer a glut of color. Pindell stretched the organizational logic of her works on paper into even less regimented territory toward the end of the 1970s. In works such as *Untitled #84* (1977), she positioned a dozen small, T-shaped paper props across the board to suspend a thread grid about an inch above the surface (fig. 67). This technique further expanded the spatial apparatus available to the chads, which clamber chaotically across the board, up the props, and along the tightrope thread.

These collaged works on paper exemplify Pindell's postminimalist concern for pushing rationality to its limits. In them, a throng of chads overcomes the grid—that signpost of late modernism, that, as art historian Rosalind Krauss has argued, lies always on the cusp of the irrational.[44] The massed chads emphasize the material aspects of the grid, rendering it a scaffold, something more akin to a clothesline than a graph (fig. 68). This proliferation of chads evokes the 1960s drawings and collages of Yayoi Kusama, who also long has deployed the round in exuberant accumulations. In both artists' works, the circle is rendered absurd through chaotic, textured multiplication. As art historian Briony Fer has argued, repetition figured in many artists' strategies for remaking modernism beginning in the late 1950s.[45] Pindell and Kusama, as well as Hesse, participated in this broader postminimalist project in works that addressed gendered tropes of rationality through their accretions.

String carries overt associations with domesticity, craft, and folk arts. In the 1970s, it appeared prominently in fine art practices, such as the work of Sheila Hicks, which gained public visibility and critical approbation. Significantly, Pindell first introduced string to the surface of her works in 1973, a year after joining A.I.R. Gallery and amid her involvement with women's consciousness-raising groups. However, she has framed her engagement with the material in relation to a folk pastime—string figures. Pindell has remarked that she thought of the material inclusion as an investigation of cat's cradle, a common string figure game she played in childhood.[46] Like many other string figure games, cat's cradle involves the manipulation of a looped length of string between two or more pairs of hands. In this sequence game, players collaboratively build off of the shapes made by their partner. When played competitively, the game ends, and a player loses, when they make a shape from which no further string formations can be formed. String games are inherently durational and ephemeral—the cat's cradle collapses into a jumble of string once the game is complete.

In the early 1970s, increased interest in global folk traditions, especially practices associated with Indigenous cultures, brought attention to string figures. Speculative lineages of string figures vary, but it is generally accepted that they have developed independently in societies globally. Franz Boas wrote the first Western anthropological text discussing them in 1888, observing that cultures in Africa, Asia, Europe, and North America all feature string figure practices, which can function as storytelling and mnemonic devices and as games. U.S. folklorist and artist Harry Smith began collecting string figure instructions and documenting their uses on Lummi and Swinomish Native reservations in the Pacific Northwest in the late 1930s. His collections of U.S. folk music and other cultural artifacts, including string figures, made him a fixture of New York countercultural scenes of the 1960s and early 1970s. Although it is unlikely Pindell encountered Smith's string figure collection in this period, their shared milieu fostered each artist's distinct concern for the objects.[47]

Smith's view of string figures exemplifies ideas expressed in a white counterculture based in the United States that construed cultural and ethnic

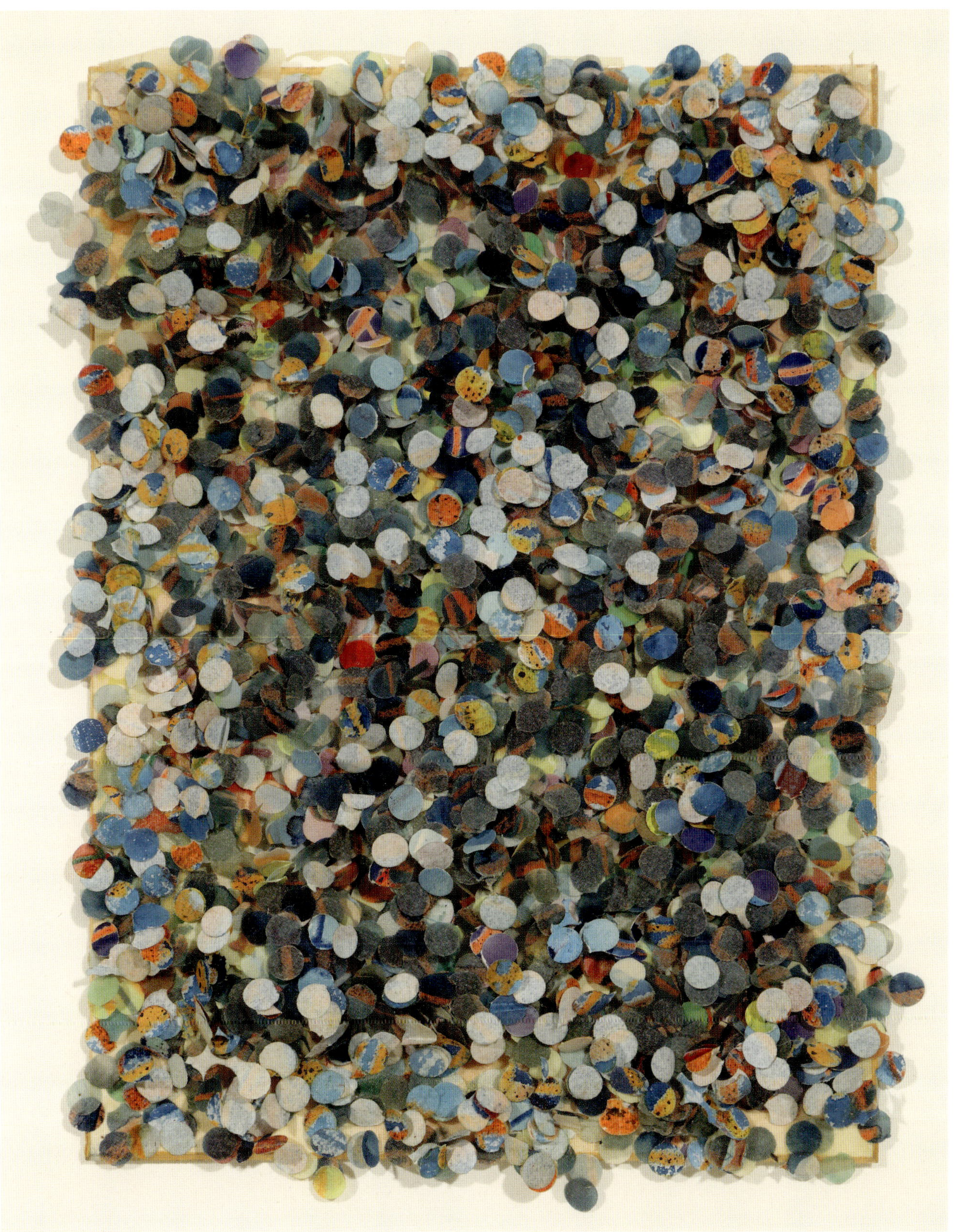

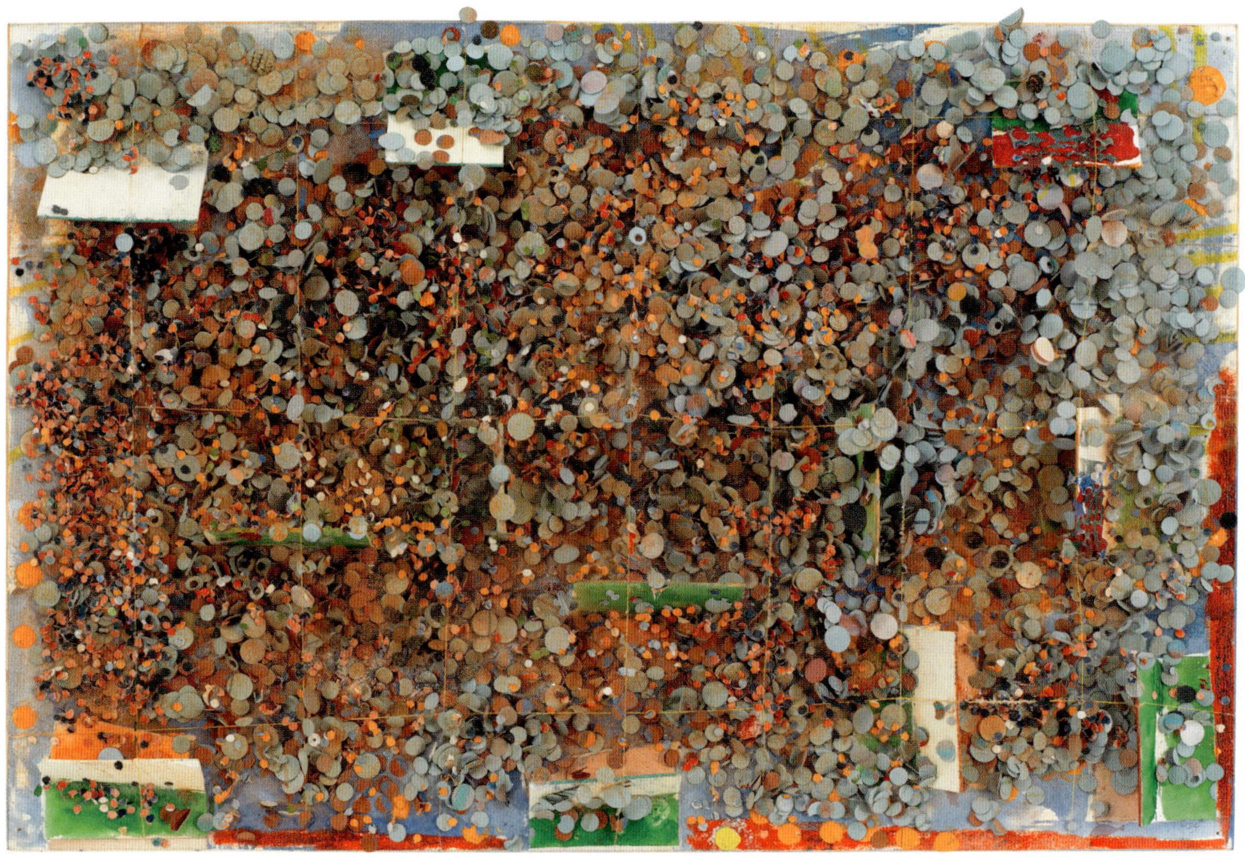

Fig. 67. Howardena Pindell, *Untitled #84,* 1977. Mixed media on board, 12½ × 18 in. (31.8 × 45.7 cm). Collection of Mr. and Mrs. Lee Broughton, Cambridge, MA.

otherness as a source of "authenticity" that had been lost to an industrialized society. Despite the prevalence of string figures as a children's pastime in societies globally, Smith hailed the figures as an idiosyncratically "primitive" tradition. He remarked in an interview, "It was the only thing that I could isolate off hand that was produced by all primitive societies and by no 'cultured' societies." By learning, collecting, and re-creating the material practices of "traditional" cultures, members of the white U.S. counterculture sought to feed a hunger for a cultural experience outside the bounds of consumer capitalism. (Of course, such ideologies created large markets for craft kits and other DIY products, such as those visible in the *Whole Earth Catalog.*) Despite their appeals to liberatory aims, these forays into otherness maintained the uneven power relations of what Black feminist theorist bell hooks has called an imperialist status quo.[48]

The invigorated appetite in the early 1970s for global folk and craft traditions arose in tandem with feminist art's reclamation of "women's work." While Smith

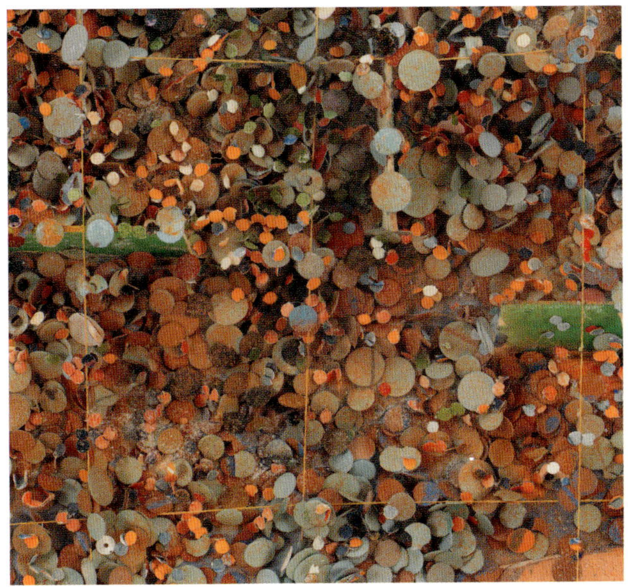

Fig. 68. Howardena Pindell, *Untitled #84,* 1977 (detail; see fig. 67).

situated string figures in broader concerns for an enlivened "primitive" culture, Pindell's examination of the forms occurred in the context of her engagements with feminine-coded materials and processes. Both as a specific reference to string figures, and as an engagement with handicraft more broadly, Pindell's use of string announces the hand as a vital, if not directly visible, component of the artwork. In string figures, digits enliven the fiber, hold it in place, and give shape and symbolic meaning to the material. These objects evoke both the domestic rhythms of childhood leisure and the skilled household labor traditionally relegated to women. The manual manipulations of string figures resemble fiber-based processes such as weaving and embroidery, while Pindell's allusion to cat's cradle suggests a domestic sociality, as two or more players are required to play the game.

String imported a childhood fascination with tactility to Pindell's oeuvre. Significantly, her earliest memories of art center on interactions with a textured surface. On a wall of their middle-class Philadelphia home, Pindell has recalled, her parents displayed a "thick, puffy reproduction" of a Van Gogh painting. Made of a thin sheet of molded plastic, this type of inexpensive print purported to convey a sense of the textured surface of the artwork it reproduced. The young Pindell made a game of sitting on her parents' desk and touching the painting. She has noted of the childhood memory that she was "sure that's why she does puffy stuff" in her own work, referring to the dense textures of her collaged works on paper and paintings.[49] The smooth, industrially made art object differed drastically from the nubby texture of Pindell's later collages. However, her comment suggests that this early physical proximity to a touchable artistic product, which was conditioned by her middle-class upbringing, educated her into tactile familiarity with art.

Pindell's use of the string figure, however, complicates its association with childhood play and craft. By contorting the material into a grid, she signals her simultaneous concerns for conceptualist idioms and the domestic. This adaptation of the string figure emphasizes its status as a system for organizing and conveying information. The gridded pattern also evokes the warp and weft of textiles—pointing to the continuity between the rational organizational system and the fibrous membranes that enrobe living bodies and everyday objects. Pindell's allusion to string figures illuminates the fact that these objects comprise a graphic semiotic system that manifests in the union between string and fingers. In other words, as a storytelling and mnemonic device, string figures function as a finger-based language.

This assertion of a domestic, tactile game as a form of knowledge transmission is reinforced by the analogous relationship between string in Pindell's mat-board works and the grid of her graph paper collages. The blue grid industrially printed on graph paper serves as an informational scaffold, a modular container for drawn or written data. Sewing thread offers a handwrought, textured alternative. The graph paper's mechanically printed lines exhibit minimal variations in spacing or thickness. They conform, and they do so effortlessly. The string grid, by contrast, attests to the artist's exertions. Small graphite marks near the edges of the board indicate where she measured its regular intervals. With great care, she cut into the edges of the mat board, creating an anchor for her strings with a slit through which they wrap around to the back. Pindell shows that string—a sometimes shapeless, jumbled, tactile line—can be transformed into a tenuously logical system. The works underscore the centrality of domestic and folkloric activity to the informational systems that have organized modern life. String figures suggested to Pindell that handiwork offered a potent conceptual mode of communication, opening onto the haptic logic of the everyday.

With her soft sculptures, Pindell introduced sewing to her oeuvre; in her slightly later collaged works on mat board, she knotted this handicraft with conceptualist idioms. However, it was with the cut and sewn paintings that she first consistently experimented with the craft technique of sewing. In a 1982 interview, Pindell addressed her recent use of sewing in her paintings: "I . . . liked sewing because of the internal geometry it gave the surface. Not only do you have the painted surface, but you also have this strange quirky geometry going on in the inside, which you may or may not notice. . . . Sometimes I allow for a separation in the thread so that you can see through the wall behind, which also gives more variety to the surface."[50] The sewing, she said, texturizes the canvas's surface, bringing paint, thread, and gaps in conversation with one another. It gives the paintings "geometry"—a term that connotes mathematical rigor and emphasizes the precision and technical knowledge required of craft practices such as sewing and quilting.

The visible stitches in Pindell's cut and sewn paintings, however, tend to be subtly uneven and large. These characteristics distinguish them from the work that a skilled seamstress would perform. Pindell deliberately sought out the

effects of visible stitching by experimenting with thread types that provided
different thicknesses and textures, including carpet thread and sail thread.
Like many U.S. women of her generation, she learned to sew as a child. Throughout the late 1960s and the 1970s, she made some of her own clothes, especially
formalwear required for events at MoMA, since she could not afford to buy readymade dresses for these occasions. Thus, Pindell "skilled down" her sewing in its
application to her abstract paintings.[51]

Sewing, as craft and handiwork, was a gendered and racialized form of labor
that artists of the 1970s wielded as a tool of feminist reclamation. It served
painters in particular as a resource for opening the traditionally vaunted
medium to associations with "experiences that did not belong to the story of
art," especially domestic labor. For instance, Ringgold's sewn panel paintings
conjure quilt-making, hair-braiding, and dressmaking. She has specifically
remarked that her move into fabric and soft sculpture entailed a deliberate
effort "to get away from" European traditions such as easel painting.[52] Ringgold
stitched together panels quilted by her mother, Willi Posey, evoking collective
handiwork practices. Pindell, by contrast, incorporated craft sewing into her
work through idioms that continued to engage with, rather than repudiate, modernist abstraction.

In this way, the cut and sewn paintings resemble the work of Pindell's
acquaintance and contemporary Al Loving, who introduced sewing to his
abstract painting practice after seeing an exhibition at the Whitney Museum of
American Art entitled *Abstract Design in American Quilts* (1971). The exhibition
reminded him of quilts his grandmother had made. Facing charges of "coopera-
tion" from Black artist-activists protesting the Whitney's *Contemporary Black
Artists in America* (1971), Loving actively sought recognizable ways to engage
with Black American cultural practices in his abstract paintings. He jettisoned
his hard-line geometric abstractions for deconstructed paintings comprised of
strips of canvas sewn together and hung loosely from a beam (fig. 69). The reference to quilting, his radiant colors, and the material textures of the unstretched
paintings allowed Loving to connect, in his own estimation, to jazz and African
religions.[53] Non-Black U.S. artists in the middle decades of the twentieth century,
such as Alan Shields and Anne Wilson, also blurred the boundaries between
quilting and painting.

Tempting though it may be to read the cut and sewn paintings as an homage
to a Black women's tradition of quilting, Pindell has resisted this interpretation
and has emphasized instead her interest in African textiles.[54] Her aversion to
the quilting comparison is somewhat unusual in her career, during which she has
remained open to a wide range of interpretive possibilities for her paintings—a
tack perhaps informed by her experience as a curator. A photograph of the artist

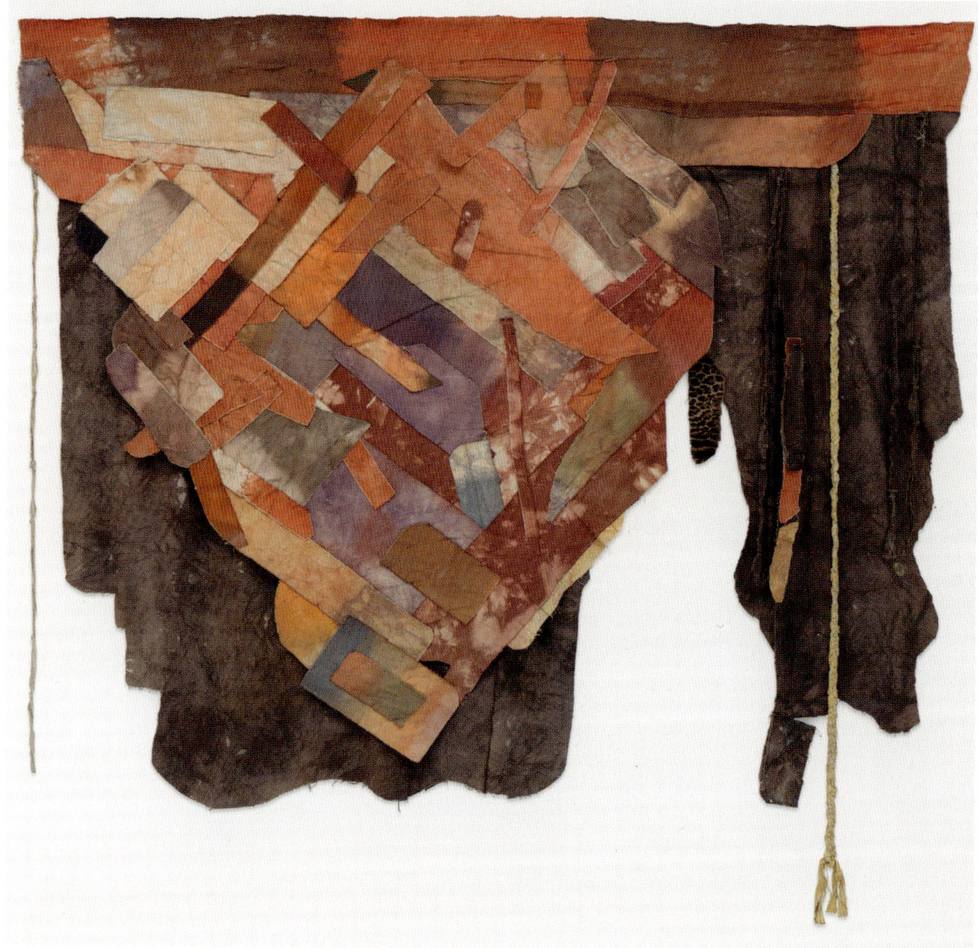

Fig. 69. Al Loving, *Untitled,* 1973. Canvas, textiles, rope, thread, and paint, 96 × 96 in. (243.8 × 243.8 cm). Collection of Peter Klimt, London.

sitting atop an in-progress cut and sewn painting from a March 1990 issue of *Elle* also suggests that she did not always shy away from the comparison—a quilt hangs prominently behind her head, on the wall of her studio (fig. 70). In the photograph, resonances between the paintings and the quilt abound; they share a geometric concern for form, hand-sewn textures, and an interest in color patterning.

Within the pages of *Elle,* this overt contextualization of the paintings within quilting practices may have been an attempt to bring them closer to the lives and interests of a broad readership; the publication is a popular culture magazine marketed toward women. However, in other contexts, Pindell eschewed the association in order to refocus her artistic authority. Her fraught relationship with quilting was catalyzed by a noxious comment a critic offered her in private sometime in the 1980s, telling her that he did not know if he liked the cut and sewn paintings but thought that he would "like to have sex under one of them." Reading the comment generously, perhaps the unnamed critic referred to the form of the canvases, whose visible seams and rectilinear form resemble a blanket or quilt, and perhaps as well to the appealingly sensuous texture of their surfaces. But his lascivious remark also reveals his inability to see Pindell as an artist. Confronted by an abstract painting that moved across several contemporary artistic discourses—postminimalism, feminist recuperations, the expansion of color field painting—the critic evoked an anti-Black stereotype of hypersexuality.[55] Pindell's refusal of the quilt, then, served to redirect viewers from the sexualizing potential of horizontality. With this notable critical reframing of her works, she defended the status of her paintings as art and her own position as an artist. The episode evinces an astonishing but all too common requirement that Black women combat their erasure as authorial figures.

Rather than being quilted—a process of drawing stitches through batting sandwiched by two layers of fabric—the cut and sewn paintings are stitched together at seams, or "pieced," as are many quilt tops. Stitches "close" the space between canvas strips in works such as *Untitled* (1977), but they also draw attention to these closures (see fig. 58). Thick, irregular pieces of thread index the movement of Pindell's hands across these junctures of the textiles, accentuating the painting's handmade origins. These stitched seams thematize the processes of fragmentation and reconstitution that went into the works' production. They show Pindell bringing elements together—the loose texture of Ghanaian textiles, the modernist grid— to make an abstract art expansive enough for her ambitions.

Pindell's works intertwine the craft practices of collage, sewing, and weaving with the industrial materials of paper, string, and office

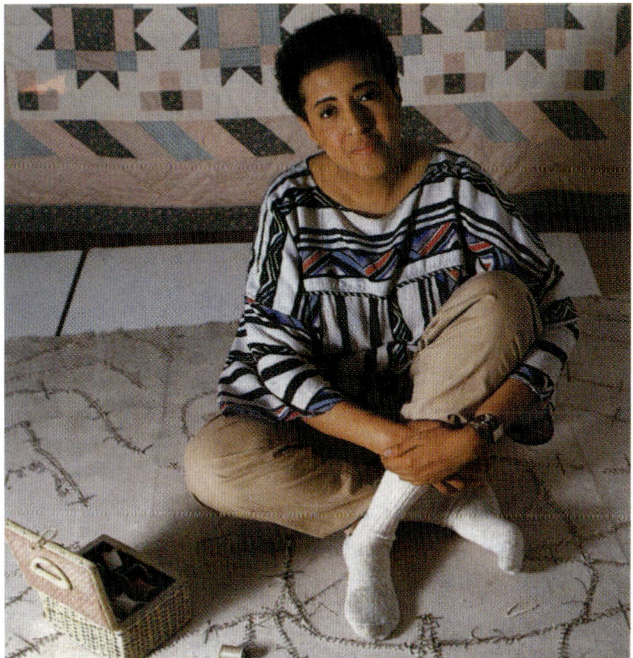

Fig. 70. Robert Pedersen, Howardena Pindell with a cut and sewn painting and quilt in her studio, c. 1990. Published in *Elle,* March 1990.

supplies. One of the most striking juxtapositions of the cut and sewn paintings occurs where the craft technique of sewing meets Pindell's ongoing allusions to administrative labor through the serial repetition of hole-punched chads. This proximity of handicraft and bureaucratic labor evokes the common perception that both comprise rote functions. However, by embracing these idioms in her production of large-scale, allover abstract paintings, Pindell asserted that each of these forms of labor could entail the highest levels of agential authority. In couching handicraft in the industrial, the paintings also offer an unresolved tension between the body and the machinic. Pindell's use of these competing protocols suggests that the aesthetic, through recourse to sensuality, can "counter," rather than reproduce, the "alienation of . . . modern life."[56]

MENDING

Through her engagement with textility and the haptic—a bodily, touch-based approach to the material world that includes but exceeds the visual—Pindell situated her paintings in a lineage of Black American women's cultural practices. She explicitly stated her desire to contribute to efforts to reclaim histories of Black women's creative authority throughout the 1970s. For instance, in "Afro-Carolinian 'Gullah' Baskets," a brief, handwritten essay published in a 1978 issue of a feminist publication on arts and politics, *Heresies,* Pindell considered several facets of U.S. cultural "amnesia," including forgetfulness around the "finer points" of anti-Black racism and the erasure of Black Americans' persistent motivation to create under these conditions. She concluded the article by grieving the loss of knowledge of African traditional crafts in her own family, which were supplanted by crafts that she felt were coded as "Anglo-American." (Pindell specified that her father taught her to knit and that her mother's sisters crocheted.)[57]

Pindell's text contributed to a discourse about Black American women's haptic practices that has spanned several decades. Art historian Huey Copeland has theorized that African diasporic women have long "turned to the haptic as a resource for self-fashioning and for the preservation of memories otherwise lost to history." He has argued that artists working in the 1970s, Pindell among them, forged Black feminist practices "predicated . . . on the feel of the subject's psychic and corporeal position."[58] Within these traditions, Black women have worked in tactile, sculptural ways that exceed the disparaging terms imposed by Euro-American scopic regimes.

Focusing on an earlier historical moment, poet Arna Bontemps and curator Jacqueline Fonvielle-Bontemps have noted that haptic perceptions have functioned as a tool for preserving and conveying cultural memory since the violent rupture of the Middle Passage because they were "more likely . . . to survive the

trauma of enslavement" than visual artistic elements. A cotton sack on display
in the inaugural exhibition of the National Museum of African American History and Culture in Washington, D.C., exemplifies the use of cloth as a vehicle
for memory. An enslaved woman named Rose filled the bag with pecans, a lock
of hair, and three tattered dresses and gave it to her daughter, Ashley, before
the girl was sold away from the Middleton Place Plantation in Charleston, South
Carolina. In 1921, Ashley's granddaughter Ruth Middleton embroidered this family history onto the fabric, fortifying the cloth bag's keepsake function and the
intergenerational passage of both handicraft practice and this particular narrative. Folklorist Gladys-Marie Fry has argued that quilting functioned largely as a
form of cultural preservation for enslaved people. For those denied literacy, quilts
could serve as a visual "diary" and a route through which to transmit symbols
derived from African cosmologies. The haptic renderings of these cultural forms
evaded detection by white slavers.[59]

These strategies have been handed down and adapted through generations
of Black women; tactile know-how has been a cornerstone of Black American
women's cultural practices for centuries. Contemporary artists such as Mark
Bradford, whose large abstract paintings feature collaged endpapers for hair,
make works that explicitly reference everyday haptic practices, in this case,
hairdressing. Art historian Freida High W. Tesfagiorgis has theorized that this
presence of "vernacular" forms associated with Black women in the work of
contemporary artists provides "evidence of historical, material, and aesthetic
links to the history of African American fine arts in the United States, and
links to the past/African heritage." The practice of claiming everyday textures
as a creative wellspring has been a critical Black feminist strategy for countering the constant erasure of Black women's cultural contributions.[60]

Amid the women's movement of the 1970s, the haptic played a particularly
prominent role in efforts to reclaim historically devalued cultural practices associated with Black women. Alice Walker, for instance, in a germinal text published
in *Ms.* in 1974, argued that intensely handworked, carefully rendered objects and
sites—quilts, baskets, gardens, and homes—are central to generations of Black
American women's cultural legacies. Walker wrote in particular of southern
Black women's creative work, generally made with "the only material she could
afford, and in the only medium her position in society allowed her to use."[61] Only
by acknowledging "low" sites of cultural production as creative labor, Walker
argued, can cultural criticism fully recognize the expansive range of Black wom
en's creative expression.

While non-Black feminists also deployed the haptic in the 1970s, embracing craft-based work traditionally associated with women, many Black women
artists related their work specifically to historically Black experiences. For

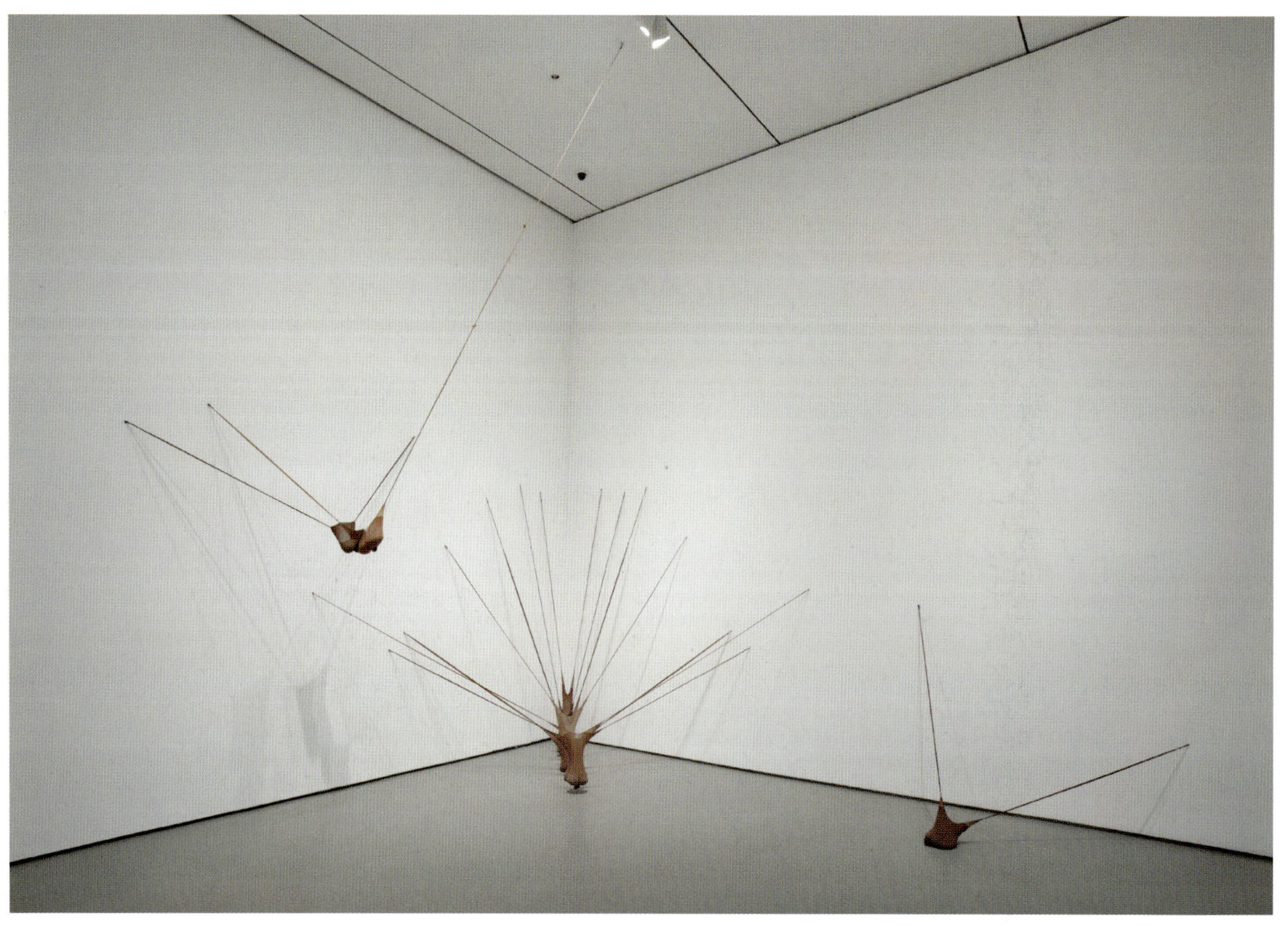

Fig. 71. Senga Nengudi, *R. S. V. P. 1,* 1977/2003. Pantyhose and sand, 10 pieces, overall dimensions variable. Museum of Modern Art, New York. Committee on Painting and Sculpture Funds, and The Friends of Education of The Museum of Modern Art. 857.2011.

instance, Senga Nengudi, a contemporary of Pindell who moved between Los Angeles and New York in the late 1970s, attends to a Black women's material history in her sculptural-performative series *R. S. V. P.* (fig. 71). Nengudi enlisted a community of women of color in her fabrication of sculptures constructed from worn pantyhose weighted with sand; she collected the pantyhose, which run a spectrum from tan to deep brown, from her friends. The abstract, though redolent, bodily gestures of the *R. S. V. P.* sculptures thematize stretch, confinement, and labor in expressive bounding arcs and drooping sacs. Their tensile activation through performance amplifies the haptic concerns permeating the sculptures. Performers manipulate the hose, stretching and bending the nylons, making literal that material's insertion of nonwhite bodies into the white box of the gallery.

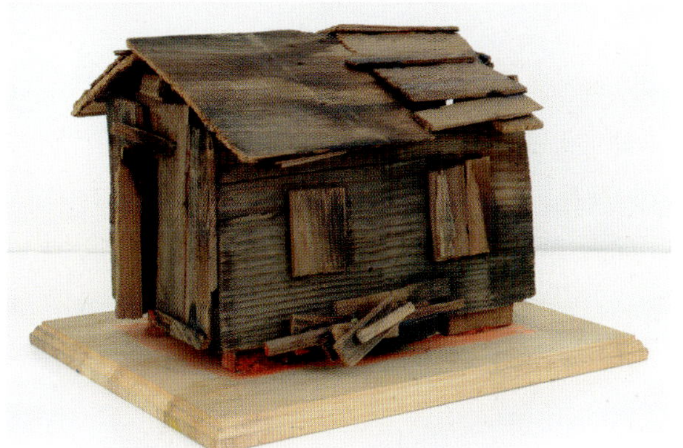

Fig. 72. Beverly Buchanan, *Patching Up,* 2009. Wood, adhesive, nails, and paint, 8 × 14 × 11 in. (20.3 × 35.6 × 27.9 cm). Andrew Edlin Gallery, New York.

Nengudi started working with pantyhose after the birth of her first child in 1974, as a way to think through the elasticity of the human body. Both nylon mesh and pregnant bodies resiliently expand to accommodate the life inside of them, and are indelibly marked by this elastic expansion. The artist understood her own pregnancy in relationship to a history of Black women's laboring bodies, drawing inspiration for her sculptures from her reflection upon "black wet nurses suckling child after child—their own as well as those of others—until their breasts rested upon their knees, their energies drained."[62] Nengudi, who was born in Chicago in 1943, connects her own pregnancy experience with that of women who have labored in intimate ways on behalf of white people who, in some cases, claimed ownership over them. The comparison raises important questions about the contemporary treatment of historical experiences and, further, about what it means to theorize Black womanhood across historical contexts. Nengudi's practice nonetheless exemplifies how artists in this period pursued a Black feminist cultural practice that could acknowledge, elevate, and draw upon a history of Black women's often overlooked and devalued labors. Consider Saar's assemblage works of the 1970s, which draw on keepsake practices. Beverly Buchanan cites her father's woodworking in her shack sculptures, which also evoke rural Black southern architectural practice (fig. 72). For many Black women artists, the haptic provided a method of situating their practice at the intersection of Black American material culture and women's handicraft traditions.

Black feminist theories of the haptic tend to position it in opposition to the visual, a realm marked by racialized and gendered caricature, stereotype, exoticization, and eroticization. Cultural critic Michele Wallace, for instance, has called the deleterious effects of visual culture on Black subjects a "negative scene of instruction."[63] The haptic, in contrast, is generally cast as a site of personal and communal empowerment. However, Black women artists' haptic approaches to art-making cannot be disentangled from the visual aspects of their works. Pindell, Nengudi, Buchanan—these are all artists choosing to work in *visual* modes. Nor can empowerment and oppression be neatly parsed along tactile and optical lines. Touch certainly has a history of violence, too. As gender studies scholar Jennifer Nash has argued, the visual offers a potential site of desire for Black women, not only "injury."[64] Pindell and other Black feminist modernists have investigated in their works precisely the entanglements of the haptic and the visual, pleasure and agony.

On one hand, Pindell's painterly embrace of textility participates in Black American feminist haptic practices that view the extra-visual as a refuge located in everyday material histories. Indeed, she explicitly has theorized her haptic aesthetic mode as a potentially "healing" practice. The dense textures of her works generate an effect she has called "surface tension"—a handworked quality that endows an artwork with potentially "empowering" properties for viewer and artist alike. Further, Pindell's use of densely textured surfaces injects her abstract paintings with quotidian materials—administrative detritus, glitter, talcum powder—bridging the aesthetic categories that so many Black American women pressurized in the 1970s. Her allusions to Ghanaian textiles exemplify Tesfagiorgis's theorization of "evidence of . . . links to the past/African heritage."[65] With these textural reference points, Pindell generated a culturally empowering context for her art.

Remarkably, Pindell's cut and sewn paintings extend her concerns for the extra-visual not only to the tactile but also to the olfactory. The "cheap perfume" she spritzed on the canvases breached the boundary between artwork and the viewer's body and carried classed as well as gendered associations. Her use of perfume created an atmosphere around the works wherein viewers could take them in, in a literal sense, for smell entails the incorporation of invisible particles into the body.[66] Perfume brought another haptic resonance to the paintings, reaching out and "touching" the viewer.

On the other hand, Pindell's paintings demand to be taken seriously as visual propositions. They engage with some of the most recognizable protocols of modernist abstraction, allover composition and the grid. With her haptic approach to abstract painting, Pindell strategically laid claim to a modernist legacy that had been harmful to people of color, especially Black women. For Pindell, the choice to work in painting—a visual medium, after all—and in abstraction was not a way around the pitfalls of the visual but a way through.

Pindell worked intentionally to produce a reparative approach to the visual, remarking that in her pursuit of haptic abstraction, she tried to "put beauty . . . where [she] found ugliness." Sedgwick's theorization of the reparative resonates with Pindell's approach to abstraction. She has posited the reparative as a mode of epistemological engagement motivated by pleasure and love in the face of an oppressive dominant culture. The reparative contrasts with the paranoid—a "tracing-and-exposure" method of journalistic-style inquiry, or a "hermeneutics of suspicion" that tends to produce a narrowing effect on thought. Reparative practices, by contrast, exhibit an accumulative logic, an impulse to gather and "confer plentitude" on cultural resources. Sedgwick has written of the politics of the reparative that these practices reveal "the many ways selves and communities succeed in extracting sustenance from the objects of a culture—even a culture whose avowed desire has often been not to sustain them."[67]

With her haptic reparative gestures, Pindell sought to mend abstraction. She deployed explicit markers of handiwork in order to situate her abstract practice in a genealogy of Black women's material culture that otherwise had been lost to her. Through these same textile resonances, she identified an African diasporic theory of painting and participated in feminist reclamations of craft. The haptic allowed her to gather from a range of sources, to bring all these meanings to a punishing visual regime and an exclusionary art world. Her practice refused to capitulate to the visual's foundational role in generating demeaning ideas about Black women. Instead, she imagined differently, reclaiming abstraction as a salient site of self-expression.

MASKING

Pindell developed the cut and sewn paintings nearly a decade into a period of fervent feminist debate about the relationship between art and gender and four years into her own experimentations with feminine-coded materials and processes. As an activist and artist, she contributed to efforts by feminists to stake out space for women's art in the New York art worlds of the 1970s. Reflecting on the gains wrought by women artists, Lippard wrote at the end of this decade, "Feminism's greatest contribution to the future of art has probably been precisely its *lack* of contribution to modernism." Pindell's art differed. In contrast to the full-throated disavowals of modernism that many of her feminist peers voiced, her practice remained rooted in the protocols of modernist abstract painting through the 1970s. Her contribution to "the future of art" was not a complete abandonment of allover abstraction but a hands-on makeover. In this way, Pindell joined several other feminist artists—Heilmann, for example—in combining paradigmatically modernist idioms with forms, materials, and methods of making associated with the feminine. These artists did so precisely in order to reroute modernism's de facto associations with masculinity.[68]

Further, in contrast to many of her white colleagues, Pindell embraced an emphatically feminine aesthetic to "signify upon" dominant notions of femininity, which in the United States have been structured around racial whiteness. Ultimately, through these works, Pindell created winking, sidelong surrogates for the "feminine" that teased out institutionalized gender and racial norms. She achieved these effects through an approach to surface drawn from masking and feminine cosmetics.

Speaking on a panel at the 1978 College Art Association (CAA) Annual Conference called "Women View the N.Y. Art Scene," Pindell declared that analyses of gender alone failed to address her day-to-day life as an artist and curator: "As a woman I have one experience, as a black woman I have another." The remark alludes to the failure of the U.S. women's liberation movement to heed the concerns of Black women, whose exposures to gendered oppression intersect with and are profoundly shaped by racism. In the 1960s and 1970s, Black women encountered familiar forms of racism in women's groups. Consider the women's movement's use of the slogan "Woman is the n—— of the world," coined by Japanese American artist Yoko Ono in a 1969 interview in *Nova* magazine. Ono and her partner, John Lennon, later released a single by the same title. Despite radio protests, the song won a "Positive Image of Women" award from the National Organization for Women in 1972—an accolade that suggests the breezily racist slogan appealed to white, middle-class women.[69]

As Black feminist scholar bell hooks has pointed out, this feminist catchphrase blatantly upholds racial hierarchies and excludes Black women from the category "women." The metaphor also diminishes the differences in social and economic opportunities granted to Black and white women. In 1970, critic Linda La Rue rejected the notion of a "common oppression" of women, calling it a "tasty abstraction designed purposely or inadvertently to draw validity and seriousness to the women's movement through a universality in plight." This appeal to universal struggle belied "the difference between being hungry and out of work, and skipping lunch and taking a day off."[70]

The insights into the feminist art movement Pindell offered on the CAA panel extended to aesthetics as well. She went on to counterpose overt, didactic art that has a feminist "message" with covert feminist art that features "feminine materials and processes" and no explicit political meaning.[71] Pindell thus laid out two dyads: Black and white women; overt and covert feminist art. These four vectors were among many in a complex web of perspectives distributed across unequal power relations that comprised feminist debates about art in the 1970s. With her cut and sewn paintings, Pindell theorized a "covert" and critically inflected Black feminism through a sidelong approach to feminine-coded aesthetics.

While the so-called feminine and feminism each constitute distinct theoretical terrain, in the 1970s, many feminist artists, including Pindell, turned to colors, materials, and methods of making culturally associated with women as a tool in the inherently political project of reconfiguring dominant aesthetic hierarchies. Her unstretched paintings introduced "feminine" colors and materials to Pindell's painting practice, marking a conspicuous aesthetic shift. Dabs of color created by chads punctuate the mostly pink field of *New York: Night Light* (1977), creating a buoyant smattering of cream, sky blue, and sea green on the textured canvas (fig. 73). Splotches of metallic glitter and opalescent sequins reflect light from the work's surface (fig. 74). This painting shares many qualities with the cut and sewn paintings, including a textured surface, but belongs to the body of unstretched works Pindell created on a single piece of canvas in the same period. *Carnival at Ostende* has a similar palette (see fig. 1). Along with glitter and paper, strands of thread are embedded *in* its protuberant surface, for this surface has textured depth. An opalescent sheen appears in patches, redolent of shimmering, pale makeup or nail polish. In case the visual cues were insufficient, the women's perfume that Pindell sprayed on the backs of several canvases originally lent an olfactory buttress to the paintings' signifiers of femininity.

Pindell understood the glitter in her work in relationship to a distinctly African aesthetic. Writing about African usage of accumulation in artistic objects, she noted that "visual textural drama is altered by both light and motion." The glitter in the cut and sewn paintings creates the impression, as gallerist Linda Goode Bryant has noted, that the paintings "wink at you."[72] This glint resists photographic capture, but in person, the glitter activates the paintings, imbuing them with a flirtatious femininity and inviting viewers to move laterally in front of the works to catch the twinkle. Thus, the cut and sewn paintings extend the choreography of viewing Pindell developed in her spray-painted canvases of the early 1970s.

Although Pindell's feminism was heartfelt and motivated by personal experience, her artworks suggest a more complicated orientation toward notions of "womanhood." The overt artificiality of the glitter, sequins, and perfume make for a "femininity" that is put-on and exaggerated, even as these markers are subsumed in an abstract composition that muffles their flirtation with camp. Pindell's cut and sewn paintings approach femininity as a form of masquerade—a theatrical (but oftentimes compulsory) performance of feminine gender. The paintings evoke practices of masking and cosmetics through their surface effects and Pindell's use of tweezers, glitter, powdered pigments, and perfume in their construction. As film theorist Mary Ann Doane has written, "It is femininity itself which is constructed as a mask—the decorative layer that conceals a non-identity. . . . The masquerade, in flaunting femininity, holds it at a distance."[73] Masking and masquerade both conceal an absence of an essential feminine identity and draw attention to the surfaces constructed by signifiers of femininity. In her unstretched canvases, Pindell deploys the enrobing textile logic of masking in order to theorize how ideas about femininity cling to "female" subjects, mediating their encounters with a public.

Carnival at Ostende repeats this concern for masquerade in its title, which refers to a 1931 poster by Belgian artist James Ensor that features masks. Pindell encountered a copy of the poster in MoMA's permanent collection of prints,

Fig. 73. Howardena Pindell, *New York: Night Light,* 1977. Acrylic and mixed media on canvas, 82½ × 96¾ in. (209.6 × 245.8 cm). Collection Albright-Knox Art Gallery, Buffalo, NY. Bequest of Arthur B. Michael, by exchange, 2014, 2014:14.2.

which she helped to oversee. This example of Ensor's work attests to his enduring interest in carnivals and frequent depiction of masks. Like Ensor's poster, Pindell's painting punctuates a pastel field with saturated primary and secondary colors.

Pindell was not alone in approaching signifiers of femininity at an oblique angle. Contemporary Ree Morton, whose works Pindell admired, created an installation entitled *Bake Sale* for a women's faculty exhibition at the Philadelphia College of Art in 1974 that included a menagerie of "dime-store materials—paper doilies, small cheap 'Old Master' reproductions, contact paper, glitter,

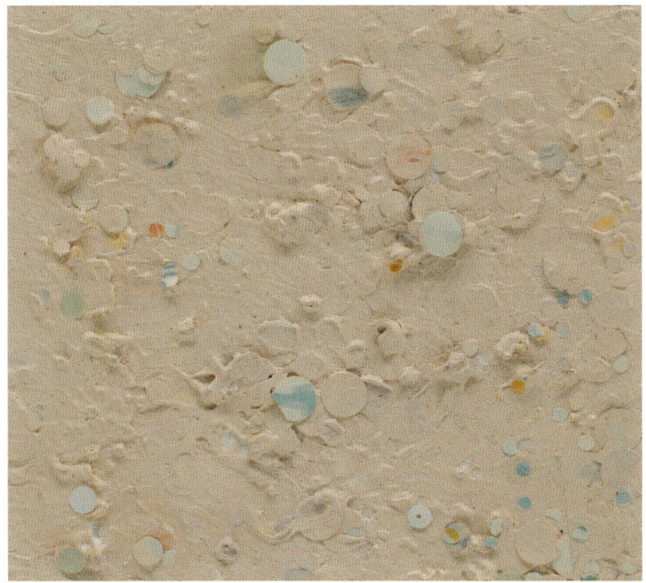

Fig. 74. Howardena Pindell, *New York: Night Light,* 1977 (detail; see fig. 73).

and candy gumdrop-like 'jujubes.'" Initially, Morton, who was a white woman, intended the pink swag and pastel bows of the no-longer extant *Bake Sale* as an ironic riposte to the premise of the exhibition, which the women faculty considered an anemic gesture toward glaring issues of gender inequity in the Art Department.[74] However, these campy, feminine-coded forms became motifs in Morton's subsequent work, such as *For Kate* (1976; fig. 75).

Pindell's and Morton's approaches to femininity, which each draw on a post-minimalist concern for bodily effects and conspicuous insertions of the hand, contrast with the more literal searches for viable feminine aesthetics undertaken by feminist artists, including those involved in the Pattern and Decoration movement, such as Joyce Kozloff.[75] (In keeping with white countercultural practices of the period, many of these feminist artists turned to the "non-Western" as a source of inspiration.) Nonetheless, Pindell and Morton also earnestly contributed to feminist efforts to expand what counted as "art," flaunting a staged femininity as they did so. The waggish presentation of bedazzled surfaces suggests that Pindell and Morton thought of femininity not only as a social code, but one whose signifiers could be playfully taken up, teased out, performed, or pinned on the gallery wall.

The cut and sewn paintings' glitzy femininity contributed to a feminist probing of the modernist suppression of the decorative. Some feminist artists in the 1970s took the outcast decorative as a productive challenge—a new women's art grounded in the very rejects of modernist criticism might truly break free from what they viewed as an inherently sexist set of aesthetic criteria. Once wryly dubbed "the only art sin" by Hesse, the decorative played a defining though ambiguous role in modernist art criticism throughout the twentieth century. Beginning with the first appearances of abstraction in twentieth-century European art, critics posited decoration's chief characteristics to be unreflective labor and dependence on a larger aesthetic scheme. These traits, they contended, distinguished it from art.[76]

As art historian Ann Gibson has noted, modernist discourse continued to associate the decorative and craft with non-white cultural and ethnic groups

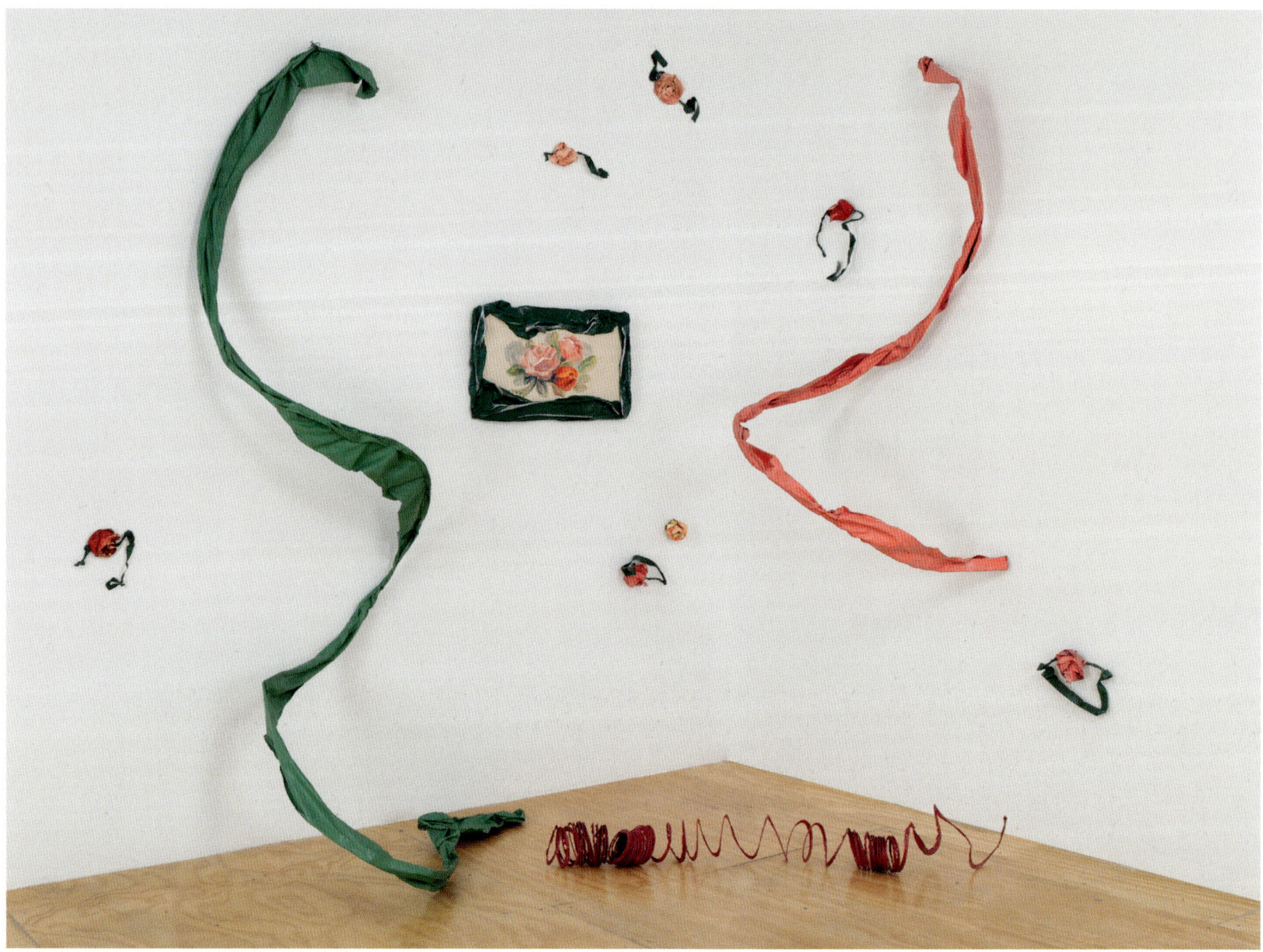

Fig. 75. Ree Morton, *For Kate,* 1976. Oil on wood and wire and enamel on celastic, dimensions variable. Private collection.

as well as with womanhood throughout the twentieth century. The decorative functioned in part as a discursive strategy for shoring up an aesthetic hierarchy that assigned value to artistic labor and tastes along social categories such as class, race, and gender. Within midcentury Greenbergian criticism, the decorative described the threatening "specter" of abstract, allover painting devolving into a uniform field of "equivalency," a wallpaper pattern that could extend indefinitely. In other words, the decorative was an inherent liability for allover abstraction, and it defined advanced art's limiting condition as "superficial ornamentation" or mere displays of craft, skill, and precision.[77]

With their confectionary surfaces, Pindell's cut and sewn paintings indisputably play with modernist notions of ornamentation. What art critic Holland Cotter has called their "adamant decorativeness" occurs in their display of materials associated with feminine masquerade, such as glitter, and the precise labor obviously required to achieve their detailed collage. The cheerfully colorful chads are redolent of confetti. Glitter and sequins evoke festive décor. Pindell further played up the decorative connotations of her materials in their idiosyncratic application; she filled plastic bottles with powdered pigments and then covered their openings with old pantyhose, dusting color onto her canvases in an evocation of cosmetics application or cake decoration. The artist has described this process as "seasoning," a cooking metaphor that recalls Lorde's insights into the potential erotic pleasures of food preparation in the vivid margarine passage of her 1978 essay "Uses of the Erotic."[78]

The coexistence of a multiplicity of sensuous, "decorative" materials on the surface of the paintings—olfactory, tactile, and visual—amplified their feminine presence. Scent in particular, with its ability to trigger the mnemonic, activated the paintings as surrogate bodies, as viewers might conjure memories of people or places associated with the odors. Shimmering, scented surfaces, the works projected their presence beyond the gallery wall, creating a three-dimensional field of light and perfume. The cut and sewn paintings simultaneously evoked an artificially enhanced feminine embodiment and, through their nod to Ghanaian textile garments, an African diasporic presence. While she refused to represent herself in a literal way in her art, Pindell used abstraction to locate a Black femininity in the realm of advanced art.

The cut and sewn paintings are at once strikingly modernist as well as feminine. The "covert" feminism of the canvases, expressed through their feminine colors, materials, and modes of making, is undergirded by the male-coded modernist forms of the grid and large, allover abstract painting. Lippard in fact once praised Pindell's works for "embodying the synthesis between women's sensibility" and these more familiar masculinist conventions of abstract art.[79] For instance, the canvases combine the putatively feminine scale of collage and the "masculine" dimensions of modernist painting. The tension between miniscule textural details and allover abstraction invites viewers to step forward, then pull back. Only by swiveling between these two scales might one appreciate both the delicate work of skilled fingers and the compositional repetition with variation. By collaging and sewing an abstract painting, Pindell consciously evokes the competing protocols of feminist art and modernist art criticism, as well as the exclusions inscribed in each.

The cut and sewn paintings' syncretism furthermore illuminates other "feminine" hauntings of modernist abstraction. Consider Pollock's *Lavender Mist,* a work whose colloquial title, through its conjuring of a mythical feminine ephemerality, could well share a name with a cosmetic spray marketed to women. The painting's titular light-gray violet dances alongside warm peach paint, contributing to a palette similar to Pindell's. While certain qualities are constructed as "feminine" in works by women artists, such as Lee Krasner, they rarely are coded as such when they appear in the art of Pollock or other male abstractionists such as Sam Francis.[80] Pindell's cut and sewn paintings ask us to see how modernist forms and the "feminine" are intertwined. Rigorous confections, they theorize a femininity culled from seemingly disparate sources that were in fact the commonplaces of the artist's life and work.

Of Pindell's abstract works, the cut and sewn paintings offer the most sustained engagements and astute explorations of the contradictions she encountered as a Black woman artist. By overlaying kente cloth, the quilt, the modernist grid, and clerical work, the paintings call for a reconsideration of received narratives that have located Black feminisms and abstraction in far-flung discursive sites. The paintings bring together disparate forms of labor that each speak to Pindell's effortful movements through the world. Craft procedures, the routines of feminine bodily adornment, the seclusion of modernist studio painting, and the paperwork of bureaucracy—Pindell navigated each of these as realities of the culture she inhabited. These works are indubitably individual in the sense that their fabrication participated in her efforts to "empower" and "heal" herself. But the aesthetic force with which they surface the tensions of late twentieth-century life, labor, and artistic formations points to her capacity to turn subjective experience into social insight.

CONCLUSION

The cut and sewn paintings subtly thematize the push and pull of experience. For a period of time after the works were made, viewers may have been drawn close by a waft of perfume, only to be repelled by cloying scents. Details such as the collaged chads invite closer inspection, while the shine of glitter deflects one's gaze through a reflection of light.[81] Dense textures of extruded pastel paint may tempt one's fingers but may not be touched. The layering of bureaucratic and domestic materials scrambles normative ideas about the site of art-work. Exuberant in their feminine beauty and their multivalent allusions, the cut and sewn paintings play with the reach of sight and hands and the viewer's ability to know and understand what is in front of her. In other words, the paintings do nothing short of asking us to look afresh at the viability of abstraction as a critical practice. With them, Pindell made abstraction all her own.

In subsequent years, Pindell carried the lessons of these paintings into a figurative practice, using collage and layered surfaces to attend to the contradictions of representation as an inherently abstracting process. Her abiding investment in textility particularly informed her engagement with mass media in a photographic series based on televisual imagery, called the *Video Drawings*, and her iconic feminist video of 1980, *Free, White and 21*. In these works, Pindell approached the figurative surface as a skin—a social and technological membrane that adheres to subjects in the public sphere. These figurative projects build on a central insight of the cut and sewn paintings; they tap into what David Joselit has identified as a defining concern of modernism—the registration on a painting's surface of psychic depth as a social condition of human subjectivity.[82] Part of the cut and sewn paintings' critical work is that they both meet and thwart this expectation that the artwork is, in a sense, a distillation of the artist herself. Pindell borrowed from her understanding of an African aesthetic of concealment and feminine notions of masquerade to interrupt the modernist model of abstract painting as a presentation of the artist's subjectivity. The cut and sewn paintings give the viewer no clear, singular, or fixed sense of where to place them or the artist. Rather, they knot and make less comfortable supposed antinomies of late twentieth-century art, creating a Black feminist modernism.

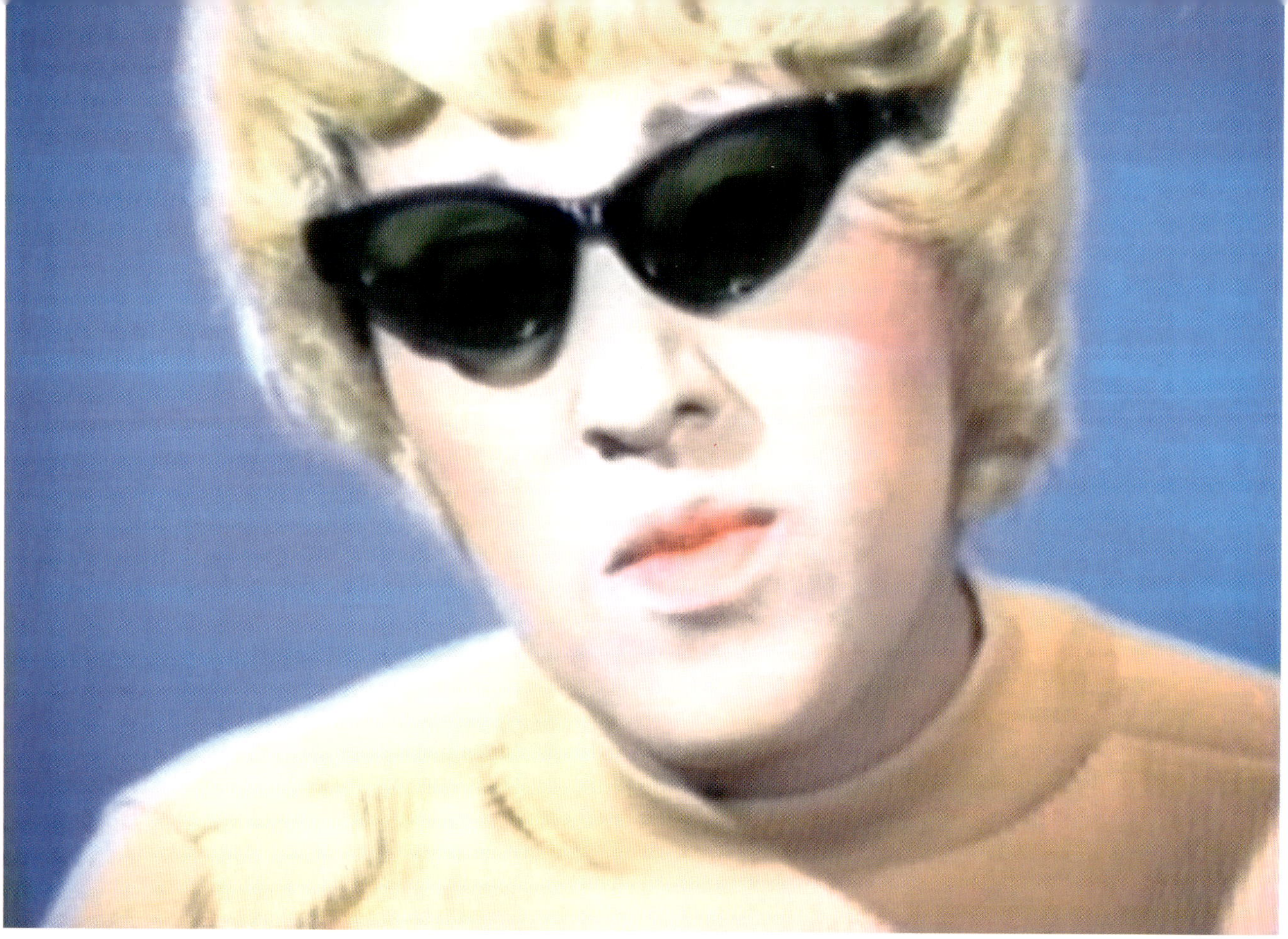

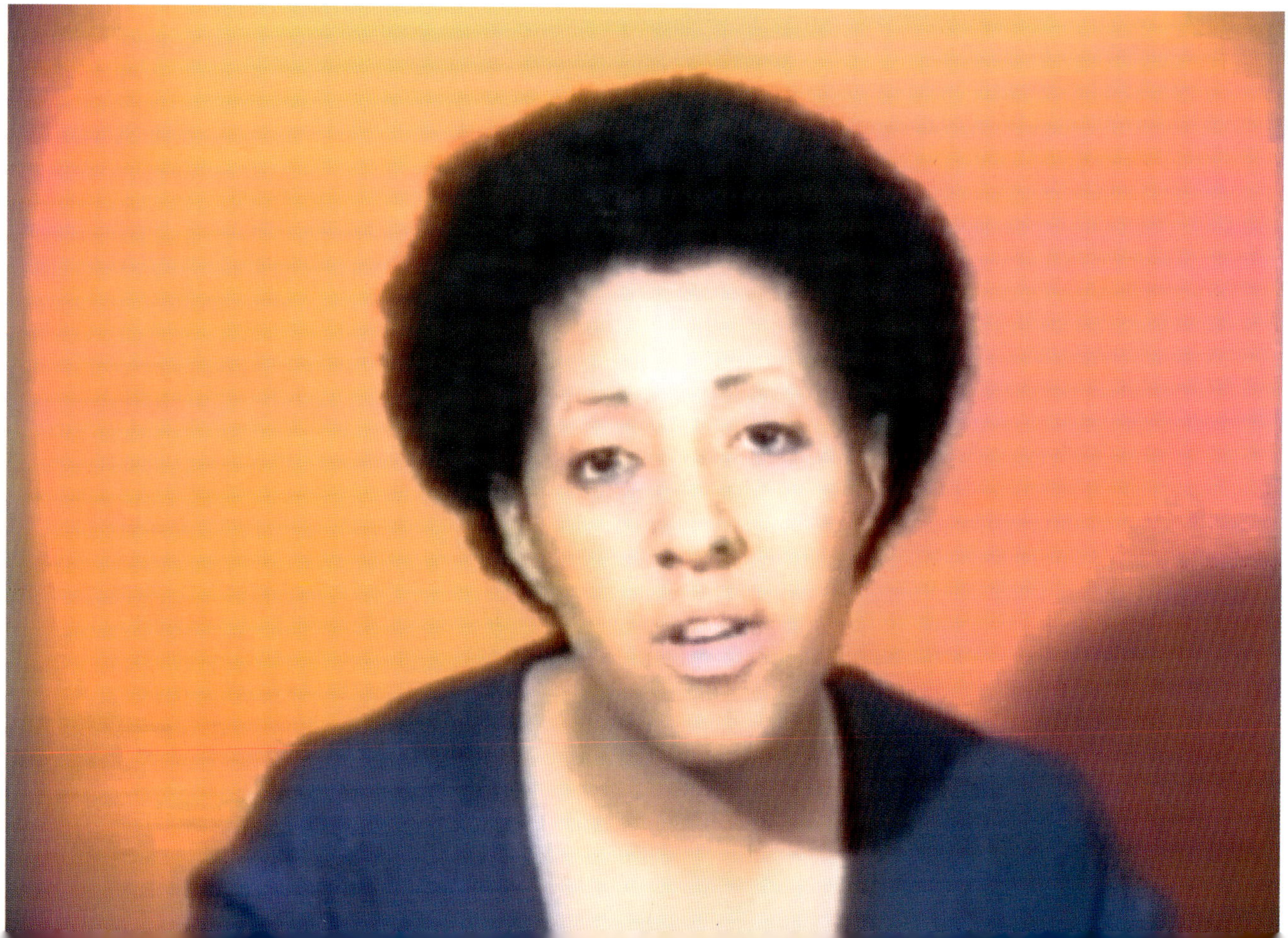

4 • Screen, Skin

In New York's record-breaking heat during the summer of 1980, Howardena Pindell "couldn't shake" an idea—she needed to see herself in a blond wig. This nagging image could not be conveyed via her usual methods of art-making; Pindell considered herself foremost a painter and long had abandoned figuration as part of this practice. She needed to make something more immediate, more biting, and more quickly executed than the laboriously collaged, allover abstract canvases she had produced in recent years. Pindell knew that it had to be video, and her conviction on this point overrode significant concerns; she considered herself "totally ignorant" of the medium, and up to this point she had dismissed it as "very narcissistic and self-involved."[1]

Free, White and 21, the twelve-minute color video that emerged from this urgent image, opens with a brief shot of Pindell in whiteface (fig. 76). Pancake makeup, dark cat-eye sunglasses, and that unremitting blond wig, styled in an outmoded bob, transform her into the character of the White Woman. The video centers on a series of verbal responses this character directs at the Artist, a Black woman also played by Pindell, who matter-of-factly recounts seven experiences of racial discrimination and harassment (fig. 77). For each shot, the Artist wears a different top against a variety of monochromatic backdrops, lending the character a collaged quality. The Artist and the White Woman engage in a conversational exchange through the use of crosscut editing. When she speaks, the Artist directs her narrations to the camera; each of her anecdotes offers a painful illustration, based on Pindell's own experiences, of the mundane, violent inequities wrought by white supremacy. She describes, for instance, being passed over for enrollment in an honors class by a teacher who told her that while she was qualified, a white student would "go further." The White Woman responds dismissively to each vignette, addressing the Artist in the second person as "ungrateful" and "paranoid," using a high-pitched, nasal tone—a vocal white-face. Through the overt artificiality of this parodic performance, Pindell strips the character of authority; she is as much a punch line as a villain. The White

Figs. 76, 77. Howardena Pindell, Still from *Free, White and 21,* 1980. Color video with sound, 12:15 min. Garth Greenan Gallery, New York.

Woman repeats the titular catchphrase, "But of course I'm free, white and 21," a recitation that she uses to defend her inability to understand both what the Artist says and why she says it. The once-common phrase saw its heyday in 1930s Hollywood cinema. Like the hairstyle the White Woman wears, it was an anachronism by 1980, but the expression would have been familiar to audiences who had lived through U.S. segregation and the civil rights movement.[2]

Although Pindell's deliberate turn to video would be fleeting, it initiated a drastic reconceptualization of audience and authorship that has been integral to her artistic legacy.[3] With *Free, White and 21,* I argue, she launched a reinvigorated artistic project that exploited the reproductive capacities and mass appeal of video to scrutinize the racial dynamics of artistic viewership. Most trenchantly, she critiqued the ways in which the evaluative systems at the center of both mass media and art criticism privilege whiteness. She also examined how she herself had internalized this white supremacist logic. The video continued the interrogation of artistic discourse that Pindell had long pursued in her abstract work, but newly approached this project through a representational idiom. The contrast between the video's excoriating critique and her earlier institutional affiliations with Yale and the Museum of Modern Art (MoMA), as well as the difference between the work's pop aesthetics and the relatively staid postminimalist abstract paintings she made in the late 1970s, enhanced the perceived radicality of *Free, White and 21.* With more cutting tools at her disposal— the blond wig is exemplary—she subjected whiteness to an exacting critical investigation.

Free, White and 21 examines the contradictions inherent to representation as a dually depictive and political project. Representation refers to depiction, as in, to re-present something in a painting. It also means delegation, or representation in the political sense—making provisions for equal presence or voice in a field. Through confrontational strategies that lampoon the emotional and intellectual blind spots inherent to white supremacy, Pindell articulates her frustrations with the contradictions of U.S. multiculturalism—a set of political and cultural agendas that encourages the growing public visibility of people of color at the same time it forecloses the range of expressions deemed beneficial to its putative goal of social harmony. In the artist's words, "The history and culture of people of color has been appropriated, distorted, and used as images and points of focus by white artists while artists of color have been excluded from speaking visually and interpreting themselves on the same platform." This is depiction without equal presence. Becoming visible in a dominant culture, even in rarefied institutions, does not guarantee power in the public sphere. In *Free, White and 21,* Pindell expresses a profound skepticism about not only mass media representations, but also the various cultural institutions that deliver them. She questions what Peggy Phelan has called the "implicit assumptions about the connections between representational visibility and political power" that dominated cultural discourse in the 1980s.[4]

Existing scholarship on Pindell's video, easily the most well-known piece in her oeuvre, has largely construed it as an arrival and a turning point—a decisive shift away from a visually compelling but politically detached abstract practice toward an affecting set of biographical disclosures and Black feminist criticism. The video, so the literature goes, launched a practice that bravely placed the artist on the surface of her works. Pindell herself credits the video with marking her transition from a practice centered largely on process to one deeply invested in autobiography and more direct political messaging. She cites *Free, White and 21* as the inaugural project in her *Autobiography* series, a body of work she pursued throughout the 1980s to explore themes of communal memory and trauma.[5] This established narrative of Pindell's career has a basis in truth. However, I want to bring some skepticism to what seems an all too familiar redemptive arc, in which an artist from a marginalized group inevitably arrives at an explicitly political practice that finally succeeds in translating her experiences for a liberal multiracial audience.

Free, White and 21 offers something much more challenging to contemporary art and the symbolically public platform of mass media. As the Artist, Pindell recounts her experiences as a woman of color, but continues to decline, as she had in her abstract practice, to "represent" herself in a straightforward way. Rather, her autobiographical disclosures come couched in a critique of white supremacy, pointing to the ways in which both mass media and the art world package the experiences of people of color for public consumption. In her articulation of whiteness and its role in her life, Pindell goes so far as to embody it for her audience. What she reveals through this performance is at turns humorous and horrifying. Whiteness appears in the video as a series of defensive gestures and cheap cover-ups, a pathological need to dominate, and what Saidiya Hartman has called "the brutal asymmetry of power," which is as vehemently defended as it is denied.[6] *Free, White and 21* investigates the pathology of U.S. whiteness and Pindell's relationship to it.

Ultimately, I argue, Pindell theorizes the abstracting set of procedures that frame the inherently racialized project of representation in the United States. Her video asserts that for people of color, both public visibility and personal legibility often involve extensive abstraction from lived experience.[7] The work also illuminates whiteness as a series of visual manipulations and psychic deflections. Amid the multiculturalism of the late 1970s and 1980s, Americans continued to turn to race as the primary lens through which to make sense of human difference. *Free, White and 21* thematizes the mediating, distorting effects of this virtual layer over human experience and interaction.

In her book about U.S.-born French entertainer Josephine Baker, Anne Anlin Cheng theorized Baker's use of "second skins" on the nude body as paradigmatic of the modernist fascination with surface. Cheng wrote, "It may not be too much of an overstatement to say that the material and metaphysical boundary of the human body—and, by implication, what constitutes the human—forms one of the central philosophical concerns of the twentieth century."[8] Through her artistic engagement with mass media in the 1970s and early 1980s, Pindell examined the intersecting surfaces of the human body and contemporary imaging technologies. In her video, she deployed several imaginative "skins," textured membranes applied to and removed from the characters' heads, to underscore the entanglement of racialization and representational practices. Skins offered an ambivalent set of surfaces with which to destabilize normative narrative processes. This tactile, collaged approach to character development echoes the techniques Pindell so ardently pursued in her abstract practice. She applied her expert knowledge of abstraction and surface to video in order to mine the potential and expose the limitations of mass media representation. Through her use of skins, Pindell extended questions about what it means to represent oneself in art to the politicized media environment of multiculturalism.

A series of occurrences beginning in 1979 led Pindell to see an urgent need for making racism visible by articulating and visualizing its effects. This chapter asks how the artist addressed her work to these changing stakes of representation. What summoned her out from "behind" her work?[9] What did it mean for her to become visible as a figure in her art in 1980? What versions of herself did she produce for the camera in this moment of crisis? The video's imagery and the content of its spoken narration draw viewers' attention to the ongoing traumatic stress of racial discrimination. They also refer to recent traumatic events that deeply touched Pindell's life—a nearly fatal car accident and a rancorous debate over the racist titling of an exhibition at an alternative art gallery in Manhattan. The latter resulted in her departure from MoMA, where she had worked for twelve years, and in her further distancing from white feminist circles.

Collectively, these events of 1979 unsettled Pindell's long-wavering faith in the predominantly white art institutions through which she had moved. She already understood MoMA and the women's collective A.I.R. Gallery, where she had been a cofounding member, as passive participants in the art world's rampant racial discrimination. Through the debates of 1979, she came to see the need for more thoroughgoing critiques of these institutions' complicity in white supremacy and, ultimately, a renunciation of them.[10] Pindell's belief in abstraction as a potential site of artistic mending was also shaken by the art world controversy that unfolded in New York that year. For a period, her privileged idiom appeared to her too disconnected from activist efforts to interrupt systemic inequities.

Hence, abstraction temporarily became a secondary concern for her, though it remained an informative conceptual and aesthetic framework in her practice.

Free, White and 21 built upon Pindell's enduring examinations of mass media as sites of artistic possibility and constraint. This chapter draws out her longer-standing engagement with mass media imagery, which coincided with her abstract practice and originated with the photographic, television-based series *Video Drawings* (1973–76). With these works, Pindell theorized a critical, ambivalent mode of mass media spectatorship that she further pursued in the video. The artist intervened in the conventions of passive viewership in order to subject markers of racial whiteness to scrutiny. This practice placed a representational burden back on whiteness, countering the demands aimed at women of color to depict themselves in ways that would be legible to white audiences. It joined other manifestations of Black feminist critique that pushed against the simultaneous "high visibility" and "almost total lack of voice" of Black women in mass media.[11] At the end of a decade that began with the promise of revolution, yet failed to redress deep and widespread racial inequities, Pindell wrestled with how to be heard and not merely depicted.

FREE, WHITE AND 21

In *Free, White and 21* Pindell stages a dialogue between the Artist and the White Woman. Although the video is a single-monitor piece that depicts only one character at a time, the White Woman seems to respond to the Artist. As the Artist, Pindell reports seven encounters with racist discrimination—a number that underscores the quotidian nature of racial oppression by suggesting an episode for each day of the week. These incidents, drawn from Pindell's own life, chart the effects of racism across various life stages. They also attest to the pervasiveness of racism as it occurs in wide-ranging spheres of experience—early childhood education, student governance, and public rites of passage.

The character of the Artist begins with a single event from her mother's life, and then narrates experiences from the first-person point of view, proceeding in chronological order so that the episodes span the arc of her own nearly middle-aged lifetime. By beginning the narration with an event from an earlier generation, Pindell indicates that racial trauma operates genealogically; it passes from one generation to the next, and stories of its infliction are part of an oral heritage shared between grandparents, parents, aunts, uncles, and children.

Pindell had written about the familial transmission of such knowledge in a 1978 publication in the feminist journal *Heresies*. The article juxtaposes her handwritten account of racist atrocities inflicted on her ancestors with typeset archival narratives of similar brutal incidents. This work exemplifies the artist's growing attention to her ancestry in the late 1970s and 1980s, when Alex Haley's

1976 influential bestseller, *Roots,* spurred many Black Americans to conduct new genealogical research.[12] Through the *Autobiography* series she initiated in 1980, Pindell began exploring how the lives of her forebearers, who were Black, white, and American Indian, intersected in U.S. histories of slavery and colonialism.

The Artist's tone in *Free, White and 21* is calm and deliberate. She chooses her words with care, occasionally pausing to formulate her sentences. Throughout, she faces the camera directly, gazing into it and blinking frequently, perhaps in response to the bright fixtures lighting her from off camera. The Artist's frankness is juxtaposed by the White Woman's oblique address. She aims her commentary exclusively at the Artist, mostly speaking to her in the second person. The White Woman frequently holds her head at an angle from the camera, either tilting her chin down in a position that obscures her mouth or sitting perpendicularly to the camera so that viewers see her in profile (fig. 78). These dissembling gestures are heightened by the accoutrements of her mask-like visage. An acid yellow wig forms a helmet over a heavily made-up face, whose cosmetic artifice is evident in the contrast between a ghostly white nose, rouged cheeks, and bubble-gum pink lips. Large, dark sunglasses shade her eyes. These visual cues reinforce the utter inaccessibility of the character's interiority. The obvious artificiality of the White Woman's costuming situates the character in an African American tradition of whiteface, which dates to the late eighteenth century. In recent decades, Black performers have used whiteface as a set of critical practices for making visible the blind spots and privileges that accompany whiteness, particularly as manifested in elite social classes.[13]

Pindell made the video for an exhibition of works by women artists of color in the United States. *Free, White and 21* debuted at a show organized by artists Ana Mendieta, Kazuko Miyamoto, and Zarina at A.I.R. Gallery, then located on Wooster Street in SoHo. Titled *Dialectics of Isolation: An Exhibition of Third World Women Artists of the United States,* it brought together the work of eight artists working across diverse idioms—Judith Baca, Beverly Buchanan, Janet Henry, Senga Nengudi, Lydia Okumura, Selena Whitefeather, Zarina, and Pindell. Many of these artists knew one another prior to the exhibition—they were friends, colleagues, and acquaintances who formed part of a small, supportive network of women artists of color showing in New York.[14] Henry displayed selections from her *Juju Bags* series, each work composed of a small doll and an assortment of handcrafted accessories reflecting the fictional figure's interests and social position. *Juju Bag for a White Protestant Male* (1979–80), for instance, features a cable-knit sweater, a pair of rowing oars, and a white female companion. These works allude to West African, particularly Nigerian, spiritual practices

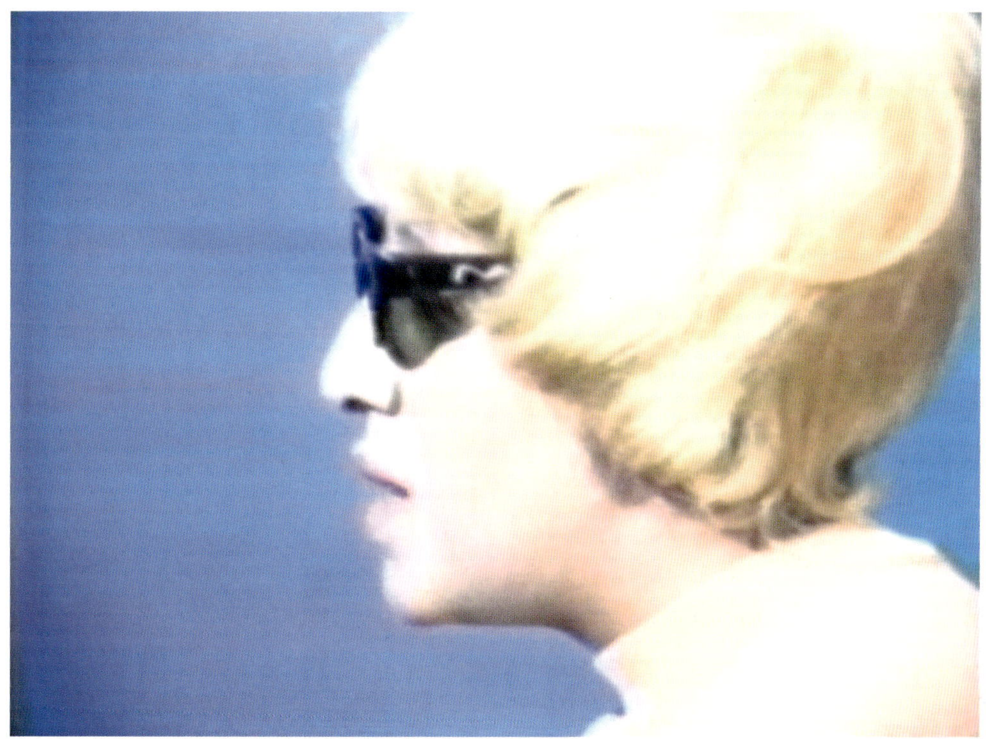

at the same time that they offer playful, pop-inflected commentary on the particular ways in which race, class, and gender are performed through consumer choices in the U.S. context. They contrasted with an arrangement of blocky concrete sculptures by Buchanan included in the exhibition, which conjured time-weathered architectural ruins (see fig. 10). Buchanan's work sat directly on the floor, evoking minimalist installations and the material experimentations of postminimalism. Pindell's was the sole video work on display and addressed racism more explicitly than its counterparts in the show.

The exhibition proposed that, despite their disparate practices, these artists shared a project as "Third World Women." The term "Third World" emerged during the Cold War to describe a collection of nations unaligned with either the political and economic structures of Soviet communism-socialism or U.S.-dominated capitalism. By the late 1960s, civil rights activists began to use the term to link the struggles of these nations, most of which were rebuilding in the aftermath of colonial occupation, to the efforts of people of color in the United States, who sought to topple the oppressive forces of a dominant white culture. Black feminist activists in the United States first adopted the moniker "Third World Women" in these same years. It signaled their solidarity with women abroad who likewise experienced the double oppressions of gender and race or ethnicity. In the context of the New York art world in which Mendieta, Miyamoto, and Zarina organized *Dialectics of Isolation,* "Third World Women" signified a rallying, if fraught, point of connection between women of color whose concerns about racism and imperialism were unheeded by largely white feminist organizations. While the term "Third World" lacked the derogatory connotations it carries today, critics argued that the concept of "Third World Women" harmfully flattened the experiences of women with drastically unequal levels of social and economic privilege.[15]

In the introduction to the exhibition catalogue, Mendieta wrote that she would like for the show to be a platform for these women artists of color to "speak" to white, middle-class feminists. She implied that these two groups were the participants of the "dialectic," or critical dialogue, staged by the show. White feminists, Mendieta noted, had "failed to remember" women of color as they politicized under the women's movement in the late 1960s and early 1970s. *Dialectics of Isolation* unapologetically directed its critique specifically at its venue, A.I.R. Gallery. The institution's largely white, middle-class membership was paradigmatic of the marginalization of women of color within the New York feminist art movement. While the critically lauded gallery had provided an important site for women to show art in the early 1970s, when well over ninety percent of artists shown in commercial galleries in New York were men, a bias toward white artists plagued the institution from its earliest days. *Dialectics of Isolation* challenged A.I.R.'s continuing failure to practice racial inclusivity.[16]

Pindell, a founding member of the cooperative who had resigned her post in 1975, was intimately familiar with her white colleagues' blind spots around issues of race and racism. By the time she left the gallery, she regarded herself as a "token" artist of color who was expected to be grateful for the opportunity to participate in the group. Thus, the exhibition served her as a return of sorts—five years after her departure, she newly articulated her frustrations with members who failed to see her as a full participant in the institution. Indeed, Pindell has noted that she imagined her video as a retort to the "white feminists" she encountered in spaces such as A.I.R. and has suggested that she drew inspiration for the White Woman's lines from interactions with some of these colleagues.

White, middle-class women long had monopolized local feminist platforms, and *Dialectics of Isolation* aimed to confront those women with the limitations of their feminist frameworks by asserting non-white experiences. By holding space for non-white feminist artists with a variety of backgrounds and aesthetic priorities, the exhibition sought to destabilize a widespread complacency with what amounted to a partial view of women's concerns. Mendieta's declaration in the catalogue's introduction that the show pointed to a "will to continue being 'other'" suggests that the "dialectic" would not resolve with the assimilation of women of color into white feminisms.[17] The women's movement would either continue with women of color and white women working in "isolation" or move forward with white feminists committing themselves to anti-racist allyship.

It bears repeating that Pindell produced *Free, White and 21* specifically for *Dialectics of Isolation*. The video shows the artist working through the exhibition's premise. First, it stages a dialogue between a woman of color and a white woman, deploying the "conversational strategy" of Third World feminism. Theorists such as Audre Lorde, Cherríe Moraga, Barbara Smith, and Beverly Smith used the dialogical mode in the late 1970s and early 1980s in publications that confronted white feminism's refusal to acknowledge white supremacy.[18] In its debut at a predominantly white institution, *Free, White and 21* established a line of communication between Pindell *specifically as a woman of color* and white viewers. In contrast to the abstract artworks that she previously had shown at A.I.R., the video contains acts of self-disclosure (her appearance on screen and use of autobiographic narratives) that assert her identity as a woman of color feminist over her affiliations with the mostly white feminists at the gallery.

As visitors to *Dialectics of Isolation* approached the back gallery of A.I.R.'s ground-floor space on Wooster, they heard the measured ticking of a metronome. Pindell installed the device atop the monitor displaying *Free, White and 21* in order to "hypnotize" her audience—to capture their attention for the duration of what she anticipated would be a difficult work of art. (The metronome did not appear in subsequent installations of the video as Pindell encountered difficulties transporting and setting it up.) The painful, detailed incidents that the Artist shares invite an emotional response from the viewer. Many viewers of color may have had traumatic experiences that resonate with the anecdotes the Artist shares. For white viewers, who may feel implicated by the White Woman's dismissive performance, it can be uncomfortable to listen to such candid testimony about the effects of racism. On a slow day, the sound of the metronome would have echoed through the high-ceilinged space in the pauses between the characters' recitations. Crowds on the weekend would have dampened the sound, perhaps rendering it imperceptible beyond a small radius of the video display. Pindell selected the video monitor for its ordinariness—it was neither large nor particularly small for a television of its time—and set it on a plinth for viewing from a standing position.[19]

Visitors also heard the voices of the Artist and the White Woman before seeing them on-screen. These characters' verbal exchanges filled the air as viewers made their way toward the back of the gallery, encountering the two-dimensional works and sculptural installations on display. Perhaps, for the informed visitor, the video's sound voiced an otherwise latent tension between the works on view and the institutional context. With this auditory lead-in, visitors could reach the monitor and begin watching *Free, White and 21* at any point during its twelve-minute run time. In dialogue with the staged conversation in the video, the metronome's insistent ticking measured the persistence of racism across time, uninterrupted by notions of historical progress, as the Artist chronicled events spanning the early to late twentieth century. The brief duration of the video, the "hypnotic" repetition of the metronome's beat, and the simmering tension between the characters on screen would have urged a viewing in its entirety. Despite these characteristics and *Free, White and 21*'s status as easily Pindell's most well-known and widely studied work, its full narrative arc has rarely been analyzed by scholars. A careful examination of the video reveals several glitches—visual seams or disturbances—that offer insight into how Pindell approached racialization as an abstracting procedure.[20]

Although the vast majority of the twelve-minute *Free, White and 21* is devoted to the Artist's narratives, the White Woman frames the work. This bookending and the video's title indicate its central investment in critically interrogating whiteness. The video opens with a title card, whose text, "Free, White and 21," primes the audience for a brief glimpse of the titular character. She appears, for just a few seconds, silently sitting with her head tilted downward. Her dark sunglasses reflect what appears to be a white piece of paper in her hands. Redolent of a script, the paper points to the scripted nature of the racist deflections the White Woman will offer.[21] Indeed, throughout the video her rehearsed affectation contrasts with the Artist's conversational pauses and hedges.

The video quickly cuts to the Artist's first appearance, in which she wears a periwinkle cardigan over a green mock turtleneck in front of a textured white wall. First, she narrates an event from her mother's childhood. Her mother received chemical burns when a white babysitter scrubbed her with lye, mistaking the darkness of her skin for stubborn dirt. As the Artist recounts this story about the babysitter's violent, racist fantasy of removing dark skin, the video cuts to the White Woman, who bites her thumb and emits a low, quick "Hmm." Curiously, the hand that reaches into the frame, clearly the actor's own appendage, is not the powdered white of the White Woman's face, but a darker tan color (fig. 79). The inclusion of Pindell's nude hand undermines the attempt at whitening narrated by the Artist and underscores the theatricality of the video's production. It also destabilizes the White Woman's racial representation, casting doubt on the reliability of this visual representation as a transmitter of fixed subject positions. Although the White Woman and the Artist serve as foil to one another, their difference is not so firmly grounded. They also operate as doubles. The White Woman's act of biting her brown thumb reinforces the violent antagonism of this relationship. Through this series of gestures, Pindell unsettles racial schema that take the epidermis as an unchanging and unambiguous signifier of racial identity.

The video cuts back to the Artist in a purple scoop-necked top against a vibrant orange backdrop. She reappears with this combination of outfit and

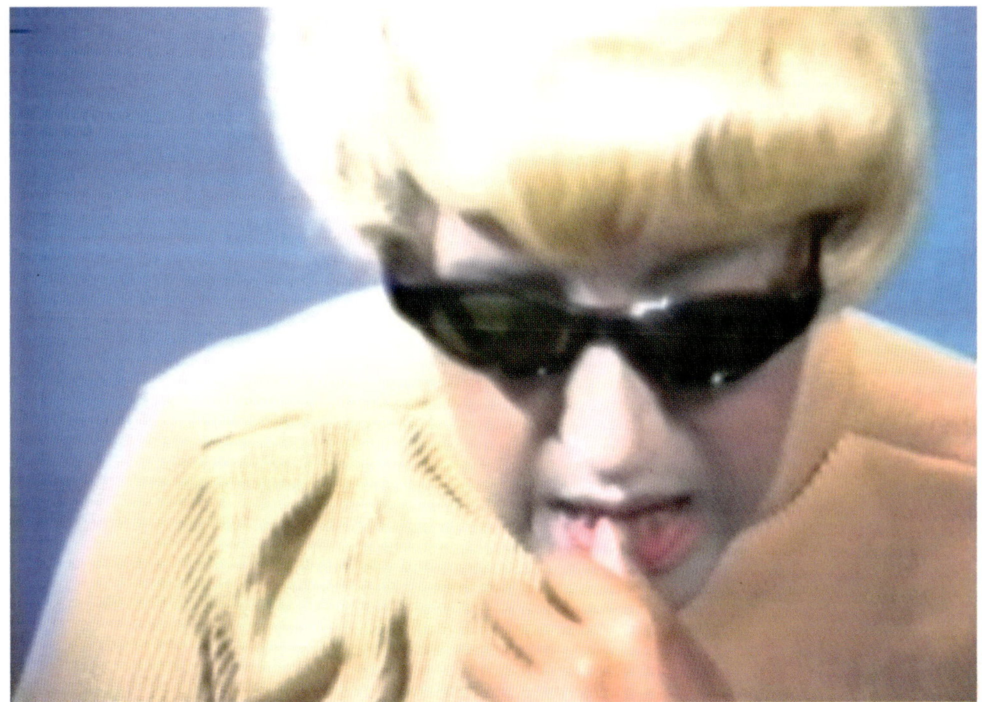

backdrop several times. These colors contrast with the White Woman's consistent yellow top and blue backdrop. The pairing of complementary colors across these shots shows Pindell approaching color as a modernist. Her training in Josef Albers's theory of color relativity taught her that these hues would intensify one another, setting up a visual tension to match the emotional tenor of the video. During this appearance, the Artist recounts an early childhood experience, a perverse event that took place in her kindergarten classroom. In response to her request to go to the restroom during a class nap, the Artist's teacher tied her to a cot with sheets, remarking that she "couldn't stand these people."

At this point in her narration, the Artist breaks her even tone with hushed, nervous laughter. The teacher left her young student there "for a couple of hours." As the Artist utters these words, she brings a roll of white gauze to her head, applying a strip down the center of her face, tucking it under her chin, around her neck, and up the back of her head. She continues to roll out the gauze, wrapping her head with it as the camera zooms in on the white fabric. Her voice largely unaffected by the gauze, the Artist continues, informing viewers that another student, perhaps a white student who had "not yet learned to differentiate" race, reported the incident to a parent. The abusive teacher was eventually fired for "bothering a student," but the Artist's tone expresses skepticism about the implications of this punishment. Perhaps she doubts that the administration at the predominantly white school realized, or would have responded to, the racial motivation behind the teacher's abusive behavior. As she concludes these

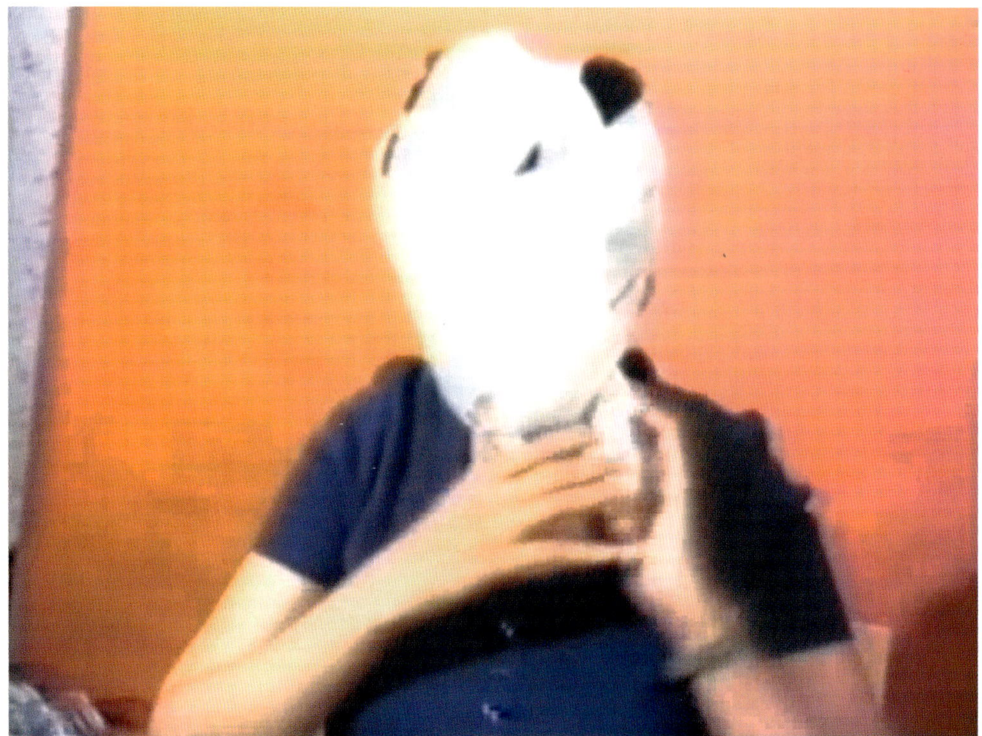

remarks, the Artist's wrapped head makes for a haunting presence, cutting a cartoonish white oblong shape against the vermillion backdrop—another form of whiteface (fig. 80). She continues wrapping in silence, covering all but a fragment of her chin and a few tufts of her hair.

The camera dwells momentarily on this uncomfortable image. This pause allows the viewer to dwell on the suffocating, damp warmth of the skin-like gauze shroud. The material cordons off the Artist's head from her body and must have muffled her perceptions of the world around her. This sense of confinement and separation evokes the restraints applied in the kindergarten classroom. The image of the Artist's wrapped head and especially her use of gauze, a medical supply, also conjure Pindell's recent car accident and subsequent convalescence. By focusing the wrapping on her head specifically, she makes direct reference to the head injury and amnesia that destabilized her life in the months following the collision. Pindell recovered under the care of her parents, who lived with her in her loft for several months following the accident.[22] This intergenerational proximity may have helped to motivate Pindell's inclusion of her mother's story in her video. The white strips of fabric that the Artist wraps around her head also evoke the textile-based artworks Pindell made immediately prior to the car accident and the video work, her cut and sewn paintings.

After a third narration in which the Artist describes her high school teacher's racially motivated denial of her request to be placed in an accelerated history course, the White Woman speaks for the first time, three and a half minutes into the video. Shot in profile, she responds to the Artist: "You know you really must be paranoid. Those things never happen to me. I don't know anyone who's had those things happen to them. But then again, they're free, white, and twenty-one, so they wouldn't have *that* kind of experience." Unable and unwilling to accept that the Artist's reality differs from her own, the White Woman defensively pathologizes her. By acknowledging that the white people she knows "wouldn't have *that* kind of experience" because "they're free, white, and twenty-one," the White Woman reveals a level of racial awareness that viewers cannot ascribe to the character, who incessantly attempts to deny the realities of racial difference. Instead, Pindell asserts her authorial voice in the parodic friction of these passages, where the White Woman's defensiveness rubs against her recognition of racial inequity. The phrase allows Pindell to name whiteness as an ideology and acknowledge its role in the character's willful ignorance.

Four scenes follow in which the Artist narrates anecdotes from her young adulthood. She attempted to run for a student government position at Boston University, where Pindell received her undergraduate degree. A college administrator and elected student officials removed her name from the ballot on the basis that it would be a "highly inappropriate" office for a Black student to hold. In response, the White Woman snipes, "Well you ungrateful little, after all we've done for you." The Artist recounts a day she witnessed discrimination against Black and Latina job searchers at a *Time-Life* magazine office in Manhattan. By way of reply, the White Woman warns, "Don't worry. We'll find other tokens." In two excruciating anecdotes, the Artist describes how white guests at a wedding in Kennebunkport, Maine, harassed her.

At this point in the video, for the first time, the Artist's vocation is clarified. The White Woman responds, "You really must be paranoid. Your art really isn't political either. You know I hear your experiences, and I think 'well, it's gotta be in her art.' That's the only way we'll validate you and it's gotta be in your art in the way that we consider valid. In fact, you won't exist until we validate you." In this passage, Pindell references her own artistic reception. The White Woman disparages the Artist's long-standing commitment to abstraction, suggesting that this idiom undermines the Artist's right to speak—"Your art isn't even political." By constantly denying the Artist's claims about her own experiences, the White Woman also forecloses the possibility that the autobiographical content of the video itself will be considered "valid." These comments render explicit the racialized expectations that Pindell had encountered since her earliest days in New York. For instance, in 1969, the director of the Studio Museum in Harlem suggested that her abstract art belonged in white galleries downtown and not in the newly established institution for living Black American artists.[23] *Free, White and 21* allowed Pindell to rehearse the transition she was then anticipating in her work, imagining how audiences might react to her newly autobiographical and explicitly political practice.

In two subsequent scenes, the Artist responds to the White Woman's complaints with a pair of oblique gestures. She removes white, skin-like membranes from her head, symbolically shedding the racist criticism. First, she appears in a yellow ribbed sweater against a blue background, echoing the color combination associated with the White Woman. With the camera zoomed on her face, the Artist pinches a bit of film at the bottom of her chin and begins peeling off a translucent mask. She works methodically, first removing the film from the right side of her face, then her forehead and left side. With care, she holds up the mask and unfolds it. Briefly, against the blue backdrop, it forms a white, twisted, clown-like mask (fig. 81). The Artist discards it, then with her eyes closed gingerly feels her face for remnants of the film. In the second shot, the Artist reappears with her head wrapped in gauze. For a moment, she sits in profile. Then, the camera cuts to a frontal view in which she begins to unwind the fabric, rolling it neatly in her hands, which move deftly around her head. Finished with this task, she stares blinkingly into the camera.

In the final minute of the video, the White Woman inverts the Artist's gestures of removing skin. She pulls tight, white pantyhose over her head. The camera zooms on her face as the stocking sets her sunglasses askew and compresses her nose. In a deeper, more emphatic voice, she says, "You ungrateful little, after *all* we've done for you. You know, we don't believe in your symbols. You must use our symbols. They're not valid unless we validate them. And you *really* must be paranoid. I've never had an experience like that, but then of course I'm free, white, and twenty-one."

With this final stream of invective delivered, the credits roll. They give special thanks to the Downtown Community Television Center (DCTV) and credit Maria Lino and Maryann De Leo with "camera and editing." Upon conceptualizing the video from that initial affecting image of a blond wig, Pindell had "asked around" about who could help her make it. Eventually, one of her friends gave the artist's contact information to DCTV, a community media center founded in 1972 by documentary film director Jon Alpert and his wife and collaborator, Keiko Tsuno. The center called Pindell, and the two parties arranged for Lino and De Leo to bring video equipment to the artist's apartment, tape the artwork, and assist her with editing.[24]

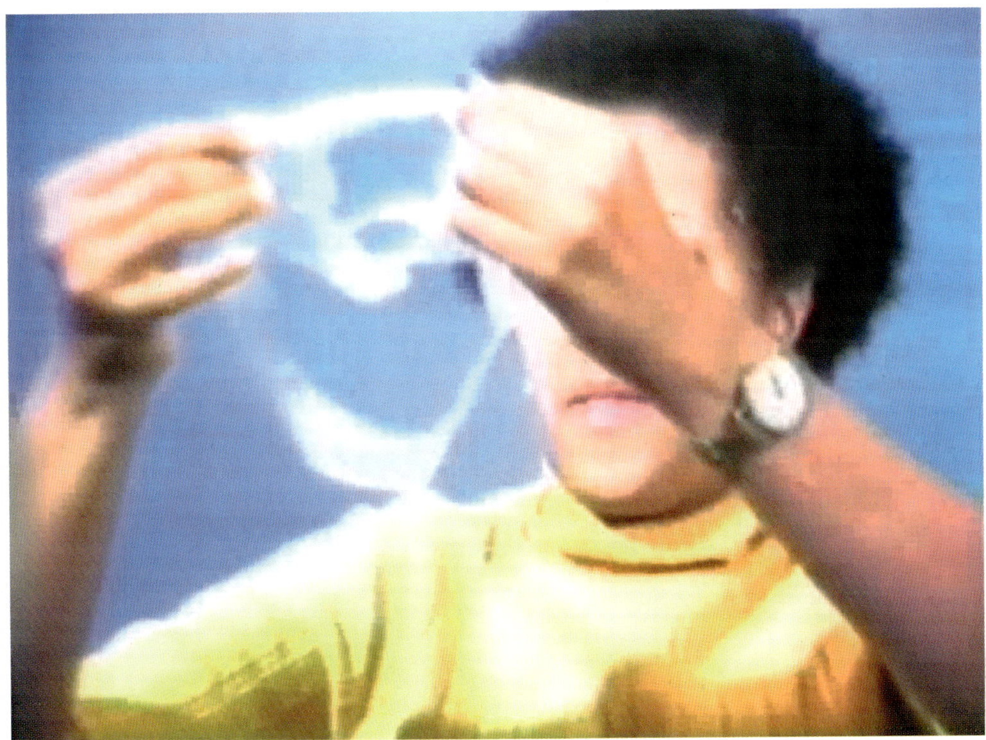

Despite the professional help Pindell enlisted for the production of her video, *Free, White and 21* bears many traces of the artist's relative inexperience as a video-maker. Ambient noise from the street outside Pindell's loft, which was located on Twenty-Eighth Street and Seventh Avenue, near a subway stop, filters audibly into the video. The artist has noted that while the camerawoman warned that the street noise presented a problem for the video's production, she (Pindell) decided to "[do] it anyway."[25] This spirit of "doing it anyway" infuses the video. Early in the piece, the camera pans to the left of the Artist, momentarily making the edge of the backdrop visible against a white wall (see fig. 80). Throughout, the camera operator somewhat clumsily deploys zoom, so that the White Woman or Artist's face appears out of focus for several seconds at a time. In one shot, the microphone becomes visible in the lower left corner (fig. 82).

Art historian Romi Crawford has theorized Black women's experimental film and video work as embracing "a paradoxical logic" of the amateur-auteur. Black women filmmakers working in the 1970s and 1980s frequently used "minor" modes of filmmaking and techniques such as video and raw sound to assert "a resolute and confident" voice.[26] For instance, Julie Dash's 1975 short film, *Four Women*, stars the dancer Linda Martina Young, who plays four personas who dance against a simple stage set in different costuming. Crawford noted that beyond emanating from uneven access to ample film budgets, this strategic use of diminished technical means reflects a desire to position one's production outside of industry norms.

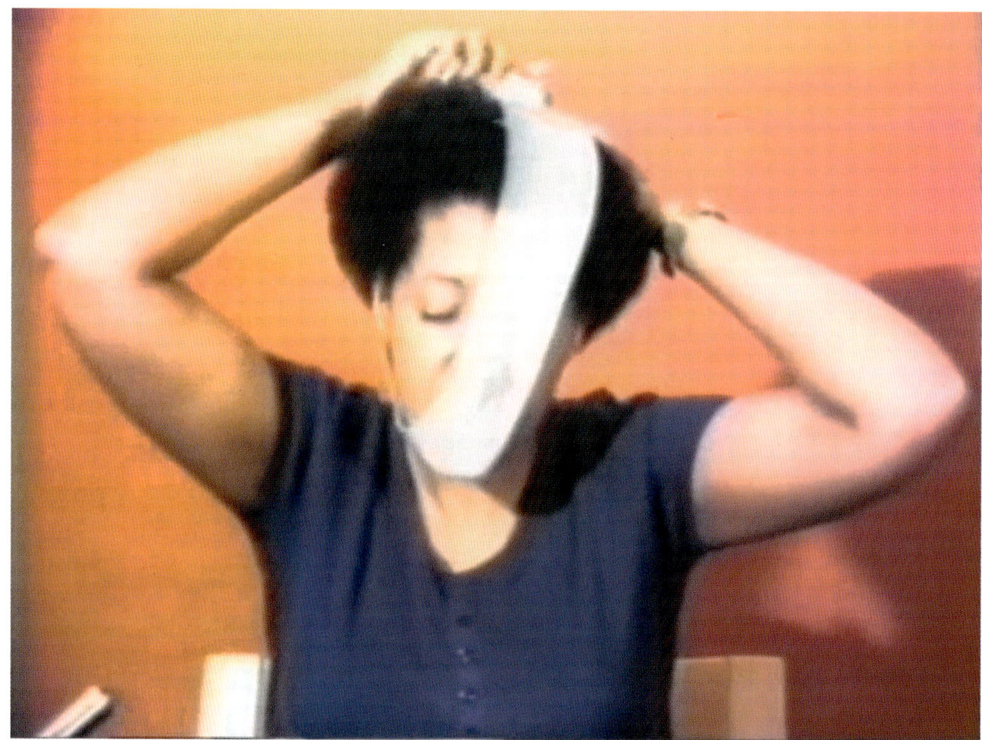

In this way, Black American women filmmakers worked in dialogue with Third Cinema, a cinematic movement emergent in the 1960s and exemplified by the work of "Third World" filmmakers such as Ousmane Sembène (Senegal), Jorge Sanjinés (Bolivia), and Miguel Littín (Chile). As cinema scholar Teshome H. Gabriel has argued, Third Cinema "built on the rejection of the concepts and propositions of traditional cinema, as represented by Hollywood. The main aim of Third Cinema is to immerse itself in the lives and struggles of the peoples of the Third World."[27] Similarly, Black American women filmmakers in the 1970s and 1980s eschewed the tropes of Hollywood representations in their explorations of the experiences of Black women. These artists also placed their work alongside films by Yoko Ono, Man Ray, and Andy Warhol, who exploited their lack of expertise as filmmakers to produce innovative artworks throughout the twentieth century.

Pindell's investment in explicit markers of amateurism situates *Free, White and 21* in a lineage of avant-garde experimentation. The excessive visibility of the video's edges, props, and technological means heighten the work's theatricality; the piece seems to comment on the conditions of its own production. These inclusions and their failure to recede into a seamless viewing experience also suggest a point of continuity in Pindell's oeuvre—just as she gathered many of her collage materials from her everyday surroundings, including the institutional detritus of MoMA, so too did she collect the materials and resources necessary to make the video from local sources. Both the Artist and the White Woman wear clothes Pindell's mother purchased at Sears, Roebuck and mailed to her when the curator struggled to make ends meet on MoMA's paltry salary. (Pindell "hated" these clothes and normally did not wear them but kept them in bags in her studio.) She purchased the blond wig at a nearby Woolworth's. The backdrops came from a local photography store.[28] Pindell's ongoing investment in cobbling together a work of art from materials at hand reflects her enduring predilection for informal networks of material, resource, and skill acquisition.

The video's aesthetic also speaks to Pindell's desire to make *Free, White and 21* expediently and to the urgency of its message. This exigency was felt in the broader project of *Dialectics of Isolation* and expressed by Mendieta in its catalogue: "Do we exist? . . . To question our cultures is to question our own existence, our human reality."[29] Pindell's video similarly voices the ontological invalidation routinely performed through white supremacy when the White Woman says to the Artist, "In fact, you won't exist until we validate you."

Recent scholarship has tended to interpret both the exhibition and the video as specifically addressing a white audience. For instance, art historian Cherise Smith has argued that the "didactic tone" of *Free, White and 21* reveals Pindell's intention to reach white viewers. Indeed, the work makes an earnest appeal to white audiences to see and hear racism. However, while Pindell anticipated a white viewership at A.I.R., she hoped with the video to expand her artistic audience beyond the white feminist circles in which she had shown regularly over the course of the previous decade. She actively sought out a wide circulation among a diverse viewership from the work's earliest days. When staff at Franklin Furnace, an alternative art space in Brooklyn that hosted the video's second presentation, told Pindell they planned to charge admission to the gallery, the artist elected to forego her honorarium in exchange for an open-door policy.[30]

Pindell's choice of medium also points to a desire for a broad viewership. Art historian Lowery Stokes Sims has argued that the mediums of video and performance serve "as a bridge between" the secluded studio or gallery and "the 'real' world, the street." A reproducible and mass medium, Pindell's video could travel and proliferate in ways that her paintings could not and thus could reach audiences whose interests were disregarded by the bulk of the New York gallery circuit, including viewers of color. Further, while early video artists generated challenging, sometimes repelling viewing conditions through aggressive modes of address and monotonous repetition, Pindell, by contrast, deployed several strategies to attract an audience.[31] Consider her use of the "hypnotic" metronome, a benign instrument of coercion meant to captivate viewers so that they would endure the discomfort of confronting racism. The vibrant coloring of the video's costuming and backdrops, the intimate mode of the Artist's address, and the clarity of her even-toned narrations also make for engrossing viewing.

Audiences for *Free, White and 21* have not always responded favorably to the video. For instance, Pindell has recalled that a jury for a 1980 video competition rejected the tape on the basis of its "divisiveness." By the end of the decade, it "became a kind of underground cult tape" shown mainly at universities, where it continued to draw occasional ire from both Black and white viewers. For instance, a white woman student in a New England university audience tauntingly asked Pindell if making the tape had made her "feel better." Pindell has noted that the older Black security guards at a New Jersey museum refused to turn on the television set that displayed the video "because they felt it was offensive to people of color." Other artists of color, Pindell reported, told her that the video "was not forceful enough" and critiqued its focus on instances of discrimination that occurred in contexts of "privilege."[32]

One of the most arresting aspects of *Free, White and 21* is how the video purports to make the artist present before the audience. In her video, Pindell speaks in the first person, in the role of the Artist, to her viewers. With her eyes trained on the camera, she appears to look directly at her audience, who return her gaze, though of course these views are highly mediated by the technological apparatus of camera and monitor. Whereas Pindell's cut and sewn paintings proliferate with multitudinous traces of the artist's handiwork, their material resplendence also distances her from their surfaces. The video, by contrast, operates through a blunt transmission of the subtle inflections of her voice and gestures.

By turning to video in 1980, Pindell inserted herself into her work in a newly literal, if mediated and performative, way. In the context of *Dialectics of Isolation,* this pivot in her oeuvre targeted white feminism's "failure to remember"; confronted with the incommensurability of the Artist's encounters with racism and their own privileged existence, viewers at A.I.R. would have to acknowledge the double oppression of women of color or else risk looking as callously aloof as the White Woman. With the video Pindell also investigated the distance between her life and its mediated representation. In her artist statement for the exhibition, she wrote: "As a Black American woman, I draw on my experience as I have lived it and not as others wish to perceive my living it as fictionalized in the media and so-called 'history' books."[33] This statement reveals Pindell's understanding of popular media representation as a form of fiction—an abstraction from reality.

A longer view of the artist's work with mass media reveals an abiding skepticism about the capacity of screen-based media to depict Black women. In 1973, Pindell initiated an extended investigation of television—exploring the tension between its ability to bring the outside world close and its distancing effects. With the *Video Drawings,* I contend, Pindell expressed a deeply ambivalent view of mass media. An analysis of these earlier works allows for a more thoroughgoing understanding of how *Free, White and 21* aimed a sharply critical eye at the abstracting procedures of representation.

Although frequently noted for its singularity in Pindell's oeuvre, *Free, White and 21* emerged from a longer engagement with mass media. In 1973, Pindell began making a body of photographic works she would later dub *Video Drawings*. Despite the titular reference to the medium, the works contain no video elements—they comprise photographs of television broadcasts overlain by drawing. Pindell began making the *Video Drawings* when she encountered difficulties in the production of her intricately collaged works on paper (see fig. 3). While the collages offered her an economical avenue of artistic production, they also generated a new problem for the artist, who worked long hours under artificial light. Her eyes became strained by the extensive detail work involved in numbering and pasting hundreds of chads onto each collage.[34] To alleviate the strain, an eye doctor recommended that she vary her focal line by occasionally training her gaze on moving objects more distant in space. Pindell's solution was to purchase her first color television set, which she could watch from across her studio.

This introduction of a stream of colorful televisual imagery to her work space stimulated several developments in her artistic practice. For one, Pindell began incorporating a range of vibrant colors to her collaged works on paper. The resonances with color television grain in works such as *Untitled #69* (1974; see fig. 66) marked a return to earlier investigations; her spray-painted canvases of the early 1970s also referenced color television. A newly intimate proximity to the technology enabled Pindell once again to address the aesthetics of electromagnetic current.

Her acquisition of a home color television set led directly to Pindell's production of the *Video Drawings*. She made the works when she became "bored" of watching programs. Borrowing elements from the notation system she was then using in her works on paper, she applied clear, skin-like acetate sheets marked with vectors and numbers to the surface of her television screen (fig. 83). With the television set flipped on, a static electric current formed, causing the plastic to cling tightly to its surface. Her thumb on the trigger of a shutter release cable, Pindell waited for compelling interactions to emerge between the publicly broadcast imagery and the illuminated drawing. She captured these fleeting, blurred alignments with her film camera. From scores of photographs taken in a single session, she selected a few from contact sheets for positive printing at a commercial lab.[35] Pindell's first forays into the photographic series, which have been exhibited most frequently, spanned 1973 to 1976; however, she has regularly experimented with the form in the decades since then.

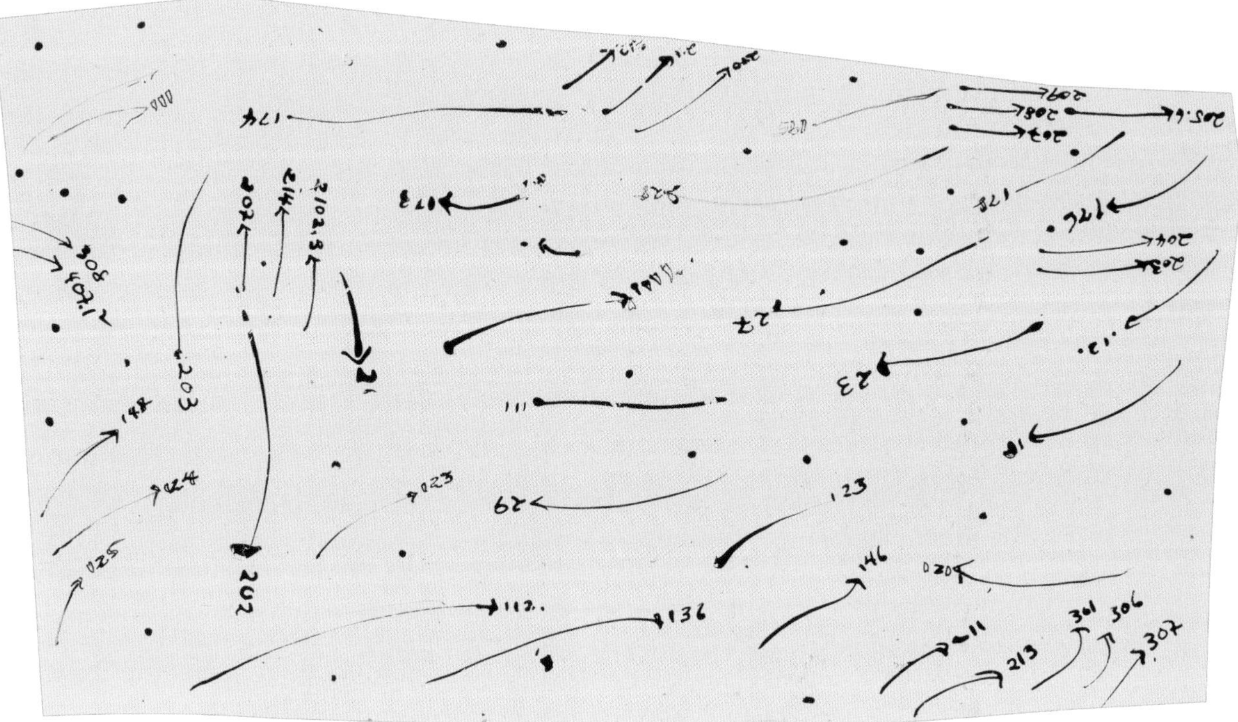

Images of athletic sporting events abound in the *Video Drawings*. More than half of the several dozen photographs Pindell made in the 1970s feature bodies in the midst of activities including track, swimming and diving, weightlifting, football, hockey, baseball, and tennis (figs. 84, 85). These athletic figures, many of whom seem to be white men, strike alert poses, prepared to execute highly choreographed motions, or they lunge, suspended mid-play (fig. 86). Others stand awkwardly, exhibiting the gawkiness of highly trained bodies performing mundane tasks between feats of physical prowess.

The *Video Drawings* predate the replete, large-scale market for televised professional and amateur sports that now characterizes U.S. broadcast offerings. In fact, Pindell stopped using sports-based imagery in the series in 1976, three years before Entertainment and Sports Programming Network (initially abbreviated as ESP, now ESPN) formed. She did not have cable in the years when she first produced the *Video Drawings,* so viewed athletic events on broadcast television rather than network stations.[36]

Pindell was not a sports fan or regular viewer of sporting events, but she found that the imagery lent itself well to her operations. In her estimation, the athletic broadcasts "transform[ed]" themselves and became "something else" through her chance-based process.[37] Her procedure pays off especially well in instances where her marks seem to direct the athletic gestures. In one example, a round encircles a runner's eye as he contorts his face in a jittery pre-race ritual (fig. 87). By suspending her notations over the television, Pindell, remarkably, made the mass medium conform to her drawings, mediating the transmitted images through her own creations.

Printed at an average size of eleven by fourteen inches, the photographs roughly mimic the dimensions of a small television screen from that era. This homology emphasizes the series' origins in televisual spectatorship at the same time that the works emphatically layer media. Through the *Video Drawings,* Pindell investigated processes of mediation. She submitted the low-fidelity transmissions of live sporting events to two layers of her own manipulations—drawing and photography. Like the works on paper she made in these same years, the photographic series functions as collage. In this case, however, the artist combines elements across mediums.

Commentators have noted similarities between Pindell's idiosyncratic notation system and symbols used to describe physical activities, including the lines of scrimmage deployed in football and labanotation, a system for recording and analyzing human movement that is often used to choreograph dance. Her use of athletic imagery, of course, amplifies these resonances. Pindell has claimed no particular familiarity with these systems. Rather, she insists that the signs used in the photographic series are "random" and that they functioned like an Etch A Sketch, quickly created and then easily removed.[38] The putative arbitrariness of these vectors and numbers foregrounds the role of chance and unpredictability in human movement. Just as Pindell awaits alignments between her drawn markings and the rapidly moving televisual image, so too must the bodies in motion on the screen operate in harmony to produce a desired outcome. Skill, of course, plays a role in the likelihood of success, but Pindell's inscrutable marks conjure the innumerable variables—wind patterns, currents, and fatigue—that operate contingently in the movement of bodies through space.

The notations that skitter across the surface of the *Video Drawings* evoke a system of critique without resolving into one. This central ambivalence of the series is heightened by the fact that the artist drew on the format of a popular television program in her development of the works. The children's program *Winky Dink and You* originally aired from 1953 to 1957, years during which Pindell was ten to fourteen years old. It was revived in 1969. The first fully interactive television program on U.S. airwaves, *Winky Dink and You* prompts its young viewers to use a marker to "draw on" their televisions with a protective acetate sheet placed on the screens (fig. 88).[39] The titular cartoon character asks his audience to help navigate puzzles and perilous situations by connecting dots to reveal hidden

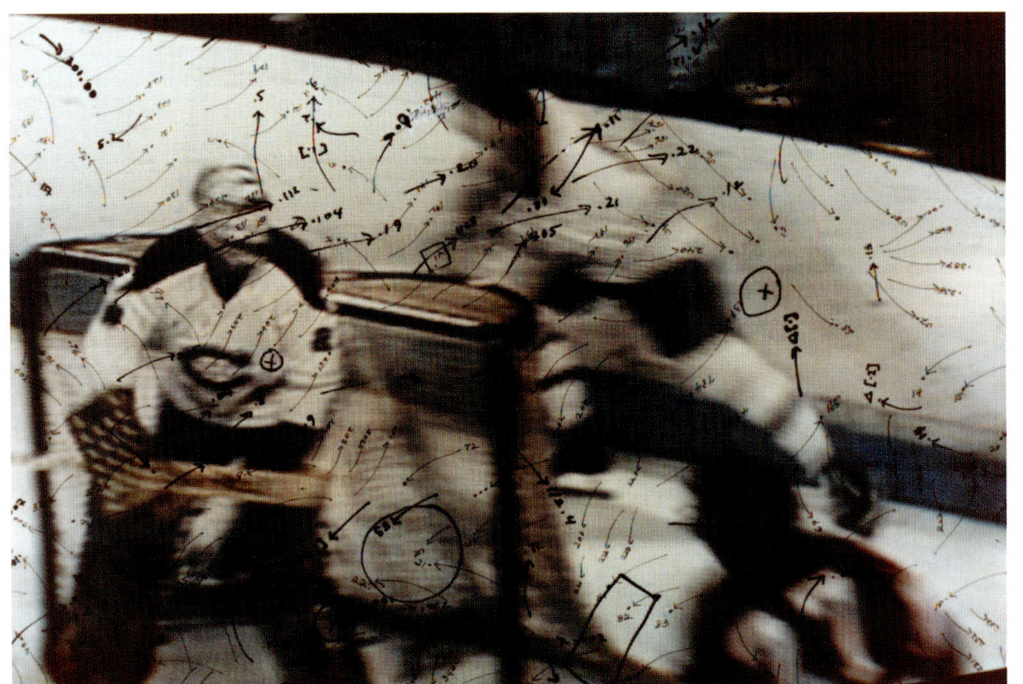

Fig. 84. Howardena Pindell, *Video Drawings: Hockey,* 1975. Chromogenic print, 13¹⁵⁄₁₆ × 16¹⁄₁₆ in. (35.4 × 40.8 cm). Museum of Contemporary Art Chicago. Anixter Art Acquisition Fund.

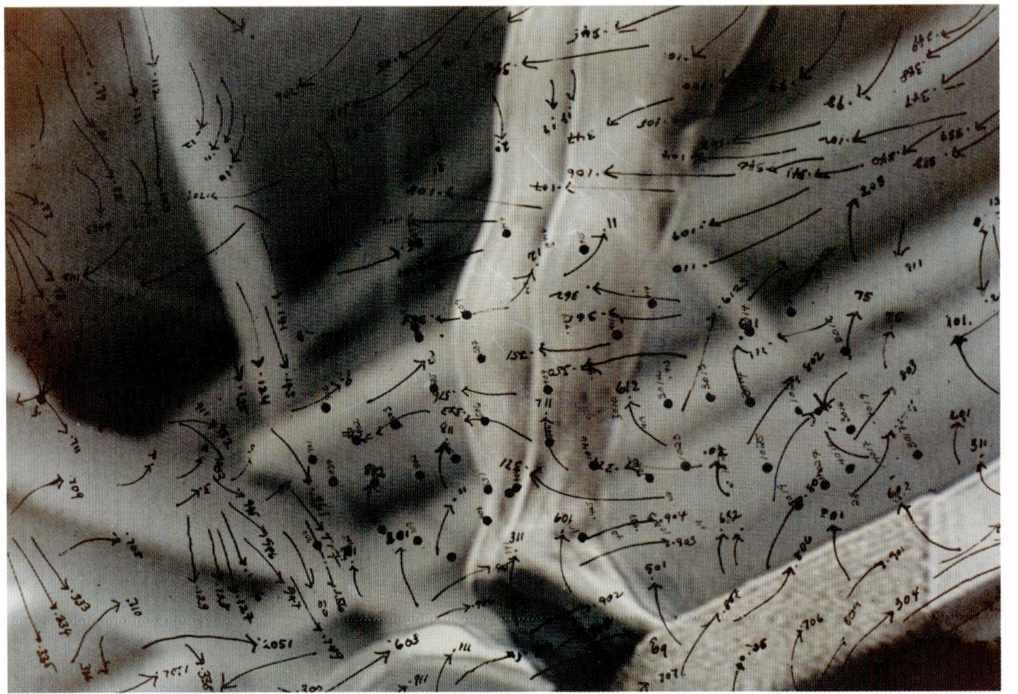

Fig. 85. Howardena Pindell, *Video Drawings: Swimming,* 1973–76. Chromogenic print, 11 × 14 in. (27.9 × 35.6 cm). Collection Walker Art Center, Minneapolis. Gift of the Peter Norton Family Foundation, 1993. 1993.51.

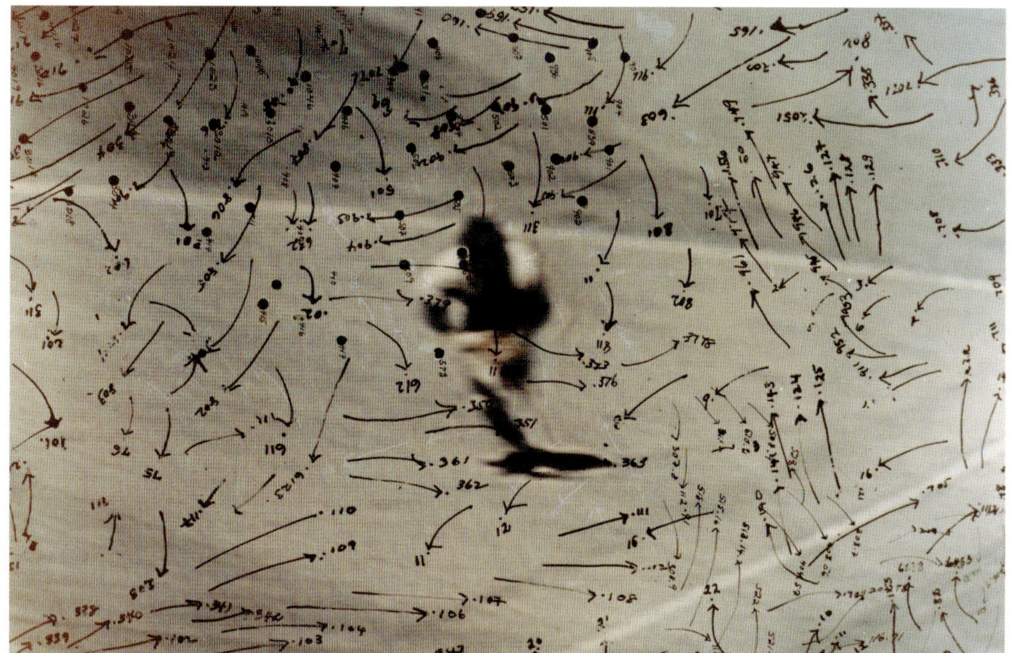

Fig. 86. Howardena Pindell, *Video Drawings: Baseball,* 1973–76. Chromogenic print, 11 × 14 in. (27.9 × 35.6 cm). Collection Walker Art Center, Minneapolis. Gift of the Peter Norton Family Foundation, 1993. 1993.49.

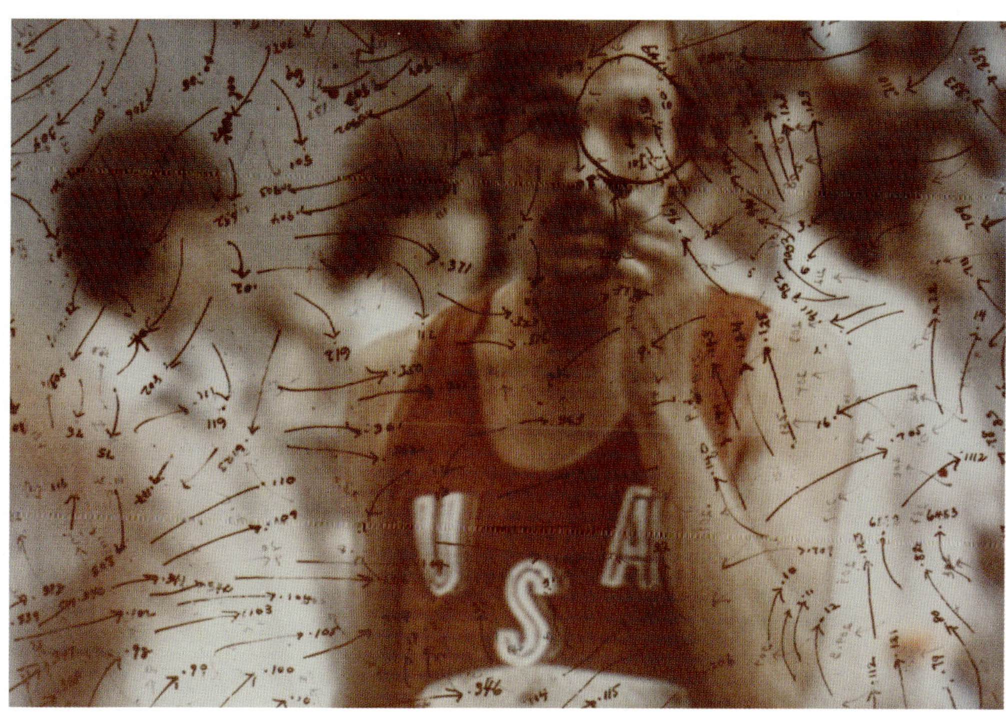

Fig. 87. Howardena Pindell, *Video Drawings: Track,* 1976. Chromogenic print, 4½ × 6½ in. (11.4 × 16.5 cm). Garth Greenan Gallery, New York.

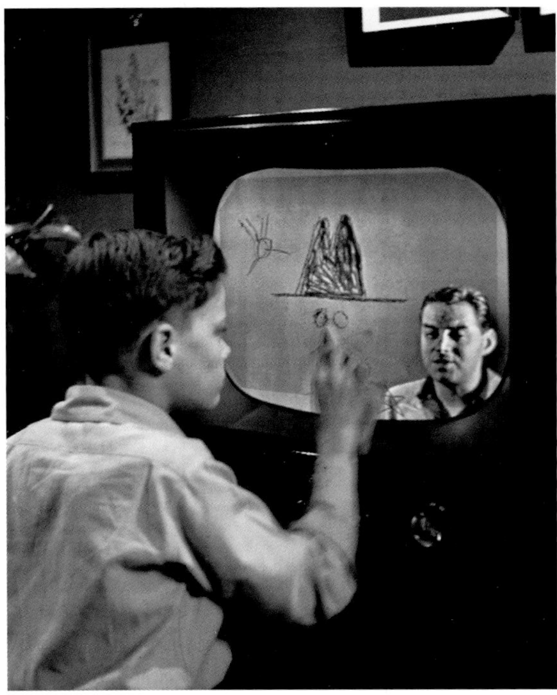

Fig. 88. *Winky Dink and You,* a children's television program, October 10, 1953. A child draws on a clear acetate sheet attached to a television screen, without damaging the actual TV screen. Show host Jack Berry is demonstrating a drawing technique.

objects or characters. In order to cohere as a series of narrative puzzles, *Winky Dink and You* requires haptic participation, drawing viewers into intimate physical proximity with the screen. This touching of the television echoes Pindell's childhood encounters with a raised plastic reproduction of a Van Gogh painting.[40] These early encounters familiarized Pindell with the idea that visual media could be experienced haptically.

As a network program, *Winky Dink and You* represents an innovative take on a nonetheless normative form of audience engagement. It requires its viewer-players to conform to its directives, to "play along." Pindell's later photographic works echo the program's seamless trans-media incorporation of drawing and the fleeting moving image. However, instead of rewarding conformity, the works raise the possibility that a viewer might reframe mass media broadcasts for her own purposes.

Pindell came of age in a period that saw the widespread dissemination of television. Between the years 1948 and 1955, more than half of U.S. homes installed a set. The technology transformed how many Americans consumed news and entertainment and how they organized their domestic lives and leisure time. These widespread social changes generated anxiety as well as optimism. By the 1960s, both critics and champions of television promoted geographic metaphors to describe how the medium had changed Americans' social-spatial orientation. Media theorist Marshall McLuhan anticipated the emergence of a democratic "global village" brought on by new flows of information. By contrast, Federal Communications Commission chairman Newton N. Minow lamented television's descent into a "vast wasteland" replete with violence and "screaming, cajoling, and offending" commercials.[41]

The contradictions inherent to television were central to Pindell's experiences with the medium from her earliest days as a viewer. Although influential for her later artistic production, television programs that were on air when she was a

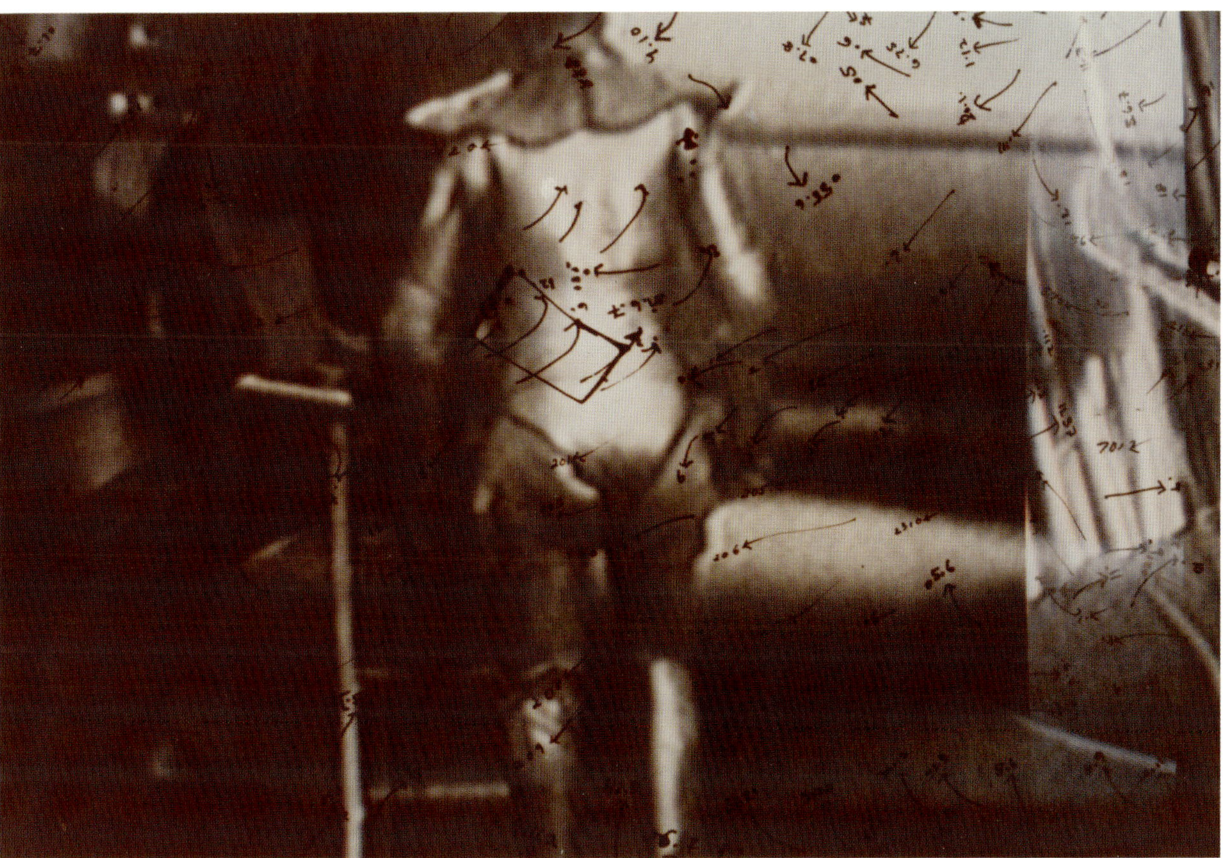

Fig. 89. Howardena Pindell, *Video Drawings: Science Fiction (Flash Gordon)*, 1976. Chromogenic print, 4½ × 6½ in. (11.4 × 16.5 cm). Garth Greenan Gallery, New York.

child, such as *The Ed Sullivan Show, The Ernie Kovacs Show, You Asked for It,* and *This Is Your Life,* seemed, in her words, to have "nothing to do" with her experiences. White hosts and actors populated these programs, which rarely depicted people or places Pindell recognized from her daily life. As film scholar Jacqueline Bobo has noted, this situation changed only slightly by the 1970s. For instance, in 1968, Diahann Carroll became the first Black actor since 1950 to star in a nationally televised program when she played the leading role in NBC's sitcom *Julia.*[42]

Pindell explores these exclusions in the *Video Drawings*. In many of the works, the distortions of multiple layers of mediation and the on-screen people's clothing and costuming obscure conventional visual racial markers such as skin tone and hair texture. The grain of the television, the blur of the photograph, and the accoutrements of athletics all abstract the human form. This is especially true of a subset of the series that draws imagery from science fiction programs such as *Flash Gordon*. In one example from 1976, Pindell's notations overlay an upright figure (fig. 89). Viewed from behind and cut off where a head should be, the body could belong to a human wearing a rigid, reflective space suit or to an android. The jet-age aesthetic of these images—their proliferation of metallic surfaces and blurred motion—evokes Afro-futurism. An aesthetic and political mode of Black cultural production, Afro-futurism centers the reparative potentiality of technology, especially as imagined in outer space.[43] By interrupting on-screen racialization through the use of technological membranes, Pindell intervenes in what she has called the "fiction" of normative racialized representation.

In cases where skin tone is visible in the *Video Drawings*, the works reflect the representational imbalance of the era by consistently presenting light skin. For instance, only two of Pindell's several dozen sports-related works depict visibly Black athletes. These televisual exclusions defy the historical reality of U.S. sports. Consider Pindell's engagement with footage from the 1976 Summer Olympic Games in Montreal. Black runners won numerous medals for the United States in the track and field events. For instance, Edwin Moses gave a world-record-smashing, gold-medal performance in the four-hundred-meter hurdles and shortly thereafter launched a winning streak that lasted nearly a decade. Nonetheless, Pindell's *Video Drawing* that utilizes imagery from the broadcasts of the track events features a white man, possibly Michael Shine, who took second to Moses (see fig. 87). The artist surely took aesthetic considerations into mind when she chose to print the photograph of the white athlete. Her hand-drawn, black marks contrast with the lightness of his skin and align with his body so that the athlete seems to hold an oversize, lopsided monocle to his left eye. All the same, Pindell's elision of Moses in favor of an athlete who performed less spectacularly highlights the underrepresentation of Black Americans in Olympic media coverage.[44]

Racial demographics have varied drastically across different professional sports in the United States. Baseball and hockey, the most frequently depicted sports in Pindell's series, exemplify these discrepancies. Black Americans in Major League Baseball (MLB) matched or exceeded the percentage of this racial demographic in the general U.S. population from the 1960s until 2000. The National Hockey League signed its first Black player, Willie O'Ree, in 1957, just ten years after the MLB; however, white players have maintained drastic overrepresentation in a league that has come under fire in recent years for a culture of racist abuse.[45] Across sports, prior to the 1980s, a consistent facet of mass media representation of U.S. athletes was the underrepresentation of people of color, including American Indian, Asian American, Black, and Latinx athletes, and of women of all races.[46]

Pindell's manipulations of mass media representations signal an understandable mistrust of a medium that failed to represent Black women through both racial and gendered exclusions. By annotating those broadcasts, however indecipherably, her photographic series asserts the presence of a critical television viewer who reframes images. Curator Grace Deveney has argued that in this series "Pindell renegotiated the psychosomatic terms of engagement with television, shifting from passive consumer to participant," thereby challenging the medium's implicit "power structure." Indeed, the relationship between Pindell's marks and the popular imagery evokes what cultural critic bell hooks has theorized in her influential text, "The Oppositional Gaze," as "black looks"—ways of looking deployed by Black Americans to assess mainstream representations of Blackness. hooks's account builds on cultural theorist Manthia Diawara's discussion of Black Americans' viewership practices, particularly the concept of "resisting spectatorship," which refers to audiences' critical analyses of racist ideologies in Hollywood films. In the *Video Drawings,* Pindell's notations evince a critical gaze possibly aimed at, among other targets, the erasures of Black womanhood on televisual airwaves.[47]

This approach to television—enacting active viewership through artistic gesture—suggests an equivocating view of the medium's potential: on one hand, television perpetuates the marginalization of people of color in U.S. society and fails to account for social difference; on the other hand, the medium leaves openings for critical agents to expose these representational failures. Pindell's ambivalence contrasts with contemporaneous artistic denunciations of television as a vehicle for capitalist indoctrination. For instance, artists Carlota Fay Schoolman and Richard Serra created *Television Delivers People* (1973) the same year that Pindell launched her series. Set against a blue backdrop, Schoolman and Serra's video consists of scrolling white text that didactically pronounces television as a tool for converting audiences into consumers: "You are consumed. You are the product of television." Schoolman and Serra's commentary echoes FCC chairman Minow's earlier lament of television as a "vast wasteland." By contrast, Pindell's series draws on the imagery and interactive modalities of popular programs in order to suggest that television can serve as a fecund site of cultural observation.

Artists in the United States began working with television as a medium in the early 1960s. Building on techniques of the historical avant-garde, Ono and Nam June Paik used the mass medium in order to strategically intervene in everyday flows of spectacular consumption. Ono's *Sky TV* (1966), for instance, used a closed-circuit television to transmit video of the sky into a gallery. Like much of Ono's work of the 1960s, it reveled in the poetic possibilities of everyday life, in this work by countering television's imbrication in consumer capitalism.[48] Pindell's fellow feminist artists who worked with video and television in the 1970s explored their ambivalence toward mass media. Made the same year that Pindell initiated her *Video Drawings,* Eleanor Antin's *Caught in the Act* (1973) juxtaposes video of the artist's clumsy, assisted attempts at ballet with photographs that capture moments of poise by editing out bodily inelegance (figs. 90, 91). The contrast between the video and photographic components of

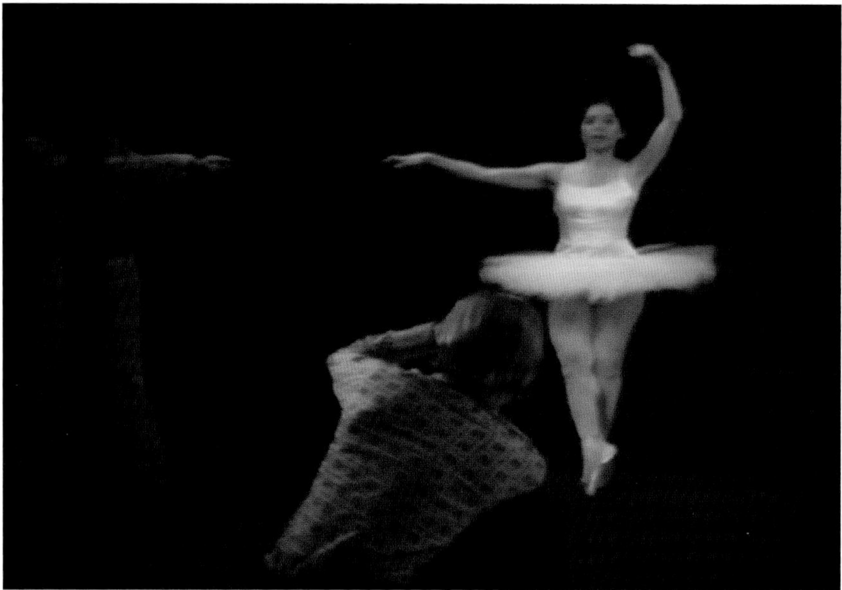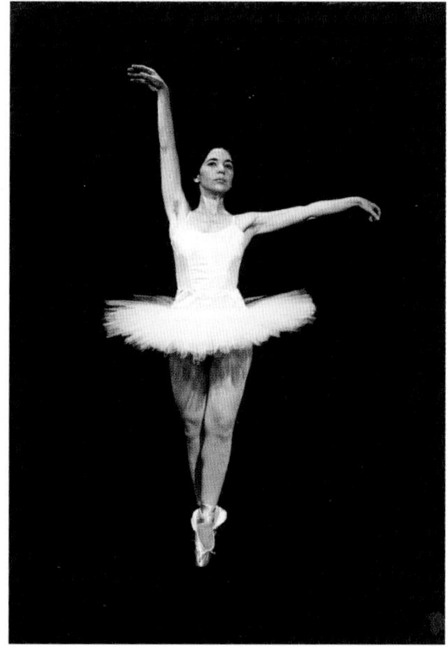

Fig. 90. Eleanor Antin, Still from *Caught in the Act,* 1973. Black and white video with sound, 36 min.

Fig. 91. Eleanor Antin, *Caught in the Act: Choreography IV—In the Grand Manner* (*Short Tutu*), 1973. Black and white photograph mounted on board, 7 × 4¾ in. (17.8 × 12.1 cm). Detail (third) from a set of four. Collection of the artist, courtesy Ronald Feldman Gallery.

Antin's work puts pressure on the truth claims of both mediums. It also suggests that each have a role to play in the production and circulation of ideas about the gendered body. Antin's work participated in a broader surge in feminist experimentations with video, exemplified by the founding in 1976 of the Los Angeles Women's Video Center at the Woman's Building.

From its nascence, television also served as a site of artistic exploration in its application as a home technology. In fact, in the early years of network television, as television historian Lynn Spigel has argued, the medium played a major role in the integration of art into everyday life. For instance, in 1952, MoMA initiated a "Television Project" that introduced family audiences to its collections. In this same period, networks hired avant-garde artists, designers, and filmmakers to develop graphics and incorporate experimental techniques into their shows. Avant-garde filmmaker Stan VanDerBeek, who used collage methods to make experimental films such as *Breathdeath* (1963) and *See, Saw, Seams* (1965), produced animations for *Winky Dink and You.* As a child, Pindell encountered this program and *The Ernie Kovacs Show,* which was hosted on various networks from 1952 through 1956 and again between 1961 and 1962. Art historian Maurice Berger has noted that *The Ernie Kovacs Show* encouraged viewers to investigate "television's transformation of reality into images." Kovacs appropriated features of surrealist, dada, and other avant-garde film, including dream sequences,

autonomously moving objects, and disorienting angles. He even invited viewers
to take photographs of his shows as they were being televised and to send these
images to the studio—a process resonant with Pindell's later layering of television and photography in *Video Drawings*. While this televisual ecology may
not have generated scenes of daily life that resonated with the young Pindell, it
framed the newly popular medium as a realm of interactive, aesthetic possibility.[49] Television offered an avenue, which ran through the middle-class U.S. home,
to modernist and avant-garde experimentation.

In contrast to projects by Antin or Ono, Pindell's series engaged with television as a source of found images, incorporating broadcasts into the *Video Drawings*. In this way, her series resonates with an early television work by Dennis
Hopper, *Kennedy Funeral* (1963). Pointing a camera directly at a television screen
broadcasting the funerary proceedings of the assassinated president, Hopper
generated blurred, low-fidelity
images that intervened in the easy
conflation of televisual representation with lived experience (fig. 92).
The four-day coverage of the events
following Kennedy's shooting offers
an early example of how television
can frame a national event, giving
far-flung viewers a sense of imme-
diacy.[50] Hopper's visually degraded
photographs and the thick, black,
rounded border of the television
screen in the frame of each photograph assert the mediated nature of
the broadcasts, thereby undermining
a viewer's intuitive sense of having
"been there." He used a photographic
technique similar to the one Pindell would deploy a decade later in order to comment directly on the mass media imagery then circulating in U.S. homes.

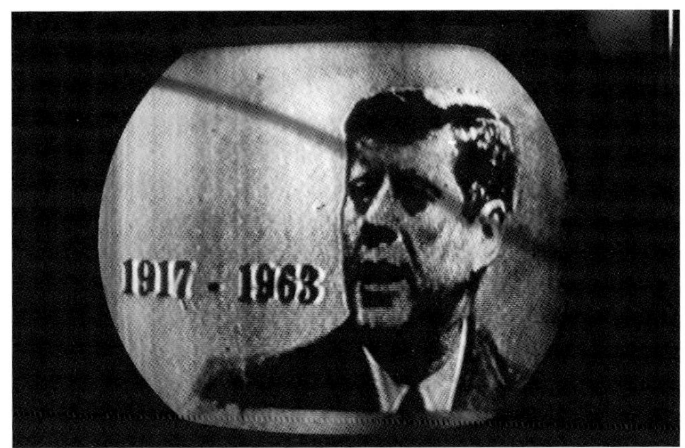

Fig. 92. Dennis Hopper, *Kennedy Funeral,* 1963. Gelatin silver print,
16 × 24 in. (40.6 × 60.9 cm). Hopper Art Trust, Los Angeles.

By 1973, when Pindell began the *Video Drawings,* televised accounts of
nationally and internationally significant events proliferated on network airwaves—for instance, the Watergate scandal, the violence inflicted on inmates
at Attica Prison, and anti–Vietnam War protests. The United States' military
involvement drew to a close that year, but broadcasts of the Vietnam War in
particular indelibly had reshaped U.S. televisual spectatorship. Dubbed the first
"living-room war" by writer Michael J. Arlen, the war was transmitted through
photographs and film to as many as twenty million television viewers in the

United States. This mediated proximity proved incendiary, as televisual depictions of the war's ghastly violence likely played a role in turning public opinion against military involvement. But by bringing war to the comfortable space of the home living room, the technology also contained and domesticated war for U.S. spectators. As art historian Carrie Lambert-Beatty has argued, television broadcasts of the Vietnam War "telescoped" the distance between Saigon and New York, both magnifying and collapsing it. The conflict became "shrunken and contained by domestic features, the bodies [of soldiers] . . . stripped of their reality." She noted that artist Martha Rosler thematized this effect in her photomontage series *Bringing the War Home: House Beautiful*. The collages combine magazine clippings depicting well-appointed, upper-class U.S. homes with images drawn from *Life* of armed soldiers and injured Vietnamese. They confront viewers with the complicity of "bourgeois aspirations" in the conflict abroad.[51]

Although not directly depicted in the *Video Drawing* series, broadcasts of the Vietnam War likely provided a salient point of reference for Pindell's commentary on televisual spectatorship. Her notation system, among its myriad evocations, conjures the symbology of antiquated military maps. The young, agile bodies in the photographed sports broadcasts belong to men ostensibly of draft age. Their physical exertions and vulnerability, then, serve as a site of displacement; these images summon and appear in lieu of spectacularized depictions of the disproportionately Black soldiers, Indigenous soldiers, Latinx soldiers, and other soldiers of color sent to perilous posts in Vietnam. This albeit tenuous relationship between athletic and wartime imagery renders the racial makeup of the sports broadcasts all the more poignant, reminding viewers how much more easily draft exemptions came to white, college-educated, and upper-class men. In a later instantiation of her *Video Drawings*, titled the *War* series (1988), Pindell explicitly works with mediated representations of military conflict. She layers vinyl lettering over images drawn from documentaries about military conflicts abroad, including in Cambodia, Ethiopia, Nicaragua, and the Persian Gulf.[52] This turn toward war imagery further indicates that the Vietnam War may have been an implicit concern of the initial series and that Pindell understood critical televisual viewership as an ethical imperative.

The *Video Drawings* enacted a new mode of address that allowed Pindell to attend more directly to the conditions of spectatorship her viewers brought to bear on her works. In one sense, this project built on the photographic practices of earlier artists, such as Hopper, who used televisual imagery to highlight the mediated status of mass communication. Pindell too generated blurred, grainy photographs as she sought to break down the televisual image "just one level" from its transmission. Sims has written that this use of visual distortion in the *Video Drawings* encourages viewers "to focus on the structure of matter transmitted as impulse." The grain of Pindell's photographs draws the viewer's attention to the physical properties and larger systems that make televisual images appear. As Deveney noted, "The breakdown of texture suggests the instability of the medium and hints at a fragility or a cracking in the facade of the homogenous and straightforward goals of much of television programming."[53]

But Pindell goes further. Through the series, she investigates how visual technologies are implicated in systems that use racist logics to ascribe differential values to human lives. By layering annotated acetate over these transmissions, she highlights the movement of televisual imagery through evaluative systems. Her use of athletic imagery emphasizes this flow of visual information through processes of approval and rejection. Sports are a form of judgment; athletic performances are scored, timed, and categorized; athletes win, lose, or are ranked. Pindell aptly uses photography—a visual technology historically used to measure and evaluate human bodies—to capture these televisual broadcasts. Her editorial annotations of the racialized visual field point to the possibility of other configurations of popular representation. By positioning herself behind the camera, Pindell shifts the stakes of representation from issues of visibility to access—from questions of who gets depicted in mass media to who gets to write, and rewrite, visual codes. She fortifies the melanin-deficient imagery of mass media with her own black marks, layering her annotated acetate skins atop the pale skins on television.

Pindell drew on her experience as a custodian of art to assert her authority as an actor who could intervene in mass media imagery. While she has welcomed the connections scholars have drawn between her notations and lines of scrimmage, labanotation, and systems used to visualize weather data, she had no training in any of these schemas. By 1973, she had, however, gained proficiency in the notation system used by conservators to record information about the condition of artworks. In her first years at MoMA, before she settled into curatorial roles, she occasionally executed condition reports for the registrar.[54] The vectors and circles of the *Video Drawings* resemble the marks used in this application. Pindell's constant exposure to artworks as physical objects needing to be managed heightened her awareness of the material nature of even fleeting images. This attunement to the tangible properties of art positioned her ideally to transform the light-based televisual signal into a stable, if blurred, physical image. By deploying a notation system with art world resonances in a series that re-imaged mass media sports broadcasts, Pindell also pointed to the evaluative systems undergirding art's circulation.

Despite the various visual rhymes between her notations and other visual systems, Pindell has insisted that her marks on the *Video Drawings* "mean nothing."[55] Thus, abstraction, and its non-reliance upon external systems of signification, remained a touchstone for the artist as she experimented with figurative elements in the photographic works. By applying her "random" notations to a medium that presented her with both the capacities of interactive viewership and the constraints of racial representation (and lack of representation), Pindell charted an ambivalent regard for mass media. With the *Video Drawings*, the artist planted seeds of skepticism about mass media representation that would blossom in *Free, White and 21*.

ARTISTS SPACE

By 1976, Pindell had paused printing photographs for her initial series of *Video Drawings*. She nonetheless applied a felt pen to an acetate sheet in 1979, writing "yes" and "no," drawing vectors and points in a work published in the feminist art and politics magazine *Heresies*. The photo-collage appeared in an issue devoted to "Third World Women: The Politics of Being Other." *Yes–No* shows Pindell's signature marks atop an image long absent from her oeuvre—the artist's face (fig. 93).[56] In three black-and-white photographs printed side-by-side on a contact sheet, she sits on a radiator in front of a light wall, wearing a striped kaftan over a cowl-neck top. Across the photographs, Pindell's mouth seems to move, she blinks, and the shot grows closer in range to her body.

Shortly after she made this work, Pindell addressed a letter to Lippard. She wrote to her close friend about a new "protest piece" she was planning. In this performance work, Pindell would cover her body with one of two materials— either oatmeal or "white dots."[57] This second material explicitly connects the would-be performance piece to the hole-punched paper scraps Pindell had collaged to abstract works on paper and paintings for nearly a decade. The artist's proposal to cover her face with these chads indicates that she viewed the surface of her abstract works as a transmutable dermis. Whether she used the oatmeal or the white dots, the intended effect was the same; Pindell noted to Lippard that the bodily covering would serve as a kind of whiteface. This performance, however, was never executed. Yet the timing of the correspondence, a month after Pindell completed *Yes–No*, suggests that this specific photographic project, and the *Video Drawings* more broadly, played a crucial role in her eventual use of whiteface in *Free, White and 21*.

Significantly, the annotated portraits appear in *Heresies* alongside Pindell's article "Criticisms/or/Between the Lines," which discusses the racial and gender bias encoded in art world criticism. In the text, Pindell draws on her experience as an art world insider to explain that criticism operates within a prestige system to authorize or exclude artists of color from the market. The juxtaposition of the article with the reproduction of the artwork suggests that such artistic judgments have a gatekeeping function.[58] In order to see Pindell, one must look through the annotated acetate "skin" that has registered critical assessments of her image. In this way, the work points to the inextricability of perception from

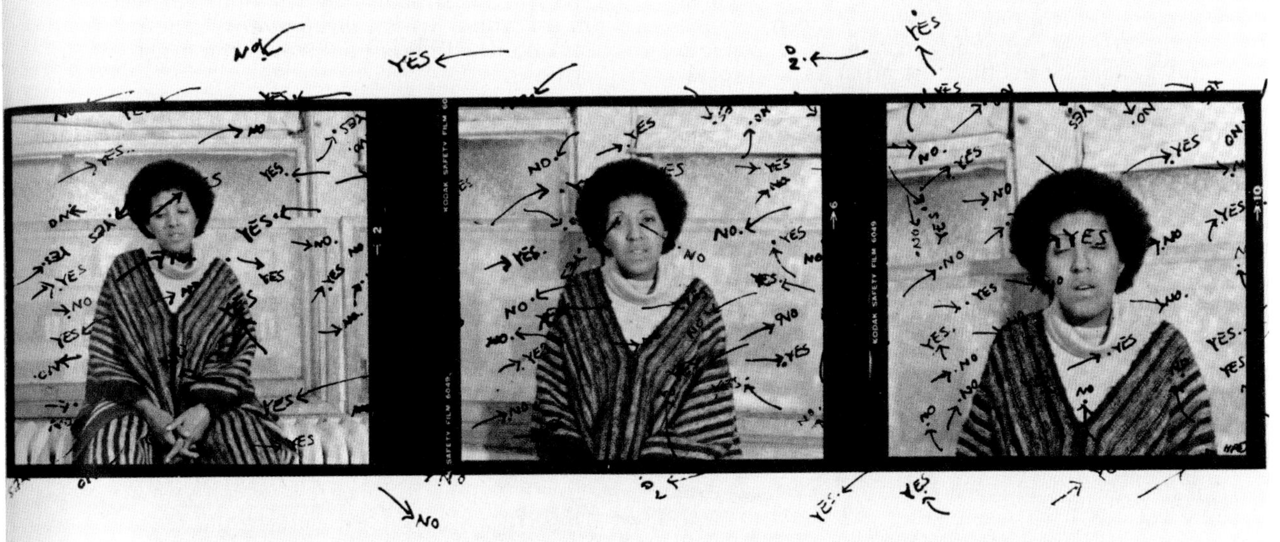

Fig. 93. Howardena Pindell, *Yes–No,* 1979. Pen and ink on acetate. Published in Howardena Pindell, "Criticisms/or/Between the Lines," special issue, "Third World Women—The Politics of Being Other," *Heresies,* no. 8 (1979).

the racialized thinking of art criticism. Pindell recontextualizes the visual principles of the *Video Drawings* to interrogate the systems that allow works of art to become visible and that, in some cases, disallow their circulation.

Both *Yes–No* and the *Video Drawings* deploy annotations in order to comment upon a system of judgments—the art world on the one hand and athletics on the other. Each of these evaluative systems broadcasts through mass media such as television and newspapers, making personal, subjective judgments into validated public commentary. However, *Yes–No* signals a significant departure from Pindell's previous, ambivalent engagement with mass media in the *Video Drawings*. The work marks her first entry into a more direct mode of critique—aimed at the art world—that would undergird *Free, White and 21.* Scholars have emphasized this pivot toward "protest" or activist art as a turning point in Pindell's career. A series of events in 1979 led to a profound shift in her understanding of the stakes of artistic production, leading her to work intently with a new mode of address.

The unrealized whiteface performance and *Yes–No* both show Pindell working through the abstracting procedures of racialization in the wake of an art world controversy that eroded her already wavering faith in predominantly white art institutions. Pindell conceived of the works in direct response to an exhibition held at Artists Space, a publicly funded "alternative" gallery located on the edge of newly redeveloped SoHo. In the first week of March 1979, Pindell learned of a one-person show on view at Artists Space from her friend Janet Henry. Both women were associated with Just Above Midtown (JAM) gallery, which Linda Goode Bryant opened in 1974 to promote Black artists working in experimental modes. Henry had gone to Artists Space to see a small exhibition featuring the work of a recent CalArts graduate named Donald Newman, who went by "Donald." His show, one of four solo exhibitions on view at the time, had opened on February 19 and displayed seven untitled triptychs measuring five by seven feet, each of which combined black-and-white photography and charcoal drawing.[59] Upon reviewing the exhibition, Henry headed directly to JAM to confer with colleagues about this otherwise unremarkable show that bore the incendiary, uncensored title *The N—— Drawings*.[60]

Henry has noted that she went to Artists Space initially to "confirm her assumption" that the show presented works by a Black artist—a possibility that required firsthand corroboration because the gallery, like other well-funded "alternative" art spaces, so rarely showed works by artists of color. During her visit to the gallery, the receptionist, Cindy Sherman, who had herself recently moved to New York to pursue an artistic career, informed Henry that "Donald" was a young white artist. She relayed to the visitor that Newman's title referred to his intensive use of the charcoal in the works on view. After hours applying thick layers of the black, friable material to the surface of his works, Newman had told Artists Space, his arms and hands became blackened, and he felt he looked like a "n——."[61] Thus, Newman embraced a purportedly accidental blackface, exploiting for artistic notoriety a "black skin" that was not his own.

As cultural critic Jeff Chang has argued, Newman pursued the white supremacist notion of "n——" in order to place himself in a local cultural scene that borrowed from a politicized punk aesthetic. In the debate that ensued, he defended his choice to follow in the footsteps of such countercultural darlings as Ono, John Lennon, and Patti Smith. All of these non-Black cultural denizens had used the term to designate and at times romanticize a subject position that they imagined to exist outside the bounds of societal acceptability.[62] In fact, Newman was not the only white artist in the orbit of Artists Space to appropriate an ostensibly racist practice as fodder for edgy artistic experimentation. Sherman had recently posed in blackface for her photographic series *Bus Riders* (1976).

Art historian Aruna D'Souza has covered in detail the factious debates that spanned from March to May 1979. Protest against the exhibition precipitated quickly thanks to the efforts of Goode Bryant, Henry, Pindell, and a multiracial group of artists and critics including Carl Andre, Cliff Joseph, Lucy Lippard, Faith Ringgold, Ingrid Sischy, and May Stevens. As D'Souza has noted, the issue took on a "pre-internet . . . form of virality," with several rounds of impassioned telegrams and letters traded between parties within days. In an open letter written on March 5, the protestor group, which called itself the "Emergency Coalition," wrote:

We assume [the title] was chosen as some sort of puerile bid for notoriety,
but we are amazed that the staff of Artists Space has lent itself to such
a racist gesture. Surely it must have occurred to you, if not to [the artist],
that this was an incredible slap in the face of Black and other artists,
of Black audiences and everyone connected in any way with one of our
leading alternative spaces. Did anyone object to these antics, or is social
awareness at such a low ebb in the art world that nobody noticed?[63]

Letters written individually by Pindell and Sims to the New York State Council
on the Arts (NYSCA) echoed this incredulous tone. They objected especially to the
use of taxpayer dollars to support the exhibition—Artists Space received sixty
percent of its funding in 1979 from the NYSCA. In her letter, Pindell, who previously served on the NYSCA visual arts advising panel, wrote, "It is appalling to
think that the staffs of institutions, alternative spaces, and some artists, have
grown so smug and secure as to think that a racial slur used under the guise of
aesthetic freedom would pass unnoticed." The council responded to the letters
with a telegraph sent to Artists Space censuring the gallery. In these initial
exchanges, protestors bemoaned the curatorial failure that had permitted such
a large public platform for what art historian Brian Wallis has identified as a
"form of hate speech." However, the subsequent debates assumed much broader
scope, bringing into focus the institutional machinations of art world racism.
Ultimately, these protests outlived the show itself, which closed as scheduled on
March 10. Henry saw the exhibition in its final days, but many of the protestors,
including Pindell, never viewed it. Pindell and Sims both noted that although
they were each on the Artists Space mailing list, neither of them received an
exhibition announcement. Both women conjectured that they may have been
intentionally excluded.[64]

Support for Artists Space and Newman's title also grew. Critics such as Douglas
Crimp contributed their renown to the cause in texts that defended the artist's
right to free speech. They also justified their support by pointing to the pliability
of language in post-structuralist thought. A statement written by Artists Space
director Helene Winer, a close friend of Pindell's prior to the controversy's eruption,
epitomized the position that linguistic meaning had become salubriously mallea-
ble: "People are neutralizing language. These words don't have quite the power
they used to—and that seems like a healthy thing."[65] To the artists and critics
who condemned the exhibition, this line of argumentation proved that Newman's
supporters were exasperatingly out of touch with the realities of ongoing racial
injustice and its manifestation in the New York alternative art world.

Protestors' frustrations mounted as Artists Space's response to their grievances failed, as Pindell noted, to acknowledge "the structural reasons that

allowed the offense to occur." For the Emergency Coalition, the gallery's heedless use of the racist epithet exemplified the endemic racism that continued to plague the art world. This included the double standard applied to white artists, whose unfettered freedom of speech Artists Space defended, and Black artists, who were systematically shut out of state-funded art institutions. Artists Space had opened in 1972 with the aim of showing avant-garde work that increasingly commercialized Manhattan galleries rarely supported. By 1979, less than four percent of artists who had shown there were Black. That year, the gallery received $74,000 in funding from the NYSCA, while the three top-funded organizations focusing on artists of color received a combined allotment of $18,500. As Henry stated in a letter to Artists Space associate director Rags Watkins, "You have to understand that [the] show was a symptom of a disease and that the malady won't disappear until something is done about it." Ephemera from the protests attest to the coalition's opposition not only to the distorting misrepresentations performed by a virulently racist title, but also to the lack of representation artists of color experienced in even "alternative" art spaces. For example, a flyer advertising a town hall–style protest on April 21 underscores this concern with the imperative, "Help Artists Space to become a true alternative space" (fig. 94). In a telegram dated April 5, Goode Bryant notified Artists Space that the Emergency Coalition would hold a teach-in at the gallery on April 14 (fig. 95). When Artists Space denied this request and protestors arrived on April 14 to a locked gallery, they picketed under a banner that read "Black Artists Locked Out of Artists Space." Art historian and Emergency Coalition member Carol Duncan wrote that the protestors' demonstrations targeted the issue of "whose images become visible," rather than white artists' freedom to make certain kinds of images. In her growing body of publications on racism, Pindell would eventually theorize this systematic exclusion of artists of color from art world circulation as "de facto censorship."[66]

Artists Space supporters, in turn, accused protestors of censorship. Crimp and critic Craig Owens, for instance, each asserted that the Emergency Coalition's exhortations to Artists Space's funder, the NYSCA, constituted a censorial ploy, with Owens writing that the group attempted "to use the governmental agency as an instrument of repression." The critics condescendingly lamented the protestors' putative "insensitivity to the complexities of both esthetics and politics" and their lack of "sophistication." These ugly remarks traded on racist ideas about the putative intellectual inferiority of the many protestors who were Black. Other aspects of the debate became racially charged as well: as D'Souza

Artists and Artworkers

Come today, Saturday, April 21, 1 pm to 105 Hudson Street to express our protest against racist practices by the staff of Artists Space

Help —

Artists Space

to become a true alternative space. Join us!

L G BRYANT
215 WEST 90 ST
NEW YORK NY 10024

western union Mailgram

4-025640E095 04/05/79 ICS IPMMTZZ CSP NYAB
2125954551 MGM TDMT NEW YORK NY 100 04-05 0913A EST

TO THE STAFF OF ARTIST SPACE
105 HUDSON
NEW YORK NY 10013

WE ARE GOING TO BE VISITING ARTIST SPACE TO SEE YOUR LATEST EXHIBITION
AND TO HOLD A TEACH-IN ON APRIL 14, 1979 WE INVITE YOU TO PARTICIPATE
AND HOPE THAT WE WILL BE WELCOMED

THE EMERGENCY COALITION

09:14 EST

MGMCOMP MGM

TO REPLY BY MAILGRAM, SEE REVERSE SIDE FOR WESTERN UNION'S TOLL - FREE PHONE NUMBERS

has observed, many Artists Space supporters, including Winer, repeatedly targeted their charges of censorship directly at Pindell rather than at white protestors such as Andre, Duncan, or Lippard. Crimp singled out Pindell's "insidious" attempts at censorship. Artist Donald Sultan berated her in a letter.[67]

In the wake of these attacks, Pindell's disillusionment with the art world establishment concretized. She felt increasingly spurned at MoMA. Most of her colleagues aligned with supporters of Artists Space who viewed her as a "censor." As a result, Pindell resigned from her post in June, as soon as she secured a job teaching studio art at Stony Brook University, leaving behind what she called a "corporate cultural agenda which is basically 'whites only'" for a state policy of "multicultural diversity."[68] She had worked at the museum for twelve years, the entirety of her professional artistic career. After years of frustrating encounters at the predominantly white institution, the Artists Space debates brought long-standing tensions to a head. Arguably, detractors such as Sultan intended for their rebukes of Pindell to have such an effect. Her most ardent critics seemed bent on villainizing her, rather than taking stock of their personal and institutional investments in racism.

As D'Souza has noted, Artists Space supporters' particular disdain for Pindell's public grievances betrayed their discomfort with and fear of Black people's indignation, especially Black women's anger. The uneasiness may have extended to the protestors as well; Lippard wrote to Winer in early March that she thought of herself as having a mollifying effect on other members of the

Emergency Coalition. Black American cultural commentators have reflected on the role of anger in responses to racism. As Michele Wallace has noted, "Being a black woman means frequent spells of impotent, self-consuming rage." In her influential essay "Uses of Anger," Lorde described the deleterious effect of white women's fear of Black women's anger within the women's movement. She emphasized the appropriateness of anger as a response to racism, writing, "Women responding to racism means women responding to anger; the anger of exclusion, of unquestioned privilege, of racial distortions, of silence, ill-use, stereotyping, defensiveness, misnaming, betrayal, and co-optation." Lorde also posited anger as a resource shared among women, arguing that feminists can make "use" of the emotion that every woman experiences when confronted with her oppression.[69]

Anger can be a resource for both creative and political work. In *Free, White and 21,* made in response to the Artists Space debates and her encounters with white feminism, Pindell uses her indignation to serve up a withering indictment of the racism of her white colleagues. The calm demeanor she deploys in her role as the Artist belies what she has called the "rage" she felt in the situations she narrates. It exemplifies what Black feminist scholar Brittney Cooper has theorized as "eloquent rage," anger that Black women communicate in ways that are "clear," "expressive," and "to the point."[70]

Pindell's outrage about her ostracization from professional circles and about the de facto censorship of Manhattan's art circuits swelled when she sustained serious injuries in an automobile accident in October 1979. In the aftermath of the collision, which occurred as the artist commuted to Stony Brook with colleagues including Art Department Chair Donald Kuspit, she faced months of rehabilitation. As she recovered from partial amnesia that temporarily damaged her short- and long-term memory, Pindell performed repetitive mnemonic exercises with postcards. She then began adhering this figurative imagery onto the surface of her collaged works. Pindell expressed her fear in the wake of the accident that she would be "silenced" by her injuries and that her critiques of art world racism would fade from public view as she recuperated. In retrospect, she noted, "I was . . . aware that there were those who were pleased: because of my injuries there was the possibility of my voice being muted. I know now that the desire to keep me silent, and to be pleased that I might be by default forced into silence, was an extension of the legacy of slavery and racism." Pindell's reflections emphasize how discourses of disability and race operate in tandem to silence or make invisible disabled people of color. As disability studies scholar Chris Bell has theorized, disability in the United States overwhelmingly has been defined as white. Pindell's decision to make her disability visible through her gesture of wrapping her head in gauze in *Free, White and 21* intervenes in these forces of erasure.[71]

The artist's fears about silence and tokenism grew in a period when national politics took a conservative turn. Ronald Reagan made a successful bid for U.S. president in 1980, after dog-whistle campaigning that repeatedly invoked the racist U.S. myth of the "welfare queen." At the same time, a corporatized version of multiculturalism gained mainstream cachet. Black women became increasingly visible in the public sphere in this period as advertisers and television networks cashed in on superficial appeals to racial diversity. As Wallace has noted, political voice or social power rarely accompanied this high visibility. These circumstances raised the stakes of anti-racist feminist politics. In this political climate, Pindell expressed a profound reluctance to continue in roles as a "token" woman of color artist and as a "superwoman." She began increasingly to understand her symbolic entry into predominantly white feminist institutions as a ploy to attest to white women's inclusivity and to set a staggering standard of entry for other women of color who might wish to join their ranks. In an influential essay originally presented at Hunter College, she described this situation as a "restraint of trade." The phrase refers to the "closed, nepotistic, interlocking system" of artistic display and sales that keeps artists of color out of galleries, museums, and art criticism.[72]

SKIN

What happens when an artist no longer trusts the institutions that deliver her work to a public? In the wake of the events of 1979, Pindell reflected on who her art served. Her frustration with the alternative New York art scene and feminist artistic circles catalyzed a growing anxiety about how viewers encountered her work. Video allowed Pindell to broadcast her discontent with the institutional art world and, potentially, to circumvent its gallery system. She exploited the capacities of the medium to counteract the forces that would silence her. Through the extended metaphor of "skins," she wrestled with racial discourse as an underlying condition of both mass media and artistic viewership.

Since its earliest days as an artistic medium, video has served as a means to investigate the changes in viewership wrought by modern technology. Art historian Anne Wagner has noted that in the early 1970s, video became a significant site for articulating "the uncertainties that . . . had begun to accumulate around 'artist' and 'viewer' as art's two correlative terms." Through video (as well as performance), artists channeled anxieties around the existence of an audience—how had and how would the rising tide of mass media in everyday life, emblemized by the ubiquitous home television, affect the terms of artistic viewership? Who would view experimental and avant-garde art if would-be audience members preferred to be at home watching TV? According to Wagner, artists in the early 1970s used the new medium in part to counter the pleasurable flows of spectatorship offered on their television screens, "urg[ing]" more skeptical modes of viewership by "aggressive[ly]" or "coercive[ly]" addressing the audience.[73] For instance, in Vito Acconci's *Undertone* (1972), the artist sits at a wooden table muttering confessions and erotic fantasies for more than forty minutes. He breaks this litany at several points to address his audience directly. Passages such as "I need you to be sitting there facing me, because I have to have someone to talk to, to address this to" both interpolate the viewer into the work and register anxiety about the availability of that audience. Artists of color and women artists throughout the twentieth century, who faced discrimination at every level of artistic training and reception, seldom took for granted that they would find mass audiences for their work.

Pindell's video borrows and complicates the "confessional" mode of address exemplified in Acconci's work. The Artist seems to speak directly to the audience, appearing alone in her shots and frequently gazing directly into the camera. In Pindell's hands, this intimate mode of address serves as a resource for exposing the limits of a form of viewership both fixated on and unable to acknowledge racial difference. The autobiographic shift in her work operates as part of an effort to unsettle the complacency of an audience that had ignored the broader circumstances of white supremacy under which Pindell labored. *Free, White and 21* triangulates the viewer in a high-stakes conversation structured by two characters' competing narratives. In fact, although the White Woman responds to and addresses the Artist, the Artist delivers her accounts of her life without acknowledging her on-screen antagonist. Instead, the viewer is left to formulate her own responses to the cantankerous White Woman's assaults.

Through this staged "dialogue," Pindell reveals issues of trust in viewership to be subject to racial discourse. As a viewer, who does one believe, and with whose point of view does one identify? As the Artist "speaks to" the audience and the White Woman responds to the Artist, to whom does the viewer choose to "talk back"? How do viewers' own racial identifications shape these responses? *Free, White and 21* critically intervenes in whiteness by requiring its white viewers to recognize the White Woman's canned phrases not only as parodies of white supremacy but also as incantations that they have heard, thought, or spoken before. In other words, the video's edge bets on the audience's awareness of the emotional and ethical obtuseness of the deflecting character, as well as white viewers' willingness to acknowledge their own cultural resemblance to the White Woman. In this mode of actively anti-racist viewership to which the video aspires, a psychologically charged audience experience contains the potential to dislodge calcified, racialized patterns of on-screen identification. White audience members are asked to recognize the White Woman in themselves and then to reject the racist logic she voices. Pindell's parodic, stiff whiteface portrayal adds a layer of humor to the performance that both heightens the absurdity of the character's deflections and allays the sting of the polemic.

Although Pindell recites autobiographical material in *Free, White and 21,* her role as the Artist must of course be viewed at a distance from the maker herself. This is especially important given the tendency in art history and criticism to read the work of women of color as straightforward commentary on the artist's individual "identity." Uri McMillan has offered the term "avatar" to theorize Pindell's use of a Black feminist strategy for mobilizing a persona in order to stretch "the subordinate roles available to black women." He noted that although Pindell narrates in the first person, she speaks her autobiographical encounters "through performed *versions* of herself." *Free, White and 21* also offers an example of the feminist strategy of "personae-play," which art historian Moira Roth has theorized as a performative tactic that combines equal parts autobiography and mythology. Consider, for instance, Adrian Piper's expanded multimedia performance of the Mythic Being—a persona she describes as "a third-world, working-class, overtly hostile male." In a 1973 performance captured on film, Piper applies the Mythic Being's garb to her body, including a mustache, Afro wig, and reflective sunglasses (fig. 96). These accoutrements evoke stereotypical representations of Black men involved in the era's Black Power movement. Dressed as the Mythic Being, the character recites entries from Piper's childhood diary and moves from the private space of her apartment to the public site of a crowded New York sidewalk. With *Free, White and 21,* Pindell compresses questions of autobiographical veracity and mythological yarn-spinning into the confrontation between her two primary characters. In the simplest terms possible, the Artist avatar deploys autobiographical anecdotes, while the White Woman gives voice to the mythology of U.S. racism. Pindell, in fact, has referred to the White Woman as a "mythical creature."[74] Just as Piper juxtaposes a redolent persona and her childhood diary entries, Pindell too extracts a character from the U.S. racial imaginary to place in dialogue with mediated, narrativized accounts of her own experiences.

Pindell enacts her on-screen personae through the use of tactile surfaces, or skins. For instance, the video theatrically cycles through costume and setting; the Artist's outfits and the vibrant-hued backdrops behind her, which both function as visual membranes or screens, change between takes. Film scholar Laura U. Marks has theorized "the skin of the film" as a metaphor for the ways that the medium can register materiality and activate haptic responses in its audience. Video, film, and other screen-based media leave psychic impressions on their viewers through these sensorial experiences.[75] The distinct materiality of Pindell's performances operates in tandem with the narrative arc of the Artist's recitations to create collaged scenes. This emphasis on the arrangement of textile surfaces to generate new contexts resonates with the tactile intensity of her paintings and

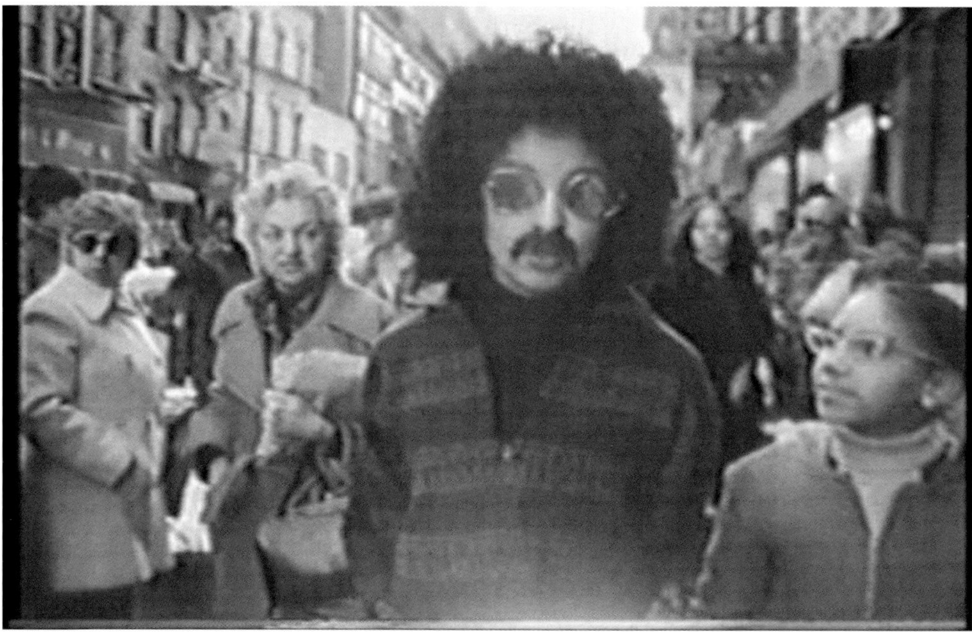

Fig. 96. Adrian Piper, *The Mythic Being,* 1973. Video, 8 min. Excerpted segment from the film *Other than Art's Sake* by the artist Peter Kennedy. Detail, video still at 6 min. 20 sec. Collection of the Adrian Piper Research Archive (APRA) Foundation Berlin.

works on canvas of the 1970s. Pindell's use of skins in *Free, White and 21* and the *Video Drawings* extends her concern for the haptic to mass media.

In her artist's statement for *Dialectics of Isolation,* Pindell identified a fraught relationship between her life "as she lived it" and its image in mass media. She explores this friction through her characters' engagements with skin-like surfaces in the video. Throughout *Free, White and 21,* the Artist and White Woman apply and remove a series of skins from their faces—gauze, facial mask, and white stocking. These operations evoke processes of racialization. For instance, the Artist peels a translucent mask from her face, transforming the substance from an imperceptible surface to a tactile material (see fig. 81). Pindell has stated in an interview that she thought of this gesture as an expression of her desire to extricate herself from whiteness. She refers here to her involvement with white feminists in spaces such as A.I.R. Perhaps in these settings she felt she had to perform a kind of whiteface in order to gain acceptance from her white peers. Pindell also has specified that in planning this gesture, she was thinking about her own multiracial ancestry, and particularly the histories of sexual assault she saw implied in her light skin.[76] Through this act of removing the mask, then, the artist alludes to more sweeping historical and cultural recuperations.

Pindell approaches the mask as a metaphor for whiteness through the procedures and materials of cosmetics—the facial mask and makeup. Her simultaneous concerns for racial identification and skincare operations point to the ways in which racial presentation and feminine masquerade coincide and overlap. By locating whiteness in these feminine-coded epidermal practices, Pindell comments on the racialized character of femininity and the gendered nature of racialization. In the White Woman, normative gender and racial codes are inextricable. This concern for imaginative, gendered, and raced skins in *Free, White and 21* evokes the adamant markers of so-called femininity the artist deployed to create masquerading effects in her cut and sewn paintings.

At the same time that the video denaturalizes the twinning of race and skin tone, it also shows that the marks of racialized oppression can be etched deeply into the flesh through a narrative skin. When the Artist tells the story of her mother, who as a child was washed with lye by a white babysitter, she says that her arms still bear marks from the burns. Parents' bodies, especially their scars, can serve as a kind of map of the larger world for the young children who sit on their laps. Perhaps the Artist begins her narrations with her mother's story not simply for the sake of chronological fidelity, but because her intimate, embodied familiarity with racism began in her scarred arms.

Within the imaginative circuit of Pindell's video, the skins that the Artist manipulates are removable. By the end of the piece, she has wrested herself from surface treatments—the gauze and the facial mask—which symbolize her injury and her imbrication in whiteness. These acts of removing the skins offer a recuperative possibility. They echo the efforts of "Third World Women," such as those gathered in *Dialectics of Isolation,* to eradicate an internalized white gaze and to establish a feminist context outside of white feminism. However, these gestures of removal are more poetic than triumphant. They occur as the Artist shares excruciating, recent encounters with racism and as Pindell continues to toggle between playing the Black Artist and the White Woman.

Skin functions differently on the face of the White Woman than on that of the Artist. The visible layer of makeup that the White Woman wears throughout the video operates, of course, as a prosthetic skin. Pindell used whiteface in *Free, White and 21* to refer to and invert Newman's alleged blackface in the production of his charcoal drawings shown at Artists Space. Her inversion of the white artist's racial appropriation exposes whiteness, undermining its authority as a ubiquitous, yet unnamed, social force. In contrast to blackface, whiteface has been a tool used to critique and dismantle white supremacy, rather than uphold it. In a paradigmatic antecedent to *Free, White and 21,* playwright Adrienne Kennedy deployed whiteface in her 1964 one-act play *Funnyhouse of a Negro.* The play centers on a young woman, Sarah, who wrestles with her mixed-race ancestry through personas including Queen Victoria, the Duchess of Hapsburg, and Patrice Lumumba. Kennedy's stage directions indicate that Queen Victoria

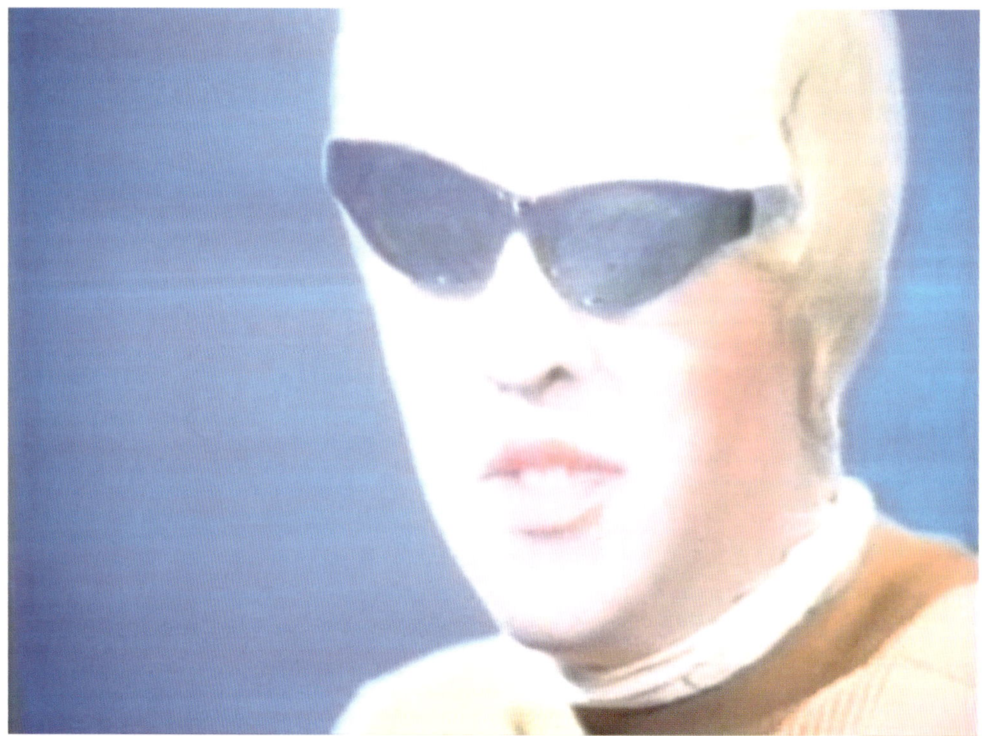

and the Duchess of Hapsburg should "wear masks or be made up to appear whitish yellow." As theater scholar Faedra Chatard Carpenter has argued, Kennedy's use of whiteface presented whiteness "as a constructed identity" and as "hypervisible, strange, and even terrifying." Kennedy, like Pindell, deployed whiteface as a way of not only critiquing whiteness as a naturalized ideology but also in order to convey "the impossibility of racial absolutes" through reference to miscegenation.[77]

The White Woman applies white pantyhose to her own face (fig. 97). Her features become distorted by the compression of the nylons—an object Pindell has likened to both a bank robber's stocking and the "polite" ladies' corollary to the white hood of the Ku Klux Klan.[78] With her use of the pantyhose, Pindell challenges the ability of racial whiteness to shapeshift and deny its own existence. Here, the crimes committed in the name of whiteness indelibly mark its benefactor.

By training the video on signifiers of whiteness, through the whiteface of makeup, white stocking, gauze, and facial mask, Pindell's project ran counter to multiculturalist calls to make racial difference visible by superficially highlighting people of color. Pindell turns the tables, submitting whiteness to exacting procedures of visibility. Her video reveals whiteness as an insidious racial ideology undergirded by violent attempts to accrue and maintain power. Whiteness appears as a series of psychological maneuvers performed through surface and deception. In *Free, White and 21,* Pindell continues to shirk demands that her art ought to provide "validated" insights into her identity. The Artist's anecdotes do more to expose the discomfort, anger, and paranoia of the white people who have harmed her than to "represent" Pindell in a straightforward way. Ultimately, her parodic ventriloquism attempts strategically to reroute the representational onus of multiculturalism. In defiance of era demands that Black women should become visible but remain silent, Pindell speaks and continues to defy the terms of literal representation.

CONCLUSION

Through the mass media technologies of television and video, Pindell explored what it might mean to become visible in her works. She maintained a characteristically critical approach to representation in the *Video Drawings* and *Free, White and 21,* enlisting her audiences in a skeptical mode of viewership. Her works prefigured significant developments in how artists confronted racism in the gallery. For instance, Piper's video installation *Cornered* (1988) echoes Pindell's deployment of a deadpan narrator who matter-of-factly addresses an audience about her own experiences with racial bias. It was with her use of skins, however, that Pindell contributed most profoundly to a Black feminist reconceptualization of distinctly American entanglements between history, biography, and representation.

Pindell's skins show her attempting to push past the binary of her lived experience and public depiction and finding it over and again. Her engagements with mass media thematize the convergence of two skins—the skin of the body and the skin of the screen. Through the membranes she deploys, Pindell theorizes the representational entanglements with which we all live. Skins both form the surface of our bodies and exceed them—they slough off and move through the world in ways that we cannot control or always foresee. They abstract from our realities. Of course, how and what specific skins represent depends on racial discourse. The screen is a social membrane, enrobing living bodies. Sometimes, as in *Free, White and 21,* the screen even aspires to register the losses and connective possibilities of representation itself. In these works, Pindell scrutinizes the deep mutual imbrication of representation and abstraction. She deploys skin in order to investigate the abstractions inherent to representation, and the need, despite this intractable infidelity, for self-authored images.

Conclusion

Pindell's orientation toward the complex spectrum of abstraction and representation began to shift in 1979. Over the next decade, her fully abstract paintings and works on paper gave way to a practice that incorporated representational and figurative elements with increasing prominence. This transition occurred amid a crisis of memory that destabilized Pindell's sense of self. In the aftermath of the head injury she sustained in a severe car accident that year, she began utilizing postcards and photo-transfers to recuperate her memory. These same materials migrated to the surface of her works. Pindell culled imagery from *National Geographic,* her travels, and her mother's postcard collection to collage onto the surface of her paintings and works on paper. The mnemonic resonances of the materials are individual and indecipherable. In *Memory: Past* (1980–81), Pindell incorporated photo-transfers of microscopic images of appendage-like biological forms (perhaps cilia, a type of sensory organelle that protrudes from some cells) and a fragmented image of what appears to be a storefront (fig. 98). Often oriented sideways or upside down, the representational elements float in a shimmering sea of paper, paint, thread, and glitter. However, their broader commentary on memory remains accessible; Pindell's scattering of pictorial elements across the expanse of an abstract plane conveys what curator Valerie Cassel Olivor has called "the difficulty of retrieving precise memories and the multifaceted nature of perspective."[1]

In addition to connecting to her past, imagistic passages also helped Pindell to secure her ability to remember future events. A detail of *Memory: Future* (1980–81) shows a sloping roofline of Japanese architecture; Pindell would spend seven months in Japan on an artist's fellowship shortly after completing this work (fig. 99). She also explored the memory of the car accident itself. Pindell retained a vivid recollection of bystanders observing her in the wreckage of the vehicle, where she was trapped, yelling for help, until rescue crews arrived.[2] She explores this memory in *Autobiography: Earth (Eyes, Injuries)* (1987; see fig. 8). Collaged eyes coolly observe a central silhouette. Like many paintings Pindell has made since the early 1980s, its ovoid canvas jettisons rectangular form.

Fig. 98. Howardena Pindell, *Memory: Past,* 1980–81. Acrylic, dye, paper, thread, tempera, photographic transfer, glitter, and powder on canvas, 10 ft. 6 in. × 7 ft. (320 × 213.4 cm). Museum of Modern Art, New York. Committee on Painting and Sculpture Funds and gift of The Friends of Education of The Museum of Modern Art. 549.2014.

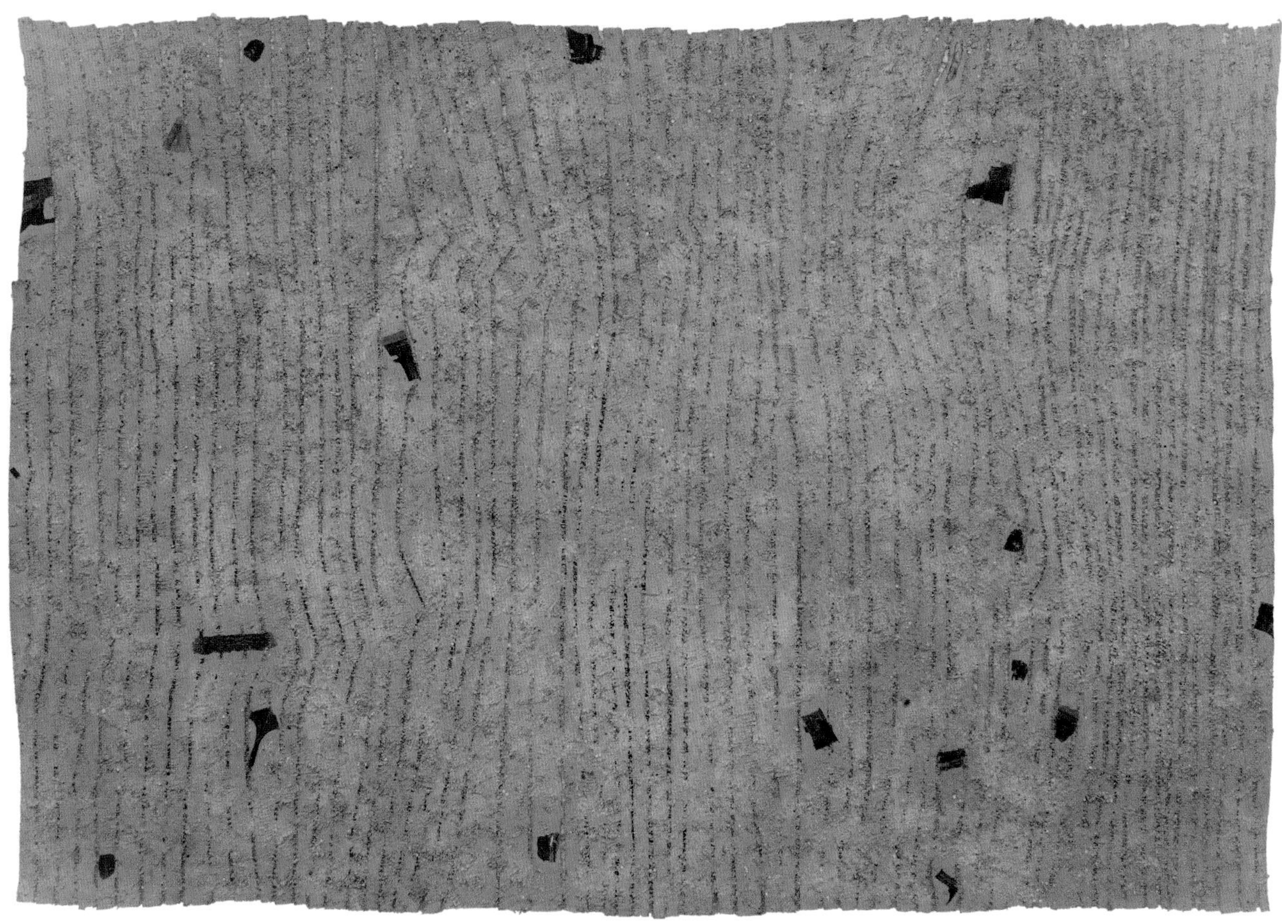

Fig. 99. Howardena Pindell, *Memory: Future,* 1980–81. Acrylic, dye, paper, thread, tempera, photographic transfer, glitter, and powder on canvas, 6 ft. 11 in. × 9 ft. 8½ in. (210.8 × 295.9 cm). Museum of Fine Arts, Boston. Museum purchase with funds donated by Barbara L. and Theordore B. Alfond through the Acorn Foundation in honor of Ann and Graham Gund Director, Matthew D. Teitelbaum 2015.2836. Photograph: © 2021 Museum of Fine Arts, Boston.

Gradually, across works in the *Memory* and *Autobiography* series, modernist questions about allover abstraction and gridded space receded from the foreground of Pindell's practice as her interest in personal, traumatic memory became increasingly imbricated in the remembrance of collective trauma. A cut and sewn painting from 1988 that uses the figure as well as abstraction, *Autobiography: Water (Ancestors/Middle Passage/Family Ghosts)*, is paradigmatic of the artist's changing concerns (fig. 100). Chattel slavery, and her ancestral connection to this U.S. practice, became a sharply focused issue for Pindell in the 1980s. *Autobiography: Water* thematizes the trauma of the Middle Passage and its persistent haunting of contemporary life. Part of her autobiographical series, the piece also explores the artist's multiracial family lineage. The eleven-foot-tall painting centers a woman's face modeled in shades of gray and based on the artist's own elegant visage.[3] A silhouetted body, traced with stitched seams, branches from the face and recedes behind an impasto-paint layer of aqueous blue hatch marks. Four pairs of arms in varying skin tones float above the head, presenting a palimpsest of human lives. Collaged photo-transfers of eyes dot the canvas, staring out at the viewer, returning the act of looking. Near the bottom left of the composition, thick paint yields to a flat, white vessel in a familiar pointed shape. This representation of a slave ship is immediately recognizable for its similarity to diagrams reproduced in history books and museum exhibitions; the painting's title primes us to find this content. Through figurative elements and vinyl text that describes atrocities of slavery, *Autobiography: Water* materializes the flotsam of a violent and unresolved history. Pindell's insistence on the relevance of these events to an audience in the late twentieth century, and on the enduring need to remember the human beings who lived under conditions of enslavement, recalls poet Elizabeth Alexander's insight that "bodily experience, both individually experienced bodily trauma as well as collective cultural trauma, comes to reside in the flesh as forms of memory reactivated and articulated at moments of collective spectatorship."[4] Through a painting that sutures the human figure to historical harms, Pindell prompts collective witnessing of an ongoing trauma.

The layers of lettering and imagery beneath the thick paint of *Autobiography: Water* lend themselves to a textual reading. Made amid the so-called culture wars, which brought a new urgency to the public visibility of Black women, the painting addresses itself to the exigencies of "re-membering." In the novel *Beloved,* Toni Morrison coined the term "rememory," a word that functions as both noun and verb. Through this concept, Morrison theorized the interconnectedness of individual and collective memories and the difficulties of reimagining one's heritage in the wake of violent histories. Pindell's *Autobiography: Water* takes on precisely this challenge through a textured visual dialogue between her body, her ancestry, and the root of U.S. culture that was planted in slavery. In her foundational text on the self-making practices of enslaved Black Americans in the nineteenth century, literary theorist and historian Saidiya Hartman built on Morrison's insights to theorize an archival and historical performative practice of "re-membering the body." Chattel slavery was designed to obliterate enslaved people's connections to an empowering culture and to their own humanity. The Middle Passage—the horrific transatlantic sea voyage during which Africans were forcibly transported to the Americas in what Hortense Spillers has called the oceanic "nowhere" of identity—functioned as a critical site for the "distortion" of humans into property. According to Hartman, to re-member the body under the conditions of slavery is an act of reconstitution

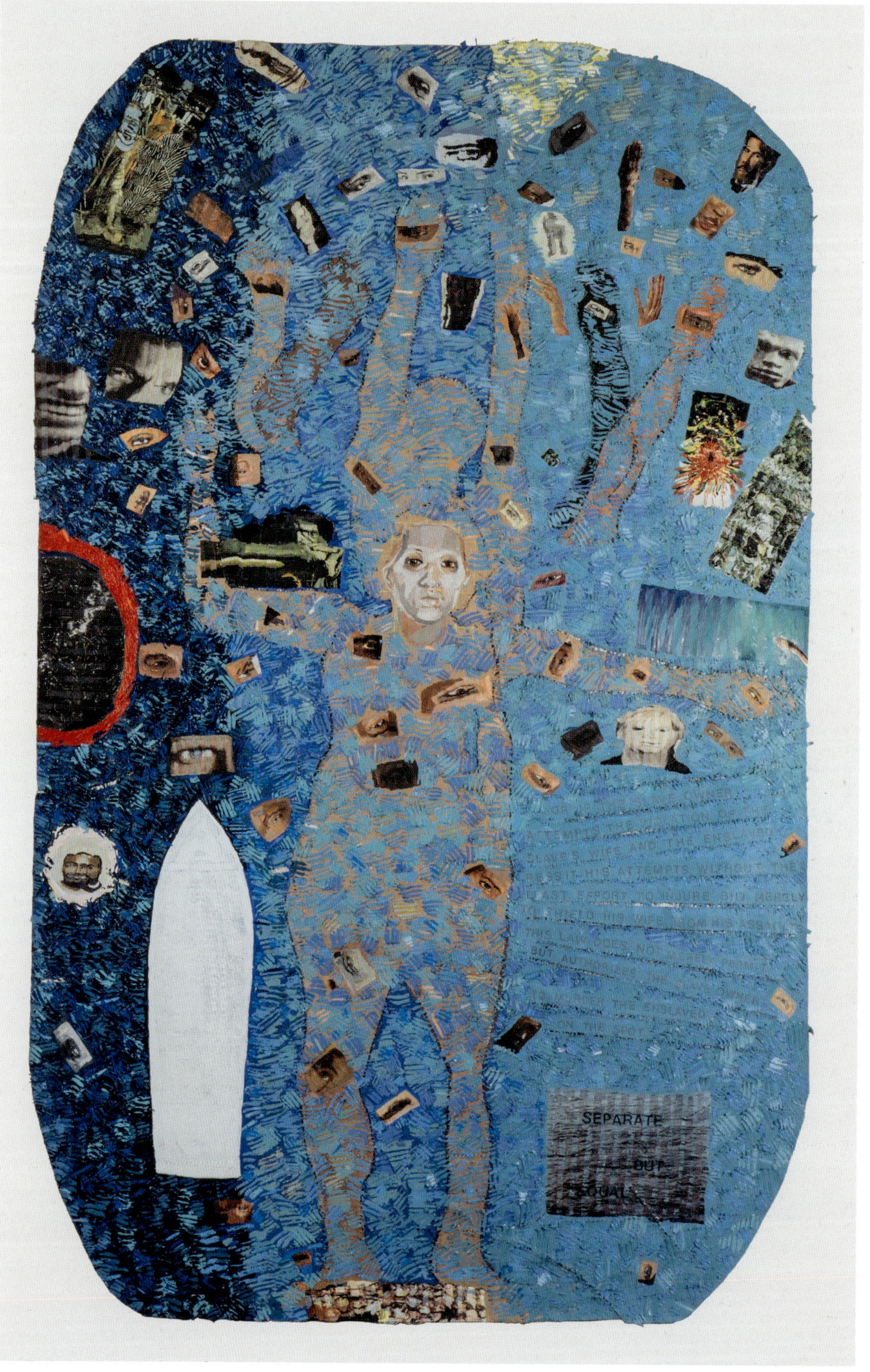

SEPARATE
BUT
EQUAL

that acknowledges "pain" and articulates the body's "violated condition," while also "[attending] to its pleasure, eros, and sociality." The body, as site of trauma, becomes a resource for self-making, for "restitution."[5]

From the late 1960s through the 1970s, Pindell pursued the belief that an artist could make something meaningful and, indeed, "healing," without recourse to figuration. She has promoted the idea that the works she made after 1979, following an art world debate about racism that caused her departure from MoMA and her recovery from life-altering injuries, increasingly centered on her own experiences and withdrew from concerns for process. Nonetheless, after this period, she maintained a conviction in the reparative possibilities of a haptic approach to art-making.[6] *Autobiography: Water* extends some of the aesthetic hallmarks of Pindell's earlier, abstract cut and sewn paintings in its extensive use of collage, sewing, and thick layers of paint. The work continues her efforts to think through the textured, handworked surface and the body as resources. Like so many of Pindell's abstract paintings, her later figurative paintings both refer to experiences of individual and collective harm and incite aesthetic pleasure. Across her Black feminist projects of mending abstraction, critiquing the representational regimes of mass media, and re-membering diasporic histories, Pindell conceived of her artistic labor as a salve and sanctuary from the persistent abrasions of everyday life.

However, *Autobiography: Water,* as an exemplar of a broader, incremental transition in Pindell's oeuvre, also supplanted many of the priorities that had marked her practice for years. The later works newly inquired into broad sociohistorical conditions. They offer explicit, public questions about the U.S. psyche, aimed at conversations beyond those of the institutional art world. Motivated by coinciding personal and social crises, these later works pursue representation as a method for interrogating individual and cultural memory and the complicity of contemporary society in historical harms, marking a profound shift away from her phenomenological examinations of modernist surface. For the first decade and a half of her career, Pindell blurred the boundaries between her artistic and activist work; in the 1980s and 1990s, she erased them all together.

Pindell launched this gradual, nonlinear shift with her video *Free, White and 21* (1980), which offers a trenchant critique of white feminism, and with

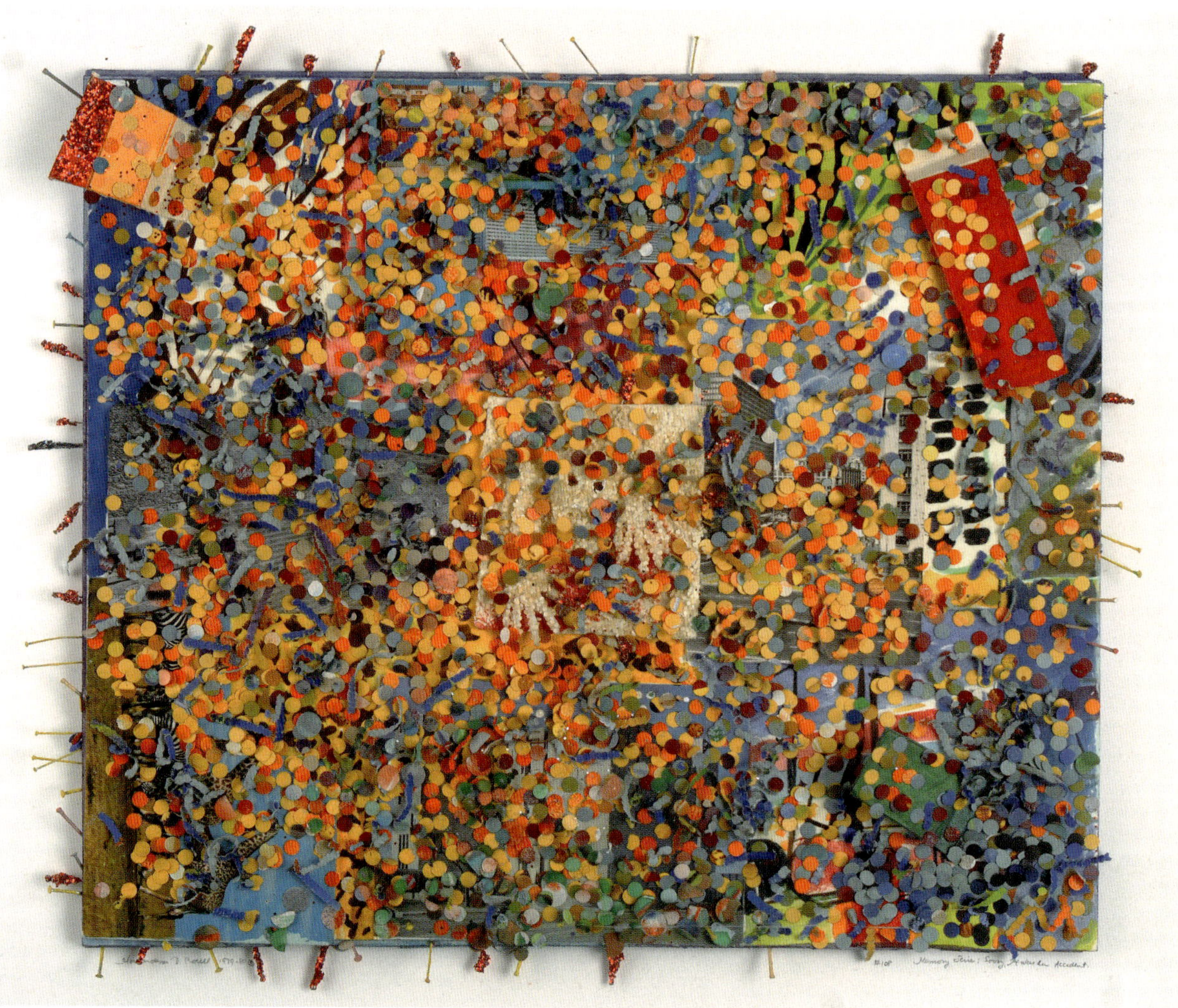

Fig. 101. Howardena Pindell, *#108 Memory Series: Sorry, It Was an Accident,* 1979. Mixed media, 14 × 17 in. (35.6 × 43.2 cm). Georgia Museum of Art, University of Georgia, Athens. The Larry D. and Brenda A. Thompson Collection of African American Art GMOA 2012.144.

a small number of collages she made in the late 1970s (see figs. 76, 77). In the collaged works, Pindell examines the psychological and representational logics of racial whiteness. A pair of delicate white hands comprised of miniscule paper chads eerily materializes from the center of the colorful collaged composition *#108 Memory Series: Sorry, It Was an Accident* (1979; fig. 101). The work evokes Pindell's fear of being silenced by white feminists following the collision. It thematizes how the interplay of disability and race shaped her treatment by others as she recovered. Another work on paper from this period, *Memory Test: Free, White and Plastic #114* (1979–80), centers a white plastic toy gorilla in a vivid hole-punched composition (fig. 102). A prize from a gumball machine, the small

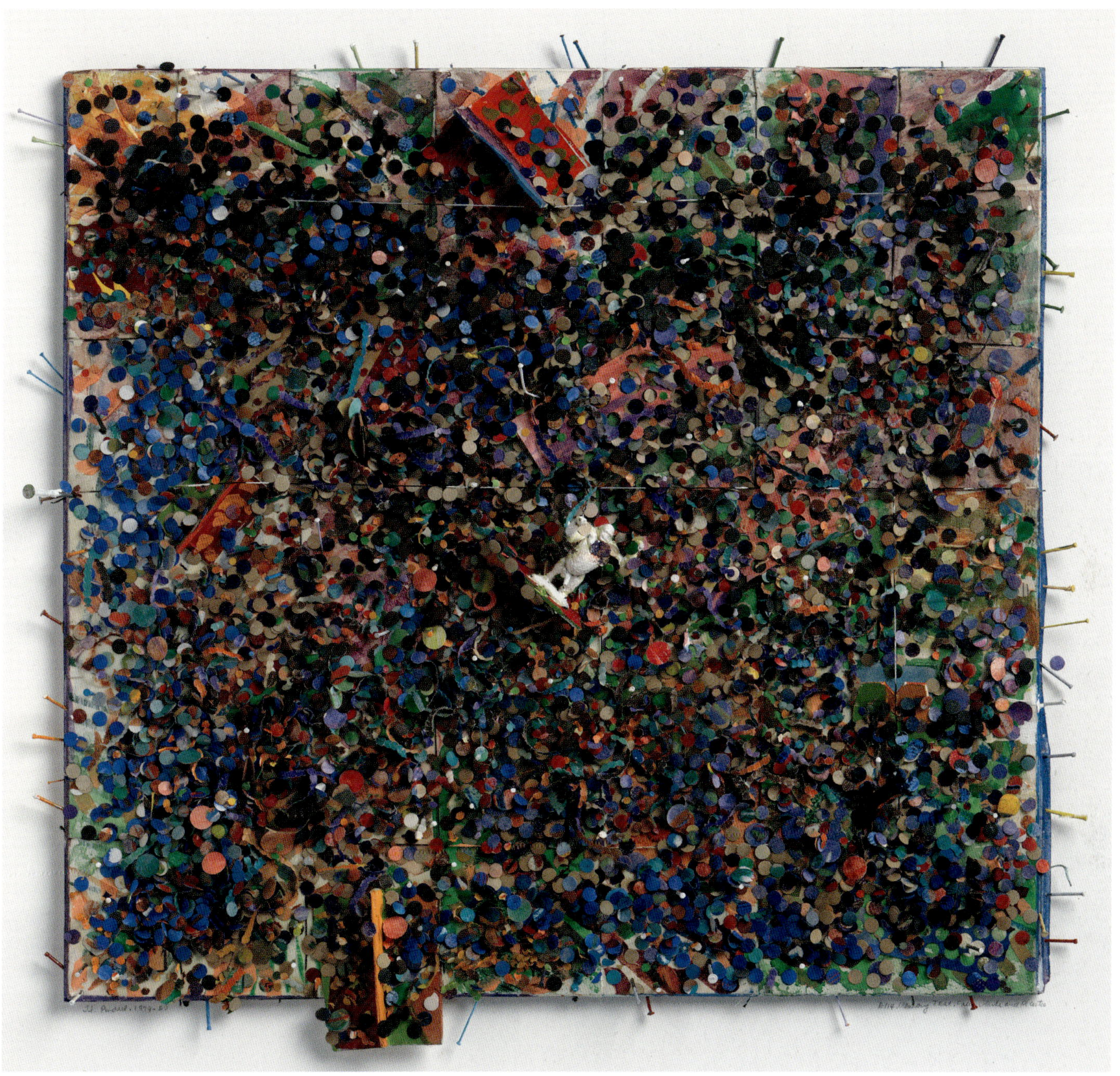

Fig. 102. Howardena Pindell, *Memory Test: Free, White and Plastic #114,* 1979–80. Cut and pasted and painted punched paper, acrylic, watercolor, gouache, ink, thread, nails, mat board, spray adhesive, and plastic on cardboard, 20⅞ × 20⅞ in. (53 × 53 cm). Metropolitan Museum of Art, New York. Arthur Hoppock Hearn Fund, 1980 (1980.150).

toy plays on and inverts anti-Black stereotypes and links whiteness to both animality and artifice. In these early instances of her reengagement with the figure, Pindell uses it as a tool for understanding and critiquing whiteness. She continues to refute the racialized expectations she encountered throughout her career, which posited abstraction as the privileged domain of whiteness and figuration as the realm in which artists of color could depict themselves.

During the 1980s and 1990s, Pindell drastically expanded the scope of her artistic and curatorial practices. She explicitly aligned her activism and art-making in works such as *Separate but Equal Genocide: AIDS* (1991–92), a two-panel painting that features vertically oriented U.S. "flags"—one black, one silver, each with a red band running along the right side (fig. 103). Stitched seams mark the boundaries between stars and stripes. These shapes are occupied by overpainted vinyl letters spelling out the first names of children and teenagers who had died of AIDS-related illnesses in New York hospitals. The painting uses some of the techniques of abstraction, collage, and craft Pindell had long embraced. Here, they combine with representational and textual elements to operate in service of a prescient political statement about the inequitable distribution of HIV/AIDS resources across non-white versus white communities. Several public-facing projects of this same period exemplify Pindell's broader reconceptualization of her practice in the aftermath of her resignation from MoMA in 1979. With her transition to a teaching career at Stony Brook, which allowed her more time for art-making, she experimented with new artistic modes. For instance, Pindell created a digitally generated light sculpture in Times Square and a sand mandala based on the drawings of students at public elementary schools in Hartford, Connecticut. She also made an artist's book about art world segregation, *ART CROW/ JIM CROW* (1988).[7] After leaving MoMA, Pindell also extended her curatorial work to more politically engaged projects. For instance, she curated *Autobiography: In Her Own Image,* a 1988–89 traveling exhibition organized by INTAR Latin American Gallery in New York that featured the work of twenty women of color, including Emma Amos, Theresa Hak Kyung Cha, Ana Mendieta, Lorna Simpson, and Kay WalkingStick. While the exhibition featured a variety of aesthetic strategies, representation was an explicit theme; Pindell's selections emphasized how the artists contended with their underrepresentation in the public sphere as women of color.[8]

Ultimately, Pindell's representational "turn" in her own artistic work proved temporary. Since the early 2000s, she has frequently worked in a fully abstract idiom. *Night Flight* (2015–16) centers many of the formal, textural concerns of Pindell's works of the 1970s (fig. 104). It combines visible seams and collaged hole punches on its irregularly shaped, unstretched canvas surface. Like many of her more recent paintings, its palette is brightly saturated—a brilliant blue in this

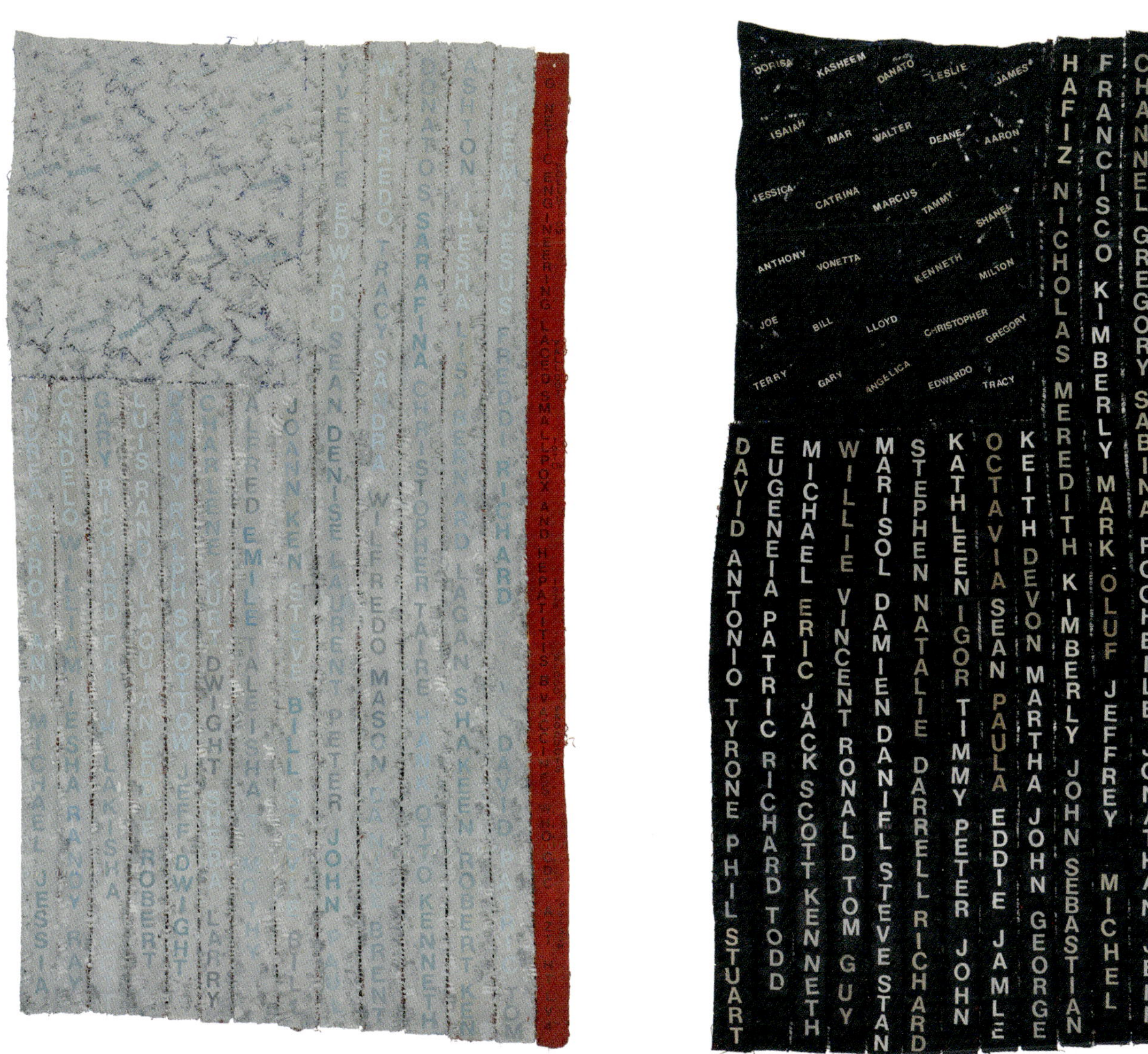

Fig. 103. Howardena Pindell, *Separate but Equal Genocide: AIDS,* 1991–92. Mixed media on canvas, 75½ × 91 in. (191.8 × 231.1 cm). Private collection, Palo Alto, CA.

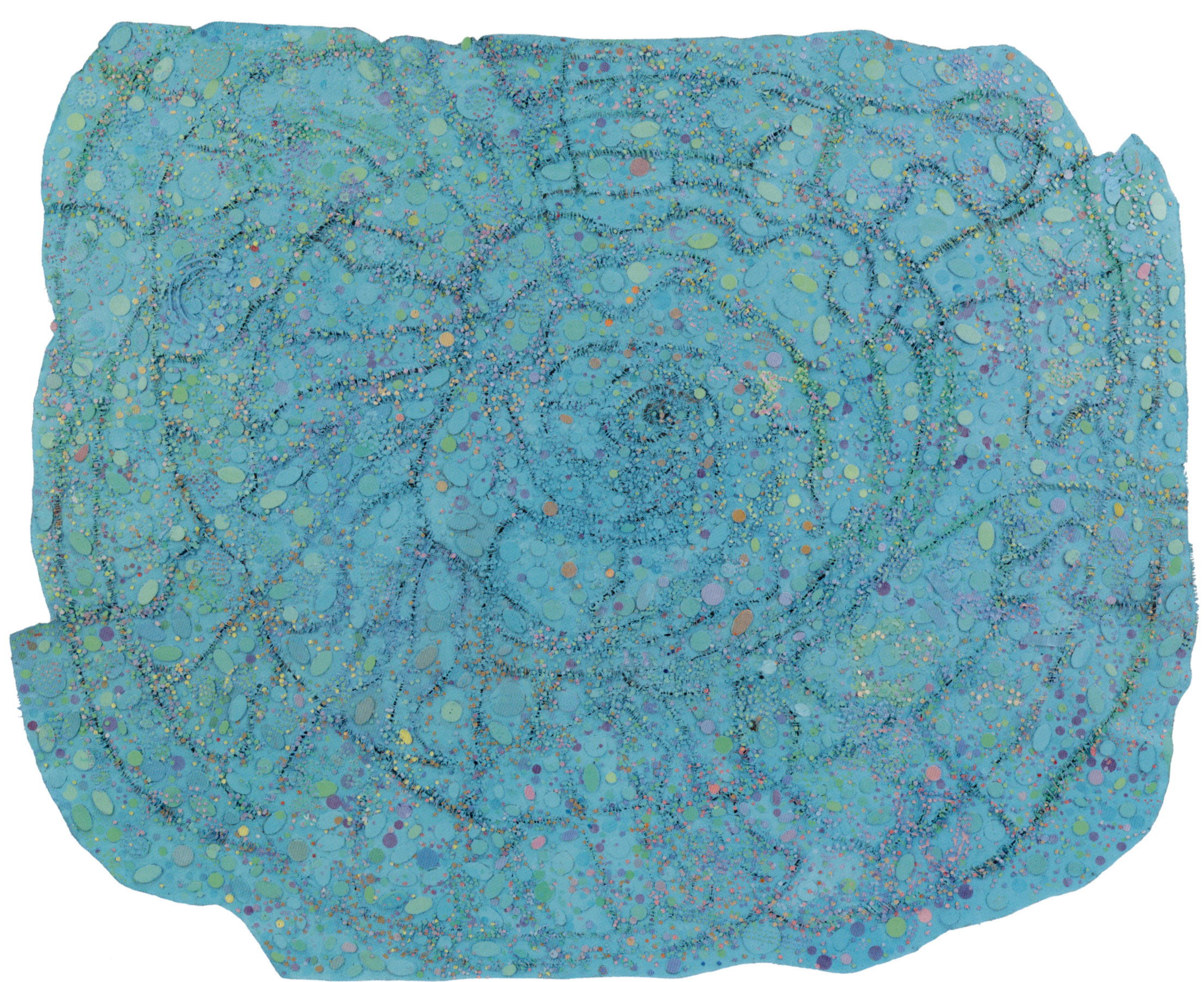

Fig. 104. Howardena Pindell, *Night Flight,* 2015–16. Acrylic, paper collage, and thread on canvas, 63 × 75 in. (160 × 190.5 cm). Collection of Philip Holzer, Frankfurt am Main, Germany.

case. Other aspects of her practice have changed. Pindell no longer fabricates her paintings by herself. Her aging body does not permit it. On her studio wall hang labeled plastic bags full of hole-punched circles and ellipses (which have returned to her oeuvre after many decades) in a variety of sizes and shapes. Assistants help her to punch and retrieve these collage materials; she attaches them to her canvases. Pindell still performs her own sewing in the cut and sewn paintings as much as possible, though. In a recent interview, she remarked that she maintains this element of her practice "for pleasure."[9]

Pindell has exhibited these abstract collaged paintings alongside content-driven, representational works in the last several years. A critically lauded solo exhibition held in 2020–21 at the Shed, part of Manhattan's newly redeveloped Hudson Yards neighborhood, reflected the span of her recent practice. *Ko's Snow Day* (2020) hung alongside abstract, densely collaged, unstretched canvases of the 1970s and the 2010s (fig. 105). In this ovoid composition, which measures approximately five feet in either direction, sprinkle-size lavender and white chads cover a system of raised tunnels and hubs. The painting extends Pindell's aesthetic concerns of the 1970s in new directions. It generates tension between the painting's handworked, encrusted surface and an underlying structure but eschews the regularity of the grid in favor of meandering forms (fig. 106). Pindell has likened the painting's surface effect to the way that plowed snow once covered parked cars on New York's streets in the days following the city's now-dwindling winter storms, thus connecting the abstract composition to her reflections on the climate crisis.[10]

At the Shed, a dozen abstract compositions appeared alongside work that directly addressed U.S. legacies of anti-Black racism, such as *Canals/Underground Railroad* (2015–16; fig. 107). Similarly to *Autobiography: Water,* this painting combines the aesthetic logic of Pindell's unstretched canvases with text and collaged imagery. These elements address U.S. chattel slavery. Pindell installed a historical pair of shackles for an enslaved child next to the canvas, a poignant artifact of slavery's human toll. The canvas's irregular shape evokes a double helix—an allusion to racial terror's embeddedness in U.S. cultural DNA and the genealogical transfer of enslavement and ownership. This interlacing of works centered, on the one hand, on aesthetic appeal and, on the other hand, on unflinching political critique is representative of how the institutional art world is narrating Pindell's legacy today.

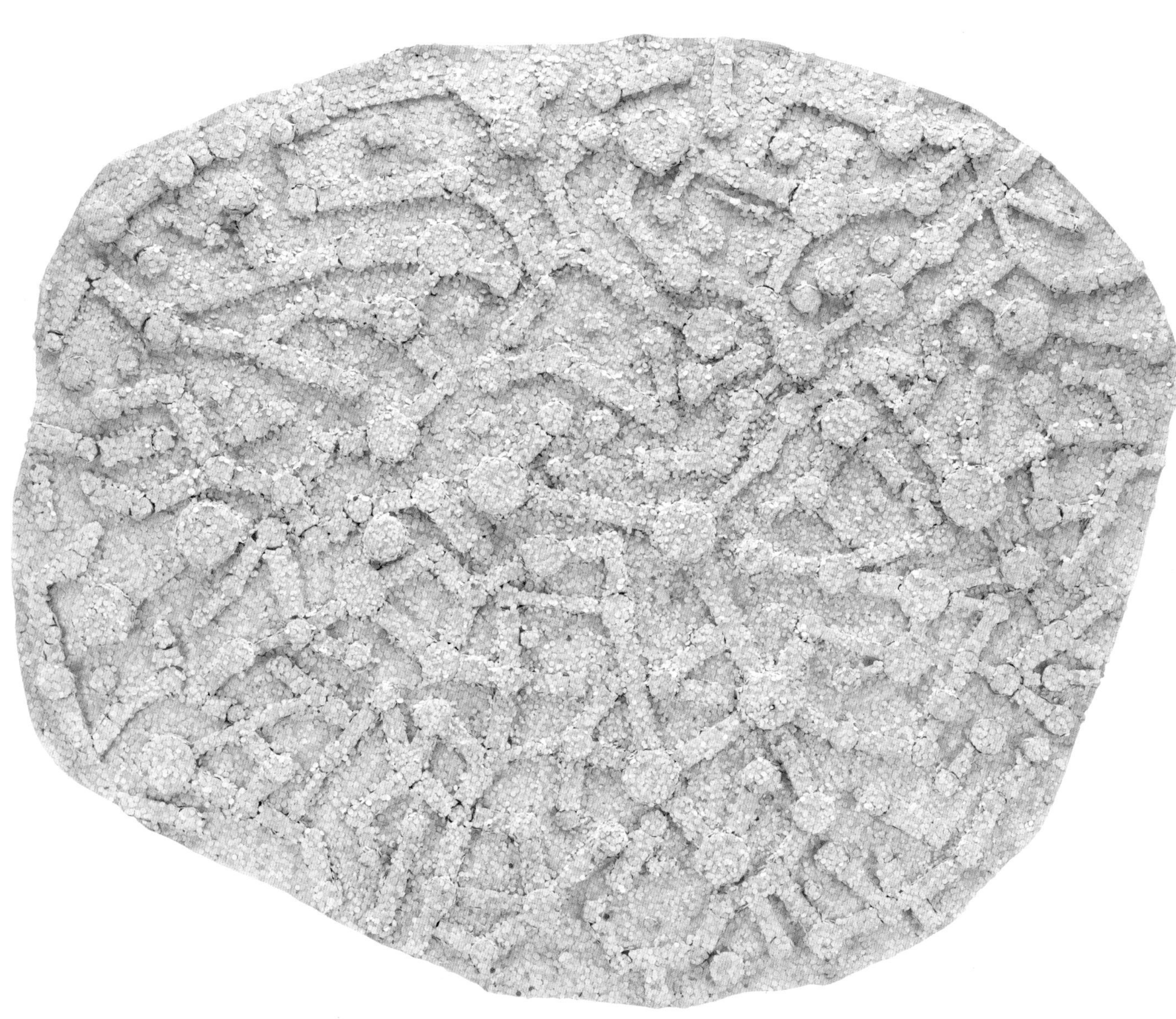

Fig. 105. Howardena Pindell, *Ko's Snow Day*, 2020. Mixed media on canvas, 55¼ × 65 in. (140.3 × 165.1 cm). Private collection, New York.

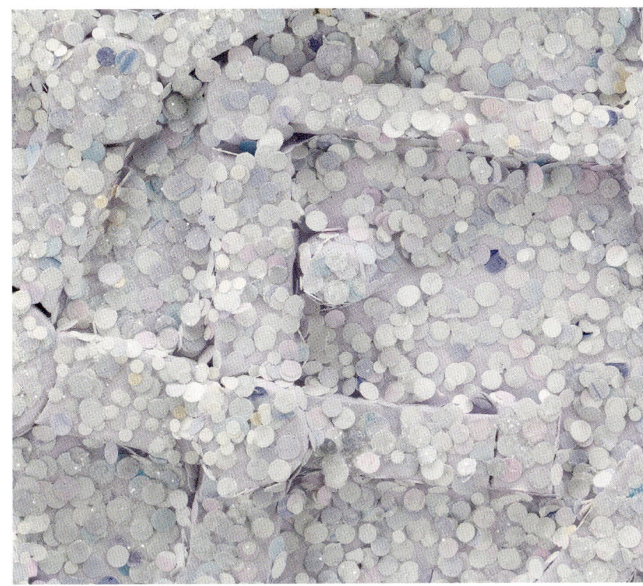

Fig. 106. Howardena Pindell, *Ko's Snow Day,* 2020 (detail; see fig. 105).

The exhibition at the Shed exemplified the unprecedented levels of professional notoriety and enthusiastic reception Pindell has enjoyed for the last decade. Since signing with Garth Greenan Gallery in 2014, her works have been shown widely in international venues, garnering big budget career retrospectives and appearing in blue chip group exhibitions. Pindell's 2018 retrospective at the Museum of Contemporary Art Chicago, curated by Naomi Beckwith and Valerie Cassel Oliver, elicited glowing critical responses. For instance, in her review of the show, art historian Jenni Sorkin deployed words I heard often when speaking to artists and curators about Pindell: "iconic," "sui generis," "trailblazer."[11]

In these critical conversations, Pindell is lauded for her range of exceptional art world engagements. She has produced activist publications demanding art world reform and curatorial meditations on modernist surface. Pindell has been a teacher, curator, cultural commentator, writer, reformer, and, above all, an artist whose oeuvre includes resolutely political artistic expressions and fully abstract, process-driven compositions. The scope of her career is remarkable, and evinces something less frequently acknowledged in her reception. Pindell defies the "special dilemma" imposed upon Black women artists, who are expected either directly to protest racism and sexism or to create art without concern for their lived experiences of discrimination.[12] Her career challenges art-historical narratives by exceeding the silos that continue to be assigned to artists, particularly those who are Black, female, or both.

Pindell developed this corrective by using modernisms' tools to undermine their own closures. Her most enduring legacy lies in her reclamation of abstraction as relevant to her interests and experiences as a Black woman. These pathbreaking efforts, which she undertook alongside others who chafed at the strictures of art world discourse in the 1970s, have normalized abstraction's availability as a politically efficacious aesthetic idiom for a younger generation of artists. A number of prominent Black artists working today, including Sadie Barnette, Torkwase Dyson, Tomashi Jackson, Samuel Levi Jones, Eric Mack, Julie

Mehretu, and Shinique Smith, have taken up this legacy in their dual commitments to an uncompromising aesthetic vision and political engagement.

Many of these artists, like Pindell, use abstraction to mine the social meanings of commonplace objects such as aluminum cans, books, and clothing. Consider Jones's gridded abstract compositions, comprised of the covers of deconstructed law books mounted on canvas. His compositions braid together the aesthetic logic of color field painting and the bureaucratic detritus that undergirds anti-Black legal systems. In one example, *Joshua* (2016), stripes of cardboard, adhesive, and paper punctuate a field of cloth in shades of vermillion (fig. 108). Jones has referred to these covers as "skins," a term that evokes Pindell's engagement with modernist surfaces as cosmetically treated surrogate embodiments. As in her cut and sewn paintings, handicraft meets modernist and industrial form in Jones's works; visible stitching organizes his abstraction into a grid, though he uses a sewing machine, rather than hand-sewing, to suture together the textile-based book covers. Jones's compositions speak to the production and circulation of white supremacist systems of knowledge, largely through his use of language, in ways that evoke Pindell's increasingly political paintings of the 1980s. A small amount of gold-printed text—"criminal," "officers and public employees"—bears witness to the legal tomes' original classificatory powers (fig. 109). The work's title evokes the state-sanctioned killing of Joshua Beal, an Indiana man who was fatally shot at his cousin's funeral by an off-duty police officer in 2016.[13] Jones thus connects an individual, contemporary example of a Black person's unjust death to the historical codification of anti-Black racism in U.S. legal institutions.

Works by artists such as Barnette further echo Pindell's in their deployment of craft-inflected materials in compositions that riff on modernist forms. In *My Father's FBI File: Government Employees Installation* (2017), for instance, Barnette generates queer- and feminine-inflected abstract gestures with hot-pink spray paint that adorns heavily redacted documents from the FBI surveillance files on her father, who founded the Compton, California, chapter of the Black Panther Party in 1968 (fig. 110).[14] Her marks, which play on graffiti and handicraft, contrast with the dry, conceptual aesthetics of the bureaucratic documents. This younger generation of artists working with abstraction, like Pindell in the 1970s, exploits the layered cultural valences of everyday materials in order to refer simultaneously to individual experiences, specific cultural formations, and large-scale social institutions.

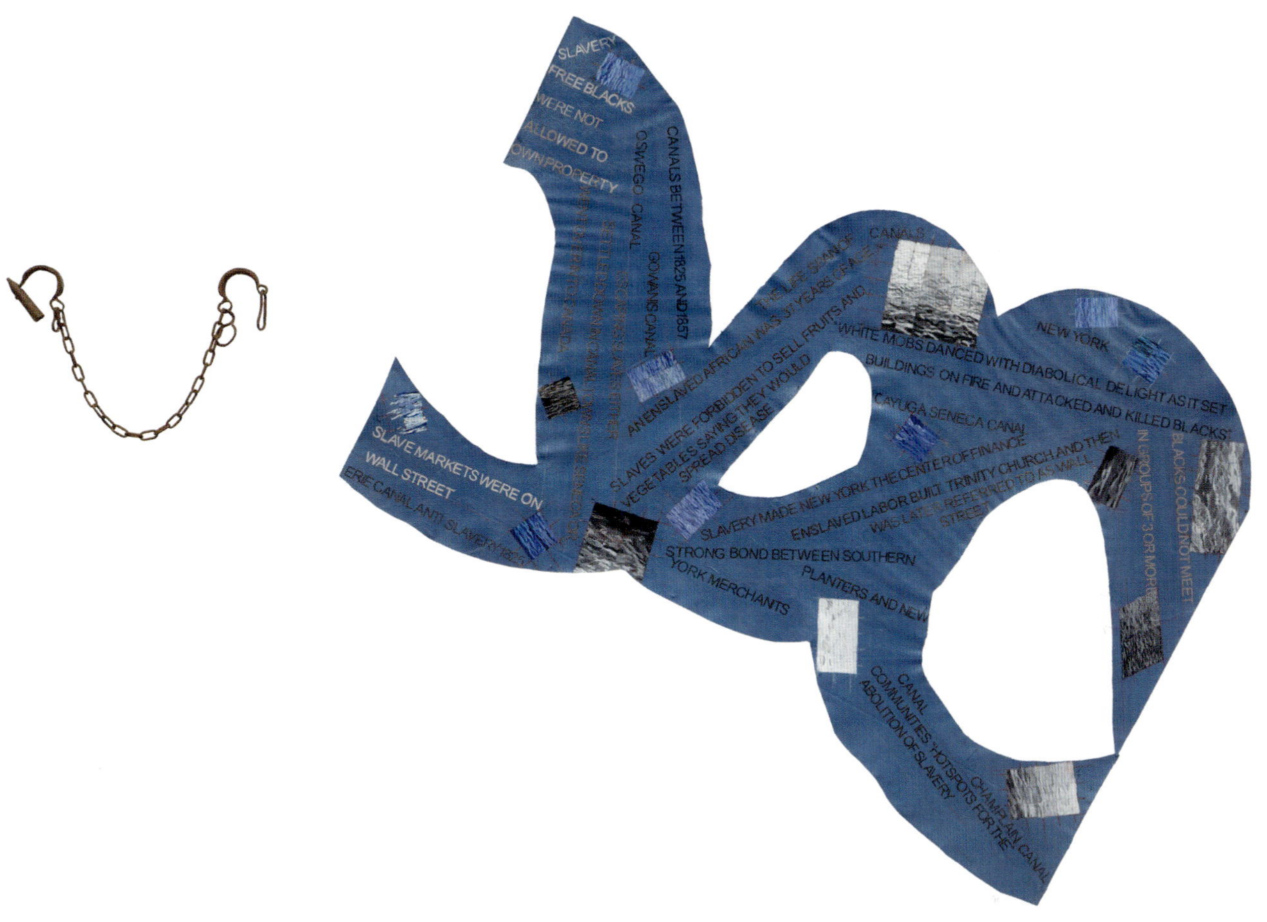

Pindell's legacy extends to her labors as an art world activist. In the late 1980s, she began compiling statistics about the representation of artists of color in major galleries and museums in New York. Combing artist lists published in *Art in America,* she found that in 1987, a majority of the most prominent galleries exclusively represented white artists. She also collected exhibition checklists from seven major New York museums covering the period 1980 to 1987. These findings were similarly alarming. MoMA, for instance, exhibited two one-person shows of works by artists of color out of 242 total exhibitions during the study period. Other museums grossly underrepresented artists of color in their programming as well. The Brooklyn Museum's fifty-one one-person exhibitions included just two for works by artists of color (Romare Bearden and Jacob Lawrence). In these same years, the feminist artist collective Guerrilla Girls and PESTS, a women-of-color corollary that focused on the intersection of racism and sexism, likewise deployed art statistics in their public-facing activism.

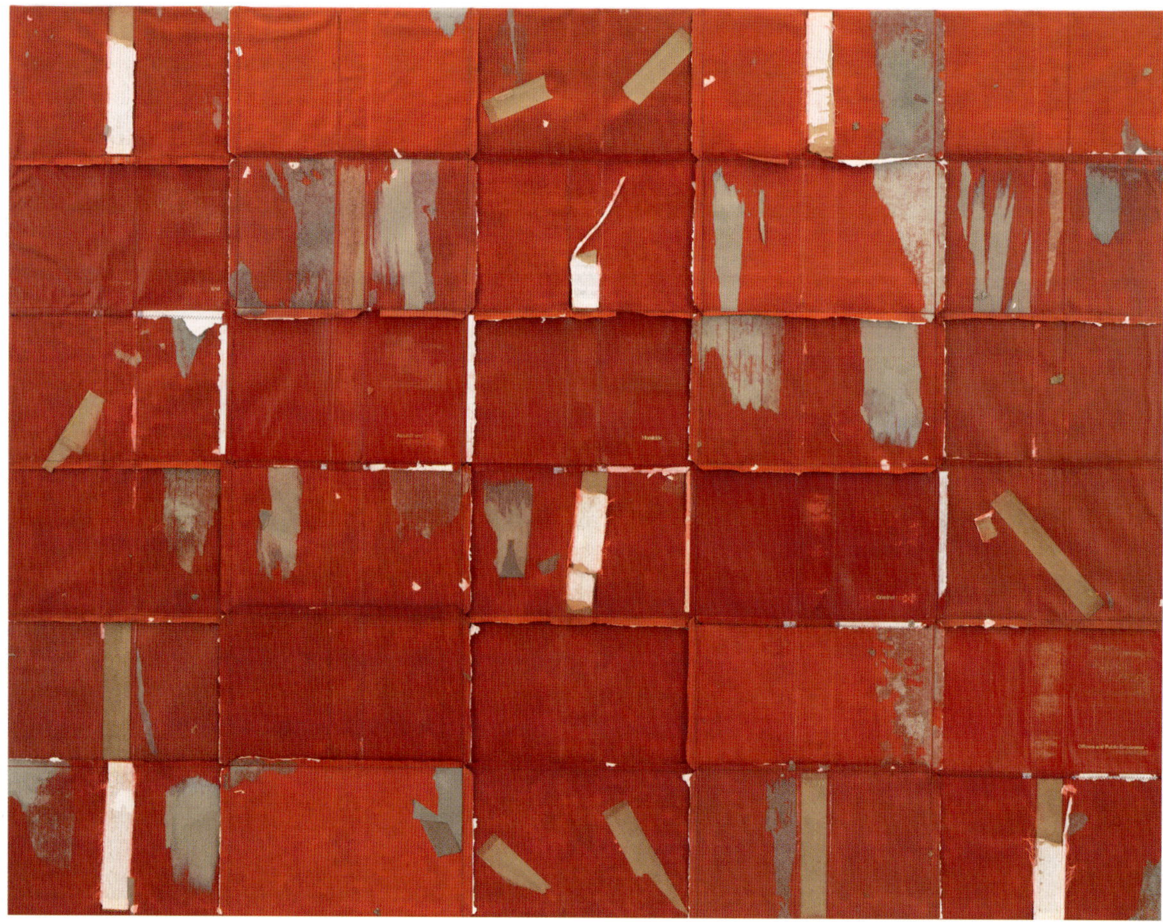

Fig. 108. Samuel Levi Jones, *Joshua,* 2016. Deconstructed Illinois law books on canvas, 61½ × 77 in. (156.2 × 195.6 cm). Chazen Museum of Art, University of Wisconsin, Madison. General Endowment Fund and Alice Drews Gladfelter Memorial Endowment Fund purchase, 2018.5.

Pindell has suggested that she participated in both of these anonymous groups, a fact that further illuminates her role in shaping feminist artist activism of the 1980s.[15]

Her activism also stands as an important model for art world workers today. In the last several years, a few major studies have examined a much larger data set than Pindell could gather through individual calls to museum offices. A group of interdisciplinary researchers at Williams College, for instance, sampled ten thousand artist records on public online collection catalogues at eighteen U.S. museums, finding that eighty-five percent corresponded to white artists and eighty-seven percent to men. In 2018, *Artnet News* and Sotheby's *In Other Words* began publishing findings of their investigations into the representation of African American artists and women artists in museums and the art market over

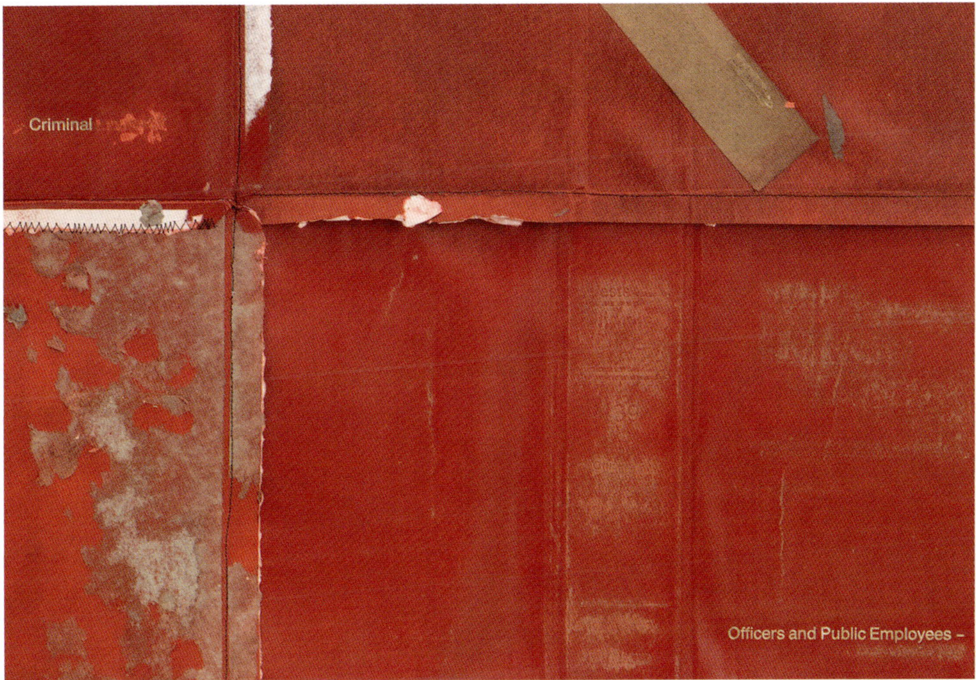

Fig. 109. Samuel Levi Jones, *Joshua,* 2016 (detail; see fig. 108), with the text "criminal" and "officers and public employees."

the span of a decade. They found that, despite a growing number of blockbuster shows and staggering sale prices for a small number of Black artists, between 2008 and 2018 work by African American artists accounted for fewer than three percent of acquisitions at thirty major museums. These recent studies, implicitly or explicitly, draw on Pindell's example. Their findings are informing the ways that museums approach efforts to increase equity and inclusion in their collection and exhibition practices.[16]

The resurgence in Pindell's career has come amid a broader shift in institutional art world priorities. Many major museums and galleries in North America have made concerted efforts in recent years to show the work of artists of color. The market for this art has grown accordingly, setting record after record, particularly for Black artists working in abstract modes. Art historian Huey Copeland has offered an illuminating interpretation of this would-be move toward art world inclusion, writing, "One might even argue that the move to recuperate black practitioners working nonrepresentationally is simply the market's way of providing a greater variety of product, now crafted by long-neglected artists whose revelatory work is implicitly 'blackened' by their identities yet still wonderfully appealing, thereby delivering alterity in safely consumable and relatively inexpensive forms."[17] In other words, the appeal of abstract work by Black artists for a predominantly white art world lies in the works' supposed ability to provide

RODNEY ELLIS BARNETTE

On June 15, 1972, Rodney Barnette was observed
embarking on American Airlines Flight 474 in the company of
Angela Davis. This flight was en route from San Francisco
to Chicago.

Observation by SAs
of the FBI
6/16/72

Fig. 110. Sadie Barnette, *My Father's FBI File: Government Employees Installation,* 2017. Archival pigment print, each 22 × 17 in. (55.9 × 43.2 cm). University of California, Berkeley, Art Museum and Pacific Film Archive. Purchase made possible through a gift of Wanda Kownacki.

"difference" in a package that bolsters claims to inclusion without threatening the underlying status quo. This cynical view on the part of collectors belies the political possibilities of abstraction and betrays how easily that potential can go ignored.

As heady market forces help to catalyze efforts at art world inclusivity, it can be tempting to dwell in the celebratory tone of self-touted art institutional progress. In the last decade, private collectors and museums have purchased Pindell's works at rates exponentially higher than during other periods in the artist's career. Research archives strive to stay atop this trend toward inclusion as well—the Smithsonian's Archives of American Art launched its three-year African American Collecting Initiative in 2017. Pindell's papers are bound for these archives, where they will join the recently acquisitioned papers of fellow Black women artists Betty Blayton, Beverly Buchanan, and Senga Nengudi. These resources promise to seed a growing body of scholarship that centers the contributions of Black women artists in U.S. art histories. How many of these institutional programs will result in permanent positions, policies, or restructuring that will benefit Black people in and out of the art world in the future? One must remember that art markets exist to accrue capital (both actual and symbolic) for a select few at the expense of others.

Pindell's words, quoted in the introduction to this book, would caution us against the view that recent art world changes reflect a permanent reconfiguration of the art world into a more egalitarian mold. She wrote: "Every ten years, the Euro-Americans come out and it's 'please tell us where you've been all this time?' Suddenly we are of great interest and then the interest dips and we hear nothing. . . . Every time the wave comes, we are there. We were there all along. We've been doing our work. We've been plodding along." As blatant forms of white supremacy have moved in recent years into the political mainstream, attention to Black women's art is an urgent political matter. However, could the current moment be another "wave" of interest in artists of color, one that will recede in more subdued political times? Discouragingly, some news reports covering this most recent surge of attention have recycled tropes of discovery, suggesting a cultural amnesia regarding these cycles.[18]

In response to a recent question about "finally" getting widespread recognition, Pindell stated, "People say to me, 'You know, you're famous,' but I do not feel like that at all. I always tell people I feel like a message in a bottle that washes up on shore. Maybe someone might find out something about me."[19] To "find out something" enduring about an artist and her art, we should not look to the celebratory crest of a wave. Pindell's "message" does not lie in the apparently effortless ways in which the story of her life and career meet the perceived needs of the current political moment. A message in a bottle carries histories. It is a durational object, traveling in some cases for many decades, with no guarantee of connecting to its imagined audiences. This book has argued that Pindell's art—her message, to follow her metaphor—defies existing scholarly narratives. Only through sustained attention do her navigations of contemporary art and life become visible, the social contradictions she has bumped up against, and the structuring tensions she astutely has investigated. Pindell has never needed discovering. To return to her words—she was already there.

Today, there is still much to understand about Pindell's practice. Future research may examine further how her career exposes the insufficiencies of the concept of the "political" as a ubiquitous interpretive framework in contemporary art history. More details about her supportive professional relationships with other Black artists working abstractly in the 1970s, such as Sam Gilliam and Melvin Edwards, or with artists associated with Just Above Midtown gallery, including David Hammons, might yield new insights into how the Black Arts movement reshaped U.S. abstraction. There are other bodies of work to consider as well—a small series of black monochrome drawings Pindell created in the early 1970s and her public-facing projects of the 1980s and 1990s. A focused study of her curatorial career might lend new insights into art institutions' responses to art world activism in the wake of the civil rights movement. Most pressingly, Pindell's career demands a reconsideration of other Black women's contributions to contemporary art. How did artists such as Betty Blayton, Beverly Buchanan, Maren Hassinger, Janet Henry, and Senga Nengudi reconfigure the artistic discourses that they encountered? If Pindell reclaimed abstraction through haptic practices, what yet-to-be theorized methods did these other artists engage with over the course of their careers?

Pindell developed her practice with awareness of the limiting ways in which her art likely would be seen, if it would be seen at all. Her career is paradigmatic of a generation of artists who strove to make art that might make some kind of difference.[20] By weaving together craft and fine art, the visual and the haptic, West African and U.S. artistic traditions, Pindell forged a Black feminist modernism that walked a tightrope of expectation. With her works of this period and the particular relationship to material that they embody, she endeavored to expand abstraction's possibilities and asked her viewers to reimagine its contours.

Notes

INTRODUCTION

Howardena Pindell, interview with Andrianna Campbell, in
"1000 Words: Howardena Pindell," *Artforum* 56, no. 6 (February 2018): 155.

1. Oral history interview with Howardena Pindell, July 10, 1972, Archives of American Art, Smithsonian Institution, Washington, DC; Howardena Pindell, interview with Kellie Jones, April 2, 1989, audiovisual recording, Camille Billops and James V. Hatch Archives, Stuart A. Rose Manuscript, Archives, and Rare Book Library, Emory University, Atlanta.

2. Howardena Pindell, interview with the author, telephone conversation, July 2020. The Trinidadian-born curator Kynaston McShine was hired by MoMA in 1959 and became associate curator in 1968. Pindell notes that McShine did not identify as African American when the two worked at MoMA.

3. See Julia Bryan-Wilson, *Art Workers: Radical Practice in the Vietnam War Era* (Berkeley: University of California Press, 2009); Susan E. Cahan, *Mounting Frustration: The Art Museum in the Age of Black Power* (Durham, NC: Duke University Press, 2016); Julie Ault, ed., *Alternative Art: New York 1965–1985* (Minneapolis: University of Minnesota Press, 2002).

4. See GerShun Avilez, *Radical Aesthetics and Modern Black Nationalism* (Urbana: University of Illinois Press, 2016); Lisa Gail Collins and Margo Natalie Crawford, eds., *New Thoughts on the Black Arts Movement* (New Brunswick, NJ: Rutgers University Press, 2006); Amy Abugo Ongiri, *Spectacular Blackness: The Cultural Politics of the Black Power Movement and the Search for a Black Aesthetic* (Charlottesville: University of Virginia Press, 2009); Lucy Lippard, "Sweeping Exchanges," *Art Journal* 40, no. 1/2 (Fall/Winter 1980): 362; Helen Molesworth, "Painting with Ambivalence," in *WACK! Art and the Feminist Revolution,* ed. Cornelia Butler and Lisa Gabrielle Mark (Los Angeles: Museum of Contemporary Art, 2007), 430; Clement Greenberg, "Modernist Painting" (1960), in *Clement Greenberg: The Collected Essays and Criticism,* vol. 4, *Modernism with a Vengeance, 1957–1969,* ed. John O'Brian (Chicago: University of Chicago Press, 1986), 85–93; Ann Eden Gibson, *Abstract Expressionism: Other Politics* (New Haven: Yale University Press, 1997), xx.

5. See Lowery Stokes Sims, "Modernism and Its Discontents," in *Challenge of the Modern: African-American Artists 1925–1945* (New York: Studio Museum in Harlem, 2003), 13, 20.

6. Darby English, *1971: A Year in the Life of Color* (Chicago: University of Chicago Press, 2016); Kellie Jones, *South of Pico: African American Artists in Los Angeles in the 1960s and 1970s* (Durham, NC: Duke University Press, 2017).

7. See Katy Siegel, "Another History Is Possible," in *High Times, Hard Times: New York Painting 1967–1975,* ed. Katy Siegel (New York: Independent Curators International, 2006), 30.

8. Lowery Stokes Sims, "The Mirror, the Other: On Politics of Esthetics," *Artforum* 28, no. 7 (March 1990): 115; Claudia Barrow, "Adrian Piper: Space, Time and Reference, 1967–1970," in *Adrian Piper* (Birmingham, UK: Ikon Gallery and Cornerhouse, 1991), 15.

9. Raymond Saunders, "Black Is a Color" (self-published pamphlet, 1967), n.p. See also Frank Bowling, "Discussion on Black Art," *Arts* 43 (April 1969): 16, 18, 20; Kimberlé Crenshaw, "Demarginalizing the Intersection of Race and Sex: A Black Feminist Critique of Antidiscrimination Doctrine, Feminist Theory and Antiracist Politics," *University of Chicago Legal Forum* (1989): 139–68.

10. Arna Alexander Bontemps and Jacqueline Fonvielle-Bontemps, "African-American Art History: The Feminine Dimension," in *Forever Free: Art by African-American Women, 1862–1890,* ed. Arna Alexander Bontemps (Alexandria, VA: Stephenson, 1980), 15.

11. See Toni Cade Bambara, ed., *The Black Woman: An Anthology* (New York: New American Library, 1970); Robin D. G. Kelley, "'This Battlefield Called Life': Black Feminist Dreams," in *Freedom Dreams: The Black Radical Imagination* (Boston: Beacon, 2002), 154.

12. Avilez, *Radical Aesthetics;* José Esteban Muñoz, *Disidentifications: Queers of Color and the Performance of Politics* (Minneapolis: University of Minnesota Press, 1999), 11–12.

13. Anne Anlin Cheng, *Second Skin: Josephine Baker and the Modern Surface* (New York: Oxford University Press, 2011); Lowery Stokes Sims, "African American Women Artists: Into the Twenty-First Century," in *Bearing Witness: Contemporary Works by African American Women Artists,* ed. Jontyle Theresa Robinson (New York: Rizzoli, 1996), 83–94.

14. See Rizvana Bradley, ed., "The Haptic: Textures of Performance," special issue, *Women and Performance* 24, no. 2–3 (2014); Olivia K. Young, "Distorting Inflections: Proprioception in Senam Okudzeto's Works-on-Paper" (lecture, College Art Association Annual Conference, Chicago, February 14, 2020).

15. See also Naomi Beckwith, "Body Optics, or Howardena Pindell's Way of Seeing," in *Howardena Pindell: What Remains to Be Seen,* ed. Naomi Beckwith and Valerie Cassel Oliver (Chicago: Museum of Contemporary Art Chicago, 2018), 87–108.

16. Howardena Pindell, "The Aesthetics of Texture in African Adornment," in *Beauty by Design: The Aesthetics of African Adornment,* ed. Marie-Thérèse Brincard (New York: African American Institute, 1984), 36–39; Howardena Pindell, interview with Joseph Jacobs, in *Since the Harlem Renaissance: 50 Years of Afro-American Art* (Lewisburg, PA: Bucknell University, 1985), 35; Pindell, interview with Jones, 1989. On Pindell's textural surfaces as repudiations of figuration, see also GerShun Avilez, "Conclusion: Queering Representation," in *Radical Aesthetics,* 167–79.

17. Laura U. Marks, *The Skin of the Film: Intercultural Cinema, Embodiment, and the Senses* (Durham, NC: Duke University Press, 2000); Eve Kosofsky Sedgwick, introduction to *Touching Feeling: Affect, Pedagogy, Performativity* (Durham, NC: Duke University Press, 2003), 1–25; Rizvana Bradley, "The Vicissitudes of Touch: Annotations on the Haptic," *b2o: an online journal,* November 21, 2020, https://www.boundary2.org/; Hortense Spillers, "To the Bone: Some Speculations on Touch" (keynote address, *There's a Tear in the World: Touch*

after Finitude, Stedelijk Museum of Art and Studium Generale Rietveld Academy, Amsterdam, March 23, 2018).

18. Roy Sieber, *African Textiles and Decorative Arts* (New York: Museum of Modern Art, 1972), 47.

19. Huey Copeland and Krista Thompson, "Afrotropes: A User's Guide," *Art Journal* 76, no. 3–4 (Fall-Winter 2017): 7.

20. Oral history interview with Pindell, 1972; Howardena Pindell, interview with Camille Billops, April 21, 1980, audiovisual recording, Billops-Hatch Archives; Pindell, interview with the author, July 2020.

21. Howardena Pindell (written anonymously), "Action against Racism in the Arts," *Heresies,* no. 8 (1979): 108–11; Pindell, interview with Billops, 1980; Pindell, interview with the author, July 2020.

22. On MoMA, see Huey Copeland, "In the Wake of the Negress," in *Modern Women: Women Artists at the Museum of Modern Art,* ed. Cornelia Butler and Alexandra Schwartz (New York: Museum of Modern Art, 2010), 480–97.

23. I censor this word throughout the book, responding to Black activists, artists, and scholars who have called on their non-Black colleagues to stop recirculating a term whose utterance has been a violent instrument of anti-Black racist ideology.

24. Howardena Pindell, "Earth: Eyes/Injuries," in *Howardena Pindell: Paintings and Drawings* (Potsdam: Roland Gibson Gallery, Potsdam College, State University of New York, 1992), 60.

25. For instance, Pindell's recent retrospective, curated by Naomi Beckwith and Valerie Cassel Oliver, was divided into two parts, with a gallery dedicated to the year 1979 connecting them. Naomi Beckwith and Valerie Cassel Oliver, eds., *Howardena Pindell: What Remains to Be Seen* (Chicago: Museum of Contemporary Art Chicago, 2018).

26. Pindell, interview with Campbell, 155.

27. Eve Kosofsky Sedgwick, "Paranoid Reading and Reparative Reading, Or, You're So Paranoid, You Probably Think This Essay Is about You," in *Touching Feeling,* 144; Howardena Pindell, interview with Linda Freeman, undated transcript, Linda Freeman Papers, 1996–2009, Archives of American Art, Smithsonian Institution; Audre Lorde, "Uses of the Erotic: The Erotic as Power," in *Sister Outsider: Essays and Speeches* (Freedom, CA: Crossing, 1984), 53–59. See also Jennifer Nash, *The Black Body in Ecstasy: Reading Race, Reading Pornography* (Durham, NC: Duke University Press, 2014); adrienne maree brown, *Pleasure Activism: The Politics of Feeling Good* (Chico, CA: AK, 2019).

28. On textility, see Nicole Archer, "Security Blankets: Uniforms, Hoods, and the Textures of Terror," *Women and Performance* 24, no. 2–3 (2014): 186–202. On textiles and contemporary art, see Julia Bryan-Wilson, *Fray: Art and Textile Politics* (Chicago: University of Chicago Press, 2017); Elissa Auther, *String, Felt, Thread: The Hierarchy of Art and Craft in American Art* (Minneapolis: University of Minnesota Press, 2010); Joan Livingstone and John Ploof, eds., *The Object of Labor: Art, Cloth, and Cultural Production* (Cambridge, MA: MIT Press, 2007); Jenni Sorkin, "Affinities in Abstraction: Textiles, Otherness, and Painting in the 1970s," in *Outliers and American Vanguard Art,* ed. Lynne Cooke (Washington, DC: National Gallery of Art, 2018), 92–105.

29. Patricia Hill Collins, "Learning from the Outsider Within: The Sociological Significance of Black Feminist Thought," *Social Problems* 33, no. 6 (October-December 1986): S14–S32; Pindell, interview with Jones, 1989; Henry Louis Gates, Jr., *The*

Signifying Monkey: A Theory of African-American Literary Criticism (Oxford: Oxford University Press, 1988); Howardena Pindell, interview with the author, telephone conversation, December 2018.

30. Daniel Moynihan, *The Negro Family: The Case for National Action* (Washington, DC: United States Department of Labor, 1965).

31. Lisa E. Farrington, "Reinventing Herself: The Black Female Nude," *Women's Art Journal* 24, no. 2 (Autumn 2003-Winter 2004): 21. See also Darcy Grimaldo Grigsby, *Enduring Truths: Sojourner's Shadow and Substance* (Chicago: University of Chicago Press, 2015); Lorraine O'Grady, "Olympia's Maid: Reclaiming Black Female Subjectivity" (1992), in *The Feminism and Visual Culture Reader,* ed. Amelia Jones (New York: Routledge, 2003), 174–86; Hortense Spillers, "Mama's Baby, Papa's Maybe: An American Grammar Book," *Diacritics* 17, no. 2 (Summer 1987): 64–81.

32. bell hooks, *Ain't I a Woman: Black Women and Feminism* (Boston: South End, 1981), 78. See also Michele Wallace, *Black Macho and the Myth of the Superwoman* (New York: Dial, 1979), 11.

33. "The Black Woman," special episode of *Black Journal,* dir. Stan Lathan (1970, WNET). See also Joyce Ladner, *Tomorrow's Tomorrow: The Black Woman* (Garden City, NY: Anchor, 1971); E. F. White, "Black Feminist Interventions," in *Dark Continent of Our Bodies: Black Feminism and the Politics of Respectability* (Philadelphia: Temple University Press, 2001), 17–77.

34. On distortion, see Spillers, "Mama's Baby, Papa's Maybe," 69, 73.

35. Oral history interview with Pindell, 1972; Catherine Morris and Rujeko Hockley, eds., *We Wanted a Revolution: Black Radical Women, 1965–85: New Perspectives* (Durham, NC: Duke University Press, 2018); Alice Walker, "In Search of Our Mothers' Gardens: The Creativity of Black Women in the South," *Ms.,* May 1974, 64–70, 105.

36. See Kay Brown, "'Where We At' Black Women Artists" (1972), in *We Wanted a Revolution: Black Radical Women, 1965–85: A Sourcebook,* ed. Catherine Morris and Rujeko Hockley (Durham, NC: Duke University Press, 2017), 62–64; Kay Brown, "The Emergence of Black Women Artists: The Founding of 'Where We At,'" *Nka: Journal of Contemporary African Art* 29 (Fall 2011): 118–27.

37. Pindell, interview with the author, July 2020.

38. Oral history interview with Pindell, 1972. Linda Goode Bryant, interview with Judith Wilson, 1979, Judith Wilson Papers, 1966–2010, Archives of American Art, Smithsonian Institution.

39. Kobena Mercer, "Black Art and the Burden of Representation," in *Welcome to the Jungle: New Positions in Black Cultural Studies* (New York: Routledge, 1994), 235; Steven Nelson, "Turning Green into Black, Or How I Learned to Live with the Canon," in *Making Art History: A Changing Discipline and Its Institutions,* ed. Elizabeth Mansfield (London: Routledge, 2007), 54–66; Darby English, *How to See a Work of Art in Total Darkness* (Cambridge, MA: MIT Press, 2007), 9.

40. Pindell, interview with the author, December 2018; Pindell, interview with Jones, 1989; Uri McMillan, *Embodied Avatars: Genealogies of Black Feminist Art and Performance* (New York: New York University Press, 2015), 161–68.

41. Howardena Pindell, "Art (World) and Racism: Testimony, Documentation, and Statistics," *Third Text* 2, no. 3–4 (1988): 160. See also Howardena Pindell, "Art World Racism," in *The Heart of the Question: The Writings and Paintings*

of Howardena Pindell (New York: Midmarch Arts, 1997), 3–28. The anthology *The Heart of the Question* contains twelve essays Pindell wrote in the 1970s, 1980s, and 1990s. On PESTS, see Guerrilla Girls Records, 1979–2013, Getty Research Institute Special Collections, Los Angeles.

42. See Michele Wallace, "Modernism, Postmodernism and the Problem of the Visual in Afro-American Culture," in *Out There: Marginalization and Contemporary Cultures,* ed. Russell Ferguson and Trinh T. Minh-ha (Cambridge, MA: MIT Press, 1990), 38–50; Nash, *Black Body in Ecstasy.* On Black American artists' turn away from visibility, see Sampada Aranke, "Material Matters: Black Radical Aesthetics and the Limits of Visibility," *e-flux,* no. 79 (February 2017): 1–10.

43. Copeland, "In the Wake of the Negress," 487; Denise Murrell, *Posing Modernity: The Black Model from Manet and Matisse to Today* (New Haven: Yale University Press, 2018); Michele Wallace, "Variations on Negation and the Heresy of Black Feminist Creativity," in *Invisibility Blues: From Pop to Theory* (London: Verso, 1990), 218.

44. Freida High W. Tesfagiorgis, "In Search of a Discourse and Critique/s that Center the Art of Black Women Artists," in *Gendered Visions: The Art of Contemporary Africana Women Artists,* ed. Salah M. Hassan (Trenton, NJ: Africa World, 1997), 73; Judith Wilson, "One Way or Another: Black Feminist Visual Theory," in *The Feminism and Visual Culture Reader,* 2nd ed., ed. Amelia Jones (New York: Routledge, 2010), 22. See also Charmaine A. Nelson, "Introduction: Toward a Black Feminist Art History," *The Color of Stone: Sculpting the Black Female Subject in Nineteenth-Century America* (Minneapolis: University of Minnesota Press, 2007), xi–xxxv.

45. See Kara Keeling, *The Witch's Flight: The Cinematic, the Black Femme, and the Image of Common Sense* (Durham, NC: Duke University Press, 2007); Hazel Carby, "White Woman Listen! Black Feminism and the Boundaries of Sisterhood," in *The Empire Strikes Back: Race and Racism in Seventies Britain* (London: Hutchinson, 1982), 212–35; Patricia Hill Collins, *Black Feminist Thought: Knowledge, Consciousness, and the Politics of Empowerment* (New York: Routledge, 1990); White, *Dark Continent.*

46. Pindell, Interview with Jones, 1989. Pindell's recent exhibitions include *Howardena Pindell: What Remains to Be Seen* (Museum of Contemporary Art Chicago, 2018); *Howardena Pindell: A New Language* (Fruitmarket, Edinburgh, UK, 2021–22); *We Wanted a Revolution* (Brooklyn Museum, 2017); *Soul of a Nation: Art in the Age of Black Power* (Tate Modern, London, 2017); *Magnetic Fields: Expanding American Abstraction, 1960s to Today* (Kemper Museum of Contemporary Art, Kansas City, MO, 2017); and *Outliers and American Vanguard Art* (National Gallery of Art, Washington, DC, 2018). She received the 2019 College Art Association Distinguished Artist Award for Lifetime Achievement.

CHAPTER 1. MOVING MODERNISMS

1. On the establishment of the Studio Museum, see Susan E. Cahan, *"Electronic Refractions II* at the Studio Museum in Harlem," in *Mounting Frustration: The Art Museum in the Age of Black Power* (Durham, NC: Duke University Press, 2016), 13–30. Pindell has recounted this experience in several interviews: Howardena Pindell, interview with Kellie Jones, April 2, 1989, audiovisual recording, Camille Billops and James V. Hatch Archives, Stuart A. Rose Manuscript, Archives, and Rare Book Library, Emory University, Atlanta; Howardena Pindell, interview with Camille Billops, April 21, 1980, audiovisual recording, Billops-Hatch Archives. This specific phrasing is quoted in Hilarie Sheets, "The Changing Complex Profile of Black Abstract Painters," *Art News* 113, no. 6 (June 2014): 62.

2. Pindell does not recall which paintings she took to the Studio Museum. Given the timeline, works like this one are most likely. Howardena Pindell, interview with the author, telephone conversation, July 2020.

3. See Amiri Baraka, "Counter Statement to Whitney Ritz Bros," in *Black Art Notes,* ed. Tom Lloyd (Ann Arbor: University of Michigan Press, 1971), 10; Margaret Burroughs, "To Make a Painter Black," in *The Black 70s,* ed. Floyd B. Barbour (Boston: Porter Sargent, 1970), 129–37; Jeff Donaldson, "Africobra: African Commune of Bad Relevant Artists, 10 in Search of a Nation," *Black World* 19, no. 12 (October 1970): 80–89; Emory Douglas, "On Revolutionary Art," *Black Panther,* January 5, 1970, 5; Larry Neal, "Any Day Now: Black Art and Black Liberation," *Ebony,* August 1969, 54–58, 62. See also Lucy Lippard, "Sweeping Exchanges: The Contribution of Feminism to the Art of the 1970s," *Art Journal* 40, no. 1–2 (Fall/Winter 1980): 362; Julia Bryan-Wilson, *Art Workers: Radical Practice in the Vietnam War Era* (Berkeley: University of California Press, 2009); Katy Siegel, "Another History Is Possible," in *High Times, Hard Times: New York Painting 1967–1975,* ed. Katy Siegel (New York: Independent Curators International, 2006), 29–91.

4. Kellie Jones, *South of Pico: African American Artists in Los Angeles in the 1960s and 1970s* (Durham, NC: Duke University Press, 2017), 17; Katherine McKittrick, *Demonic Grounds: Black Woman and the Cartographies of Struggle* (Minneapolis: University of Minnesota Press, 2006), x.

5. Darby English has written that "art affords a space, maybe the *one* space, in which possibility trumps necessity." In Darby English, *1971: A Year in the Life of Color* (Chicago: University of Chicago Press, 2016), 39. On "institutional modernism," see Patricia Mainardi, "The Political Origins of Modernism," *Art Journal* 45, no. 1 (Spring 1985): 11–14. Charles Gaines, "Howardena Pindell: Negotiating Abstraction," in *Howardena Pindell: What Remains to Be Seen,* ed. Naomi Beckwith and Valerie Cassel Oliver (Chicago: Museum of Contemporary Art Chicago, 2018), 143.

6. English, *1971,* 48.

7. For instance, the BECC responded to the Metropolitan Museum of Art's failure to exhibit or involve contemporary, Harlem-based artists in the landmark exhibition *Harlem on My Mind* in 1969.

8. One of Pindell's painting instructors at Yale was Al Held, best known for his large-scale, hard-edge paintings. Peter Bradley, who produced atmospheric color field paintings, and William T. Williams, a hard-edged painter, each graduated the year after Pindell. Oral history interview with Howardena Pindell, July 10, 1972, Archives of American Art, Smithsonian Institution, Washington, DC. See also Howardena Pindell, "Problems Encountered and Posed in My Development as a Painter," 1967, Yale University Records, School of Art, New Haven.

9. Oral history interview with Pindell, 1972.

10. "Authority," in *New Oxford American Dictionary,* ed. Angus Stevenson and Christine A. Lindberg (Oxford: Oxford University Press, 2010), https://www.oxfordreference.com.

11. Howardena Pindell, interview with Sally Swenson, in *Lives and Works: Talks with Women Artists,* ed. Lynn F. Miller

and Sally S. Swenson (Metuchen, NJ: Scarecrow, 1981), 136. See also Howardena Pindell, interview with Helen Ramsaran, in Siegel, *High Times, Hard Times,* 105; Howardena Pindell, interview with Andrianna Campbell, "1000 Words: Howardena Pindell," *Artforum* 56, no. 6 (February 2018): 155. Swenson may have been referring to Lucy Lippard, *From the Center: Feminist Essays on Women's Art* (New York: Dutton, 1976), or *26 Contemporary Women Artists* (Ridgefield, CT: Aldrich Museum of Contemporary Art, 1971).

12. Pindell, interview with Swenson, 136.

13. Ibid., 136, 137.

14. "Abstraction or Essence: Three African-American Perspectives," June 17, 1997, Sound Recordings, 97.29a, Museum of Modern (MoMA) Art Archives, New York. Many Black Americans relied on *The Negro Motorist Green Book,* first published in 1936 by New York mail carrier Victor Hugo Green, to identify food and lodging amenable to non-white customers amid racial segregation.

15. Pindell, interview with Jones, 1989; oral history interview with Pindell, 1972; Sarah Cowan, "Clearly Seen: A Chronology," in Beckwith and Oliver, *What Remains to Be Seen,* 34. See also Matthew J. Countryman, *Up South: Civil Rights and Black Power in Philadelphia* (Philadelphia: University of Pennsylvania Press, 2006), 98; "Pickets Empty Woolworth's at Peak Store Hours," *Philadelphia Tribune,* February 23, 1960.

16. Pindell, interview with Jones, 1989; quoted in Pindell, interview with Ramsaran, 105.

17. The women both worked on the Byers Committee, discussed below. Pindell, interview with Billops, 1980.

18. See Buckminster Fuller, *Operating Manual for Spaceship Earth* (Carbondale: Southern Illinois University Press, 1969); Norbert Wiener, *The Human Use of Human Beings: Cybernetics and Society* (New York: Doubleday, 1954). In 1966, Stewart Brand, founder of the *Whole Earth Catalog,* initiated a public campaign to pressure NASA to release satellite photographs of Earth as seen from space. See Nicholas Mirzoeff, "Introduction: How to See the World," in *How to See the World: An Introduction to Images, from Self-Portraits to Selfies, Maps to Movies, and More* (New York: Basic, 2016), 1–17; Fred Turner, *From Counterculture to Cyberculture: Stewart Brand, the Whole Earth Network, and the Rise of Digital Utopianism* (Chicago: University of Chicago Press, 2006).

19. While Pindell would soon set aside these references to outer space, she returned to astrological themes in later works such as *M64* (1982).

20. Oral history interview with Pindell, 1972; Robert E. Abrams, "3 Modern American Painters," *Harvard Crimson,* April 30, 1965, n.p. Each work on view measured at least six feet in height. See also Michael Fried, introduction to *Three American Painters: Kenneth Noland, Jules Olitski, Frank Stella* (1965; repr., New York: Garland, 1978), 3–53. The essay was also printed as Michael Fried, "Three American Painters: Kenneth Noland, Jules Olitski, Frank Stella," in *Art and Objecthood: Essays and Reviews* (Chicago: University of Chicago Press, 1998), 213–65. Subsequent citations will use page numbers from this printing.

21. See Karen Wilkin, *Color as Field: American Painting, 1950–1975* (New York: American Federation of Arts, 2007).

22. Lisa Farrington, "Color Field Painting," in *African-American Art: A Visual and Cultural History* (Oxford: Oxford University Press, 2016), 224–27.

23. Oral history interview with Pindell, 1972; Pindell, interview with Swenson, 133; Pindell, interview with Jones, 1989.

24. Fried, "Three American Painters," 214; Abrams, "3 Modern American Painters."

25. Courtney J. Martin, "The Re-Selection of Ancestors: Genealogy and American Abstraction's Second Generation," in *Energy/Experimentation: Black Artists and Abstraction, 1964–1980,* ed. Kellie Jones (New York: Studio Museum in Harlem, 2006), 82–83; Clement Greenberg, "Post Painterly Abstraction," in *Post Painterly Abstraction* (Los Angeles: F. Hensen, 1964), 5–8. See also Christa Noel Robbins, *Artist as Author: Action and Intent in Late-Modernist American Painting* (Berkeley: University of California Press, 2021).

26. See the exhibition booklet, *Paintings and Drawings by Howardena Pindell and Vincent Smith, November 7–21, 1971* (Atlanta: Coordinated Art Program of the Atlanta University Center, 1971), in Evans-Tibbs Collection, National Gallery of Art Library, Washington, DC.

27. "Collection Highlights," Spelman College Museum of Fine Arts, July 27, 2013, https://museum.spelman.edu/collection-highlights. For historical exhibitions, see issues of the *Spelman Messenger* in Spelman College Archives, Atlanta.

28. *Spelman Messenger,* May 1971, 43.

29. Clyde Burnett, "Burnett on Art," *Atlanta Journal,* December 2, 1971, 2-F. Unfortunately, there are no known photographs of the exhibition.

30. Pindell, interview with Jones, 1989.

31. The catalogue for *Three American Painters* makes no mention of Helen Frankenthaler, a white woman whose stained canvases inspired the men in the show, most especially Noland and Olitski. Pindell, interview with Jones, 1989; oral history interview with Pindell, 1972.

32. Fried, "Three American Painters," 230, 229, 248.

33. Rosalind Krauss, "'Specific' Objects," *RES: Anthropology and Aesthetics* 46 (Autumn 2004): 223.

34. Pindell developed a "supportive relationship" with Gilliam, Benny Andrews, and Melvin Edwards upon her return from a trip to Egypt in 1974. Lorna Simpson, "Chronology," in *Howardena Pindell: Odyssey* (New York: Studio Museum in Harlem, 1986), 15.

35. Sound Recordings, 97.29a, MoMA Archives. Pindell notes that Sillman presented the same curriculum that Albers had taught in the painting department at Yale in the 1950s. See also Michael Craig-Johnson, "The Teaching of Josef Albers: A Reminiscence," *Burlington* 137, no. 1105 (April 1995): 248–52; Josef Albers, *Interaction of Color* (1963; repr., New Haven: Yale University Press, 1971), 1, 2.

36. On this development, see, for instance, Clement Greenberg, "Collage" (1959), in *Collage: Critical Views,* ed. Katherine Hoffman (Ann Arbor: UMI Research Press, 1989), 67–77.

37. Fried, "Three American Painters," 247.

38. Oral history interview with Pindell, 1972; Andrea D. Barnwell, "Been to Africa and Back: Contextualizing Howardena Pindell's Abstract Art," *International Review of African American Art* 13, no. 3 (1996): 43.

39. Pindell, interview with the author, July 2020; Yve-Alain Bois and Christopher Lyons, trans., "What Is There to See? On a Painting by Ad Reinhardt," *MoMA* 8 (Summer 1991): 3.

40. Sampada Aranke, "Blackouts and Other Visual Escapes," *Art Journal* 79, no. 4 (Winter 2020): 62–75. See also Fred Moten, *In the Break: The Aesthetics of the Black Radical Tradition* (Minneapolis: University of Minnesota Press, 2003); Édouard

Glissant, *Poetics of Relation,* trans. Betsy Wing (Ann Arbor: University of Michigan Press, 1997); Adrienne Edwards, "Blackness in Abstraction," *Art in America,* January 5, 2015; Sampada Aranke, "Material Matters: Black Radical Aesthetics and the Limits of Visibility," *e-flux,* no. 79 (February 2017): 1–10.

41. Merce Cunningham, *Changes: Notes on Choreography* (New York: Something Else, 1968), n.p.; Carolyn Brown, "Summerspace: Three Revivals," *Dance Research Journal* 34, no. 1 (Summer 2002): 74–82; Michelle Potter, "'A License to Do Anything': Robert Rauschenberg and the Merce Cunningham Dance Company," *Dance Chronicle* 16, no. 1 (1993): 1–43.

42. Potter, "'License to Do Anything,'" 11.

43. Fried, "Three American Painters," 224.

44. See English, *1971,* for a discussion of "color" as both a late modernist and racialist concept and tool. See GerShun Avilez, *Radical Aesthetics and Modern Black Nationalism* (Urbana: University of Illinois Press, 2016); Lisa Gail Collins and Margo Natalie Crawford, eds., *New Thoughts on the Black Arts Movement* (New Brunswick, NJ: Rutgers University Press, 2006); Margo Natalie Crawford, *Black Post-Blackness: The Black Arts Movements and 21st Century Black Aesthetics* (Urbana: University of Illinois Press, 2017); Amy Abugo Ongiri, *Spectacular Blackness: The Cultural Politics of the Black Power Movement and the Search for a Black Aesthetic* (Charlottesville: University of Virginia Press, 2009); Leigh Raiford, "Attacked First by Sight," in *Imprisoned in a Luminous Glare: Photography and the African American Freedom Struggle* (Chapel Hill: University of North Carolina Press, 2011), 129–208.

45. Neal, "Any Day Now," 57–58. The capitalization of "Black" was not widely implemented in this period, as it is today.

46. For instance, the Spiral collective formed in 1963, in response to the March on Washington for Jobs and Freedom. Its members interrogated what the politics of the civil rights movement demanded of them as artists. See Courtney J. Martin, "From the Center: The Spiral Group, 1963–1966," *Nka: Journal of Contemporary African Art* 29 (Fall 2011): 86–99. In the 1920s, W. E. B. DuBois, Alain Locke, and James Porter debated about the relationship between aesthetics and politics in the context of the New Negro movement. See Mary Ann Calo, "Alain Locke and American Art Criticism," *American Art* 18, no. 1 (Spring 2004): 88–97. For a discussion of Stevens, who was a member of the Chicago-based collective AfriCOBRA (African Commune of Bad Relevant Artists), see Barbara Jones-Hogu, "Inaugurating AfriCOBRA: History, Philosophy, and Aesthetics," *Nka: Journal of Contemporary African Art* 30 (Spring 2012): 90–97.

47. When possible, I use country- and culture-specific language to describe the African cultural materials with which Pindell engaged. In other cases, I resort to "African," despite the limitations of this term, which refers to innumerable cultures and practices, in order to maintain the language commonly used by cultural critics throughout the 1970s. Notably, the most canonical white abstractionists in the first half of the twentieth century, Pablo Picasso and Jackson Pollock, mined non-white cultural resources, including African and African diasporic practices, to generate abstraction from sources not widely granted the honorific designation of "abstract art." See Ann Eden Gibson, *Abstract Expressionism: Other Politics* (New Haven: Yale University Press, 1997). See also artist Hank Willis Thomas's screen print *Colonialism and Abstract Art* (2019), which traces the historical relationship between colonialism and abstraction by reconfiguring Alfred H. Barr, Jr.'s familiar 1937 diagram "Cubism and Abstract Art."

48. Baraka, "Counter Statement," 10; Lowery Stokes Sims, "The Mirror, The Other: On the Politics of Esthetics," *Artforum* 28, no. 7 (March 1990): 115.

49. Kellie Jones, "'It's Not Enough to Say "Black Is Beautiful"': Abstraction at the Whitney, 1969–1974," in *Discrepant Abstraction,* ed. Kobena Mercer (Cambridge, MA: MIT Press, 2006), 158.

50. The statistic is published in "Art: Situation Report," in "The American Woman," special issue, *Time,* March 20, 1971, 77. See also Lisa Gail Collins, "The Art of Transformation: Parallels in the Black Arts and Feminist Art Movements," in Collins and Crawford, *New Thoughts on the Black Arts Movement,* 273–96; Michele Wallace, *Black Macho and the Myth of the Superwoman* (New York: Dial, 1979).

51. See, for instance, Clement Greenberg, "Avant-Garde and Kitsch" (1939) and "Towards a Newer Laocoön" (1940), in *Clement Greenberg: The Collected Essays and Criticism,* vol. 1, *Perceptions and Judgments, 1939–1944,* ed. John O'Brian (Chicago: University of Chicago Press, 1986), 5–22, 23–37.

52. Phillip Brian Harper, *Abstractionist Aesthetics: Artistic Form and Social Critique in African American Culture* (New York: New York University Press, 2015), 62, 28.

53. English, *1971,* 16–17. Tom Lloyd, "Black Art–White Cultural Institutions," in *Black Art Notes,* 5. The Studio Museum in Harlem's inaugural exhibition was a one-person show featuring Lloyd's abstract light-based sculptures. In an encounter that no doubt informed his later explicit articulation of the political relevance of his own works and his criticism of other Black abstract artists, local community members derided Lloyd's abstractions as white art. See Cahan, *"Electronic Refractions II,"* 13–30.

54. Hans Bhalla, introduction to *Paintings and Drawings by Howardena Pindell and Vincent Smith* (Atlanta: Coordinated Art Program of the Atlanta University Center, 1971), i–ii.

55. Ibid, i.

56. Ibid, i.

57. Hans Bhalla, "The Dilemma of Afro-American Artists," *Spelman Messenger,* February 1972, 12–17, quotes on 16.

58. James Oles, "Noguchi in Mexico: International Themes for a Working-Class Market," *American Art* 15, no. 2 (Summer 2001): 10–33. See Avilez, *Radical Aesthetics.*

59. Pindell, interview with Billops, 1980; see document titled "List of Committees Formed with Art Workers Coalition, Meeting of November 25, 1969," John B. Hightower Papers, III.1.8, MoMA Archives; Bryan-Wilson, *Art Workers;* Michele Wallace, "Reading 1968: The Great American Whitewash" (1990), in *Invisibility Blues: From Pop to Theory* (New York: Verso, 2016), 195–96.

60. "The Byers Committee: Highlights of a Forthcoming Report to the Board of Trustees of the Museum of Modern Art," Carroll Greene Papers, unprocessed, Stuart A. Rose Manuscript, Archives, and Rare Book Library, Emory University; Pindell, interview with Billops, 1980.

61. Pindell, interview with Billops, 1980.

62. J. Frederic Byers III, Chairman, "Report to the Trustees of the Museum of Modern Art: The Committee to Study Afro-American, Hispanic, and Other Ethnic Art," Carroll Greene Papers, unprocessed, Stuart A. Rose Manuscript, Archives, and Rare Book Library, Emory University. See, for instance, Howardena Pindell, "Art World Racism" and "Covenant of Silence," in *The Heart of the Question: The Writings*

and Paintings of Howardena Pindell (New York: Midmarch Arts, 1997), 3–28, 32–50.

63. Howardena Pindell, quoted in Jack Flam, ed., *Western Artists/African Art* (New York: Museum for African Art, 1994), 56. As a child, Pindell encountered African art during trips to the Egyptian wing of the Philadelphia Museum of Art and through visits to her parents' home by Ethiopian exchange students. See Howardena Pindell, "Ancestral Memories and Visual Coincidences," 1994, unpublished manuscript in Samella S. Lewis Papers, Stuart A. Rose Manuscript, Archives, and Rare Book Library, Emory University.

64. The exhibition has been written about extensively in recent years. See Susan E. Cahan, "*Contemporary Black Artists in America* at the Whitney Museum of American Art," in *Mounting Frustration*, 109–70; Darby English, "Making a Show of Discompose," in *1971*, 123–90; and Jones, "It's Not Enough."

65. Quote from Jones, "It's Not Enough," 173. Twenty-four of the seventy-eight artists invited to participate withdrew from the show. Cahan, *Mounting Frustration*, 109. Correspondence in the Whitney's exhibition files indicates that Doty reached out to artists, heads of art departments, and scholars around the country with greater expertise in Black American art. Many of the artists included in the exhibition were brought to his attention by these unpaid, outsourced advisors. *Contemporary Black Artists in America*, exhibitions files, Whitney Museum of American Art, New York.

66. Cahan, *Mounting Frustration*, 161. John Canaday, "Black Artists on View in 2 Exhibitions," *New York Times*, April 7, 1971, 52. See also Lawrence Alloway, "Art," *Nation*, May 10, 1971, 604–5.

67. John Dowell et al., "Politics," *Artforum* 9, no. 9 (May 1971): 12. Cahan, *Mounting Frustration*, 149–50.

68. Kellie Jones, "To the Max: Energy and Experimentation," in *Energy/Experimentation*, 24. Sam Gilliam, interview with Joseph Jacobs, in *Since the Harlem Renaissance: 50 Years of Afro-American Art* (Lewisburg, PA: Bucknell University, 1985), 21; Donald Miller, "Hanging Loose: An Interview with Sam Gilliam," *Art News* 72, no. 1 (January 1973): 43; Henri Ghent, "Notes to the Young Black Artist: Revolution or Evolution," *Art International* 15 (June 1971): 33.

69. Pindell, interview with Campbell, 155.

70. Pindell, interview with Billops, 1980; Pindell, interview with Swenson, 148.

71. Pindell, interview with Billops, 1980.

72. Pindell, interview with Swenson, 139.

73. John I. H. Baur, letter to Ad Hoc Women Artists' Committee, November 12, 1971, exhibition files, Whitney Museum of American Art Archives; Faith Ringgold, *We Flew over the Bridge: The Memoirs of Faith Ringgold* (Durham, NC: Duke University Press, 2005), 175–78; Grace Glueck, "Women Artists Demonstrate at the Whitney," *New York Times*, December 12, 1970, A19.

74. Marcia Tucker, "Painters for the Annual: Women Painters," n.d., exhibition files, Whitney Museum of American Art Archives. Pindell's inclusion in the 1972 Painting Annual was complicated when Tucker attempted to rescind her invitation on the basis of a museum policy that an artist could not show in two exhibitions within any twelve-month period. (*Contemporary Black Artists in America* had closed in May 1971, and the annual was set to open in January 1972.) Letters show that Pindell, based on her familiarity with museum protocol, balked at what she considered a thinly veiled act of discrimination. Ultimately, Pindell showed in both exhibitions. Howardena Pindell, letter to Lucy Lippard, December 2, 1970, Lucy R. Lippard Papers, 1930s–2010, bulk 1960s–1990, Archives of American Art, Smithsonian Institution.

75. Pindell, interview with Swenson, 148.

76. Jones, "It's Not Enough," 172.

77. See for instance, Lucy Lippard, "Top to Bottom, Left to Right," in *Grids Grids Grids Grids Grids Grids Grids Grids* (Philadelphia: Institute of Contemporary Art, University of Pennsylvania, 1972), n.p.

78. Pindell, interview with Swenson, 136.

79. John Elderfield, "Grids," *Artforum* 10, no. 9 (May 1972): 53, 54.

80. Elderfield, "Grids," 52–59; Lippard, "Top to Bottom," i.

81. Rosalind Krauss, "Grids," *October* 9 (Summer 1979): 50, 52.

82. Krauss, "Grids," 52; Elderfield, "Grids," 53.

83. Naomi Beckwith, "Body Optics, or Howardena Pindell's Ways of Seeing," in Beckwith and Oliver, *What Remains to Be Seen*, 93.

84. Rosalind Krauss, "The Originality of the Avant-Garde" (1981), in *The Originality of the Avant-Garde and Other Modernist Myths* (Cambridge, MA: MIT Press, 1985), 158.

85. Oral history interview with Pindell, 1972. Larry Poons, interview with Phyllis Tuchman, "An interview with Larry Poons," *Artforum* 9, no. 4 (December 1970): 45.

86. Lippard, "Top to Bottom," i.

87. Ibid., ii.

88. Michael S. Harper, "Apollo Vision: The Nature of the Grid," in *History Is Your Own Heartbeat* (Urbana: University of Illinois Press, 1971), 90–91; Michael S. Harper, "Michael Harper," in *Interviews with Black Writers*, ed. John O'Brien (New York: Liverlight, 1972), 106.

89. Harper, *Abstractionist Aesthetics*, 34, 42.

90. McKittrick, *Demonic Grounds*, x, xxiii.

91. Pindell, interview with Billops, 1980. English, *1971*, 10.

92. This occurs even as the disciplinary divide between these two "camps," once deeply entrenched, has become permeable over the course of the past decades, and it is not only commonplace, but expected that scholars operate between these two modes. Huey Copeland, "Flow and Arrest," *Small Axe* 48 (November 2015): 220. See also James Meyer, *Minimalism: Art and Polemics in the Sixties* (New Haven: Yale University Press, 2001), 9.

CHAPTER 2. PAPER WORK

1. Howardena Pindell, interview with Joseph Jacobs, in *Since the Harlem Renaissance: 50 Years of Afro-American Art* (Lewisburg, PA: Bucknell University, 1985), 35.

2. See Thomas Crow, *The Rise of the Sixties: Modern Art in the Era of Dissent* (New York: Abrams, 1996); Katherine Hoffman, ed., *Collage: Critical Views* (Ann Arbor: UMI Research Press, 1981); Kobena Mercer, "Romare Bearden, 1964: Collage as *Kunstwollen*," in *Cosmopolitan Modernisms*, ed. Kobena Mercer (Cambridge, MA: MIT Press, 2005), 124–45; Christine Poggi, *In Defiance of Painting: The Invention and Early Practice of Collage, 1912—1919* (Ann Arbor: UMI Research Press, 1991); Gwen Raaberg, "Beyond Fragmentation: Collage as Feminist Strategy in the Arts," *Mosaic* 31, no. 3 (September 1998): 154.

3. Howardena Pindell, interview with the author, telephone conversation, July 2020.

4. Kellie Jones, *South of Pico: African American Artists in Los Angeles in the 1960s and 1970s* (Durham, NC: Duke University Press, 2017), 68; Clement Greenberg, "Collage" (1959), in Hoffman, *Collage: Critical Views*, 67–77; Lucy Lippard, "Sweeping Exchanges," *Art Journal* 40, no. 1/2 (Fall/Winter

1980): 362–65; Fredric Jameson, "Postmodernism, or the Cultural Logic of Late Capitalism," *New Left Review* 146 (July–August 1984): 59–92.

5. See Rachel Farebrother, *The Collage Aesthetic in the Harlem Renaissance* (Burlington, VT: Ashgate, 2009); Harriet Grossman Janis, *Collage: Personalities, Concepts, Techniques* (Philadelphia: Chilton, 1962); Daniel Louis Haxall, *Cut and Paste Abstraction: Politics, Form, and Identity in Abstract Expressionist Collage* (Ann Arbor: UMI Dissertation Services, 2009); Judy Loeb, ed., *Feminist Collage: Educating Women in the Visual Arts* (New York: Teachers College, Columbia University, 1979).

6. Lucy Lippard, *The Pink Glass Swan: Selected Feminist Essays on Art* (New York: New Press, 1995), 136; Raaberg, "Beyond Fragmentation."

7. Mary Schmidt Campbell, *American Odyssey: The Life and Work of Romare Bearden* (New York: Oxford University Press, 2018), 8. See also Kevin Young, *The Grey Album: On the Blackness of Blackness* (Minneapolis: Graywolf, 2012).

8. "Abstraction or Essence: Three African-American Perspectives," Sound Recordings, 97.29a, Museum of Modern Art (MoMA) Archives, New York.

9. Howardena Pindell, "Ancestral Memories and Visual Coincidences," 1994, unpublished manuscript in Samella S. Lewis Papers, Stuart A. Rose Manuscript, Archives, and Rare Book Library, Emory University, Atlanta; Benjamin H. D. Buchloh, "Conceptual Art 1962–1969: From the Aesthetic of Administration to the Critique of Institutions," *October* 55 (Winter 1990): 105–43.

10. Judith Wilson, "Howardena Pindell Makes Art that Winks at You," *Ms.*, May 1980, 69.

11. Greenberg, "Collage," 67.

12. See Matthew Biro, *The Dada Cyborg: Visions of the New Human in Weimar Berlin* (Minneapolis: University of Minnesota, 2009); John G. Frey, "From Dada to Surrealism," *Parnassus* 8, no. 7 (December 1936): 12–15; Rosalind Krauss, "The Photographic Conditions of Surrealism," *October* 19 (Winter 1981): 3–34; Lucy Lippard, "Dada into Surrealism," *Artforum* 5, no. 1 (September 1966): 10–15. Quote from Raaberg, "Beyond Fragmentation," 154. See also Lucy R. Lippard, "Max Ernst: Passed and Pressing Tensions," *Hudson Review* 23, no. 4 (Winter 1970–1971): 701–9.

13. Albert Gleizes and Jean Metzinger, "On Cubism" (1912), in *Modern Artists on Art: Ten Unabridged Essays*, ed. Robert Herbert (Englewood Cliffs, NJ: Prentice-Hall, 1964), 1–18; Clement Greenberg, "Modernist Painting" (1960), in *Clement Greenberg: The Collected Essays and Criticism*, vol. 4, *Modernism with a Vengeance, 1957–1969*, ed. John O'Brian (Chicago: University of Chicago Press, 1993), 85–93.

14. *Dada, Surrealism, and Their Heritage* included collage works by Kurt Schwitters and Yves Tanguy. William S. Rubin, *Dada, Surrealism, and Their Heritage* (New York: Museum of Modern Art, 1968); *Printed, Cut, Folded, and Torn*, Museum of Modern Art press release, 1974, Records of the Department of Public Information, II.A.634. MoMA Archives. See also the interviews about printmaking that Pindell and Shields conducted in 1974: Alan Shields and Howardena Pindell, "Tales of Brave Ulysses," *Print Collector's Newsletter* 5, no. 6 (January–February 1975): 137–43.

15. Howardena Pindell, interview with Sally Swenson, in *Lives and Works: Talks with Women Artists*, ed. Lynn F. Miller and Sally S. Swenson (Metuchen, NJ: Scarecrow, 1981), 147.

16. I use the term "African American" throughout this section to retain the language employed by the scholars under discussion. Patricia Hills, "Cultural Legacies and the Transformation of the Cubist Collage Aesthetic by Romare Bearden, Jacob Lawrence, and Other African-American Artists," *Studies in the History of Art* 71 (2011): 223.

17. See Alain Locke, *Negro Art: Past and Present* (Washington, DC: Associates in Negro Folk Education, 1936); Alain Locke, *The Negro in Art: A Pictorial Record of the Negro Artist and of the Negro Theme in Art* (Washington, DC: Associates in Negro Folk Education, 1940).

18. Hills, "Cultural Legacies," 223, 240.

19. Mercer, "Romare Bearden," 125, 126, 131. On Bearden's collages, see also Campbell, *American Odyssey*.

20. Howardena Pindell, interview with Camille Billops, April 21, 1980, audiovisual recording, Billops-Hatch Archives, Stuart A. Rose Manuscript, Archives, and Rare Book Library, Emory University.

21. See Malcolm McLaughlin, *The Long, Hot Summer of 1967: Urban Rebellion in America* (New York: Palgrave Macmillan, 2014).

22. *African Textiles and Decorative Arts*, Museum of Modern Art press release, 1972, Public Information Records, II.A.557, MoMA Archives. Pindell discusses the show in Howardena Pindell, interview with Kellie Jones, April 2, 1989, audiovisual recording, Billops-Hatch Archives, Stuart A. Rose Manuscript, Archives, and Rare Book Library, Emory University. The exhibition subsequently traveled to the Los Angeles County Museum of Art, the de Young Museum in San Francisco, and the Cleveland Museum of Art. Although Pindell was employed by MoMA at the time, she did not work on the exhibition. Howardena Pindell, interview with the author, telephone conversation, December 2018.

23. Sieber, in fact, helped her to plot her itinerary; Sound Recordings, 97.29a, MoMA Archives. Pindell also had viewed African objects at the Brooklyn Museum. Andrea D. Barnwell, "Been to Africa and Back: Contextualizing Howardena Pindell's Abstract Art," *International Review of African American Art* 13, no. 3 (1990). 43.

24. Pindell, "Ancestral Memories and Visual Coincidences."

25. See Tobias Wofford, "Feedback: Between American Art and African Art History," *Nka: Journal of Contemporary African Art* 41 (November 2017): 154–64; Arnold Rubin, "Accumulation: Power and Display in African Sculpture," *Artforum* 13, no. 9 (May 1975): 35–47; Howardena Pindell, "The Aesthetics of Texture in African Adornment," *Beauty by Design: The Aesthetics of African Adornment*, ed. Marie-Thérèse Brincard (New York: African American Institute, 1984), 36–39.

26. Rebecca VanDiver, "The Diasporic Connotations of Collage: Loïs Mailou Jones in Haiti, 1954–1964," *American Art* 32, no. 1 (Spring 2018): 26–27. See also Rebecca VanDiver, *Designing a New Tradition: Loïs Mailou Jones and the Aesthetics of Blackness* (University Park: Pennsylvania State University Press, 2020).

27. VanDiver, "Diasporic Connotations of Collage," 27.

28. See Melissa Meyer and Miriam Schapiro, "Waste Not, Want Not: An Inquiry into What Women Saved and Assembled," *Heresies* 4 (1978): 66–69; Linda Nochlin, "Why Have There Been No Great Women Artists?" (1971), in *The Feminism and Visual Culture Reader*, ed. Amelia Jones (New York: Routledge, 2003), 229–34.

29. Pindell, interview with Swenson, 149. See A.I.R. Gallery Archives, ca. 1972–2008, MSS 184, Fales Library and Special

Collections, New York University; "A Short History," A.I.R. Gallery, https://www.airgallery.org/history/; oral history interview with Howardena Pindell, July 10, 1972, Archives of American Art, Smithsonian Institution, Washington, DC; Carolee Schneemann, "Inside the Art Bars," *Art in America*, November 27, 2013, https://www.artnews.com/art-in-america. On the sites of women's art-making practices in these years, see Lucy Lippard, *From the Center: Feminist Essays on Women's Art* (New York: Dutton, 1976), 4.

30. Pindell, interview with Billops, 1980. The Women's Slide Registry was developed by the Art Workers' Coalition's Ad Hoc Women's Committee, which Lippard helped to organize. Carey Lovelace, "Optimism and Rage: The Women's Movement in Art in New York, 1969–1975," *Women's Art Journal* 37, no. 1 (Spring/Summer 2016): 6.

31. Pindell, interview with Jones, 1989; Pindell, interview with Swenson, 148.

32. Pindell, interview with Jones, 1989; oral history interview with Pindell, 1972; Lucy Lippard, *26 Contemporary Women Artists* (Ridgefield, CT: Aldrich Museum of Contemporary Art, 1971).

33. Pindell, interview with Swenson, 143. The A.I.R. Gallery Archives at Fales Special Collections at New York University contains no record of the exhibition's checklist; however, a set of installation photographs indicate that Pindell showed a number of small-scale collaged works and an unstretched canvas.

34. Oral history interview with Harmony Hammond, September 14, 2008, Archives of American Art, Smithsonian Institution. See also Lovelace, "Optimism and Rage," 8. On postminimalism, see Briony Fer, *The Infinite Line: Remaking Art after Modernism* (New Haven: Yale University Press, 2004); Lucy Lippard, "Eccentric Abstraction" (1966), in *Changing: Essays in Art Criticism* (New York: E. P. Dutton, 1971); Robert Pincus-Witten, *Postminimalism* (New York: Out of London, 1977).

35. Pincus-Witten, *Postminimalism*, 16.

36. As elaborated below, Pindell ran out of space to store her paintings and was short on funds to purchase canvas when she turned to collage.

37. Hammond constructed sculptures in the early 1970s from old bags and textiles collected from friends. Norvell presented a "hair quilt" at A.I.R. made from strands provided by women in her consciousness-raising group. Oral history interview with Hammond; Lovelace, "Optimism and Rage," 7.

38. Oral history interview with Pindell, 1972; Pindell, interview with Jones, 1989.

39. Naomi Schor, *Reading in Detail: Aesthetics and the Feminine* (New York: Methuen, 1987), 4. See also Lippard's assertion that Eva Hesse's work "transcends the cliché of 'detail as women's work'" in *Eva Hesse* (New York: New York University Press, 1976), 209; Miriam Schapiro, "Femmage," in Hoffman, *Collage: Critical Views,* 306.

40. Muriel Castanis, "Behind Every Artist There's a Penis," *Village Voice,* March 19, 1970, 15–16, 60; quote from Pindell, interview with Swenson, 137; Nicole Fleetwood, "Excess Flesh: Black Women Performing Hypervisibility," in *Troubling Vision: Performance, Visuality, and Blackness* (Chicago: University of Chicago Press, 2010), 107–11.

41. Jones, *South of Pico,* 108–15; Lippard, "Sweeping Exchanges"; Meyer and Schapiro, "Waste Not, Want Not"; Norma Broude, "Miriam Schapiro and 'Femmage': Reflections on the Conflict between Decoration and Abstraction in Twentieth-Century Art," in *Feminism and Art History: Questioning the Litany,* ed. Norma Broude and Mary D. Garrard (New York: Harper and Row, 1982), 315–29.

42. Quote from Elizabeth Alexander, "'Coming out Blackened and Whole': Fragmentation and Reintegration in Audre Lorde's *Zami* and *The Cancer Journals,*" *American Literary History* 6, no. 4 (Winter 1994): 696; on "biomythography," see Audre Lorde, *Zami: A New Spelling of My Name* (Freedom, CA: Crossing, 1982); Audre Lorde, *The Cancer Journals* (San Francisco: Spinsters, 1980); quote beginning "Collage is born of interruption" from Lippard, *Pink Glass Swan,* 136.

43. There is also a single untitled abstract collage dated 1970. See Naomi Beckwith and Valerie Cassel Oliver, eds., *Howardena Pindell: What Remains to Be Seen* (Chicago: Museum of Contemporary Art Chicago, 2018), 245.

44. Pindell, interview with Jacobs, 35–36; Wilson, "Howardena Pindell Makes Art," 69.

45. Manila folders, whose name derives from the Philippine city, also reference histories of colonialism and imperialism. Claire Lui, "A Manila Envelope: The Inspiration behind an Exhibition's Graphic Identity," Guggenheim, April 2, 2021, https://www.guggenheim.org/.

46. "At a Glance," *MoMA,* no. 4 (977): 7; Pindell, interview with Billops, 1980.

47. Julia Bryan-Wilson, *Art Workers: Radical Practice in the Vietnam War Era* (Berkeley: University of California Press, 2009), 14; Sol LeWitt, "Serial Project #1, 1966," *Aspen,* no. 5–6 (Fall–Winter 1967): n.p.

48. Max Weber, "Bureacracy" (1922), in *Economy and Society: An Outline of Interpretive Sociology,* ed. Guenther Roth and Claus Wittich (Berkeley: University of California Press, 2013), 975.

49. On the notion of the "executive artist," see Caroline Jones, *Machine in the Studio: Constructing the Postwar American Artist* (Chicago: University of Chicago Press, 1996), 2.

50. Pindell, interview with Billops, 1980.

51. Toni Morrison, "What the Black Woman Thinks about Women's Lib," *New York Times Magazine,* August 22, 1971, 64. See also Saidiya Hartman, "The Belly of the World: A Note on Black Women's Labors," *Souls* 18, no. 1 (2016): 166–73.

52. Lucy Lippard, introduction to *955,000* (Vancouver: Vancouver Art Gallery, 1970), n.p.; Benjamin Buchloh, "Conceptual Art 1962–1969: From the Aesthetic of Administration to the Critique of Institutions," in *Conceptual Art: A Critical Anthology,* ed. Alexander Alberro and Blake Stimson (Cambridge, MA: MIT Press, 1999), 532; Lucy Lippard, *Six Years: Dematerialization of the Art Object from 1966 to 1972, A Cross-Reference Book on Some Esthetic Boundaries* (New York: Praeger, 1973).

53. Howardena Pindell, interview with Linda Freeman, undated transcript, Linda Freeman Papers, 1996–2009, Archives of American Art, Smithsonian Institution. Thanks to Olivia K. Young for suggesting the phrase "anti-erasure gesture." Michele Wallace, "Variations on Negation and the Heresy of Black Feminist Creativity," in *Invisibility Blues: From Pop to Theory* (New York: Verso, 1990), 215; Lorraine O'Grady, "Olympia's Maid: Reclaiming Black Female Subjectivity" (1992), in *The Feminism and Visual Culture Reader,* ed. Amelia Jones (New York: Routledge, 2003), 177; Roland Barthes, "The Death of the Author," *Aspen,* no. 5–6 (1967): n.p.

54. Skowhegan Lecture Archive, 282, MoMA Archives, Long Island City, Queens; Pindell, interview with Swenson, 143–46.

55. Wilson, "Howardena Pindell Makes Art," 69.

56. Oral history interview with Pindell, 1972; Pindell, interview with Jones, 1989.

57. Sound Recordings, 97.29a, MoMA Archives; Pindell, interview with Jones, 1989; Alison Dillulio (associate director, Garth Greenan Gallery), email correspondence with the author, March 2017.

58. Oral history interview with Pindell, 1972; Pindell, interview with Swenson, 143; Skowhegan Lecture Archive, 282, MoMA Archives.

59. Pindell, interview with the author, December 2018. In a letter dated September 25, 1989, Pindell wrote to Wadsworth Atheneum Museum of Art curator Andrea Miller-Keller: "One of my paintings in the 1970s was peed on by one of my cats. I think after the Serrano business I should list it as a medium." The letter is housed in the Wadsworth Atheneum Museum of Art curatorial files, Hartford, CT.

60. Carolee Schneemann, quoted in Thyrza Nichols Goodeve, "'The Cat Is My Medium': Notes on the Writing and Art of Carolee Schneemann," *Art Journal* 74, no. 1 (Spring 2015): 10. In 1974, Schneemann went so far as to declare, "The cat is my medium!" Carolee Schneemann, letter to Margaret Fisher, July 17, 1974, in *Correspondence Course: An Epistolary History of Carolee Schneemann and Her Circle,* ed. Kristine Stiles (Durham, NC: Duke University Press, 2010), 218.

61. See Helen Molesworth, "House Work and Art Work," *October* 92 (Spring 2000): 71–97.

62. Abby Lane and Katherine Gallagher Robbins, "The Wage Gap over Time," *National Women's Law Center,* May 3, 2012, https://nwlc.org; Solomon W. Polacheck and John Robst, "Trends in the Male–Female Wage Gap: The 1980s Compared with the 1970s," *Southern Economic Journal* 67, no. 4 (April 2001): 869–88; Pindell, interview with Billops, 1980.

63. Kobena Mercer, "Tropes of the Grotesque in the Black Avant-Garde," in *Pop Art and Vernacular Cultures,* ed. Kobena Mercer (Cambridge, MA: MIT Press, 2007), 137, 152, 154.

64. Linda Goode Bryant and Marcy S. Philips, *Contextures* (New York: Just Above Midtown, 1978), 39; see also "Dear S/F: Interview with Fred Moten and Stefano Harney," interview with artist MPA in *MPA: The Interview. Red, Red Future,* ed. Rose D'Amora and Patricia Restrepo (Houston: Contemporary Arts Museum Houston, 2016), 2; Mark Godfrey, "Notes on Black Abstraction," in *Soul of a Nation: Art in the Age of Black Power,* ed. Mark Godfrey and Zoé Whitley (London: Tate, 2017), 188.

65. See Brian O'Doherty, *Inside the White Cube: The Ideology of the Gallery Space* (1976; repr., Berkeley: University of California Press, 1999).

66. For an exception, see Lowery Stokes Sims, "Synthesis and Integration in the Work of Howardena Pindell, 1972–1992: A (Re)Consideration," in Beckwith and Oliver, *What Remains to Be Seen,* 54–78.

67. Pindell, "Ancestral Memories and Visual Coincidences."

68. Pindell, interview with Billops, 1980.

69. Oral history interview with Pindell, 1972; Pindell, interview with Billops, 1980; Pindell, interview with Freeman.

70. Pindell, interview with Freeman; Adrian Piper, "The Triple Negation of Colored Women Artists" (1990), in *The Feminism and Visual Culture Reader,* 2nd ed., ed. Amelia Jones (London: Routledge, 2010), 273; Freida High W. Tesfagiorgis, "In Search of a Discourse and Critique/s that Center the Art of Black Women Artists," in *Gendered Visions: The Art of Contemporary Africana Women Artists,* ed. Salah M. Hassan (Trenton, NJ: Africa World, 1997), 75; Barbara Christian, "But What Do We Think We're Doing Anyway: The State of Black Feminist Criticism(s) or My Version of a Little Bit of History" (1989), in *New Black Feminist Criticism, 1985–2000,* ed. Barbara Christian and Gloria Bowles (Urbana: University of Illinois Press, 2007), 11.

71. David Joselit, "Notes on Surface: Toward a Genealogy of Flatness," *Art History* 23, no. 1 (March 2000): 24.

72. Pindell, interview with Jacobs, 35; Pindell, interview with Jones, 1989; Pindell, "Aesthetics of Texture," 37.

73. Eve Kosofsky Sedgwick, *Touching Feeling: Affect, Pedagogy, Performativity* (Durham, NC: Duke University Press, 2003), 14.

74. See especially Pindell, "Aesthetics of Texture"; Pindell, interview with Jones, 1989; Pindell, interview with Jacobs, 35. Examples of this literature include Arnold Rubin, "Accumulation: Power and Display in African Sculpture," *Artforum* 13, no. 9 (May 1975): 35–47; Sharon F. Patton, "The Stool and Asante Chieftaincy," *African Arts* 13, no. 1 (November 1979): 76; Patrick R. McNaughton, "The Shirts that Mande Hunters Wear," *African Arts* 15, no. 3 (May 1982): 54–58, 91. Pindell also saw Mande garments in *African Textiles.* Pindell's theory of African diasporic art as "spiritual" was shared by other Black feminist creatives in this period. For instance, see Alice Walker, "In Search of Our Mothers' Gardens: The Creativity of Black Women in the South," *Ms.,* May 1974, 66.

75. Pindell, undated interview with Freeman; Orna Guralnik and Daphne Simeon, "Depersonalization: Standing in the Spaces between Recognition and Interpellation," *Psychoanalytic Dialogues* 20, no. 4 (2010): 401.

76. Pindell, interview with Freeman. Though Pindell did not read Lorde's work until the 1980s, she was "familiar with" her poetry and ideas by the late 1970s. Maggie Hire (representative, Garth Greenan Gallery), email correspondence with the author, August 2017; Audre Lorde, interview with Karla Hammond, *American Poetry Review* (March–April 1980): 18; Lorde, *Zami;* Lorde, *Cancer Journals.* See also Jennifer Nash, *The Black Body in Ecstasy: Reading Race, Reading Pornography* (Durham, NC: Duke University Press, 2014)

77. Audre Lorde, "Uses of the Erotic: The Erotic as Power," *Sister Outsider: Essays and Speeches* (Freedom, CA: Crossing, 1984), 53–59, quotes from 53, 54. Quote beginning "the necessity for certification," Estella Lauter, "Re-Visioning Creativity: Audre Lorde's Refiguration of Eros as the Black Mother Within," in *Writing the Woman Artist: Essays on Poetics, Politics, and Portraiture,* ed. Suzanne W. Jones (Philadelphia: University of Pennsylvania Press, 1991), 415.

78. Lorde, "Uses of the Erotic," 57–58.

79. Pindell, interview with Freeman; Gina Dent, "Black Pleasure, Black Joy," in *Black Popular Culture: A Project by Michele Wallace,* ed. Gina Dent (Seattle: Bay, 1992), 18.

80. Sound Recordings, 97.29a, MoMA Archives; MoMA PS1 Archives, III.B.52, MoMA Archives.

81. *Information,* Museum of Modern Art checklist, 1970, Public Information Records, II.B.813, MoMA Archives.

82. Ibid.; Hilton Kramer, "Show at the Modern Raises Questions," *New York Times,* July 2, 1970, 26; Pindell, interview with Jones, 1989.

83. See Lippard, *Six Years.*

84. Wilson, "Howardena Pindell Makes Art," 69; Pindell, interview with Jacobs, 35; Lucy Lippard, "Hanne Darboven: Deep in Numbers," *Artforum* 12, no. 2 (October 1973): 35.

85. Wilson, "Howardena Pindell Makes Art," 69.

86. Howardena Pindell, quoted in Wilson, "Howardena Pindell Makes Art," 69; Sound Recordings, 97.29a, MoMA Archives; Howardena Pindell, "Numbering: Counting on My Fingers and Toes," *International Review of African American Art* 19, no. 3 (2004): 42–43.

87. Skowhegan Lecture Archive, 282, MoMA Archives.

88. *Jasper Johns Lithographs,* Museum of Modern Art press release, 1970, Public Information Records, II.B.866, MoMA Archives.

89. Pindell, interview with Jacobs, 36.

90. Lippard, *Pink Glass Swan,* 181, 209.

91. See Lorde, *Zami* and *Cancer Journals.*

CHAPTER 3. MENDING ABSTRACTION

1. The first of these paintings is no longer extant. Pindell dates it to circa 1976. Other early cut and sewn paintings are dated 1977. Alison Dillulio (associate director, Garth Greenan Gallery), email correspondence with the author, March 2017.

2. The artist continued making cut and sewn paintings well after this period, but began incorporating figurative elements in the works, initially through the use of collaged photo-transfers. Howardena Pindell, interviews with the author, telephone conversations, July 2015, May 2018, December 2018.

3. See Naomi Beckwith, "Body Optics, or Howardena Pindell's Way of Seeing," in *Howardena Pindell: What Remains to Be Seen,* ed. Naomi Beckwith and Valerie Cassel Oliver (Chicago: Museum of Contemporary Art Chicago, 2018), 87–108.

4. Eve Kosofsky Sedgwick, *Touching Feeling: Affect, Pedagogy, Performativity* (Durham, NC: Duke University Press, 2003), 14; Hypatia Vourloumis, "Ten Theses on Touch, or, Writing Touch," *Women and Performance* 24, no. 2–3 (2014): 232–38.

5. Rizvana Bradley, "The Vicissitudes of Touch: Annotations on the Haptic," *b2o: an online journal,* November 21, 2020, https://www.boundary2.org; Hortense Spillers, "To the Bone: Some Speculations on Touch" (keynote address, *There's a Tear in the World: Touch after Finitude,* Stedelijk Museum of Art and Studium Generale Rietveld Academy, Amsterdam, March 23, 2018). See also Laura U. Marks, *The Skin of the Film: Intercultural Cinema, Embodiment, and the Senses* (Durham, NC: Duke University Press, 2000).

6. Howardena Pindell, "Ancestral Memories and Visual Coincidences" (1994, unpublished manuscript of lecture, College Art Association Annual Conference, San Antonio, TX, January 27, 1995), Samella S. Lewis Papers, Stuart A. Rose Manuscript, Archives, and Rare Book Library, Emory University, Atlanta; Howardena Pindell, "The Aesthetics of Texture in African Adornment," in *Beauty by Design: The Aesthetics of African Adornment,* ed. Marie-Therese Brincard (New York: African American Institute, 1984), 36–39; Howardena Pindell, interview with Joseph Jacobs, in *Since the Harlem Renaissance: 50 Years of Afro-American Art* (Lewisburg, PA: Bucknell University, 1985), 35; Howardena Pindell, interview with Kellie Jones, April 2, 1989, audiovisual recording, Camille Billops and James V. Hatch Archives, Stuart A. Rose Manuscript, Archives, and Rare Book Library, Emory University.

7. I am grateful to Naomi Beckwith for sharing this insight. For a discussion of Black artists' use of bodily surrogates in their works, see Huey Copeland, *Bound to Appear: Art, Slavery, and the Site of Blackness in Multicultural America* (Chicago: University of Chicago Press, 2013), 10.

8. Howardena Pindell, "Rope/Fire/Water Reading Room," *Shed* (October 2020), https://theshed.org.

9. A printed poster called *Carnival at Ostende* (1931) by Belgian artist James Ensor was accessioned by MoMA in 1962. Jasper Johns's screen print *The Dutch Wives* (1977) was accessioned in 1978. "James Ensor, Poster for *Carnival at Ostende,* 1931," Museum of Modern Art, https://www.moma.org; "Jasper Johns, *The Dutch Wives,* 1977," Museum of Modern Art, https://www.moma.org.

10. Frank Bowling, "It's Not Enough to Say 'Black Is Beautiful,'" *ARTnews* (April 1971): 55. Bowling's terminology predates Henry Louis Gates, *The Signifying Monkey: A Theory of African-American Literary Criticism* (New York: Oxford University Press, 1988).

11. Howardena Pindell, postcard to Lucy Lippard and Charles Simonds from Nairobi, Kenya, July 24, 1973, Lucy R. Lippard Papers, 1930s–2010, bulk 1960s–1990, Archives of American Art, Smithsonian Institution, Washington, DC. I use country- and culture-specific language to describe the African cultural materials with which Pindell engaged whenever possible. Occasionally, I resort to "African," despite the limitations of this term, which refers to innumerable cultures and practices, in order to maintain the language that Pindell and many others used throughout the 1970s.

12. Howardena Pindell, "Mandeleo Ya Wanawake" and "Notes from Africa," in *The Heart of the Question* (New York: Midmarch Arts, 1997), 51–59; Pindell, "Aesthetics of Texture," 36–39; Howardena Pindell, "Afro-Carolinian 'Gullah' Baskets," *Heresies* 1, no. 2 (1978): 22. On Pindell's artistic engagement with African cultural practices, see also Andrea D. Barnwell, "Been to Africa and Back: Contextualizing Howardena Pindell's Abstract Art," *International Review of African American Art* 13, no. 3 (1996): 42–49; Sarah Louise Cowan, "Texturing Abstraction: Howardena Pindell's Cut and Sewn Paintings," *Art Journal* 79, no. 4 (Winter 2020): 26–43.

13. This was not Pindell's first trip abroad. She had traveled to Sweden as a high school student as part of an exchange program. After the trip to Africa, Pindell became a voracious traveler, visiting Egypt in 1974 and Japan, Brazil, India, and Paris in subsequent years. The cultures, religions, and cosmologies she encountered on these trips became prominent themes in her works of the 1980s.

14. Pindell was thirty and Sims was twenty-three when they went on this trip. Howardena Pindell Papers, Public Information Records, II.C.162, II.C.163, Museum of Modern Art (MoMA) Archives, New York; Pindell, interview with Jones, 1989; Pindell, "Notes from Africa," 55–57; Pindell, "Ancestral Memories and Visual Coincidences."

15. Roy Sieber, introduction to *African Textiles and Decorative Arts* (New York: Museum of Modern Art, 1972), 10. For an exemplary review of the exhibition, see Diane L. Zimmerman, "What Tarzan Missed: The Arts of Africa," *New York News,* November 5, 1972, 55, 57, 60. Pindell eventually became aware of Africanist Robert Farris Thompson's work. He was a professor at Yale when she was in the MFA program, but she did not take any classes with him. Howardena Pindell, interview with Camille Billops, April 21, 1980, audiovisual recording, Billops-Hatch Archives, Stuart A. Rose Manuscript, Archives, and Rare Book Library, Emory University.

16. Public Information Records, II.A.557, MoMA Archives. See Susan E. Cahan, *Mounting Frustration: The Art Museum in the Age of Black Power* (Durham, NC: Duke University Press, 2016), 203–4; Kellie Jones, "'It's Not Enough to Say "Black Is Beautiful"': Abstraction at the Whitney, 1969–1974," in *Discrepant Abstraction,* ed. Kobena Mercer (Cambridge, MA: MIT Press, 2006), 154–80.

17. On the AWC, see Julia Bryan-Wilson, *Art Workers: Radical Practice in the Vietnam War Era* (Berkeley: University of California Press, 2009). The AWC demands appear in "Program for Change: Black and Puerto Rican Culture," John B. Hightower Papers, III.2.16, MoMA Archives. "Magic, Anybody?" *Warwick Valley Dispatch,* November 21, 1972, 23.

18. Sieber helped Pindell plot her itinerary. Howardena Pindell, "Abstraction or Essence: Three African-American Perspectives," June 17, 1997, Sound Recordings of Museum-Related Events, 97.29a, MoMA Archives. Quote from Pindell, "Ancestral Memories and Visual Coincidences."

19. Doran H. Ross, *Wrapped in Pride: Ghanaian Kente and African American Identity* (Los Angeles: UCLA Fowler Museum of Cultural History, 1998), 9. I am grateful to Ivy Mills for sharing her insights into West African textiles and their relationship to the human body. See also Sieber, introduction to *African Textiles.*

20. Howardena Pindell, interview with the author, telephone conversation, July 2020.

21. Howardena Pindell, interview with Sally Swenson, in *Lives and Works: Talks with Women Artists,* ed. Lynn F. Miller and Sally S. Swenson (Metuchen, NJ: Scarecrow, 1981), 144. None of the extant paintings are entirely woven. Pindell made one such painting but found the doubled layers of canvas too heavy to roll up and transport by herself. Howardena Pindell, interview with the author, July 2015, Garth Greenan Gallery, New York.

22. Pindell, interviews with the author, July 2015, December 2018. Pindell remarked that the cat hair ended up in her paintings "serendipitously" and that she allowed it to become part of the work. See Howardena Pindell, untitled lecture transcript, summer 1980, 5, Skowhegan Lecture Archive, 282, MoMA Archives, Long Island City, Queens; Pindell, interview with Jones, 1989.

23. See Katy Siegel, ed., *High Times, Hard Times: New York Painting, 1967–1975* (New York: Independent Curators International, 2006).

24. Pindell, "Ancestral Memories and Visual Coincidences."

25. Doreen St. Félix, "The Embarrassment of Democrats Wearing Kente-Cloth Stoles," *New Yorker,* June 9, 2020. On kente, see Ross, *Wrapped in Pride,* 19, 29. On "the wake" of the Middle Passage, see Christina Sharpe, *In the Wake: On Blackness and Being* (Durham, NC: Duke University Press, 2016).

26. On the central role of textiles in modern and contemporary art, see Elissa Auther, *String, Felt, Thread: The Hierarchy of Art and Craft in American Art* (Minneapolis: University of Minnesota Press, 2010); Julia Bryan-Wilson, *Fray: Art and Textile Politics* (Chicago: University of Chicago Press, 2017); Jenni Sorkin, "Affinities in Abstraction: Textiles, Otherness, and Painting in the 1970s," in *Outliers and American Vanguard Art,* ed. Lynne Cooke (Washington, DC: National Gallery of Art, 2018), 92–105; K. L. H. Wells, *Weaving Modernism: Postwar Tapestry between Paris and New York* (New Haven: Yale University Press, 2019).

27. Arnold Rubin, "Accumulation. Power and Display in African Sculpture," *Artforum* 13, no. 9 (May 1975): 35–47; Sharon F. Patton, "The Stool and Asante Chieftaincy," *African Arts* 13, no. 1 (November 1979): 76; Patrick R. McNaughton, "The Shirts that Mande Hunters Wear," *African Arts* 15, no. 3 (May 1982): 54–58, 91; Pindell, "Aesthetics of Texture," 37.

28. Jonathan C. Randal, "African Festival: Protecting Values," *Washington Post,* January 15, 1977, C1. Vivian E. Browne,

quoted in Vivian Browne, interview with James V. Hatch, March 31, 1972, audiovisual recording, Billops-Hatch Archives, Stuart A. Rose Manuscript, Archives, and Rare Book Library, Emory University. See also Tobias Wofford, "Feedback: Between American Art and African Art History," *Nka: Journal of Contemporary African Art* 41 (November 2017): 154–64; Mark Godfrey, "Notes on Black Abstraction," in *Soul of a Nation: Art in the Age of Black Power,* ed. Mark Godfrey and Zoé Whitley (London: Tate, 2017), 142.

29. "Betye Saar," in *Now Dig This!: Art and Black Los Angeles, 1960–1980,* ed. Kellie Jones (Los Angeles: Hammer Museum, 2011), 152. See also Betye Saar, interviews with Karen Anne Mason, 1990, Center for Oral History Research, University of California, Los Angeles, Library. Saar, like Pindell, was especially moved by textured tunics that she saw in a museum context. She had read Rubin's article on accumulation in African sculpture.

30. Lowery Stokes Sims, "Synthesis and Integration in the Work of Howardena Pindell, 1972–1992," in *Howardena Pindell: Paintings and Drawings* (New York: Roland Gibson Gallery at Potsdam College of the State University of New York, 1992), 14.

31. See Michele Wallace, *Black Macho and the Myth of the Superwoman* (New York: Dial, 1979); bell hooks, *Ain't I a Woman: Black Women and Feminism* (Boston: South End, 1981); Angela Davis, *Women, Class, and Race* (New York: Vintage, 1981); Kimberly Springer, "Black Feminists Respond to Black Power Masculinism," in *The Black Power Movement: Rethinking the Civil Rights–Black Power Era,* ed. Peniel E. Joseph (New York: Routledge, 2006), 105–18.

32. Pindell, "Ancestral Memories and Visual Coincidences."

33. Ibid. On African concealment practices, Pindell cites Mary H. Nooter, "African Art that Conceals and Reveals," *African Arts* 26, no. 1 (January 1993): 54–69, 102. Kevin Young, *The Grey Album: On the Blackness of Blackness* (Minneapolis: Graywolf, 2012), 23; Howardena Pindell, quoted in Jack Flam, ed., *Western Artists/African Art* (New York: Museum for African Art, 1994), 56. Pindell's few encounters with African art as a child included trips to the Egyptian wing of the Philadelphia Museum of Art and visits to her parents' home by Ethiopian exchange students.

34. See April Kingsley, *Afro-American Abstraction* (New York: April Kingsley, 1981).

35. Pindell, "Ancestral Memories and Visual Coincidences"; I am referencing Kobena Mercer's articulation of a "double-voiced mode of address" in Kobena Mercer, "Tropes of the Grotesque in the Black Avant-Garde," in *Pop Art and Vernacular Cultures,* ed. Kobena Mercer (Cambridge, MA: MIT Press, 2007), 137.

36. On postminimalism, see, for instance, Briony Fer, *The Infinite Line: Remaking Art after Modernism* (New Haven: Yale University Press, 2004); Lucy Lippard, "Eccentric Abstraction" (1966), in *Changing: Essays in Art Criticism* (New York: E. P. Dutton, 1971); Robert Pincus-Witten, *Postminimalism* (New York: Out of London, 1977). On the inherent tension between the handmade and the industrial embodied by textiles, see Bryan-Wilson, *Fray,* 8.

37. Pindell, interview with the author, 2018.

38. Katy Siegel, "Another History Is Possible," in *High Times, Hard Times,* 42; Gregory Battcock, "Painting Is Obsolete," *New York Free Press,* January 23, 1969, 7.

39. "Spring Exhibition—'26 Contemporary Women Artists' Opens April 18," Aldrich Museum of Contemporary Art press release,

April 1, 1971; Lucy Lippard, introduction to *26 Contemporary Women Artists* (Ridgefield, CT: Aldrich Museum of Contemporary Art, 1971), n.p.; Pindell, interview with Jones, 1989.

40. Pindell, interview with the author, 2015.

41. Ibid. Pindell also was inspired by the textures of Hesse's sculptural surfaces to work with talcum powder. The two artists were acquainted before Hesse's death; Skowhegan Lecture Archive, 282, MoMA Archives. Jack Whitten conceived of his paintings' surfaces as "skin" in the late 1970s. See *More Dimensions than You Know: Jack Whitten, 1979–1989*, September 27–November 18, 2017, Hauser and Wirth, London, 2017, https://www.hauserwirth.com; Sampada Aranke, "Blackouts and Other Visual Escapes," *Art Journal* 79, no. 4 (Winter 2020): 66.

42. Robert Farris Thompson, *Flash of the Spirit: African and Afro-American Art and Philosophy* (New York: Random House, 1983), 209.

43. Sound Recordings, 97.29a, MoMA Archives; oral history interview with Howardena Pindell, July 10, 1972, Archives of American Art, Smithsonian Institution.

44. Rosalind Krauss, "Grids," *October* 5 (Summer 1979): 50–64.

45. See Frances Morris, ed., *Yayoi Kusama* (London: Tate, 2012). Fer, *Infinite Line*, 2.

46. Beckwith, "Body Optics," 94.

47. See Franz Boas, "The Central Eskimo," *Sixth Annual Report of the Bureau of Ethnology, 1884–85* (Washington, DC: Government Printing Office, 1888). Rani Singh, "Harry Smith, an Ethnographic Modernist in America," in *Harry Smith: The Avant-Garde in the American Vernacular*, ed. Andrew Perchuk and Rani Singh (Los Angeles: Getty Research Institute, 2010), 49–50.

48. Harry Smith, "John Cohen—Chelsea Hotel, NYC [*Sing Out!* 19, no. 1 (1969)]," interview with John Cohen, in *Think of the Self Speaking: Harry Smith—Selected Interviews*, ed. Rani Singh (Seattle: Elbow/Cityful, 1999), 15; Bryan-Wilson, *Fray*, 54; bell hooks, "Eating the Other: Desire and Resistance," in *Black Looks: Race and Representation* (Boston: South End, 1992), 22, 25.

49. Sound Recordings, 97.29a, MoMA Archives; Pindell, interview with Jones, 1989. In the Jones interview, Pindell specifies that the reproduction was of Van Gogh's *Wheatfield with Crows* (1890).

50. Pindell, interview with Jacobs, 34.

51. Pindell, interview with Jones, 1989; Howardena Pindell, email correspondence with the author, March 2019. Pindell first learned to sew on a machine. Her parents enrolled her in classes held by the Singer Sewing Corporation in Philadelphia when she was "ten or twelve years old." She has never considered herself a skilled seamstress, but performed the work out of necessity. She continues to incorporate hand sewing into her artworks, she has noted, for the "pleasure" of it. On amateurism and art, see Julia Bryan-Wilson and Benjamin Piekut, eds., "Amateurism," special issue, *Third Text* 34, no. 1 (2020).

52. Siegel, "Another History Is Possible," 30; Faith Ringgold, quoted in Lowery Stokes Sims, "African-American Women Artists: Into the Twenty First Century," in *Bearing Witness: Art by Contemporary African-American Women*, ed. Jontyle Theresa Robinson (New York: Rizzoli, 1996), 86.

53. April Kingsley, "Alvin Loving: On a Spiraling Trajectory," in *Al Loving: Color Construct*, ed. Judy Collischan and April Kingsley (Purchase, NY: Neuberger Museum of Art, 1998), 7; Godfrey, "Notes on Black Abstraction," 148–49. Bowling's

54. Pindell, "Ancestral Memories and Visual Coincidences." According to Pindell, no one in her family quilted.

55. Pindell, interview with the author, July 2015. On the topic of the interlocking notions of Black female sexuality as both excessive and invisible, see Evelyn Hammonds, "Black (W) holes and the Geometry of Black Female Sexuality," *Differences: A Journal of Feminist Cultural Studies* 6, no. 2–3 (1994): 127–45.

56. I am referencing Anne M. Wagner, *Three Artists (Three Women): Modernism and the Art of Hesse, Krasner, and O'Keeffe* (Berkeley: University of California Press, 1996), 275.

57. Pindell, "Afro-Carolinian 'Gullah' Baskets," 22. See also Pindell, "Aesthetics of Texture" and "Ancestral Memories and Visual Coincidences." Pindell, interview with Jones, 1989; Pindell, interview with Jacobs.

58. Huey Copeland, "In the Wake of the Negress," in *Modern Women: Women Artists at the Museum of Modern Art*, ed. Cornelia Butler and Alexandra Schwartz (New York: Museum of Modern Art, 2010), 490. See also Sharbreon S. Plummer, "Haptic Memory: Resituating Black Women's Lived Experiences in Fiber Art Narratives" (PhD diss., Ohio State University, 2020); Lowery Stokes Sims, "African-American Women Artists," 83–94; Freida High W. Tesfagiorgis, "In Search of a Discourse and Critique/s that Center the Art of Black Women Artists," in *Gendered Visions: The Art of Contemporary Africana Women Artists*, ed. Salah M. Hassan (Trenton, NJ: Africa World, 1997), 73–92; Tina M. Campt, *Listening to Images* (Durham, NC: Duke University Press, 2017).

59. Arna Alexander Bontemps and Jacqueline Fonvielle-Bontemps, "African-American Art History: The Feminine Dimension," in *Forever Free: Art by African-American Women, 1862–1890*, ed. Arna Alexander Bontemps (Alexandria, VA: Stephenson, 1980), 12; wall text, *Slavery and Freedom*, National Museum of African American History and Culture, Washington, DC; Gladys-Marie Fry, *Stitched from the Soul: Slave Quilts from the Ante-Bellum South* (New York: Dutton Studio, 1990), 1, 6–7.

60. Tesfagiorgis, "In Search of a Discourse," 86.

61. Alice Walker, "In Search of Our Mothers' Gardens: The Creativity of Black Women in the South," *Ms.*, May 1974, 70.

62. Linda Goode Bryant and Marcy S. Philips, *Contextures* (New York: Just Above Midtown, 1978), 46.

63. Michele Wallace, "Modernism, Postmodernism and the Problem of the Visual in Afro-American Culture," in *Out There: Marginalization and Contemporary Cultures*, ed. Russell Ferguson and Trinh T. Minh-Ha (Cambridge, MA: MIT Press, 1990), 41–45. See also Patricia Hill Collins, "Mammies, Matriarchs, and Other Controlling Images," in *Black Feminist Thought: Knowledge, Consciousness, and the Politics of Empowerment* (New York: Routledge, 1991), 67–90; Lisa Farrington, "Reinventing Herself: The Black Female Nude," *Women's Art Journal* 24, no. 2 (Autumn 2003–Winter 2004): 15–23; Nicole Fleetwood, *Troubling Vision: Performance, Visuality, and Blackness* (Chicago: University of Chicago Press, 2010); Lorraine O'Grady, "Olympia's Maid: Reclaiming Black Female Subjectivity" (1992), in *The Feminism and Visual Culture Reader*, ed. Amelia Jones (New York: Routledge, 2003), 174–86. On Black American artists' turn away from visibility, see

Sampada Aranke, "Black Radical Aesthetics and the Limits of Visibility," *e-flux*, no. 79 (February 2017): 1–10.

64. Jennifer Nash, *The Black Body in Ecstasy: Reading Race, Reading Pornography* (Durham, NC: Duke University Press, 2014), 3.

65. Pindell, "Ancestral Memories and Visual Coincidences"; Pindell, interview with Jacobs, 35; Pindell, interview with Jones, 1989; Pindell, "Aesthetics of Texture," 37; Tesfagiorgis, "In Search of a Discourse," 86.

66. Pindell, interview with the author, July 2015. On scent as a process of incorporating invisible particles into the body, see Mel Y. Chen, *Animacies: Biopolitics, Racial Mattering, and Queer Affect* (Durham, NC: Duke University Press, 2012), 198–203.

67. Howardena Pindell, interview with Linda Freeman, undated transcript, Linda Freeman Papers, 1996–2009, Archives of American Art, Smithsonian Institution; Eve Kosofsky Sedgwick, "Paranoid Reading and Reparative Reading, Or, You're So Paranoid, You Probably Think This Essay Is about You," in *Touching Feeling*, 123–51.

68. Lucy Lippard, "Sweeping Exchanges," *Art Journal* 40, no. 1/2 (Fall/Winter 1980): 362; Helen Molesworth, "Painting with Ambivalence," in *WACK! Art and the Feminist Revolution*, ed. Cornelia Butler and Lisa Gabrielle Mark (Los Angeles: Museum of Contemporary Art, 2007), 428–39.

69. Howardena Pindell, quoted in "Special Report: Women's Caucus for Art/College Art Association 1978 Annual Meetings," *Womanart* (Spring 1978): 25; Yoko Ono, quoted in Irma Kurtz, "IN THE BAG (Personal-type, single, retiring in company, for the use of) YOKO ONO," *NOVA*, January 1969, 52–57; Laurie Johnston, "Women's Group to Observe Rights Day Here Today," *New York Times*, August 25, 1972, 40.

70. hooks, *Ain't I a Woman*, 142; Linda La Rue, "The Black Movement and Women's Liberation," *Black Scholar* 1, no. 1 (May 1970): 36–37.

71. Pindell, "Special Report," 25.

72. Pindell, "Aesthetics of Texture," 37. Linda Goode Bryant, quoted in Judith Wilson, "Howardena Pindell Makes Art that Winks at You," *Ms.*, May 1980, 69. On glitter, see Nikki Greene, *Grime, Glass, and Glitter: The Body and the Sonic in Contemporary Black Art* (Durham, NC: Duke University Press, 2022); and Krista Thompson, *Shine: The Visual Economy of Light in African Diasporic Aesthetic Practices* (Durham, NC: Duke University Press, 2015).

73. Susan Sontag, "Notes on Camp," *Partisan Review* (1964): 515–30; Mary Ann Doane, "Film and the Masquerade: Theorising the Female Spectator," *Screen* 23, no. 3–4 (September–October 1982): 81. See also Luce Irigaray, *This Sex Which Is Not One* (Ithaca, NY: Cornell University Press, 1985), 220; Joan Rivière, "Womanliness as Masquerade," *International Journal of Psychoanalysis* 10 (1929): 303–13; Abigail Solomon-Godeau, "The Legs of the Countess," *October* 39 (Winter 1986): 65–108.

74. Howardena Pindell, "Artist's Statement," in Katy Siegel, *High Times, Hard Times,* 105; Allan Schwartzman and Kathleen Thomas, "Ree Morton: A Critical Overview," in *Ree Morton Retrospective, 1971–77,* ed. Allan Schwartzman and Kathleen Thomas (New York: New Museum, 1980), 40–41.

75. See Anne Swartz, *Pattern and Decoration: An Ideal Vision of American Art, 1975–1985* (Yonkers, NY: Hudson River Museum, 2007).

76. Cindy Nemser, *Art Talk: Conversations with 12 Women Artists* (New York: Charles Scribner's Sons, 1975), 217. See Albert Gleizes and Jean Metzinger, "On Cubism" (1912), in *Modern Artists on Art: Ten Unabridged Essays,* ed. Robert Herbert (Englewood Cliffs, NJ: Prentice-Hall, 1964), 1–18; Adolf Loos, "Ornament and Crime" (1908), in *Programs and Manifestoes on 20th-Century Architecture* (Cambridge, MA: MIT Press, 1970), 19–24.

77. Ann Eden Gibson, *Abstract Expressionism: Other Politics* (New Haven: Yale University Press, 1999), 36; Clement Greenberg, "Milton Avery" (1957), in *Clement Greenberg: The Collected Essays and Criticism,* vol. 4, *Modernism with a Vengeance,* ed. John O'Brian (Chicago: University of Chicago Press, 1986), 43. See also Clement Greenberg, "The Crisis of the Easel Picture" (1948), in ibid., vol. 2, *Arrogant Purpose,* ed. John O'Brian (Chicago: University of Chicago Press, 1986), 221–24; Elissa Auther, "The Decorative, Abstraction, and the Hierarchy of Art and Craft in the Art Criticism of Clement Greenberg," *Oxford Art Journal* 27, no. 3 (2004): 342.

78. Holland Cotter, "A Resolutely Global Journey: The Life and Work of Howardena Pindell," in *Howardena Pindell: Paintings and Drawings,* 11. Sound Recordings 97.29a, MoMA Archives; Audre Lorde, "Uses of the Erotic: The Erotic as Power," *Sister Outsider: Essays and Speeches* (Freedom, CA: Crossing, 1984), 53–59.

79. Susan L. Stoops, "From Eccentric to Sensuous Abstraction: An Interview with Lucy Lippard," in *More than Minimal: Feminism and Abstraction in the '70s,* ed. Susan L. Stoops (Waltham, MA: Rose Art Museum, Brandeis University, 1996), 28.

80. See Anne M. Wagner, "Lee Krasner as L.K.," *Representations* 25 (Winter 1989): 42–57.

81. Thompson, *Shine,* 225.

82. David Joselit, "Notes on Surface: Toward a Genealogy of Flatness," *Art History* 23, no. 1 (March 2000): 19–34.

CHAPTER 4. SCREEN, SKIN

1. Howardena Pindell, quoted in Leslie King Hammond and Lowery Stokes Sims, "Reflections on Art as a Verb: Twenty Years Later, in the New Millennium," in *Cinema Remixed and Reloaded: Black Women Artists and the Moving Image since 1970,* ed. Andrea Barnwell Brownlee and Valerie Cassel Oliver (Houston: Contemporary Art Museum Houston/Atlanta: Spelman College Museum of Fine Art, 2008), 15–17. Pindell's view of video evokes Rosalind Krauss, "Video: The Aesthetics of Narcissism," *October* (Spring 1976): 50–64.

2. See Andrew Heisel, "The Rise and Fall of an All-American Catchphrase: 'Free, White and 21,'" *Jezebel*, September 10, 2015, https://pictorial.jezebel.com.

3. Pindell has made two other works in the medium: *Doubling* (1995), about war atrocities, which has not been exhibited widely, and *Rope/Fire/Water* (2020), which debuted at Pindell's solo exhibition at the nonprofit art space the Shed in New York.

4. On visibility and multiculturalism, see Stuart Hall, *Representation and the Media,* dir. Sut Jhally (1997; Northampton, MA: Media Education Foundation, 2002), DVD; Kobena Mercer, "Diaspora Aesthetics and Visual Culture" in *Black Cultural Traffic: Crossroads in Global Performance and Popular Culture,* ed. Harry Justin Elam and Kennell A. Jackson (Ann Arbor: University of Michigan Press, 2005); Jeff Chang, *Who We Be: The Colorization of America* (New York: St. Martin's, 2014); Huey Copeland, *Bound to Appear: Art, Slavery, and the Site of Blackness in Multicultural America* (Chicago: University of Chicago Press, 2013); Howardena

Pindell, "Autobiography: In Her Own Image," in *The Heart of the Question: The Writings and Paintings of Howardena Pindell* (New York: Midmarch Arts, 1997), 72; Peggy Phelan, *Unmarked: The Politics of Performance* (New York: Routledge, 1993), 1.

5. See, for instance, Uri McMillan, "Is This Performance about You? The Art, Activism, and Black Feminist Critique of Howardena Pindell," in *Embodied Avatars: Genealogies of Black Feminist Art and Performance* (New York: New York University Press, 2015), 153–95; Brian Wallis, "Coming to Voice: Howardena Pindell's *Free, White and 21*," in *Howardena Pindell: What Remains to Be Seen*, ed. Naomi Beckwith and Valerie Cassel Oliver (Chicago: Museum of Contemporary Art Chicago, 2018), 169–80; Howardena Pindell, "Howardena Pindell: Some Reminiscences and a Chronology," in *Howardena Pindell: Paintings and Drawings* (Potsdam, NY: Roland Gibson Gallery at Potsdam College of the State University of New York, 1992), 20; Howardena Pindell, interview with Kellie Jones, April 2, 1989, audiovisual recording, Camille Billops and James V. Hatch Archives, Stuart A. Rose Manuscript, Archives, and Rare Book Library, Emory University, Atlanta.

6. Saidiya Hartman, *Scenes of Subjection: Terror, Slavery, and Self-Making in Nineteenth-Century America* (New York: Oxford University Press, 1997), 55.

7. See Phillip Brian Harper, *Abstractionist Aesthetics: Artistic Form and Social Critique in African American Culture* (New York: New York University Press, 2015), 2.

8. Anne Anlin Cheng, *Second Skin: Josephine Baker and the Modern Surface* (New York: Oxford University Press, 2011), 8. See also Uri McMillan, ed., "Skin, Surface, Sensorium," special issue, *Women and Performance* 28, no. 1 (2018); Michelle Ann Stephens, *Skin Acts: Race, Psychoanalysis, and the Black Male Performer* (Durham, NC: Duke University Press, 2014).

9. Anne M. Wagner, "Performance, Video, and the Rhetoric of Presence," *October* 91 (Winter 2000): 74.

10. Pindell has described her video as in part a response to "yet another run-in with white feminists." Howardena Pindell, "Free, White and 21," in *Heart of the Question*, 66.

11. Michele Wallace, "Negative/Positive Images," in *Invisibility Blues: From Pop to Theory* (New York: Verso, 1990), 5.

12. Howardena Pindell, "Afro-Carolinian 'Gullah' Baskets," *Heresies* 1, no. 2 (1978): 22; Lisa Gail Collins, *The Art of History: African American Women Artists Engage the Past* (New Brunswick, NJ: Rutgers University Press, 2002).

13. See Marvin Edward McAllister, "Liberatory Whiteness: Early Whiteface Minstrels, Enslaved and Free," in *Whiting Up: Whiteface Minstrels and Stage Europeans in African American Performance* (Chapel Hill: University of North Carolina Press, 2011), 19–49; Faedra Chatard Carpenter, *Coloring Whiteness: Acts of Critique in Black Performance* (Ann Arbor: University of Michigan Press, 2014); John Strausbaugh, *Black Like You: Blackface, Whiteface, Insult and Imitation in American Popular Culture* (New York: Penguin, 2006).

14. For instance, Pindell knew Henry through the gallery Just Above Midtown and became friends with Buchanan following the exhibition. She included Henry and Mendieta (posthumously) in the 1988 traveling exhibition she curated, titled *Autobiography: In Her Own Image*. See Howardena Pindell, *Autobiography: In Her Own Image* (New York: INTAR Latin American Gallery, 1988).

15. See Komozi Woodard, "Amiri Baraka, the Congress of African People and Black Power Politics from the 1961 United Nations Protest to the 1972 Gary Convention," in *The Black Power Movement: Rethinking the Civil Rights-Black Power Era*, ed. Peniel E. Joseph (New York: Routledge, 2006), 55–78; Stephen Ward, "The Third World Women's Alliance: Black Feminist Radicalism and the Black Power Movement," in Joseph, *Black Power Movement*, 119–44; Lowery Stokes Sims, "Third World Women Speak," *Women Artists News* 4, no. 6 (December 1978): 1, repr. in Catherine Morris and Rujeko Hockley, eds., *We Wanted a Revolution: Black Radical Women, 1965–85: A Sourcebook* (New York: Brooklyn Museum, 2017), 190–93; Editorial Statement, "Third World Women: The Politics of Being Other," special issue, *Heresies*, no. 8 (1979): 1.

16. Ana Mendieta, introduction to *Dialectics of Isolation: An Exhibition of Third World Women Artists of the United States* (New York: A.I.R. Gallery, 1980), n.p., repr. in Morris and Hockley, *We Wanted a Revolution*, 214. See also Editorial Statement and Heresies Collective Statement in "Racism Is the Issue," *Heresies*, no. 15 (1982): 1, repr. in Morris and Hockley, *We Wanted a Revolution*, 198; "Art: Situation Report," in "The American Woman," special issue, *Time*, March 20, 1971, 77; Stephanie Weissberg, "Ana Mendieta's *Dialectics of Isolation*," and Aruna D'Souza, "Early Intersections: The Work of Third World Feminism," both in Morris and Hockley, *We Wanted a Revolution*, 210–13 and 73–96.

17. Pindell, "Free, White and 21," 65–66; Mendieta, introduction to *Dialectics of Isolation*, n.p., repr. in Morris and Hockley, *We Wanted a Revolution*, 214.

18. Cherise Smith, *Enacting Others: Politics of Identity in Eleanor Antin, Nikki S. Lee, Adrian Piper, and Anna Deveare Smith* (Durham, NC: Duke University Press, 2011), 101; Cherríe Moraga and Gloria Anzaldúa, eds., *This Bridge Called My Back: Writings by Radical Women of Color* (Watertown, MA: Persephone, 1981).

19. The image of *Free, White and 21* in the catalogue for *Dialectics of Isolation*, which shows two monitors, was from a test Pindell performed prior to the exhibition. *Free, White and 21* is a single-monitor piece and was displayed on a single television monitor at A.I.R. Howardena Pindell, interview with the author, telephone conversation, December 2018.

20. See Nicole Fleetwood, "Visible Seams: The Media Art of Fatimah Tuggar," in *Troubling Vision: Performance, Visuality, and Blackness* (Chicago: University of Chicago Press, 2010), 179.

21. See Robin Bernstein, "Dances with Things: Material Culture and the Performance of Race," *Social Text* 27, no. 4 (2009): 67–94.

22. Howardena Pindell, interview with the author, telephone conversation, July 2020.

23. Pindell, interview with Jones, 1989.

24. Howardena Pindell, quoted in Hammond and Sims, "Reflections on Art as a Verb," 15.

25. Ibid.

26. Romi Crawford, "Amateurism and Auteurism: Contrary Instincts in Black Women's Experimental Film Forms," in Barnwell Brownlee and Oliver, *Cinema Remixed and Reloaded*, 30. See also Jacqueline Bobo, preface to *Black Women Film and Video Artists* (New York: Routledge, 1998), xi.

27. Teshome H. Gabriel, *Third Cinema in the Third World: The Aesthetics of Liberation* (Ann Arbor: UMI Research Press, 1982), xi.

28. Pindell, interview with the author, December 2018. Pindell
recalls that she made about $5,000 a year at MoMA. This
income was well below the median U.S. household income in
the 1970s, which ranged from $9,870 (1970) to $15,060 (1978).
See "Median Family Income Up in 1970," *Consumer Income,
A United States Department of Commerce Publication* P-60,
no. 70 (May 1971): 1–2; "Money Income in 1978 of Households
in the United States," *Consumer Income*, P-60, no. 121 (February 1980): 1.

29. Mendieta, introduction to *Dialectics of Isolation,* n.p.

30. Smith, *Enacting Others*, 103; Weissberg, "Ana Mendieta's *Dialectics of Isolation*," 212; Pindell, interview with the author,
December 2018.

31. Lowery Stokes Sims, "Aspects of Performance by Black American Women Artists," in *Feminist Art Criticism: An Anthology,*
ed. Arlene Raven, Cassandra L. Langer, and Joanna Frueh
(Ann Arbor: UMI Research Press, 1988), 208; see Wagner,
"Performance, Video, and the Rhetoric of Presence," 59–80.

32. Pindell, "Free, White and 21," 66–67.

33. Howardena Pindell, "Artist's Statement," in *Dialectics of
Isolation,* n.p.

34. Howardena Pindell, interview with Sally Swenson, in *Lives
and Works: Talks with Women Artists,* ed. Lynn F. Miller and
Sally S. Swenson (Lanham, MD: Rowman and Littlefield,
1996), 143.

35. Pindell, interview with the author, December 2018; Pindell,
interview with Swenson, 143.

36. Pindell, interview with the author, December 2018.

37. Ibid.

38. See, for instance, Camille Ann Brewer, "Moving Pictures:
Video Drawings by Howardena Pindell," in *Howardena
Pindell: Video Drawings, 1973–2007* (Boston: Howard
Yezerski Gallery, 2013), n.p.; Grace Deveney, "Interrupting the
Broadcast: Howardena Pindell's *Video Drawings*," in Beck-
with and Oliver, *What Remains to Be Seen*, 151–68; Pindell,
"Some Reminiscences and a Chronology," 30; Skowhegan Lec-
ture Archive, 282, Museum of Modern Art (MoMA) Archives,
Long Island City, Queens.

39. Skowhegan Lecture Archive, 282, MoMA Archives; Ian Smith,
Fiona Stewart, and Phil Turner, "Winky Dink and You:
Determining Patterns of Narrative for Interactive Television
Design," in *Proceeding of the Second European Conference
on Interactive Television*, ed. J. Masthoff, R. Griffiths, and
L. Pemberton (2004), http://citeseerx.ist.psu.edu.

40. Howardena Pindell, "Abstraction or Essence: Three African-American Perspectives," June 17, 1997, Sound Recordings,
97.29a, MoMA Archives, New York.

41. Marshall McLuhan, *Understanding Media: The Extensions of
Man* (New York: Signet, 1964); Newton N. Minow, "Television
and the Public Interest," May 9, 1961, National Association
of Broadcasters, Washington, DC, American Speech Bank,
https://www.americanrhetoric.com/speechbank.htm. See
also Lynn Spigel, "Installing the Television Set: Popular
Discourses on Television and Domestic Space, 1948–1955,"
in *Private Screenings: Television and the Female Consumer,*
ed. Lynn Spigel and Denise Mann (Minneapolis: University of
Minnesota Press, 1992), 3.

42. Pindell, "Some Reminiscences and a Chronology," 20; Bobo,
Black Women Film and Video Artists, 6; Aniko Bodroghkozy,
"Is This What You Mean by Color TV?': Race, Gender, and Con-
tested Meanings in NBC's *Julia*," in Spigel and Mann, *Private
Screenings*, 143–67; Herman Gray, *Watching Race: Television

43. There are also several works in the *Video Drawings* series sub-
titled "Abstraction," whose imagery appears to be drawn from
close-ups of natural matter such as sea life. On jet-age aesthetics, see Vanessa R. Schwarz, *Jet Age Aesthetic: The Glamour
of Media in Motion* (New Haven: Yale University Press, 2020).
On "Afro-futurism," see Mark Dery, "Black to the Future: Interviews with Samuel R. Delany, Greg Tate, and Tricia Rose," in
Flame Wars: The Discourse of Cyberculture, ed. Mark Dery
(Durham, NC: Duke University Press, 1994), 179–222; "25 Years
of Afrofuturism and Black Speculative Thought: Roundtable
with Tiffany E. Barber, Reynaldo Anderson, Mark Dery, and
Sheree Renée Thomas," *TOPIA: Canadian Journal of Cultural
Studies,* no. 39 (Spring 2018): 136–44.

44. "Moses Launches Epic Era with Hurdles Record—Athletics,"
International Olympic Committee News Archive, July 25,
1975, https://www.olympic.org/news.

45. Mark Armour and Daniel R. Levitt, "Baseball Demographics,
1947–2016," Society for American Baseball Research, https://
sabr.org/. See the widely reported open letter written by
Nigerian-born, Canadian-Ukrainian NHL player Akim Aliu,
"Hockey Is Not for Everyone," *Players' Tribune*, May 19, 2020,
https://www.theplayerstribune.com/.

46. See W. Perman, "Race on the Sports Page," *Review of Sport
and Leisure* 3, no. 2 (1978): 54–68; Samantha N. Sheppard,
*Sporting Blackness: Race, Embodiment, and Critical Muscle
Memory on Screen* (Berkeley: University of California Press,
2020); Nicole Fleetwood, "The Black Athlete: Racial Precarity
and the American Sports Icon," in *On Racial Icons: Blackness
and the Public Imagination* (New Brunswick, NJ: Rutgers
University Press, 2015), 81–110.

47. Deveney, "Interrupting the Broadcast," 157, 167. bell hooks,
"The Oppositional Gaze: Black Female Spectators," in *Black
Looks: Race and Representation* (Boston: South End, 1992),
117; Manthia Diawara, "Black Spectatorship: Problems of
Identification and Resistance," *Screen* 29 (1988): 66–79.

48. John Alan Farmer, "Pop People," in *The New Frontier: Art
and Television, 1960–65* (Austin: Austin Museum of Art,
2000), 49, 56.

49. Lynn Spigel, introduction to Maurice Berger, *Revolution of
the Eye: Modern Art and the Birth of American Television*
(New Haven: Yale University Press, 2014), xii; Pindell, "Some
Reminiscences and a Chronology," 20; Maurice Berger, "Rev-
olution of the Eye," in *Revolution of the Eye*, 59, 81, 86; David
Joselit, *Feedback: Television against Democracy* (Cambridge,
MA: MIT Press, 2007).

50. Farmer, "Pop People," 49, 56. Elizabeth Ferrer, foreword to
Farmer, *New Frontier*, 11.

51. Chang, *Who We Be*, 55; Michael J. Arlen, "Living-Room War,"
New Yorker, October 15, 1966, 200–202; Michael J. Arlen,
Living-Room War (New York: Viking, 1969); Daniel C. Hallin,
The "Uncensored War": The Media and Vietnam (New York:
Oxford University Press, 1986), 4–5; Carrie Lambert-Beatty,
Being Watched: Yvonne Rainer and the 1960s (Cambridge,
MA: MIT Press, 2008), 149; Jayne Wark, "Conceptual Art
and Feminism: Martha Rosler, Adrian Piper, Eleanor Antin,
and Martha Wilson," *Woman's Art Journal* 22, no. 1 (Spring–
Summer 2011): 44–45.

52. Deveney, "Interrupting the Broadcast," 165.

53. Lowery Stokes Sims, "Synthesis and Integration in the Works
of Howardena Pindell, 1972–1992," in *Howardena Pindell:*

Paintings and Drawings, 15; Deveney, "Interrupting the Broadcast," 161.

54. Howardena Pindell, interview with the author, Garth Greenan Gallery, New York, July 2015.

55. Skowhegan Lecture Archive, 282, MoMA Archives.

56. Most recently, Pindell had created a pair of self-portraits as an undergraduate in the early to mid-1960s, one of which is now in the collection of the Metropolitan Museum of Art. Howardena Pindell, "Criticism/or/Between the Lines," in special issue, "Third World Women: The Politics of Being Other," *Heresies,* no. 8 (1979): 2–4.

57. Lucy R. Lippard Papers, 1930s–2010, bulk 1960s–1990, Archives of American Art, Smithsonian Institution, Washington, DC.

58. Pindell, "Criticism/or/Between the Lines," 2–4; D'Souza, "Early Intersections," 83.

59. This account of the exhibition and the surrounding controversy draws heavily from letters, memos, and other materials found in the Artists Space Archives at Fales Special Collections at New York University, including *The N—— Drawings* press release, Artists Space Archives, 1973–2009, MSS.291. Fales Special Collections, New York University (NYU). See also the extended discussions of the protests in Aruna D'Souza, "Act II: *The N—— Drawings,* Artists Space, 1979," *Whitewalling: Art, Race and Protest in 3 Acts* (New York: Badlands Unlimited, 2018), 65–100; Chang, "Color Theory: Race Trouble in the Avant-Garde," in *Who We Be,* 79–97; Howardena Pindell (written anonymously), "Action against Racism in the Arts," *Heresies,* no. 8 (1979): 108–11. See also Julie Ault, ed., *Alternative Art New York, 1965–1985* (Minneapolis: Minnesota University Press, 2002).

60. I have chosen to censor this word, including when it appears in the context of proper names, publication titles, and quotes, in response to the calls of countless Black activists, artists, and scholars to their white colleagues to stop reproducing a term uniquely embedded in the violent exertion of white supremacist ideologies.

61. Janet Henry, letter to Jim Reinish, March 6, 1979, Artists Space Archives, Fales Special Collections, NYU; D'Souza, "Act II," 74.

62. Chang, *Who We Be,* 85. See also Richard Goldstein, "Art Beat: The Romance of Racism," *Village Voice,* April 2, 1979, 43–44.

63. D'Souza, "Act II," 73; Emergency Coalition, open letter, March 5, 1979, Artists Space Archives, Fales Special Collections, NYU.

64. D'Souza, "Act II," 68, 78; Howardena Pindell, letter to NYSCA, Artists Space Archives, Fales Special Collections, NYU; Jim Reinish, telegram to Artists Space, Artists Space Archives, Fales Special Collections, NYU; Wallis, "Coming to Voice," 177.

65. Douglas Crimp et al., "Commentaries on Artists Space's Exhibit of 'N—— Drawings,'" *Art Workers News,* June 1979, 12. Helene Winer, Statement, Artists Space Archives, Fales Special Collections, NYU.

66. D'Souza, "Act II," 78–79, 94; Chang, *Who We Be,* 91; Janet Henry, letter to Rags Watkins, Artists Space Archives, Fales Special Collections, NYU; Carol Duncan, quoted in Elizabeth Hess, "Art-World Apartheid," *Seven Days* 3, no. 6 (May 18, 1979): 27; Howardena Pindell, "Covenant of Silence" (1990), in *Heart of the Question,* 32–49.

67. Craig Owens, "Black and White," *Skyline,* April 1979, 16; Crimp, "Commentaries on Artists Space's Exhibit," 16; D'Souza, "Act II," 91; Donald Sultan, letter to Howardena Pindell, Artists Space Archives, Fales Special Collections, NYU.

68. Howardena Pindell, interview with Camille Billops, April 21, 1980, audiovisual recording, Billops-Hatch Archives, Emory University; Kellie Jones, "Interview with Howardena Pindell," *EyeMinded: Living and Writing Contemporary Art* (Durham, NC: Duke University Press, 2011), 222.

69. D'Souza, "Act II," 91; Lucy Lippard, letter to Helene Winer, Artists Space Archives, Fales Special Collections, NYU. Michele Wallace, "Anger in Isolation," in *Invisibility Blues,* 23; originally published as Michele Wallace, "Anger in Isolation: A Black Feminist's Search for Sisterhood," *Village Voice,* July 28, 1975, 6–7. Audre Lorde, "The Uses of Anger: Women Responding to Racism," in *Sister Outsider* (New York: Ten Speed, 1984), 124–33. Lorde originally delivered the text as a keynote presentation at the National Women's Studies Association Conference, Storrs, CT, June 1981. See also bell hooks, *Killing Rage: Ending Racism* (New York: Henry Holt, 1995).

70. Andrea Barnwell Brownlee, "The Skin I'm In: Black Women, Color, and Video Art," in Barnwell Brownlee and Oliver, *Cinema Remixed and Reloaded,* 47; Brittney Cooper, *Eloquent Rage: A Black Feminist Discovers Her Superpower* (New York: St. Martin's, 2018), 4.

71. Pindell, interview with Jones, 1989; Pindell, interview with Billops, 1980; Pindell, "Free, White and 21," 65; Chris Bell, "Introducing White Disability Studies: A Modest Proposal," in *The Disability Studies Reader,* 2nd ed., ed. Lennard J. Davis (New York: Routledge, 2006), 275–82. See also Mel Y. Chen, *Animacies: Biopolitics, Racial Mattering, and Queer Affect* (Durham, NC: Duke University Press, 2012), 199–201.

72. Michele Wallace, "Negative Images: Towards a Black Feminist Cultural Criticism," in *Invisibility Blues,* 241–42; Pindell, "Free, White and 21," 67; Howardena Pindell, "Art World Racism: A Documentation," repr. in *Heart of the Question,* 3–27.

73. Wagner, "Performance, Video, and the Rhetoric of Presence," 60, 73–75, 79.

74. Jennifer A. González, *Subject to Display: Reframing Race in Contemporary Installation Art* (Cambridge, MA: MIT Press, 2008); McMillan, "Is This Performance about You?," 12, 171; Wallis, "Coming to Voice," 172; Moira Roth, cited in Smith, *Enacting Others,* 37; Adrian Piper, "The Mythic Being: Getting Back," in *Out of Order, Out of Sight,* vol. 1, *Selected Writings in Meta-Art, 1968–1992* (Cambridge, MA: MIT Press, 1996), 147; Pindell, interview with Jones, 1989.

75. Laura U. Marks, *The Skin of the Film: Intercultural Cinema, Embodiment, and the Senses* (Durham, NC: Duke University Press, 2000), xi–xii.

76. Barnwell Brownlee, "Skin I'm In," 47; Aimee Meredith Cox, *Shapeshifters: Black Girls and the Choreography of Citizenship* (Durham, NC: Duke University Press, 2015), 146; Pindell, "Free, White and 21," 69.

77. Adrienne Kennedy, *Funnyhouse of a Negro* (New York: Samuel French, 1969), 5–6; Carpenter, *Coloring Whiteness,* 18–19. Kennedy's use of the color yellow alludes to the concept of a "high yellow" complexion belonging to a light-skinned person of Black and white ancestry.

78. Pindell, "Free, White and 21," 65.

CONCLUSION

1. Howardena Pindell, interview with Kellie Jones, April 2, 1989, audiovisual recording, Camille Billops and James V. Hatch Archives, Stuart A. Rose Manuscript, Archives, and Rare Book Library, Emory University, Atlanta. See also Howardena Pindell, interview with Andrea Miller-Keller, June 1989, curatorial files, Wadsworth Atheneum Museum of Art, Hartford, CT. Valerie Cassel Oliver, "The Tao of Abstraction:

Howardena Pindell's Paper Works," in *Howardena Pindell: What Remains to Be Seen,* ed. Naomi Beckwith and Valerie Cassel Oliver (Chicago: Museum of Contemporary Art Chicago, 2018), 130.

2. Howardena Pindell, interview with the author, telephone conversation, December 2018. Pindell wrote about her time in Japan in Howardena Pindell, "An American Black Woman Artist in a Japanese Garden," *Heresies* 15, no. 4 (February 1983): 54–55.

3. Pindell, interview with Miller-Keller, June 1989.

4. Elizabeth Alexander, "'Can You Be BLACK and Look at This?': Reading the Rodney King Video(s)," *Public Culture* 7, no. 1 (Fall 1994): 80. See also Cheryl Finley, *Committed to Memory: The Art of the Slave Ship Icon* (Princeton, NJ: Princeton University Press, 2018); Christina Sharpe, *In the Wake: On Blackness and Being* (Durham, NC: Duke University Press, 2016).

5. Toni Morrison, *Beloved* (New York: Knopf, 1987); Caroline Rody, "Toni Morrison's *Beloved:* History, 'Rememory,' and a 'Clamor for a Kiss,'" *American Literary History* 7, no. 1 (Spring 1995): 92–119; Hortense Spillers, "Mama's Baby, Papa's Maybe: An American Grammar Book," *Diacritics* 17, no. 2 (1987): 72, 69, 73; Saidiya Hartman, "Redressing the Pained Body: Toward a Theory of Practice," in *Scenes of Subjection: Terror, Slavery, and Self-Making in Nineteenth-Century America* (New York: Oxford University Press, 1997), 76–77, 74.

6. See Howardena Pindell, "Ancestral Memories and Visual Coincidences," 1994, unpublished manuscript in Samella S. Lewis Papers, Stuart A. Rose Manuscript, Archives, and Rare Book Library, Emory University; Howardena Pindell, "Howardena Pindell: Some Reminiscences and a Chronology," in *Howardena Pindell: Paintings and Drawings* (Potsdam, NY: Roland Gibson Gallery at Potsdam College of the State University of New York, 1992), 20; Judith Wilson, "Howardena Pindell Makes Art that Winks at You," *Ms.,* May 1980, 69.

7. See Michael Winerip, "Computerized Billboard Brightens up Times Sq. with Art-of-the-Month," *New York Times,* August 26, 1983, B1, B4; press release for "Howardena Pindell: Making of a Mandala," January 1996, Charter Oak Cultural Center Gallery, Hartford, CT, curatorial files, Wadsworth Atheneum Museum of Art. Howardena Pindell, interview with the author, telephone conversation, July 2020. Pindell phoned hospitals in New York to ask for these first names. She had lost thirteen friends, including a cousin, to AIDS-related illnesses.

8. See Howardena Pindell, *Autobiography: In Her Own Image* (New York: INTAR Latin American Gallery, 1988).

9. Howardena Pindell, interview with the author, Garth Greenan Gallery, New York, July 2015; Howardena Pindell, email correspondence with the author, March 2019.

10. *Howardena Pindell: Rope/Fire/Water* (Cologne: Buchhandlung Walther und Franz König, 2020), 84.

11. These exhibitions include Catherine Morris and Rujeko Hockley, curators, *We Wanted a Revolution* (Brooklyn Museum, 2017); Fiona Bradley, curator, *Howardena Pindell: A New Language* (Fruitmarket, Edinburgh, UK, 2021–22); Mark Godfrey and Zoé Whitley, curators, *Soul of a Nation: Art in the Age of Black Power* (Tate Modern, London, 2017); Melissa Messina and Erin Dziedzic, curators, *Magnetic Fields: Expanding American Abstraction, 1960s to Today* (Kemper Museum of Contemporary Art, Kansas City, MO, 2017); Lynne Cooke, curator, *Outliers and American Vanguard Art* (National Gallery of Art, Washington, DC, 2018); Jenni Sorkin, "Howardena Pindell," *Artforum* 56, no. 10 (Summer 2018): 313.

12. Arna Alexander Bontemps and Jacqueline Fonvielle-Bontemps, "African-American Art History: The Feminine Dimension," in *Forever Free: Art by African-American Women, 1862–1890,* ed. Arna Alexander Bontemps (Alexandria, VA: Stephenson, 1980), 15.

13. Leigh Raiford, "Burning All Illusion: Abstraction, Black Life, and the Unmaking of White Supremacy," *Art Journal* 29, no. 4 (Winter 2020): 77–91.

14. Sadie Barnette, "Dear 1968 . . . ," *Sadie Barnette,* April 2017, sadiebarnette.com.

15. Howardena Pindell, "Art World Racism," in *The Heart of the Question: The Writings and Paintings of Howardena Pindell* (New York: Midmarch Arts, 1997), 3–28. Pindell originally published this report in 1987 under the title "Statistics, Testimony and Supporting Documentation." She delivered this report on June 28, 1987, at the Agendas for Survival Conference at Hunter College, New York. It appeared in *Third Text* the following year: Howardena Pindell, "Art (World) and Racism: Testimony, Documentation, and Statistics," *Third Text* 2, no. 3–4 (1988): 157–90. Uri McMillan, *Embodied Avatars: Genealogies of Black Feminist Art and Performance* (New York: New York University Press, 2015), 183–95. See also materials on PESTS in Guerrilla Girls Records, 1979–2013, Getty Research Institute Special Collections, Los Angeles.

16. Chad M. Topaz et al., "Diversity of Artists in Major U.S. Museums," *PLoS One* (March 2019), https://doi.org/10.1371/journal.pone.0212852; Julia Halperin and Charlotte Burns, "African American Artists Are More Visible than Ever. So Why Are Museums Giving Them Short Shrift?," *Artnet News,* September 20, 2018, https://news.artnet.com. Sotheby's has a vested interest in addressing the underrepresentation of works by African American artists in U.S. museums, as this exclusion drives down sale prices. See also Julia Halperin and Charlotte Burns, "Methodology: How We Gathered and Analyzed Our Data on Women in the Art World," *Artnet News,* September 19, 2021, https://news.artnet.com; Alex Greenberger, "White Cubes: Do Exhibitions at U.S. Museums Reflect Calls for Diversity?," *ARTnews,* August 5, 2019, https://artnews.com; Tessa Solomon, "Museums Can Track Gender Breakdown in Collections with New Software," *ARTnews,* November 13, 2019, https://artnews.com. Elisabeth Smith (collections records associate, Seattle Art Museum), email correspondence with the author, September 2021.

17. Huey Copeland, "One-Dimensional Abstraction," *Art Journal* 78, no. 2 (Summer 2019): 116.

18. Pindell, interview with Jones, 1989; Hilarie M. Sheets, "Discovered after 70, Black Artists Find Success, Too, Has Its Price," *New York Times,* March 23, 2019, https://www.nytimes.com.

19. Howardena Pindell, quoted in Greenberger, "White Cubes," 85.

20. On the concept of modernists making art that makes a difference, see Anne M. Wagner, *Three Artists (Three Women): Modernism and the Art of Hesse, Krasner, and O'Keeffe* (Berkeley: University of California Press, 1996), 242.

Index

Illustration Credits